Roman Forts

For in a camp, well chosen and entrenched, the troops both day and night lie secure within their works, even though in view of the enemy. It seems to resemble a fortified city which they can build for their safety wherever they please.

(Vegetius, I, 21)

Roman Forts

of the
1st and 2nd centuries AD
in Britain and the German Provinces

ANNE JOHNSON

Adam & Charles Black · London

First published 1983 by A & C Black (Publishers) Ltd
35 Bedford Row, London WC1R 4JH

ISBN 0-7136-2223-7
© Anne Johnson 1983

British Library Cataloguing in Publication Data

Johnson, Anne
    Roman forts.
    1. Fortification, Roman—England
    2. Fortification, Roman—Germany
    I. Title
    623'.12'09362   UG429.G7
    ISBN 0-7136-2223-7

Typeset in Monophoto Ehrhardt
by Latimer Trend & Company Ltd, Plymouth
Printed in Great Britain
by BAS Printers Ltd, Over Wallop, Hampshire

Contents

List of Illustrations   vii

Acknowledgements   xiii

Preface   xv

Introduction   1

1   The Roman Army   17

2   The Fort Plan   27
    Classical sources   27
    Legionary fortresses and auxiliary forts   31
    Typical anatomy of a permanent fort   34

3   The Construction of the Fort   36
    Siting   36
    Preparation of the site   38
    Survey and layout   40
    Responsibility for fort construction   43

4   The Defences   45
    Ditches   45
    Obstacles   53
    The berm   55
    Ramparts   56
    Stone-built defences   66
    Angle and interval towers   72
    Gates   77
    Catapult platforms   94

5   The Internal Buildings   97
    Building methods   97
    The headquarters building   104
    The commander's house   132
    The granaries   142
    The hospital   157
    Barracks   166

Stables 176
The workshop 183
Storebuildings 188
Other internal buildings 191

6 Food and the Water Supply 195
The military diet 195
Preparation and cooking 197
Water supply 202
Drainage 210
Latrines 211

7 External Structures 215
The parade ground 215
The bathhouse 220

8 The Development of the Fort Plan 222
Republican camps 222
Augustus 228
Claudius 234
Nero 247
The Flavian Emperors 249
Trajan 266
Hadrian 269
Antoninus Pius 274
The later second century 284
Septimius Severus 287

9 Fort Types and Garrisons 291
Fort area 292
Granary capacity 293
Barrack accommodation 294

List of abbreviations 298

Notes 300

Select bibliography of forts 339

Bibliography 346

Index 359

List of Illustrations

Half-tone illustrations are indicated by an asterisk in this list.

In order to keep the written dimensions in the text to a minimum plans have been prepared to uniform scales to aid comparison, unless otherwise indicated in captions.

Legionary fortresses	1:5000
Auxiliary forts	1:2000
Internal buildings	1:1000
Gates	1:500

1. *The fort at Housesteads from the air. — xx
2. *Fragment of papyrus recording annual strength of garrison stationed in Lower Moesia, in early years of second century AD. — 5
3. *Fragment of writing tablet from Chesterholm-Vindolanda. — 6
4. *Scene from Trajan's Column showing soldiers engaged in camp construction. — 7
5. *Stone dedication slab from the south gate at Risingham. — 8
6. *Military discharge certificate dated AD 107, from Weissenburg. — 9
7. *Plan of fort at Benningen, near Stuttgart, by Simon Studion, 1597. — 11
8. William Stukeley's sketch of the fort at Greatchesters on Hadrian's Wall, 1725. — 12
9. *Saalburg Roman fort, reconstructed between 1898 and 1907. — 13
10. *Reconstruction drawing of Chesters Roman fort, by Alan Sorrell. — 15
11. *The fort at Beckfoot, on the Cumbrian coast, from the air. — 15
12. *Tombstone of a centurion of *legio XX* from Colchester. — 18
13. *Tombstone of a trooper of the *ala Longiniana* from Gaul. — 18
14. *Tombstone of an auxiliary soldier of the *cohors Raetorum*. — 24
15. The Polybian Camp. — 28
16. The Hyginian Camp. — 29
17. The legionary fortress at (a) Inchtuthil, Scotland, and — 32
   (b) Neuss, Lower Germany. — 33
18. The *numerus* fort at Hesselbach. — 34
19. The principal features of an auxiliary fort. — 34
20. Changes in siting of successive forts near Leintwardine, Hereford and Worcester. — 38
21. *Scene from Trajan's Column showing legionaries felling and transporting timber for construction. — 39
22. The use of the *groma* in surveying. — 41
23. Part of a *groma* and a footrule. — 42

24. *Scene from Trajan's Column showing legionaries engaged in fort construction.   46
25. Selection of tools found at the Saalburg Roman fort.   46
26. Profile of a *fossa fastigata* and a *fossa Punica*.   47
27. The defensive earthworks of a Roman fort.   48
28. *Aerial photograph of the multiple ditches of the fort at Whitley Castle, Northumberland.   49
29. *Scene from Trajan's Column showing a tented enclosure with gateway defenced by a *clavicula*.   50
30. Entrances defended by the *clavicula* and *titulum*.   51
31. The remains of bridge timbers found at Theilenhofen.   52
32. Foundation slots within ditch at Gelligaer, which supported a timber bridge in front of gate.   53
33. The use of thorn branches as obstacles in ditches.   54
34. *Defensive traps found at Antonine Wall fort of Rough Castle, in 1904.   54
35. *Scene from Trajan's Column showing legionaries building in turf.   60
36. Types of rampart construction.   61
37. *Scene from Trajan's Column showing a turf rampart surmounted by a log walkway.   64
38. *A portion of experimental turf rampart and ditch reconstructed in 1966 at The Lunt, Baginton, Warwickshire.   64
39. Detail of the construction of the experimental turf rampart at The Lunt.   65
40. *Staircases on either side of reconstructed gate at The Lunt.   67
41. Part of the curtain wall and west gate at Urspring.   68
42. An unusual method of rampart construction *murus Gallicus* seen at the Saalburg, constructed c. AD 135.   68
43. Part of the fort wall at Wörth which had collapsed into the ditch.   70
44. Centurial building stone from Carvoran on Hadrian's Wall, c. AD 136–138.   71
45. Towers and gates illustrated on Trajan's Column.   73
46. *Foundations of the curtain wall and south-east angle tower at Unterböbingen.   74
47. *Replica stone tower and section of wall at Chesterholm-Vindolanda.   74
48. *Replica towers in timber and stone constructed at Chesterholm-Vindolanda.   75
49. *Foundations of the curtain wall and an interval tower at Unterböbingen.   75
50. Suggested reconstruction of successive towers at the south-east angle of fort at Künzing.   76
51. Bridge-type gateways.   79
52. Gates with towers flush with the rampart.   80
53. The groundplans of some Republican and Augustan gates.   82
54. Gates with internal towers.   83
55. Suggested reconstructions of timber gateways at Rödgen and Künzing.   83
56. View through gate portals of Flavian fort showing threshold beams.   84
57. Suggested reconstruction of a principal gate at Rottweil.   84
58. *Royal Engineers erecting reconstruction of timber east gate at The Lunt, Baginton.   85
59. *The completed gateway at The Lunt.   86
60. *Scene from Trajan's Column showing a camp with timber gate and angle towers.   86

61. *Foundations of curtain wall and south gate at Buch, Raetia.   87
62. The south gate at Chesters on Hadrian's Wall.   88
63. The south-east gate at Hesselbach.   88
64. The remains of the north gate of fort of Bu Njem in Libya, illustrated by G. F. Lyon in 1819.   89
65. *Decorative door-head from a gatetower at Hesselbach.   90
66. *Detail of a mosaic depicting gateway of a Roman town.   90
67. Suggested reconstruction of the principal gate at Hesselbach.   91
68. *The east gate at Birdoswald on Hadrian's Wall.   92
69. *Detail of east gate at Birdoswald.   92
70. Gatetowers which projected in front of the curtain wall.   93
71. An inscription from High Rochester, Northumberland, recording the restoration of an artillery platform in AD 225–235.   95
72. Artist's impression of an auxiliary fort.   96
73. Successive stages in the rebuilding of the fort at Corbridge.   98
74. *The timber foundations of part of courtyard-plan workshop of Claudian fort of Valkenburg.   98
75. Detail of timber construction techniques revealed at Valkenburg.   100
76. Commanders' houses at Niederbieber and Cadder.   102
77. Detail of wall foundations at Valkenburg.   103
78. Section drawn through a typical *principia*, showing main features.   104
79. *An inscription from Lower German fort of Remagen, recording the repair of the fort clock.   105
80. *Column bases, capitals and shafts from courtyard portico of *principia* at Bar Hill, on Antonine Wall.   107
81. *The courtyard of the reconstructed *principia* at the Saalburg fort.   107
82. A keystone, found in the courtyard at South Shields.   107
83. Surviving portion of the cross-hall wall of legionary *principia* at Burnum, recorded in 1774.   110
84. *Bronze military standard from Chesterholm-Vindolanda.   113
85. *Key to a *signifer*'s paychest, found at legionary fortress of Neuss.   114
86. The location of the regimental treasury.   114
87. Headquarters with part-stone and part-timber construction.   116
88. Successive designs of the *principia* at Künzing.   116
89. *The strongroom of *principia* at Chesters.   117
90. The strongroom of *principia* at Brough by Bainbridge.   118
91. *Sandstone statue from *principia* at Niederbieber.   119
92. *Principia* of legionary fortress at Lambaesis, North Africa.   121
93. *Principia* forehalls with elaborate entrances.   122
94. *Interior of reconstructed forehall of *principia* at the Saalburg.   123
95. *Principia* with forehalls.   124
96. Headquarters of Republican camps.   126
97. Headquarters of Augustan forts.   128
98. Developments in *principia* plan: Claudian, Neronian, Late Flavian.   129
99. Developments in *principia* plan: Hadrianic, Antonine, Severan.   131
100. *Tombstone from Birdoswald recording death of infant son of the garrison commander.   133
101. The commander's house: comparison with civilian houses.   135
102. Groundplan of commander's house at Housesteads.   136
103. Reconstruction drawing of commander's house at Housesteads.   137
104. Commanders' houses with adjoining compounds.   138
105. Types of timber granaries.   146
106. Types of stone-built granaries.   147

107. *Longitudinal sleeper walls supporting floor of granary at Corbridge. 148
108. *Granary at Housesteads. 148
109. *Granary at Corbridge. 150
110. *Granary at Corbridge, showing the loading platform, portico column and drain. 151
111. *The granary at The Lunt, Baginton. 154
112. *Reconstruction drawing of timber granary at The Lunt, Baginton, by Alan Sorrell. 154
113. *A pair of stone granaries reconstructed at the Saalburg. 155
114. Reconstruction drawing of stone-built granary. 156
115. *A grain ship shown on wall painting from Ostia. 157
116. *Scene from Trajan's Column showing soldier receiving medical attention. 158
117. Groundplans of legionary hospitals. 160
118. *Model of the legionary hospital at Vetera. 161
119. *Surgical instruments from a doctor's grave at Bingen. 162
120. *Lead stopper from a medicine jar found at Haltern. 162
121. Possible hospital plans within auxiliary forts. 163
122. The corridor-plan building found at Beaufront Red House, near Corbridge. 164
123. *Fragments of marble plan of Rome. 165
124. Details of storebuildings shown on marble plan of Rome. 165
125. *Scene from Trajan's Column showing tents within a fortified enclosure. 166
126. Arrangement of the century's tents within the marching camp, according to Hyginus. 167
127. A typical auxiliary barrack block. 167
128. *Pair of reconstructed timber barracks on stone foundations at the Saalburg. 168
129. Comparative plans of auxiliary barracks. 169
130. *Panel of painted wall plaster, found in officer's rooms in a timber barrack at Echzell, Upper Germany. 170
131. Reconstruction drawing of interior of a barrack room. 172
132. Double barrack block at Valkenburg, in three successive periods. 174
133. *Aerial photograph of excavations at Heidenheim, showing foundation trenches of timber barracks. 175
134. Stables found in auxiliary forts. 178
135. *Part of a small pottery lamp found at Valkenburg. 179
136. Stables at Hod Hill. 181
137. Possible stables at Künzing. 181
138. Workshops in legionary fortresses. 184
139. Workshop of legionary fortress at Inchtuthil. 184
140. Auxiliary workshop plans. 186
141. Hammerhead from Bar Hill, on the Antonine Wall. 189
142. Workshops or storebuildings. 190
143. Plan of the *gyrus-vivarium* at The Lunt, Baginton. 191
144. *The *gyrus-vivarium* at The Lunt, Baginton. 192
145. Miscellaneous internal buildings. 193
146. Internal bathhouses. 193
147. *Stores list on wooden writing tablet, from Chesterholm-Vindolanda. 197
148. Bakehouse at Stockstadt. 198
149. *Suggested reconstruction of a corn mill, from Zugmantel. 198

150. Circular structures, possibly millhouses, found at Chesterholm-Vindolanda. 200
151. Small millstone found at the Saalburg. 200
152. *Stone-built oven preserved at Antonine fort of Birrens. 201
153. Buckets and winding gear preserved in wells at the Saalburg. 203
154. A type of well lining, based on example found at the Saalburg. 204
155. Timber well construction: an example of a prefabricated design from Krefeld-Gellep. 205
156. Impression of postholes and timbers found in wells. 205
157. *Inscription found at Öhringen, referring to the fort aqueduct. 207
158. Types of water channels. 208
159. The water-settling tank in courtyard of *principia* at Benwell. 209
160. Stone drain cover from Housesteads. 210
161. *Latrine at Housesteads. 211
162. Plan of Housesteads latrine. 212
163. Latrines in auxiliary forts. 214
164. Plan of fort and parade ground at Hardknott. 216
165. *Aerial photograph of fort at Hardknott, Cumbria. 216
166. *Altar from Auchendavy, Scotland, dedicated to the goddesses of parade ground. 217
167. *Parade armour from Straubing; bronze face masks. 218
168. *Parade armour from Straubing; bronze protective plates for horses' faces. 218 & 219
169. Principal components of auxiliary bathhouse. 221
170. *Bathhouse at Chesters. 221

Fort Plans
171. Renieblas, Numantia, Camps I, III, V. 224
172. Castillejo, Numantia, c. 133 BC. 226
173. Peña Redonda, Numantia, c. 133 BC. 227
174. Beckinghausen, Augustan. 231
175. Rödgen, Augustan (timber). 232
176. Haltern, Augustan (timber). 233
177. Hofheim, Claudian (timber). 235
178. Vindonissa, Claudian legionary fortress (stone). 236
179. Valkenburg, c. AD 40 (timber). 236
180. Oberstimm, c. AD 40 (timber). 238
181. Roman fort built within defences of Iron Age hillfort at Hod Hill. 241
182. Hod Hill, c. AD 43–44 (timber). 242
183. Plan of defences and timber internal building of fort at Stanway, plotted from aerial photographs. 243
184. *Aerial photograph of defences and timber internal buildings of fort at Stanway. 243
185. Longthorpe vexillation fortress, c. AD 44/8 (timber). 245
186. Vetera 1, Neronian (stone). 246
187. Nanstallon, c. AD 60 (timber). 248
188. Baginton, c. AD 64, (timber). 248
189. Rottweil 3, c. AD 72/3 (timber). 251
190. Pen Llystyn, c. AD 78/9 (timber). 253
191. Fendoch, c. AD 82–4 (timber). 256
192. Newstead, c. AD 80. 258
193. Oakwood, c. AD 80. 259

194. Künzing, c. AD 90 (timber). 264
195. Wiesbaden, c. AD 90 (stone). 264
196. Heidenheim, c. AD 90 (stone *principia*, timber barracks). 265
197. Caerleon, legionary fortress, c. AD 100 (stone). 267
198. Gelligaer, c. AD 103–111 (stone). 268
199. Housesteads, Hadrianic (stone). 271
200. Benwell, Hadrianic, (stone). 272
201. Wallsend, Hadrianic (stone). 272
202. Ambleside, Hadrianic (stone). 273
203. Hesselbach, Hadrianic (timber). 273
204. Mumrills, Antonine (principal buildings stone). 276
205. Balmuildy, Antonine (principal buildings stone). 277
206. Bearsden, Antonine (stone granaries, other internal buildings timber). 278
207. Birrens, Antonine (stone). 279
208. Newstead, Antonine, 1 and 2 (stone). 281
209. Unterböbingen, Antonine (stone). 283
210. Niederbieber, c. AD 185 (principal buildings stone). 285
211. Osterburken, c. AD 180 (stone). 286
212. Bewcastle, Severan (stone). 288
213. Supply base at South Shields, Severan (stone). 289

List of Maps

Britain and the German Provinces xiv
Augustan sites in the Rhineland 229
German–Raetian frontier, Augustus–Vespasian (19 BC–AD 79) 237
Conquest period forts in southern England 240
Flavian forts in Wales and northern Britain, c. AD 74–84 254
German–Raetian frontier, Domitian–Antoninus Pius AD 81–mid 2nd century AD 260
Lower Germany 262
Hadrian's Wall 270
The Antonine Wall 275

Acknowledgements

The author and publishers are grateful to the following persons and institutions for permission to reproduce illustrations:

Aesculap-Werke AG and Stadtverwaltung Bingen/Rhein, 119; Prof. Dr D. Baatz and the Saalburg Museum, 9, 25, 65, 67, 130, 149, 151, 153; Bayer. Landesamt für Denkmalpflege, München and Dr J. Prammer, Gäuboden-museum Straubing, 167, 168; The British Library, 2; Albrecht Brugger, 133; D. Charlesworth and the Carlisle Archaeological Unit, 56; The Clarendon Press and R. P. Wright, 44, 71; Colchester and Essex Museum, 12; Committee for Aerial Photography, Cambridge University, 1, 10, 28, 165; Coventry City Museums, 38, 111, 112, 144; Crown Copyright, reproduced by permission of the Controller of Her Majesty's Stationery Office, 11, 103, 108, 161; P. Crummy and Colchester Archaeological Trust Ltd, 183; Derbyshire Archaeological Society, 90; P. W. H. Gentry, 47, 68, 89, 110, 170; Gesellschaft pro Vindonissa, Brugg, 83; B. Hobley, 39; Hunterian Museum, Glasgow and the Glasgow Archaeological Society, 80, 166; Instituut voor Prae-en Protohistorie, Universiteit van Amsterdam, and Dr M. D. de Weerd, 74, 132, 135; A. E. Johnson, 22, 27, 33, 45, 69, 72, 78, 81, 86, 94, 107, 109, 113, 114, 128, 131, 154, 155, 156, 158, 160; L. J. F. Keppie, Professor A. S. Robertson, Mrs M. Scott and the Hunterian Museum, Glasgow, 141; Lancaster City Council Museum and the Museum of Antiquities of the University and Society of Antiquaries of Newcastle upon Tyne, 100; Museum of Antiquities of the University and Society of Antiquaries of Newcastle upon Tyne, 5; Museum Calvet, Bibliothèques et Musées, Avignon, 66; National Monuments Record Air Photograph, Crown Copyright Reserved, 184; D. S. Neal, 103; Dr D. Planck and the Landesdenkmalamt Baden-Württemberg, 46, 49, 57, 61; Prähistorische Staatssammlung, München, 6; Rheinisches Landesmuseum, Bonn, 13, 14, 79, 85, 91, 118; Lady I. Richmond, 181; Professor Anne S. Robertson, 152; Römisch-Germanische Kommission, and Prof. Dr H. Schönberger, 50, 55, 88; Royal Commission on the Ancient and Historical Monuments of Scotland, and the Society of Antiquaries of Scotland, 34; Oscar Savio Fotografo, 123; Dr G. Simpson, 159; Konrad Theiss Verlag, Stuttgart, 133; Titus Wilson and Son Ltd, Kendal, 8; University of Newcastle upon Tyne and The Vindolanda Trust, 3, 48, 84, 147; Westdeutscher Verlag GmbH and Prof. H. von Petrikovits, 17, 178, 197; Westfälisches Museum für Archäologie, Münster, and Römisch-Germanischen Museum, Haltern, 120; Württembergische Landesbibliothek, 7; Württembergisches Landes-museum, Stuttgart, and Dr Ph. Filtzinger, 157. The remaining uncredited illustrations were drawn by the author.

Britain and the German Provinces

Preface

The subject of the Roman army and its military achievements in Britain, Germany and elsewhere in the empire has been studied extensively by both historians and archaeologists. The aim of this book is to focus upon just one aspect of Roman military organisation, its permanent fortifications, and to relate the available literary and epigraphic evidence with the discoveries made from the archaeological investigation of numerous fort sites.

Such a vast amount of Roman frontier research has been carried out in the past hundred years that this review of Roman forts in the first and second centuries AD has necessarily been very selective. There will inevitably be mistakes and omissions, as research and excavations currently in progress are continually adding to our understanding. I have drawn on the work of a large number of specialists in a variety of disciplines, and owe a considerable debt to both excavators and scholars who have studied the literary, epigraphic, ceramic and numismatic evidence.

This book developed from my research in preparation for a Ph.D. thesis on the subject of Roman fort planning for the University of Wales, Cardiff, and I am greatly indebted to Professor M. G. Jarrett who has encouraged and fostered my interest in Roman military studies.

I owe a debt of gratitude to the many excavators with whom I have corresponded, and who have generously provided information and photographs. I am also most grateful to the many kind archaeologists who gave freely of their time and advice during my study tour of Germany, particularly Prof. Dr H. Schönberger of the Römisch-Germanische Kommission in Frankfurt, Drs D. Planck and A. Rüsch of the Landesdenkmalamt Baden-Württemberg, Stuttgart, Dr Ph. Filtzinger of the Württembergisches Landesmuseum in Stuttgart, Dr J. Prammer of the Gäubodenmuseum, Straubing, and especially Prof. Dr D. Baatz of the Saalburgmuseum, who has been so generous in his advice both during my studies in Germany and subsequently during the preparation of the text on the continental material.

I also wish to thank two members of staff at University College, Cardiff, Mrs S. Pollard of the Arts and Social Sciences Library for her tenacity in obtaining all the references I asked for, however obscure, and Sabina Thompson, Secretary to the Department of Archaeology, for all her assistance. The photographs of Trajan's Column (from C. Cichorius, *Die Reliefs der Traianssäule*, Berlin 1896 and 1900) were kindly taken by Mr R. Watkiss of Penzance.

Above all I should like to thank my husband Tony who drew several excellent reconstruction drawings and provided a number of photographs and, having first suggested that I should write the book, has lived with Roman forts for longer than he cares to remember.

Dowran, St. Just-in-Penwith, September 1982

1. The fort at Housesteads on Hadrian's Wall from the air. Visible in the central range is the headquarters building flanked on the left by the commander's house and on the right by the granaries, with perhaps a hospital behind, and, in the right foreground, three barrack blocks.

Introduction

> Whenever the Romans enter upon hostile ground, they never think of
> fighting till they first make their camps, which they do not rear up at a
> venture, or without rule.
>
> (Josephus, *Bell. Jud.* III, 76)

When on campaign the Roman army normally constructed a ditched
enclosure every night, within which were pitched rows of leather tents laid
out in a strict rectilinear pattern. This layout remained constant, whatever
the nature of the ground, so that each man upon entering the camp could
readily identify his own tent.

In the second century BC the historian Polybius described in some detail
a camp suitable for two legions, which was rectangular in shape and
defended by a ditch and an earthen bank with a palisade of wooden stakes on
the top, enclosing a regular internal arrangement of tents. Camps of this date
with a similar uniform internal layout have been excavated at Numantia in
Spain, although here they were set within polygonal defensive circuits.[1] The
origins of this type of marching camp are rather obscure, and there is some
conflict in the literary evidence, but the tradition can be traced back to at
least the fourth century BC when colonies, walled towns with regularly laid-
out street plans, were built by Rome to consolidate her initial expansion into
Italy. It is probable that the form evolved gradually, as the Romans
characteristically assimilated and modified the best defensive ideas of other
armies with whom they came into contact.

The Republican army was originally composed of part-time soldiers,
Roman citizens who enlisted in the legions for summer campaigns and who
returned to their homes at the end of each season. But, as the army became
more and more successful and Roman conquests expanded overseas, from
the third century BC onwards, to Spain, Greece, North Africa, Asia Minor
and Gaul, it became increasingly necessary for the army to stay abroad for
several years at a time to consolidate its gains, which led to changes both in
the recruitment of more professional soldiers and the need for more
permanent winter accommodation.[2] The temporary camps occupied during
the summer campaigns (*castra aestiva*) were therefore supplemented by
winter quarters (*hiberna*), which were built either in the territory of friendly
allies or in the newly conquered lands. These provided more substantial
accommodation, perhaps with stone or turf huts and timber store buildings
and had stronger defences, housing one or more legions and their allied
troops and cavalry.

The concept of a frontier had not developed at this time, for there was no idea of any limits to Roman expansion. The legions engaged the enemy in the field and almost invariably defeated them, often striking deep into their territory, only to negotiate peace, perhaps take a few hostages, and ultimately return to their winter quarters in anticipation of the next season's campaigns. Unfortunately, although the most successful general, Julius Caesar, described the camps which he built in Gaul during the campaigns of the 50s BC none have so far been located on the ground, and it is not until the reign of the emperor Augustus that we begin to find traces of the earth-and-timber supply depots and semi-permanent bases built by his generals during successive campaigns (from c. 16 BC to AD 16) against the Germans in the Rhineland. The crushing defeat of the general Varus and his loss of three legions in the German Teutoburg forest in AD 9 so profoundly shocked the emperor Augustus that for the first time a halt to Roman expansion was contemplated; he advised his successor, Tiberius, not to extend the limits of the empire any further.

As a result of this policy, by AD 16 the rivers Rhine and Danube became effectively the frontiers of the empire in Germany, and for the first time legionary bases and permanent earth-and-timber forts were established to house the newly formed auxiliary infantry and cavalry (non-Roman specialist troops). By the time of the Claudian invasion of Britain in AD 43 a clear distinction between the permanent fort/fortress and the temporary summer marching camp was emerging. The conquest of southern England was characterised by the establishment of a series of small earth-and-timber forts connected by a network of good military roads, which may initially have housed a combined detachment of legionaries and auxiliaries to impose swift control over the native population. This strategy was continued in the Flavian period, first in Wales and later in the north of England and Scotland, with auxiliary forts normally spaced within a day's march of each other, frequently overlooking important road crossings and junctions, with the larger legionary bases established at the rear.

For the purpose of this study a fort is defined as a permanent fortification ranging in size from c. 1 to 5 hectares in internal area, which normally housed a unit of auxiliary infantry or cavalry of 500 or 1000 men, or very occasionally a combined auxiliary and legionary force, whilst a legionary fortress of some 20 hectares was designed to house a full legion of between 5000 and 6000 men.

The boundaries of the Upper German and Raetian frontiers were extended first during the Flavian period and later under Antoninus Pius. Both extensions consisted of a frontier line marked with a timber palisade and intermediate watchtowers, with a regular series of auxiliary forts close by; as the frontiers became permanent the forts, and later part of the frontier in Raetia, were re-built in stone. The northern frontier of Britain was consolidated under Hadrian by a mural frontier linking the Tyne and the

Solway estuaries, with a series of sixteen stone-built auxiliary forts added to police it. This was replaced for a while under Antoninus Pius by a turf wall running from the Forth to the Clyde, again with an integral series of auxiliary forts.

Auxiliary forts were also constructed for specific purposes, providing more than just another link in a frontier chain. On the Danube, for example, at Oberstimm and on the Rhine, at Valkenburg, forts were built in c. AD 40 which contained workshops considerably larger than those required by their garrisons alone. They probably provided supplies, equipment, and possibly preserved foodstuffs to neighbouring forts along their respective frontiers, and to other forts which lay upon navigable rivers and estuaries; in coastal harbours they sometimes functioned as supply bases. The fort at South Shields, at the mouth of the River Tyne, with eighteen or twenty granaries provided a supply depot for the Severan campaigns in Scotland at the beginning of the third century, probably in conjunction with a similar base at Cramond on the Forth estuary, and forts with harbour facilities are also known on the Welsh and northern coasts of Britain.[3] Many of the forts along the frontiers of Germania and Raetia could be supplied from the Rhine and the Danube. The harbour at Dover was selected as the base for the British fleet (*Classis Britannica*). The Trajanic fort in London may have performed a ceremonial role, housing the guard of the provincial governor of Britain, and Baginton, with its circular arena (*gyrus*) may also have played a specialist role in cavalry training, the detention of hostages and prisoners, or perhaps the collection of wild animals for a *vivarium*.

Several forts have been linked with mineral extraction. At Pumsaint in Wales, for example, the fort lay close to the gold workings at Dolaucothi, and the fort at Charterhouse in Somerset was associated with the Mendips lead mines.[4] Two lead ingots from this area, one dated AD 49 and the other stamped by *legio II Augusta* provide evidence of the early extraction of lead (and therefore silver) from the new province of Britain.[5] Finds of lead and lead ore from Brough on Noe, and lead ingots (pigs) found near the fort of Brough on Humber suggest a connection with the lead mines of Derbyshire, and it is probable that the forts of Brough under Stainmore, Whitley Castle and Kirkby Thore in Westmorland had connections with lead mining on nearby Alston Moor.[6]

The documentary and epigraphic evidence

The most important Classical literary sources relating to Roman castramentation and the organisation of the auxiliary troops are an incomplete text, *de munitionibus castrorum*, included in a manuscript of a surveyor called Hyginus Gromaticus (believed to refer to the reign of Marcus Aurelius) and the *epitoma rei militaris* of Flavius Vegetius Renatus, written probably in the late fourth or early fifth century AD, but drawing upon much earlier sources, some of which extended as far back as the middle Republic.[7]

The work of Hyginus was intended mainly as a surveying manual in which he set out formulae and a framework for the siting and laying out of a camp which could theoretically accommodate every type of unit that his students might have to deal with; thus within his 'model' camp are housed not only three legions but a selection of Praetorians, auxiliary cavalry and infantry, marines, scouts, irregular troops and a camel corps. Although his camp is essentially a hypothetical and temporary one, designed for a very large number of men, the principles of organisation, the functions of the various components, and the terminology also hold true for the smaller permanent auxiliary fort. There are many corruptions in the text which obscure some of the details, but nevertheless it provides a clear general outline of the arrangement of a legionary marching camp, together with the numbers involved in both the legions and the auxiliary troops.

Flavius Vegetius Renatus also deals mainly with legionary camps and he provides a wealth of detail about the organisation and tactics of the legions, and also deals with the duties of the various ranks of officers, the selection and building of camps, and the training of recruits. However, he draws on a wide variety of sources ranging in date from the mid Republican period to the end of the third century AD, so his authority must be accepted only with extreme caution. Here he is quoted only where his words can be substantiated from the archaeological or epigraphic evidence.

Important details about Roman camps and their defences are given by several other Classical authors. The historian Polybius described the marching camp of the late third to middle second centuries BC and Julius Caesar fully documented his campaigns a century later in the Civil War, and in Africa, Gaul and Spain, giving details of camp construction and siege tactics.[8] Josephus described the camps built by the Roman army during the Jewish War of AD 72.[9] Equally valuable are the writings of Flavius Arrianus, a former governor of the province of Cappadocia, and a contemporary of the emperor Hadrian, who wrote a manual of cavalry training and recorded information about the composition of auxiliary cavalry units at this period.[10]

Fragments of military documents giving everyday lists of men available for duty, guard rosters, receipts for military stores, pay lists, records of leave or secondment, etc., written on papyri, parchment or inscribed potsherds (*ostraca*) are occasionally preserved under favourable conditions, especially in Egypt and Syria. The most important surviving documents which relate to an auxiliary garrison are the remains of papyri from the archives of *cohors XX Palmyrenorum*, stationed at Dura Europos in Syria, which were found in 1931–2.[11] They span a period of over fifty years and give a remarkable insight into the everyday life of the soldiers there. Other important documents include *ostraca* and papyri from Pselcis, which record receipts

2. Fragment of papyrus from a military document recording the annual strength
(*pridianum*) of a garrison stationed in the province of Lower Moesia (modern
Romania) in the early years of the second century AD. (Hunt's *Pridianum*:
British Museum Papyrus 2851)

3. Fragment of a wooden writing tablet from Chesterholm-Vindolanda in Northumberland, part of a private letter which mentions the dispatch of a parcel containing shoes, socks and underpants. (Vindolanda writing tablet no. 15)

for stores and grain rations, and from the Wâdi Fawâkhir, on which are preserved requests and thanks from individual soldiers for food and additional items of equipment from home.[12] Another extremely important group of documents, written on wooden tablets and preserved in water-logged deposits, has recently been discovered at Chesterholm in Northumberland; they include military documents such as stores lists, together with personal correspondence, such as the tablet recording the dispatch of a parcel containing shoes, socks and underpants.[13] (Ill. 3) These documents are very valuable as they provide details of routine life within the fort and often give minutiae which could not be gleaned from any other source. They have the added advantage of offering the historian and archaeologist first-hand accounts which have been neither corrupted by later copying nor distorted for propaganda purposes.

Trajan's Column, erected in Rome in c. AD 113 to commemorate the emperor's victories in Dacia, consists of a series of sculptured panels which depict the army, mostly the legions, in battle, and engaged in the construction of temporary camps. It is upon these illustrations that most of the reconstructions of defensive features and internal buildings are based.[14]

Having constructed a new building, or largely rebuilt an old one, it was customary to set up a dedication slab recording the name of the emperor, the

4. Scene from Trajan's Column showing legionary soldiers engaged in camp construction. (Scenes XVIII/XIX)

unit responsible for the project, the commanding officer, and perhaps the actual nature of the work completed.[15] These inscriptions can give important information about the actual unit which was in garrison, its title and type, often at a specific date, and it is occasionally possible from archaeological excavation to uncover the building to which it referred; although only in stone-built forts, for the dedication slabs from timber forts, which were presumably cut in timber, do not survive. Altars may also give the name of the unit in garrison, perhaps with its commanding officer, and tombstones from the vicinity of the fort can be of importance for they sometimes depict the deceased in his military uniform and, if a craftsman,

7

may illustrate the tools of his trade. In the absence of stone inscriptions a clue to the garrison's identity may sometimes be given by roofing or hypocaust tiles stamped with the unit's name. There may, though, be difficulties in interpretation as it is known that some auxiliary cohorts (for example the *cohors IIII Vindelicorum* stationed at Gross-Krotzenburg in Upper Germany) operated large tile works supplying tiles to neighbouring forts, all of which bore their stamp.[16] Discharge diplomas (*diplomata*

5. Stone dedication slab from the south gate at Risingham, Northumberland (*RIB* 1234), which reads: *[Imp(eratoribus) Caes(aribus) L(ucio) Sept(imio) Severo Pio Pertinaci Arab(ico) Adi]ab(enico) Part(h)[i]co Maxi(mo) co(n)s(uli) III et M(arco) Aurel(io) Antonino Pio c(n)s(uli) II Aug(ustis) et P(ublio) Sept(imio) Getae nob(ilissimo) Caes(ari) portam cum muris vetustate dilapsis iussu Alfeni Senecionis v(iri) c(larissimi) co(n)s(ularis) curante Oclatinio Advento proc(uratore) Aug(ustorum) n(ostrorum) coh(ors) I Vangion(um) m(illiaria) eq(uitata) cum Aem[i]l(io) Salviano trib(uno) suo a solo restit(uit)*

'For the Emperor-Caesars Lucius Septimius Severus Pius Pertinax, conqueror of Arabia, conqueror of Adiabene, Most Great Conqueror of Parthia, three times proclaimed consul, Augustus, and Marcus Aurelius Antoninus Pius, twice consul, Augustus, and for Publius Septimius Geta, most noble Caesar, the First Cohort of Vangiones, one-thousand strong, part-mounted, restored from ground level this gate with its walls, which had fallen down through old age, at the command of Alfenus Senecio, of senatorial rank, the consular governor, under the charge of Oclatinius Adventus, procurator of our Emperors, together with its tribune Aemilius Salvianus' (AD 205-207).

militaria), recording the grant of Roman citizenship to an auxiliary soldier upon his retirement after twenty-five years' service, can also give valuable information, as upon them were inscribed not only the details of the recipient, but also the name of the emperor, the province, the governor, and the names of all the other auxiliary units within the province at that date which had retiring soldiers receiving such grants at the same time.[17] From a study of these diplomas it is sometimes possible to trace the movements of various auxiliary units from one province to another, with considerable accuracy.

6. Military discharge certificate (*diploma*) dated June 30th AD 107, from Weissenburg in Raetia. The *diploma*, comprising a pair of small bronze plates fastened together, was conferred on an auxiliary soldier upon his honourable discharge from the army, and records the official grant of citizenship made to him by the emperor. On one side (a) are inscribed details of the emperor, the province, the governor, and the names of all the other auxiliary units which were discharging soldiers at the same time, and on the other (b, overleaf) the names of the individuals concerned. Each leaf measures 16.3 × 13 cm. (*CIL* XVI 51, no. 55)

6. (b) names of individual soldiers.

The archaeological background

The excavation of Roman forts has figured prominently in British and German archaeology since the middle of the last century. In previous centuries an increased awareness and interest in Roman antiquities, stimulated by the Renaissance, had been concentrated upon digging for relics to add to collections of inscriptions, sculptures and coins and little systematic excavation, and even less detailed recording, was attempted. An exception may be seen in Simon Studion, who collected inscriptions in the Stuttgart area and who, in 1597, produced an excavation plan giving dimensions of part of the auxiliary fort at Benningen.

Antiquarian work during the seventeenth and eighteenth centuries was concerned predominantly with fieldwork—in recognising the remains of a Roman site and recording its surviving remains, together with any finds from the vicinity. This field survey approach began with William Camden in England when in 1600 he published his volume *Britannia*, which included the observations he had made upon his own travels, supplemented in later editions from information supplied by local correspondents. The tradition was continued by a succession of local historians, including William Stukeley, who described and sketched many of the Hadrian's Wall forts, published posthumously in his *Iter Boreale* in 1776.

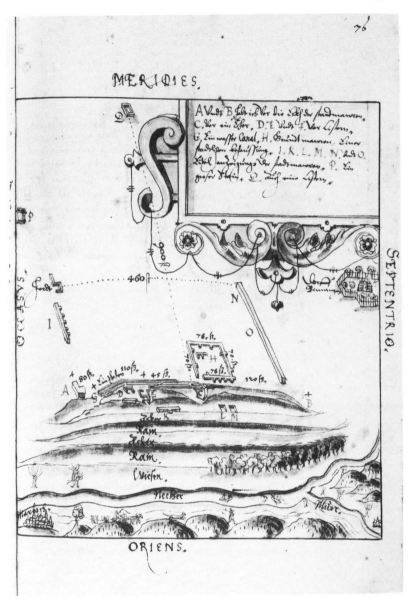

7. Plan of the Roman fort at Benningen, near Stuttgart, in Upper Germany which was drawn by Simon Studion in 1597.

8. William Stukeley's sketch of the fort at Greatchesters on Hadrian's Wall, in 1725.

At this time substantial remains of ruined internal buildings were still visible within several forts in the north of Britain and in the more densely forested parts of the Upper German frontier. The defences of the fort at Housesteads on Hadrian's Wall, for example, were evidently still in use, as the site provided a base for the Armstrong family, a notorious band of horse thieves; such was their reputation that Camden declined to visit this part of the frontier during his tour of 1599. At Carvoran, also on the Wall, the buildings of the fort and the adjacent civilian settlement were well preserved too, and in 1708 it was recorded as 'a square Roman City, with a deep Vallum or Trench around it, one hundred and twenty yards one way, and one hundred and sixty or one hundred and seventy yards the other. Great Ruins of old Housesteeds (buildings) are very visible, with the tracks of the Streets; and without the South side Trench, are likewise several long streets, and foundations of houses'.[18] When William Stukeley visited Maryport, on the Cumbrian coast, he was able to 'trace many square plots of the houses, and of the streets, paved with broad flag stones that are visibly worn with use'.[19] These descriptions are particularly important because the building of a military road across several Hadrian's Wall forts by General Wade in 1751, together with continual stone robbing and increasing cultivation later denuded these sites extensively.

Upon the northern British frontier the emphasis placed on theoretical interpretation from field work alone continued until the turn of the nineteenth century. The Reverend Anthony Hedley, after investigating the east gate of the fort at Chesterholm in 1818, and publishing the results, stressed the need for more excavation within Roman forts for, as he pointed out, since Camden's time 'nothing or next to nothing, has been done towards systematically clearing the ground plan of one of these stations'. Excavation would 'throw a very interesting and desirable light on the stationary economy of the Romans, and on the form and arrangement of their castra stativa'.[20] Increasingly there was small-scale digging at a number of sites; the first British fort to be excavated in detail was High Rochester, from 1852 to 1855. Programmes of excavation followed at Housesteads and other Hadrian's Wall forts at the end of the nineteenth century, at Birrens in southern Scotland in 1895, and on the Antonine Wall from 1896 to 1903, with work at Gelligaer in Wales (1899–1901), Newstead in the Scottish Lowlands (1905–8), Hardknott in the Lake District and Melandra Castle near Manchester (1898–1902).

The pattern of antiquarian enquiry and research was much the same in Germany, where there was increasing local interest and exploration in the nineteenth century, culminating in the establishment, in 1884, of the Reichs-Limes Kommission, inspired largely by the scholar Theodor Mommsen. Under the auspices of the Kommission from 1892 onwards

9. Saalburg Roman Fort. The stone-built defences, headquarters, two barracks and part of the commander's house were reconstructed at the instigation of Kaiser Wilhelm II, between 1898 and 1907.

almost a hundred forts along the Upper German and Raetian frontier were systematically excavated, a project which was sponsored by the German government. The results of these researches were published between 1894 and 1937 in fourteen volumes of frontier research, *Der Obergermanisch-rätische Limes des Römerreiches*. It was at this time also (1898–1907) that the stone walled defences and several of the internal stone buildings of the fort at the Saalburg, in the Taunus mountains, were restored by Kaiser Wilhelm II. Archaeological investigation of the Lower German frontier upon the left bank of the Rhine was concentrated primarily during the latter part of the last century and the first half of this century upon the excavation of the legionary fortresses of Neuss-Novaesium, Vetera and Bonn, and there has been a considerable amount of excavation of auxiliary forts here since the 1940s.[21]

Most of the forts excavated in the last century were wholly or partially stone-built, and it was only with the work of such brilliant excavators as J. P. Bushe-Fox at the Claudian supply base of Richborough in Kent in the 1920s and 1930s that a complex of timber buildings was recognised on a large scale for the first time.[22] The increasing pace of redevelopment since the Second World War has resulted in a considerable growth in the number of forts recognised and excavated, and at the same time improved archaeological excavation techniques have ensured that more and more earth-and-timber forts have been recorded. A move away from the practice of examining the fort defences and interior in a narrow hand or machine-dug trench towards investigation in a large open area, has resulted in the discovery of unique structures such as the circular enclosure (*gyrus-vivarium*) at Baginton, and the large workshop and assorted specialist buildings at Oberstimm. A major contribution to the study of Roman forts has been made since 1945 by aerial photography which has led to recognition of new fort sites, and helped to clarify the internal and external arrangements of previously known sites and place them in their topographical context.[23]

At present approximately 250 auxiliary forts are known in Britain and over 200 in Germany, and there are numerous other probable sites which have yet to be confirmed by excavation—but despite the great wealth of information available only a relatively small number of sites has been excavated in detail using modern techniques. The following pages are intended as an introduction to this fascinating and complex subject. I have attempted to pick out the most important archaeological discoveries and to combine them with the available literary and epigraphic evidence to give as full a picture as possible of the construction, layout and possible reconstruction of the forts' defences and internal buildings. It has not been possible to provide here detailed information on individual sites, although a comprehensive gazetteer of Roman forts is in preparation.

The dates of the forts considered here span the first and second centuries AD and the geographical limits are defined within the provinces of *Britannia*,

10. Reconstruction drawing of Chesters Roman fort by Alan Sorrell, showing the bridge across the North Tyne, the external bathhouse, and the civilian settlement on the slope between the fort and the river.

11. The fort at Beckfoot, on the Cumbrian coast, from the air, looking south-east. The differential ripening of the crop provides a remarkably clear picture of the underlying stone buildings, and broadly reveals the internal arrangements of the fort.

Germania Inferior, Germania Superior and *Raetia*. Forts and frontiers in these provinces developed on similar lines during the first and second centuries AD, and they shared a common climate, which may be relevant to constructional techniques. It is possible to trace the progress, very occasionally, of particular auxiliary units from one province, and from one fort, to another. The first part of the book deals with the composition of the various units within the Roman army and the fort layout, and goes on to consider the construction of the fort, the individual components of the defences and the internal buildings. The second part deals with the development of the fort plan from the temporary marching camp of the Republican period and the early Augustan forts and legionary bases of the Rhineland to the more 'standard' rectangular layout of the permanent fort. The latest forts included are those built during the reign of Septimius Severus (AD 193–211), for during the third century the defensive problems of the Roman army were changing and the composition of the Roman army itself was in transition, so that the forts began to change in plan and function.[24] Finally there is a brief consideration as to how far a study of the size and planning of the auxiliary fort can be used to indicate the size and type of the unit in garrison.

There is no discussion here of the civilian settlements (*canabae, vici*) which developed outside all but the most temporary of forts. These flourished particularly during the third and fourth centuries, accommodating the soldiers' families, veteran soldiers, and the various tradesmen and service industries. Guest houses and inns were found here. Outside the forts also lay cemeteries, temples, bathhouses and, occasionally, fortified annexes. Recent work on these extra-mural settlements, both from archaeological excavation and aerial photography makes their reconsideration long overdue.[25]

I   The Roman Army

The Legions

The legion was the most prestigious of the various Roman armed forces and formed the backbone of the imperial army. It comprised a force of some 5300 well-equipped and highly trained infantry soldiers whose status, pay and conditions of service were far better than their auxiliary counterparts. Recruitment to the legions was restricted exclusively to Roman citizens who served normally for twenty-five years, receiving upon retirement a grant of land or money from the emperor.

The legion was divided into ten cohorts, each containing six centuries of eighty men. Within the century mess groups of eight men shared a barrack room. During the early empire all the cohorts were of equal size but during the Flavian period, probably by c. AD 80, the first cohort was almost doubled in size and reorganised to contain five centuries of 160 men, giving it a total strength of 800 whilst cohorts II–X had 480 men each. In addition to the infantry a small contingent of 120 cavalry was assigned to each legion; the cavalrymen mainly acted as dispatch riders and couriers and were dispersed throughout the individual centuries.[1]

The commander of the legion (*legatus Augusti legionis*) and his second-in-command, the senior tribune (*tribunus militum legionis laticlavius*), were not long-serving professional soldiers but were rather administrators, of senatorial rank, in their thirties and twenties respectively, to whom a legionary appointment represented a step up the promotion ladder of the imperial service. Similarly five junior tribunes (*tribuni militum angusticlavii*) of equestrian status were attached to the legionary staff on short-term commissions as a step in their civil service careers.[2] The senior experienced army officer was the *praefectus castrorum* (or *praefectus legionis*), the third-in-command, who was a former centurion and had spent his whole career in the army. He bore considerable responsibility for the administration of the legion, and supervised all its engineering, construction and industrial projects. Within the ranks the main responsibility for military discipline and training fell upon the shoulders of the sixty centurions, who were ranked in each cohort according to seniority, the most senior in the legion being the principal centurion of the First Cohort, the *primus pilus*.[3] In addition the

12. Tombstone of a centurion of *legio XX* from Colchester (*RIB* 200), which dates probably before the Boudiccan rebellion of AD 60–61. It reads:

M(arcus) Favoni(us) M(arci) f(ilius) Pol(lia tribu) Facilis c(enturio) leg(ionis) XX Verecundus et Novicius lib(erti) posuerunt h(ic) s(itus) e(st)

'Here lies Marcus Favonius Facilis, son of Marcus, of the Pollian voting-tribe, centurion of the Twentieth Legion. His freedmen Verecundus and Novicius set this up.'

13. Tombstone of a trooper of the *ala Longiniana* from Gaul, found in Bonn, which dates before AD 70. It reads:

Vonatorix Duconis f(ilius) eques ala Longiniana annorum XLV stipendiorum XVII h(ic) s(itus) e(st)

'Here lies Vonatorix, son of Duco, trooper of the ala Longiniana, aged 45 years, with 17 years' service.'

18

century included several non-commissioned officers, the *optio*, *tesserarius* and *custos armorum*. Specialist skills were provided by the *immunes*, men who pursued their particular craft or trade within the legion, such as surveyors, armourers, hospital orderlies or clerks, who were exempted from the routine duties of the ordinary soldiers.[4]

There were generally no more than twenty-eight legions in the whole empire at any one time. Tacitus tells us that in the early first century (in AD 23) there were eight legions stationed in the Rhineland; four each in *Germania Inferior* and *Germania Superior*, although this number was later reduced to two legions in each province.[5] The conquest of Britain in AD 43 needed four legions, three of which remained in the province permanently. The legions were matched and often surpassed in numbers by supporting auxiliary troops. Until the middle of the first century AD both the legions and auxiliaries were closely linked and often shared the same camps, but as gains were consolidated and the frontiers of the empire drawn it fell to the auxiliaries to garrison the frontier forts of the newly won territories, acting under the jurisdiction of the legions who were now based in permanent fortresses behind the front lines.

Numerous inscriptions show that the legions were active in engineering and constructional projects. Detachments from all three legions stationed in Britain built Hadrian's Wall and its attendant milecastles and forts, whilst elsewhere legionaries are recorded engaged in a wide variety of activities including lime kilns, quarries, tileries, sawmills, arsenals, overseeing mines, and aqueduct and road construction. The legions also supplied experienced officers to take charge of auxiliary units, from time to time, or to supervise maintenance or repair work, and centurions might also have been seconded to serve on the staff of the provincial governor or his officials.

The Auxiliary Units

Although they were crack infantry troops, the heavily armed legionaries had always been weak in cavalry and in more versatile light-armed soldiers. Consequently the Roman generals found it increasingly necessary to supplement their armies by recruiting native troops from the newly conquered provinces (or even from outside the empire). These troops had specialist skills—sometimes with particular weapons, such as archers and slingers, or in horsemanship, and the recruits were known as allies (*socii*). The earliest recorded instance of a native force giving such aid (*auxilium*) to Roman legions dates from the First Punic War, from 264–241 BC, when Gallic horsemen were employed. The number of these units multiplied rapidly during the later Republic, and they were organised into regular army units (*auxilia*) by the emperor Augustus.

Auxiliary soldiers were usually non-citizens (*peregrini*) from the provinces who received a grant of Roman citizenship for themselves and their families upon discharge after twenty-five years' service. The *auxilia* were composed of units which consisted either entirely of cavalry (*alae*) which were the most prestigious in terms of status and pay, infantry (*cohortes peditatae*), or a combination of the two (*cohortes equitatae*). Each unit bore a number and was often named from the native people amongst whom it was recruited (such as the *cohors Hispanorum*, or *ala Thracum*), or from the name of the original native commander (*ala Longiana*). It may perhaps have taken the name of the imperial house under which it was raised (*ala Flavia*), or occasionally after the distinctive weapons or type of warfare used (*cohors sagittariorum*, archers or *cataphractarii*, armoured cavalry). Having been raised the new auxiliary unit was sent away from its homeland to serve elsewhere in the empire. Its regional identity became quickly submerged, as new recruits usually came from the province in which the unit was normally stationed, perhaps the only remaining link with the original recruiting ground being the garrison's name.

Each *ala* or cohort had a nominal strength of either 500 (*quingenaria*) or 1000 men (*milliaria*). The milliary unit was probably not created until the Flavian period, at the same time as the legionary first cohort was reorganised and almost doubled in size.[6] It is necessary to examine briefly the size and composition of the six different types of auxiliary unit, as the number of men and horses to be accommodated is important when considering the probable garrison of a particular fort (see Chapter 9, p. 294). Although the organisation of the legion is reasonably well documented there is much less evidence for the *auxilia*. In his treatise on Roman camps Hyginus gives the number of centuries and cavalry troops in each of the cohorts and *alae* (see Table 1) but unfortunately neglects to clarify the number of men in each, which has led to some confusion. He does tell us that each century contained eighty men, but the context of his statement is legionary and so it is uncertain whether the absence of any reference to the auxiliary century implies that there was no difference in size, or whether this omission was an oversight on his part. The difficulties in reconciling this figure of eighty men per century with the strengths indicated by the titles quingenary and milliary have led some modern scholars to believe that the number of men per century varied amongst the different units, with three sizes involved, of sixty, eighty and a hundred men.[7] Similarly the number of thirty-two men per cavalry troop (*turma*) given by Hyginus and other Roman authorities has not been thought sufficient for a thousand-strong cavalry unit (*ala milliaria*) which, on this reckoning would number less than eight hundred men, and therefore a larger *turma* strength has been suggested.[8]

This apparent discrepancy may be more easily explained if the number of men per century or cavalry troop is taken as constant within both the legionary and auxiliary forces, each having eighty and thirty-two men respectively, with the terms 'milliary' and 'quingenary' being used much less precisely. The basic auxiliary cohort would therefore be modelled directly upon the legionary pattern, with six centuries of eighty men (cavalry were added in a ratio similar to the legionary *equites*, in multiples of 120 riders). The milliary auxiliary cohort may well have been based upon the legionary first cohort which, although also termed milliaria, was not actually double the size of the remaining cohorts, as it had five double centuries giving, in comparison with them, a ratio of 10:6 centuries: similarly the ratio of centuries between the milliary and quingenary cohorts of the *auxilia* was also 10:6. It is equally probable that the strength of the cavalry *turma*, whether milliary or quingenary, remained constant at thirty-two men, so that the *ala milliaria* with an increase from sixteen to twenty-four *turmae* was not double the size of the quingenary *ala*, which should demand thirty-two *turmae*, but was only half as big again. On present evidence it seems most likely that despite its nominal strength of one thousand the milliary unit was not double but rather one and a half the size of its quingenary counterpart.[9] Table 1 (overleaf, p. 22) summarises the strength and organisation of the various auxiliary units with the total numbers of men based upon these figures; alternative figures are shown in brackets.

Cavalry (*Alae*)

ala quingenaria   Commanded by a *praefectus*. This unit, according to Arrian, contained 512 men who, Hyginus tells us, were divided into sixteen troops (*turmae*), giving thirty-two men per *turma*, the same number which is given by Vegetius for a *turma* of legionary cavalry.[10] It is not known whether the *turma* comprised thirty or thirty-two actual troopers, depending upon whether two junior officers, the *duplicarius* and the *sesquiplicarius*, were included in Arrian's calculation, although the commander of each troop, the *decurio*, certainly was not.

ala milliaria   This unit was commanded by a *praefectus* and was divided into twenty-four *turmae*, each under the command of a *decurio*.[11] The number of men in the milliary *ala* is unknown, but if the figure of thirty-two men per *turma* given for the quingenary *ala* is applied to it the total number of men would be 768. As this figure has been considered too low for a nominally thousand-strong force an alternative *turma* strength of forty-two men has been suggested.

The *ala milliaria* was always rare in the Roman army. In a survey of the composition of the army during the second half of the second century AD only ten of these units have been traced in comparison with ninety *alae quingenariae*.[12]

The *praefectus* of the milliary *ala* ranked above the other auxiliary commanders, and the scarcity of these appointments made promotion to them highly competitive. Only one milliary *ala* is known from Britain, the

Table 1 The strength and organisation of the auxiliary units: (after Breeze and Dobson, 1976)

	Infantry			Cavalry			
	No. of centuries	Men per century	Total infantry	No. of turmae	Men per turma	Total cavalry	Total strength
ala milliaria	–	–	–	24	32 (42)	768 (1008)	768 (1008)
ala quingenaria	–	–	–	16	32	512	512
cohors milliaria peditata	10	80 (100)	800 (1000)	–	–	–	800 (1000)
cohors quingenaria peditata	6	80	480	–	–	–	480
cohors milliaria equitata	10	80	800	8 (10)	32	256	1056
cohors quingenaria equitata	6	80 (60)	480 (360)	4	32	128	608 (488)

(alternative figures placed in brackets)

ala Petriana, which probably lay at Stanwix in the third century AD. Raetia also had a milliary *ala*, the *ala II Flavia milliaria*, which was stationed at Heidenheim during the Flavian period, and was transferred to a new fort at Aalen in the middle of the second century.

Infantry

cohors quingenaria peditata   Commanded by a *praefectus* and organised, according to Hyginus, into six centuries, giving a total of 480 men.[13]

cohors milliaria peditata   Commanded by a *tribunus*. This unit comprised ten centuries, giving a total of probably 800 men, although it has been suggested that the size of the century of this type of cohort was increased to 100 men to bring it up to its nominal strength.[14] The earliest dated reference to this type of unit appears on a military diploma from Pannonia, dated AD 85.[15]

Part-mounted cohorts

cohors quingenaria equitata   Commanded by a *praefectus*. Hyginus states that this unit comprised six centuries and 120 cavalrymen, excluding the officers.[16] Evidence for the organisation of this type of unit into six centuries and four *turmae* comes also from an inscription on which the decurions of the four *turmae* are mentioned[17] and from three papyri which give the annual strength (*pridianum*) of similar units, which were stationed in the provinces of Moesia and Egypt.[18] If the centuries contained eighty men there would have been 480 infantry together with 120 troopers and their officers, giving a total strength of 600 men. It has been argued, however, that this figure is too high for a 'five hundred strong' unit, and that the cavalry numbers should be subtracted from this figure, leaving six centuries of sixty infantrymen.[19]

The discovery of papyri giving the actual number of men in three of these cohorts should throw light on this problem, although examination of the figures which they provide tends to confuse further rather than resolve the difficulties. A recently published *pridianum* of an unnamed *cohors quingenaria equitata* from Egypt appears to support the smaller infantry contingent; it lists a net total of 457 men, consisting of six centurions, four decurions, 334 infantrymen, thirteen camel drivers (*dromedarii*), and 100 cavalry. This example may, however, be misleading, as it is believed to represent the depleted forces of the unit soon after an uprising and subsequent massacre.[20] The *pridianum* of *cohors I Hispanorum veterana quingenaria equitata* from Moesia (c. AD 105) records a total strength of 546 men, including 119 cavalry, whilst that of *cohors I Augusta praetoria Lusitanorum equitata*, stationed in Egypt in AD 156, lists 363 infantrymen (*pedites*), six centurions, four decurions, nineteen camel drivers and 114

14. Tombstone of an auxiliary
soldier of the *cohors Raetorum*
found at Andernach, dating to
the middle of the first century
AD. It reads:

> *F(irmus) Ecconis f(ilius)*
> *mil(es) ex coh(orte)*
> *Raetorum natione Montanus*
> *ann(orum) XXXVI*
> *stip(endiorum) X . . II heres*
> *e[x] tes(tamento) po[sui]t*

'Firmus, son of Ecco, soldier
of the cohors Raetorum, of
the tribe of Montani, aged
36 years, with ? 12 years'
service. His heirs set this up
according to his will.'

cavalrymen (*equites*). In both cases the figures for the cavalry are close to the 120 quoted by Hyginus, but the evidence for the infantry numbers remains ambiguous—if we assume that 360 was the normal infantry strength the two examples show respectively sixty-seven and nine soldiers too many on the books. On the other hand, if 480 was the correct 'paper strength', which seems more probable, the units were 53 and 111 men short.[21]

cohors milliaria equitata   Commanded by a *tribunus*. Hyginus records that this unit was divided into ten centuries and ten *turmae*, with a total number of 240 cavalry.[22] If the centuries were of legionary size there would have been 800 infantry, giving a total force of 1040 men, excluding the officers. Hyginus' statement implies that there were twenty-four men per *turma*, but if the size of the *turma* was consistent with the *alae* there would more probably have been eight *turmae* each with thirty troopers.

Irregular Troops

By the end of the first century AD the auxiliary units, which had been recruited as specialist provincial troops to complement the legions, had become so much a part of the establishment of the regular army that the need was again felt to employ irregular units of native soldiers to patrol and man the frontiers and outposts of the empire, and to act as a buffer between the Romanised provinces and the hostile barbarians beyond. New irregular troops were recruited from the frontier zones, consisting of both infantry— called simply units (*numeri*)[23]—and cavalry (*cunei*). Just like the original auxiliaries the *numerus* soldiers were allowed to retain their native weapons and identity, and probably also their own commanders.

Very little is known about the strength and organisation of these troops, nor of their commanders or conditions of service, although we do know that citizenship was not conferred upon discharge. It is probable that the organisation of the individual *numeri* varied considerably. The best documented examples of such troops are the *numeri* of Britons who were recruited in northern Britain and sent to man outpost forts and signal towers upon the Odenwald frontier of Upper Germany in the early second century AD. Recent excavations here, at Hesselbach, have revealed four barrack blocks within the 0.4 hectare fort, suggesting that the *numerus* was organised into four parts. As centurions of *numeri Brittonum* are known from inscriptions found in the vicinity it is believed that these divisions represent four individual centuries. The sizes and internal arrangements of these barracks vary, so that it is difficult to estimate the total strength of the garrison.[24]

Numeri may also have been attached to regular auxiliary cohorts in a frontier zone. Close association between the two can be seen, for example, on the Upper German frontier at Neckarburken, where a *numerus* fort lay only 200 metres from that of an auxiliary cohort, and at Osterburken, where, from the reign of Commodus, a *numerus* was accommodated alongside the fort of *cohors III Aquitanorum* in a walled annexe (see Chapter 8, p. 286 and illustration 211). In the third century AD such units were added to some of the garrisons of the Hadrian's Wall forts. For example, *cohors I Tungrorum milliaria* stationed at Housesteads was supplemented by a *numerus Hnaudifridi* from Germany and a *cuneus Frisiorum* from the Low Countries, although whether they were housed in an independent *numerus* fort, within the auxiliary fort, or in less formal native settlements outside, remains unknown.[25]

Inscriptions describe these irregular troops in a variety of roles—as frontier patrols and police, manning outpost forts, providing cavalry, as scouts (*exploratores*), and even acting as bargemen.[26]

2 The Fort Plan

Classical Sources

Most of our knowledge about the internal layout and terminology of the Roman camp derives from two Classical authors. The earliest surviving description of a temporary marching camp is given by Polybius, writing in the middle of the second century BC, who details the accommodation required by two legions with their associated cavalry and allied troops. In the third century AD a surveyor known as Hyginus (*hyginus gromaticus*) wrote a theoretical surveying manual which was intended to provide the appropriate accommodation for every type of army unit which his students were likely to encounter; his camp houses three legions, praetorians, auxiliary cavalry and infantry, pioneers, scouts and even a camel corps. Despite being written five hundred years apart both accounts are still broadly comparable, with differences in detail reflecting, in general, the changes in the organisation of the army itself during such a long period.[1] Excavation has clearly demonstrated that the basic principles laid down by these writers were incorporated into the planning of both legionary fortresses and auxiliary forts from the late Republic until well into the third century AD. In addition, both writers provide valuable information about the methods of surveying, the organisation and terminology of the various elements of the camp plan, which can be applied directly to the study of permanent forts.

The Polybian camp   The Polybian camp,[2] designed for two legions and a full complement of allied troops (totalling altogether some 16 800 infantry and 1800 cavalry), was square, with sides of 2017 Roman feet, surrounded by a ditch and a rampart of earth and turf surmounted by a palisade of wooden stakes. The surveyors (*metatores*) placed a white flag upon the site chosen for the general's tent (*praetorium*) and from this point the detailed surveying and allocation of space was carried out. In front of the *praetorium* lay the tents of the twelve legionary tribunes, six from each legion. The camp was traversed by three major streets. The main street (*principia*) ran in front of the tribunes' tents and was 100 Roman feet wide, and parallel to it in the front part of the camp lay a second street only half as

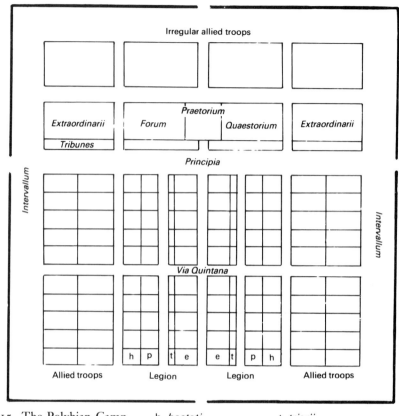

Irregular allied troops

Extraordinarii | Forum | Praetorium | Quaestorium | Extraordinarii
Tribunes

Principia

Intervallum

Intervallum

Via Quintana

Allied troops | Legion | Legion | Allied troops

15. The Polybian Camp.   h–*hastati*   t–*triarii*
                           p–*principes*   e–*equites*

wide, known as the *via quintana*. Running along the central axis of the camp at right-angles to them was another street 50 Roman feet wide which divided the space in front of the *praetorium* in two; each half accommodated the tents of one legion and those of its allied cavalry.

Polybius tells us that the main fighting unit of the Republican army in the second century BC was the maniple, which was the equivalent of two centuries.[3] Each legion comprised thirty maniples, divided equally into three lines of battle, the younger recruits (*hastati*), the more experienced fighting men (*principes*), and the tried veterans (*triarii*). These divisions were retained in the camp layout, where the legionary cavalry lay adjacent to the central road and behind lay the tents of first the *triarii*, then the *principes* and finally the *hastati*. On the outside, nearest to the defences, were quartered the allied cavalry and infantry.

On each side of the general's tent lay the *quaestorium* and the *forum*, which were flanked in turn by the tents of the cavalry (*extraordinarii equites*) and infantry who accompanied the general and his staff on the march, and acted as a bodyguard. Behind them lay the remainder of the *extraordinarii equites* and *pedites*, and all the other irregular allied forces accompanying the legions. All round the camp between the rampart and the tents lay an open space, the *intervallum*, which was 200 Roman feet wide and designed to give good access for the troops, to house booty and cattle, and to ensure that the tents were pitched well out of the range of burning missiles. In his account Polybius also records details of the camp routine, such as the camp oath, the allocation of duties, guard duty, parades, watchwords and the procedure for breaking camp.

The Hyginian camp The Hyginian camp, designed for three legions and assorted auxiliary units (estimated at approximately 40 000 men), was rectangular in shape with rounded corners, measuring 2320 × 1620 Roman feet, and so was much more crowded than the Polybian example. The camp was surrounded by a ditch at least 5 Roman feet wide × 3 feet deep, with a rampart of earth, turf or stone 8 Roman feet wide and 6 feet high; additional ditches were dug to protect the gateways (*tituli*).

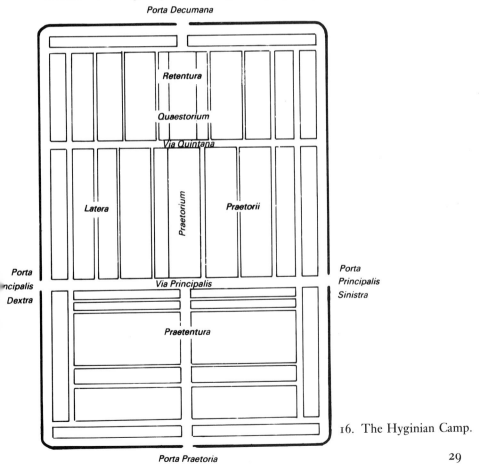

Porta Decumana

Retentura

Quaestorium

Via Quintana

Latera

Praetorium

Praetorii

Porta Principalis Dextra

Via Principalis

Porta Principalis Sinistra

Praetentura

16. The Hyginian Camp.

Porta Praetoria

The principal street, the *via principalis*, was 60 Roman feet wide and extended across the width of the camp, with gates at either end, the *porta principalis sinistra* and the *porta principalis dextra*. The two other gates, set in the centre of the shorter sides of the camp, were the *porta praetoria*, which lay nearest to the enemy, and the *porta decumana*, at the rear of the camp. A space 720 × 180 Roman feet was allocated for the general's quarters, the *praetorium*, which occupied a central position fronting onto the *via principalis*. This street, together with another running parallel at the rear of the *praetorium*, the *via quintana*, 40 Roman feet wide, divided the camp into three parts.

The central portion (*latera praetorii*) comprised the *praetorium*, the *auguratorium* for religious sacrifices, the *tribunal* from which the general addressed his men, and the tents of the general's personal staff and those of the praetorian troops, which were flanked on the outside by the first cohort and *vexillarii* of one of the legions in garrison.

The front part of the camp, from the *via principalis* to the front gate (*porta praetoria*) was termed the *praetentura*, in which were drawn up first, fronting the main street, the tents of the legionary legates and tribunes together with the *scholae* or meeting places of the first cohorts, then the auxiliary *alae*, the hospital (*valetudinarium*) for soldiers, the *veterinarium* for sick horses, the workshop (*fabrica*) and the quarters of the various companies of marines, pioneers and scouts. The legionary cohorts, being the most trustworthy, were drawn up in lines nearest to the rampart around the perimeter of the camp, encircling the tents of the auxiliary soldiers.

The rear third of the camp was known as the *retentura*, which housed the *quaestorium* of the camp prefect, where booty and prisoners were kept, together with an assortment of auxiliary troops (including a camel corps). Legionaries were again housed adjacent to the rampart. The *intervallum* was 60 Roman feet wide, with a street, the *via sagularis*, close by running all round the inside of the camp. Ancillary streets between the tent rows (*viae vicinariae*) were 20 Roman feet wide.

A standardised plan was vital when dealing in a single overnight camp with such large numbers of men and animals as those described by Polybius and Hyginus. It was essential that, whatever the nature of the ground, the layout should remain constant so that each unit, and indeed every individual, would know exactly where to pitch their tents with a minimum of delay and confusion, especially if under threat of attack. Organisation was equally important when breaking camp, and the accommodation of the various legions and auxiliaries was arranged in a way which would allow them to break camp in marching order.

Legionary Fortresses and Auxiliary Forts

Both legionary fortresses and auxiliary forts of the first and second centuries AD conformed broadly in their planning to the basic principles laid down by these two authors, with divergences due mainly to the differing needs of an army in permanent garrison as opposed to a temporary camping site.

Hyginus recommended that the legionary camp should have proportions of length to breadth of 3:2 (*tertiata*),[4] and generally by the early Flavian period most legionary fortress and auxiliary fort defences conformed either to this rectangular shape with rounded corners, reminiscent of a playing card, or to a regular square (see Chapter 8, p. 250). The permanent legionary base accommodated at the most two legions, as at Vetera (Xanten), but from the middle of the first century AD usually only one, occupying an area of some 20 hectares. The internal area of the auxiliary fort varied in size according to its garrison, from about one hectare for the smallest unit of 500 foot soldiers (*cohors quingenaria peditata*) to 5 or 5.5 hectares for the thousand-strong cavalry units (*alae milliariae*) stationed at Heidenheim and Aalen in Raetia; within these limits the majority ranged from 1 to 2.5 hectares. *Numerus* forts normally occupied an area, within the ramparts, of between 0.4 and 0.9 hectares.

The plan and design of the permanent fort had developed from the marching camp and preserved its main defensive features. The shallow ditch and palisade of the temporary camp were, however, replaced by more substantial earthworks in the permanent fortification, often with two or more V-shaped ditches and either an earth or turf rampart surmounted by a timber breastwork, or a stone wall with an earth bank behind. The four gateways were retained, which in the permanent fort were defended by gate towers, and further defensive towers were added at the four angles and at intervals between. As in the marching camp there was a tripartite division of the internal accommodation, with the same wide streets and a roadway running all round the fort within the defensive perimeter, and the regular tent lines were replaced with timber, and later stone, buildings. The layout of the auxiliary fort, especially from the end of the first century AD was standardised, but a close examination of fort layouts shows that there were considerable differences in detail between individual fort plans, and between the same types of building at different sites. Surprisingly, despite the obvious similarities, no two excavated forts are identical.

Comparison of the timber fortress at Inchtuthil, in Scotland, with the stone example from Neuss, in Lower Germany, will demonstrate the typical layout of the legionary fortress, although it is clear that they were far from identical in detail. The interior was divided into three parts by two transverse streets, with the front and rear portions further subdivided by a longitudinal street. The need for increased office space for the administration of the permanent garrison led to the separation of the commander's office from his residence. This meant the administrative headquarters, known as the *principia*, was sited in a central position at the junction of the two principal streets, which was the traditional place for the general's tent in the marching camp. The commander's residence, which retained the title *praetorium*, lay either directly behind, as at Neuss, or next door. It is uncertain where the *praetorium* was to be at Inchtuthil, as the decision to abandon the fortress was taken before construction work on it had begun, although vacant plots were left both beside and behind the *principia*.

On a permanent site the army had to cope with the logistics of supplying and storing food for the entire garrison often for long periods. Food stores and granaries were needed, which were usually sited near the gates to provide convenient access. A bathhouse was provided at Neuss next to the *principia*; at Inchtuthil it lay outside the fortress. Other buildings within the central range included a hospital, workshop and equipment store and, in addition, the barracks of the first cohort lay on the right-hand side of the *principia*, with the houses of the five senior centurions adjacent to the main

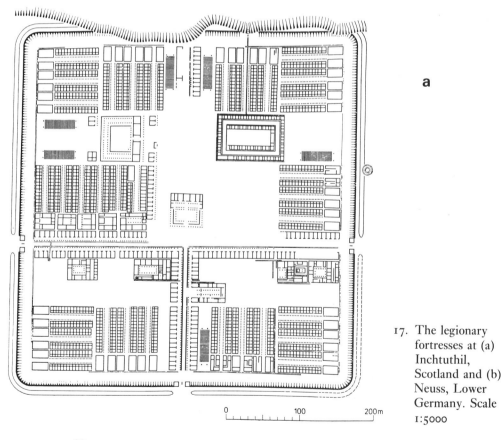

a

17. The legionary fortresses at (a) Inchtuthil, Scotland and (b) Neuss, Lower Germany. Scale 1:5000

street; another cohort lay on the left-hand side. Facing the main street in the front part of the fortress (the *praetentura*) lay the houses of the six military tribunes and the *schola*, or meeting place, of the first cohort, although at Inchtuthil only four of the tribunes' houses had been completed. The legion stationed at Neuss was further reinforced by an auxiliary *ala* whose barracks lay behind the houses of the tribunes.[5] The barracks of the remaining legionary cohorts occupied the front of the *praetentura* and the whole of the *retentura*. Fronting the major streets of both fortresses lay rows of small square rooms, apparently open to the street, whose precise function is unknown; they may have provided extra storage or perhaps workshop facilities.[6]

The layout of the auxiliary fort was essentially a miniature of this plan. The main differences are seen in the grouping of the *principia*, *praetorium* and granaries together in the central range, with barrack accommodation normally confined to the *praetentura* and *retentura*. Workshops were present in most forts, although hospitals were probably seldom provided, and the garrison's bathhouse was usually sited outside the fort.

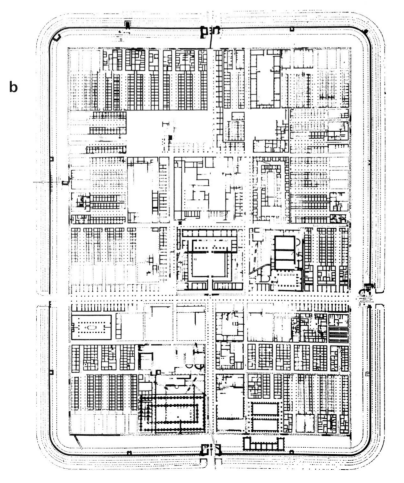

b

33

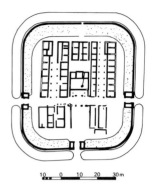

18. The *numerus* fort at
Hesselbach, Upper
Germany. Scale
1:2000

Only one *numerus* fort has been excavated in detail, at Hesselbach in
Upper Germany. In this timber-built fort the *principia*, with the *praetorium*
behind, was flanked on both sides by two pairs of barracks; there was no
retentura. In the *praetentura* lay buildings of uncertain function, which are
thought to have been stables and a storebuilding.

A descriptive anatomy of a typical auxiliary fort follows (see Figure 19).

Defences

1. One or more ditches (*fossae*) encircling the fort. The ditches may be continuous
   with timber bridges in front of the gates, or may have had earthen causeways.
2. Additional defences may include stakes or obstacles within or between ditches,
   or in pits beyond (*lilia*).
3. (a) Rampart (*vallum*) of earth, turf or upcast from the ditches, revetted with
   timber or turf, founded upon perhaps a corduroy of logs or a stone base. Angle
   and interval towers set within the body of the rampart.
   (b) Possible stone wall (*murus*) with an earth backing, which may be free
   standing or more usually cut into the front of an existing rampart. Stone-built
   angle and interval towers.
4. *Intervallum*. The open space between the rear of the rampart and the built-up
   area, occupied by cookhouses, latrines, ovens and hearths. Bordered by a road
   (*via sagularis*).

Gates and roads

1. The main fort street (*via principalis*) leading on the left-hand side to the gate
   known as the *porta principalis sinistra*, and on the right to the *porta principalis
   dextra*.
2. The *via praetoria* is the street leading from the *principia* to the front gate, the
   porta praetoria.
3. *Via decumana*, the street leading from the rear of the *principia* to the rear gate, the
   porta decumana.
4. The street, the *via quintana*, runs parallel with the *via principalis* behind the
   central range.
5. The *via sagularis* runs around the edge of the *intervallum*.
6. The minor roads between barracks and stables are known as *viae vicinariae*.

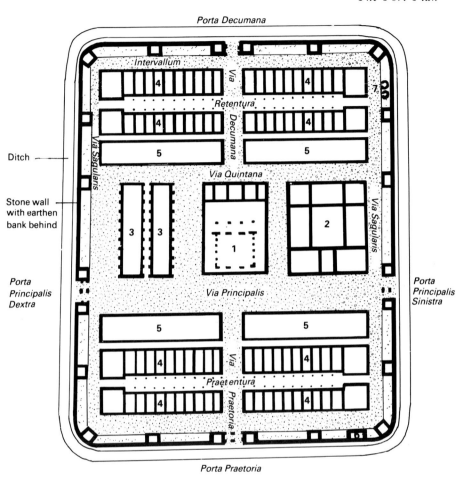

19. The principal features of an auxiliary fort.

1 The headquarters (*principia*)
2 Commander's house (*praetorium*)
3 Granaries (*horrea*)
4 Barracks (*centuriae*)
5 Storebuildings or stables
6 Latrine
7 Rampart ovens

The interior

1. *Latera praetorii*, the central range situated between the *viae principalis* and *quintana*. At the centre the headquarters building (*principia*), flanked by the commanding officer's house (*praetorium*), granary (*horreum*), and perhaps a workshop (*fabrica*) or hospital (*valetudinarium*).

2. *Praetentura*. The front portion of the fort from the *via principalis* to the front gate. Barracks (*centuriae*), stables and storebuildings aligned either parallel with the main street (*per scamna*), or at right-angles to it (*per strigas*).

3. *Retentura*. The rear part of the fort from the *via quintana* to the rear gate, with barracks, stables and stores aligned either *per scamna* or *per strigas*.

3 The Construction of the Fort

Siting

'A camp, especially in the neighbourhood of an enemy, must be chosen with great care. Its situation should be strong by nature, and there should be plenty of wood, forage and water. If the army is to continue in it for a considerable time, attention must be paid to the salubrity of the place. The camp must not be commanded by any higher grounds from whence it might be insulted or annoyed by the enemy, nor must the location be liable to floods which would expose the army to greater danger.'[1] According to Vegetius these were the priorities in the siting of legionary camps—considerations which are also relevant to the siting of the permanent auxiliary fort. The *praefectus castrorum* of the legion was usually responsible for selecting the position of the camp, although Tacitus describes how the general Agricola chose his own camp sites and explored the terrain himself when on campaign in northern Britain.[2]

The auxiliary fort in the first and second centuries AD was not intended primarily as a highly defensible and unassailable stronghold in the same way as, for example, a medieval castle. Defensive walls or ramparts with ditches were constructed, but the fort was essentially a base from which its garrison could control the surrounding countryside and fight, if necessary, on open ground. It was more likely to be sited, as recommended by Hyginus, upon a 'slight prominence on gently sloping land' and close to a river than upon a naturally well defended and inaccessible summit.[3] Ease of communications, a good water supply and timber for both building and firewood were extremely important considerations which influenced the selection of the site. The favourite location was undoubtedly at the end of a spur or on a small plateau with falling ground on three or four sides, at the confluence of two streams or a river with a tributary, commanding extensive views along both valleys: marshy ground often protected access on at least one side. This siting was especially important in upland regions where the roads followed the river valleys, and in the Highlands of Scotland, where a strategically placed fort could control the approaches to a major mountain pass.[4] Auxiliary forts were often sited to protect a river crossing at a bridge or ford, or an important road junction, and in some cases it may have been necessary to sacrifice good visibility to the requirement for close supervision of the crossing. Water was usually readily available from the nearby river, and each fort was linked with its neighbours only a day's march away by a first-class network of roads, which ensured good communications and regular supplies.

Vegetius' advice[5] was that the site should not be placed at a disadvantage, either near a wood where a hostile force could congregate, overlooked by higher ground within arrow-shot or on ground liable to flood but in a few cases this appears to have been disregarded. Forts which were overlooked by higher ground, such as Chesterholm or Risingham in northern Britain, were generally out of the range of enemy missiles, although this certainly was not the case at Osterburken in Upper Germany, where the mid-second-century cohort fort lay at the bottom of a very steep slope. Here, considerations of a good water supply and communications must have outweighed the obvious disadvantage, which was rectified in the reign of Commodus when the entire slope was enclosed by a stone defensive wall and occupied as a *numerus* fort.

The effects of flooding have been detected at a few low-lying sites. At Bochastle in Scotland, for example, the northern defences had been inundated and eroded by the River Leny, which resulted in the retraction of the defences on this side above the flood level of the river. Possible flood barriers have been found at Ambleside, where a gravel bank ran from the fort towards the shore of Lake Windermere, and at the Welsh fort of Caersŵs, where an outer gravel bank on the north-west side of the fort may have provided protection against the River Carno.

Occasionally the original site chosen proved to be unsuitable, for one reason or another, and the fort had to be moved to an alternative location. Such a move may have been dictated by a change in the size of the garrison, by a shift in strategic considerations, or perhaps because the site had proved too prone to flooding. The Trajanic fort at Gelligaer was built just 50 metres away from its larger Flavian predecessor, a change which probably reflects a reduction in the size of the garrison. The Flavian fort of Easter Happrew in Scotland was abandoned in favour of a site on the opposite side of the river, at Lyne, in the Antonine period. Although its predecessor commanded better visibility the transfer to Lyne was made necessary when a main road was built, linking the Lowland forts of Newstead and Castledykes, as the most convenient route happened to be on the opposite bank of the river from the original fort site.[6]

Changing strategic requirements at different dates are reflected in the transfer of the fort at Llwyn-y-Brain, in the upper Severn valley, from the crest of a ridge with a commanding position, down to lower ground one kilometre to the west, at Caersŵs. The move shows that the first requirement was a strong tactical position, giving extensive views across several valleys during the initial pacification of the area; later, in more settled times, a permanent base was needed to supervise an important road junction

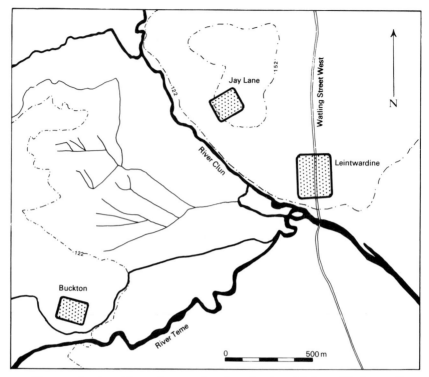

20. Changes in the siting of successive forts in the vicinity of Leintwardine, Hereford and Worcester.

at a river confluence. The fort site near the village of Leintwardine in Herefordshire was moved twice, from Jay Lane to Buckton, and then to Leintwardine itself. The first move, as at Caersŵs, may have been devised to secure a base suited to local needs rather than a tactical base for a conquering army. The second move has been variously explained as either the result of flooding, or possibly the desire to be closer to the major supply route of Watling Street West, which ran through Leintwardine.[7]

Preparation of the Site

The selected site was cleared of trees and scrub in preparation for the surveying and demarcation of the defences and the internal buildings.

Examination of pollen and plant remains from the original ground surface sealed by the rampart, or from within the rampart turves, can give valuable information about the local vegetation prior to the construction of the fort, though few forts have so far yielded this environmental evidence. Pollen samples from Brough on Humber and Pen Llystyn have suggested

21. Scene from Trajan's Column showing legionaries felling and transporting timber for construction. (Scene XV)

that both forts were built in clearings close to mixed forest.[8] These analyses do present problems, however, as pollen grains may have been blown a considerable distance and can be misleading. Although twigs and small branches provide more reliable indicators as they are unlikely to have been transported far, they unfortunately survive only rarely in waterlogged conditions. It is probable that the fort builders were often faced with much tree felling and clearance, especially in the highland zone of Britain and in the forests of the Upper German frontier, and a recent study has indicated that in Britain mixed oak forest would have been extensive in the lowlands and the more fertile highland valleys, with Scots pine and birch predominant elsewhere, up to a height of at least 750 metres.[9] Sufficient clearance would also have been needed in the vicinity to give a clear sight from the ramparts, and to avoid giving cover to hostile forces too close to the fort. The construction of a fort with an internal area of c. 1.6 hectares, for example, would require a considerable open space around it which, allowing for the depth of the defences and from 35 to 45 metres beyond the ditches would amount to a total area cleared of some 5.7 hectares.[10]

39

When building an earth-and-timber fort suitable local timber was felled and used regardless of whether it had been seasoned. To provide an external rampart revetment, gates, towers and internal buildings for a 1.6 hectare fort somewhere in the region of 650 cubic metres (23 000 cubic feet) of structural timber would be required which, in a frontier region, would not be transported any farther than was absolutely necessary; the area of mature woodland which would have to be felled to meet these requirements could range from 6.5 up to 12 hectares, depending upon its density.[11]

Having felled any trees suitable for structural timbers the vegetation may have been burnt off, as was the case at Buckton or Ebchester, or the whole site may have been stripped of turf to provide suitable material for building the rampart revetments.[12] In some cases it was necessary to level the site before construction work could begin. At Bowness on Hadrian's Wall, for example, a layer of white clay was laid upon the subsoil to provide a level base for the fort buildings, and at Birdoswald, another Hadrian's Wall fort, where the site chosen had been previously occupied by a native promontory fort defended on three sides by marshy ground, the Roman builders had to infill hollows and drain the marshes to provide a dry and level fort platform.[13] Where the site of an earlier fort was selected for rebuilding the opportunity may have been taken, where necessary, to raise the ground level with a dumped layer of earth, clay or debris to a depth of up to 0.6 metres to minimise the risks of flooding, a remedy which was used at Caersŵs, Binchester and Brough on Noe.[14]

Survey and layout

Paternus mentions surveyors (*mensores*) in his list of legionary *immunes*, men who were exempted from routine duties in order to pursue a particular craft or skill, and Vegetius describes how 'the *mensores* work out the ground by measure for the tents in an encampment, and assign the troops their respective quarters in the garrison'.[15] In addition the 'dimensions must be exactly computed by the engineers, so that the size of the camp may be proportioned to the number of troops. A camp which is too confined will not permit the troops to perform their movements with freedom, and one which is too extensive divides them too much.'[16] Manuals must have been available to the surveyors to enable them to calculate both the defensive circuit appropriate to the intended garrison and purpose of the fort, and the requisite dimensions of the internal buildings.

Such a handbook was compiled by Hyginus. He recommended that the length of the camp should exceed its breadth by one third, for if the proportions were much greater bugle signals could not be heard in every part of the camp.[17] Vegetius, on the other hand, observed that the shape of the fort should be determined by the terrain rather than strictly by the rulebook: 'after these precautions the camp is formed square, round, triangular or oblong, according to the nature of the ground. For the form of a camp does not constitute its goodness.'[18] Generally, by the early Flavian period, the auxiliary fort was laid out as a regular square or with a rectangular 'playing card' shape (see above, p. 31), although exceptions do occur where the site chosen imposed restrictions upon the layout, as at Fendoch, in the Highlands of Scotland, where the only suitable site was upon a glacial moraine which dictated a long, narrow rectangular plan (see Chapter 8, p. 256).

Hyginus states that the *porta praetoria* should lie nearest to the enemy, advice which is echoed by Vegetius, who adds that alternatively the camp should face east or in the direction of the proposed route of march.[19] This was not strictly adhered to in the permanent fort where considerations of transport and communications, access and water supply, were more pressing. Polybius tells us that the *porta decumana* lay at the rear of the fort and provided access for procuring wood, water and other provisions in relative safety; it was also the gate through which soldiers passed on their way to punishment or execution.[20] According to Hyginus this gate should lie at the highest part of the site overlooking the interior of the camp. Both Vitruvius and Hyginus also commented upon the necessity of taking the prevailing wind direction into consideration when aligning streets so that the wind might blow away stale air.[21]

Having decided upon the aspect of the fort the surveyors laid out its two principal axes, the *cardo maximus* and the *cardo decumanus*, and marked out their courses with coloured flags. A surveying instrument, known as a *groma*, was used to establish right-angles, which consisted of a cross frame with four arms set at ninety degrees to each other with a plumb-line suspended from the end of each arm.[22] The instrument was supported upon a staff, which was positioned off-centre to enable the surveyor to sight through the opposing plumb-lines and thus survey straight lines and right-angles. Another line hung from the centre of the frame so that it could be set up over

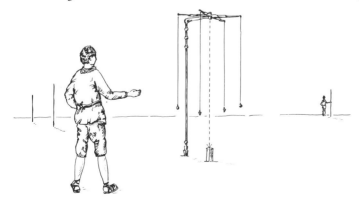

22. The use of the *groma* in surveying.

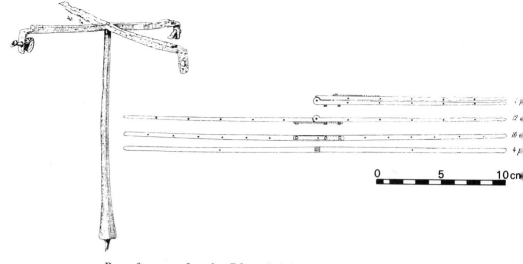

0   5   10cn

23. Part of a *groma* found at Pfünz (height 32 cm; each arm c. 14 cm long) and a foot-rule from Weissenburg.

an exact point on the ground. Occasionally difficulties seem to have been experienced in obtaining true right-angles with this instrument, and the rhomboidal plan of the Flavian fort of Easter Happrew in Scotland, and irregularities in the plan of the Welsh fort of Caernarfon have been attributed to faulty surveying. Part of an iron *groma* was found in a granary at the Raetian fort of Pfünz, and a case containing a surveyor's bronze measuring rod was discovered at Alphen-Zwammerdam in Lower Germany.[23] Poles, known as *metae* or *signi*, were used to sight straight lines, whilst linear measurements were made with graduated ten-foot rods (*decempedae*), foot rules or with strings and markers. From a study of Roman methods and units of measurement employed at Gelligaer in South Wales it has been possible to demonstrate that a ten-foot (Roman feet) staff had been used, as the dimensions of the internal buildings occurred usually in multiples of five or ten Roman feet;[24] the Roman foot (*pes*) was equivalent to 0.296 metres.[25]

The point from which all the measurements were taken, in the very middle of the *via principalis*, was also called the *groma*. From this point the two axes of the fort could be laid out. The *cardo maximus* provided the line of the *via principalis*, the *cardo decumanus* that of the *via praetoria* at the front and the *via decumana* at the rear of the fort. The position of the four gates could then be determined. The space allocated to the central buildings would have been marked out with poles, flags or strings, bordered at the rear by a second major transverse street, the *via quintana*; the position of the barracks and the other minor streets would have been laid out in the same way. It appears that a ritual foundation deposit was sometimes laid in the centre of the fort before any construction work began. At Pen Llystyn, for example, there lay at the entrance to the *principia* crosshall a shallow pit filled with carbonised material and covered with clean silt. This deposit lay within one Roman foot of the exact centre of the fort, upon the longitudinal axis of the headquarters building, and 75 Roman feet from the central axis of the *via principalis*.[26] Similarly, in the centre of the earth-and-timber fort at the Saalburg, in Upper Germany, lay a square setting with four postholes, thought by its excavator to have been the remains of a temporary altar.[27]

The actual methods used to mark the chosen lines of the defensive ditches and the rampart are unknown. Strings may have been laid, or perhaps turves from the line of the ditches removed and placed as guides. Shallow spade-dug trenches (lockspits), such as those found at Buckton and Caersŵs, could have been used to fix the intended line of the rampart. They may also have been dug to determine the course of the ditches, although this is usually impossible to establish as normally all evidence would have been removed when the ditch was dug. However, a stretch of unfinished ditch found near the south gate at Birdoswald was marked out in this manner.[28]

Responsibility for Fort Construction

Within the legion the *praefectus castrorum* supervised all construction work, and was responsible not only for the 'position of the camp, the direction of the entrenchments, the inspection of the tents or huts of the soldiers, and the baggage' but also 'the proper tools for sawing and cutting wood, digging trenches, raising parapets, sinking wells and bringing water into the camp'.[29] The legion contained a wide range of skilled men including 'ditch-diggers, architects, glaziers, roof-tile makers, plumbers, stonecutters, lime-burners, and woodcutters',[30] but there is no evidence amongst the auxiliary ranks for the same skilled technicians and craftsmen, and no inscriptions recording work by them until the Hadrianic period, in northern Britain. Trajan's Column includes several scenes showing camp construction, but it is legionary troops and not auxiliaries who are engaged in the building work and the procuring of raw materials. It is generally supposed, therefore, that the *auxilia* played little or no part in the construction of their own forts, at least until the Hadrianic period, and that this task was left to the legions, who had the necessary training and experience.

The earliest evidence for auxiliaries involved in building work comes from Benwell, on Hadrian's Wall, where in AD 122–6 a detachment of the British fleet (*Classis Britannica*) built a granary, and Carvoran, on the same frontier, where rampart building was completed by its auxiliary garrison, *cohors I Hamiorum*, in AD 136–8.[31] From then on inscriptions recording auxiliary building projects appear more and more frequently,[32] and it is probable that increasingly the legions delegated some of the responsibility for fort construction (or at least for individual buildings) providing the craftsmen and basic blueprints for the layout but allowing the auxiliaries to shoulder the heavy routine work. That they were fully trained in the construction of camps can be seen from the large number of practice camps and earthworks found in the vicinity of some forts, notably on Haltwhistle and Llandrindod Commons.[33]

Each legion had its own plans and methods of working, this having been demonstrated by a detailed examination of the work of the three legions which built Hadrian's Wall, *legio II Augusta*, *legio XX Valeria Victrix*, and *legio VI Victrix*. Their individual styles can be seen in constructional details such as the shape or type of gateways in the milecastles, different positions used for setting-out lines, whether doorways were placed on the right or left hand side of the turrets, or even where the offsets occurred on the curtain wall itself.[34] If legionaries were involved either directly or indirectly in the building of auxiliary forts and if their design was drawn up in the legionary *fabrica* it should be possible to detect the hand of different legions in the excavated structures and fort plans. This is the case with the twelve original Hadrian's Wall forts, whose groundplans fall into two groups according to their size and shape. One group is generally longer and narrower than the rest, which is thought to reflect a difference between the legionary builders (in this case *legio II Augusta* and *legio VI Victrix*).[35]

The legionary workshop probably had a standard blueprint for the construction of a fort which might vary in detail according to the size of the intended garrison or any particular local requirements, and which could be scaled down to cover *numerus* forts also. This may be seen in the close correspondence between the gates of the cohort fort of Oberscheidental, in Upper Germany, and those of the neighbouring tiny *numerus* fort at Hesselbach, which are almost identical in plan, although the latter is on a much smaller scale.[36] A building inscription found in the small *numerus* fort of Böhming, in Raetia, attests a combination of legionary and auxiliary builders. In AD 181 the fort walls were built by a detachment of *legio III Italica*, which then returned to its base at Regensburg, leaving behind a centurion to supervise the construction of the gates with gatetowers by *cohors I Breucorum*, from the neighbouring fort of Pfünz.[37]

4 The Defences

Most auxiliary forts of the first century AD were defended by an earth or turf rampart, with a timber breastwork and walkway, and surrounded by one or more ditches. Timber towers set within the body of the rampart flanked the four gateways, stood at the angles, and were further spaced at regular intervals around the perimeter. During the course of the second century it became customary to newly construct or rebuild forts in stone with a defensive wall, interval and angle towers, and often impressive stone gateways, still retaining a single or multiple ditch system, according to the vulnerability of the site.

Despite broad similarities, excavation has shown that there can be considerable variation in the construction and layout of the defences of individual forts. The variations depended mainly upon local conditions and may be reflected, for example, by differences in the number, size or spacing of the ditches, or in the materials chosen for the rampart. These factors will be discussed in this chapter.

Ditches (*Fossae*)

Vegetius describes the methods of entrenching both the temporary and the permanent camp. In the former a trench was dug around the camp 5 Roman feet wide and 3 feet deep which provided material for a defensive bank if there was a lack of suitable turf available. Permanent camps received more care and attention; here the soldiers used to 'range their shields and baggage in a circle about their own colours and, without other arms than their swords, open a trench 9, 11 or 13 feet broad. Or if they are under great apprehensions of the enemy, they enlarge it to 17 feet (it being a general rule to observe odd numbers)'.[1] Individual centuries were allocated a specified length of ditch to dig or rampart to construct, and their work was measured and supervised by the centurions. The two activities must have been concurrent, with the spoil from the ditches forming the core of the rampart. On Trajan's Column there are several scenes in which soldiers are engaged upon ditch digging. The tools depicted on this column, and surviving examples often found in auxiliary forts, are very similar to their modern

24. Scene from Trajan's Column showing legionaries engaged in fort construction. In the foreground the soldiers can be seen digging ditches and transporting the earth in wicker baskets. (Scenes XIX/XX)

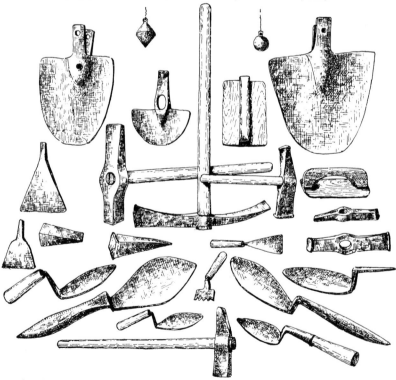

25. A selection of tools found at the Saalburg Roman Fort, in Upper Germany.

counterparts, and included crescent-bladed turf cutters, various entrenching tools and pickaxes (the *dolabra* and the *ligo*), the iron or iron-shod spade (*pala*) and shovel (*rutrum*); the soil was removed from the ditches either with a shovel or, as illustrated on Trajan's Column, in wicker baskets.[2] Ill. 25 shows a variety of such tools which have been reconstructed from fragmentary originals by the Saalburg Museum. From his examination of an unfinished section of ditch at the practice camp of Cawthorn, in Yorkshire, Professor Ian Richmond concluded that a trench was first dug along the central axis of the proposed ditch line and the sides then cut back with a depth and slope appropriate to the subsoil.[3]

Two types of military ditch are described by Hyginus, the *fossa fastigata* and the *fossa Punica*.[4] The *fossa fastigata* was V-shaped in cross section, the profile most commonly found in fort ditches. Sometimes they had narrow channels in the bottom whose function has been explained as perhaps ankle breakers for the unwary or drainage channels. We know from papyri that routine fort duties included ditch cleaning and these channels may have been caused unintentionally by running a spade along the base of the ditch during the periodic removal of silt and vegetation.[5] The second type of ditch was the *fossa Punica* which had a steep, almost vertical, outer scarp with a gentler inner slope. This profile may have been intended to lure an attacker within range of missiles from the rampart with an apparently easy slope to climb; the steeper outer scarp, however, being far more difficult to negotiate, hindered his retreat and kept him within missile range for as long as possible.[6] The Punic ditch usually formed the outermost of a fort's ditch sequence and this fact has prompted the observation that its distinctive profile may have been connected with the need for an unrestricted view from the top of the rampart to the bottom of the outermost ditch; this could best be achieved with a gently sloping inner scarp. W-shaped ditch profiles have also been recorded from excavation, but there is often some uncertainty as to whether they were originally dug like this or whether they represent subsequent recuttings upon slightly different lines of a normal V-shaped *fossa fastigata*.[7]

There are considerable variations in the number of ditches provided, in their widths and in their spacing. The width and depth depended to some extent upon the subsoil into which they were dug. Widths generally varied

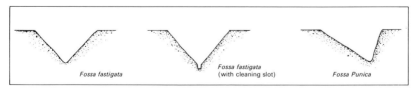

26. Profile of a *fossa fastigata* and *fossa Punica*.

between 2.5 and 6 metres. When only a single ditch was used a width of 3.7 to 5 metres was common, whilst the ditches in double and multiple systems tended to be slightly smaller. On sites with a loose or sandy subsoil or where the water table was particularly high a deep ditch would not have been practicable even if, as at Caerphilly, the sides were lined with clay. The need for a clear line of sight between the defender on the rampart and the bottom of every ditch, to ensure that an attacker could not take refuge there prior to a fresh assault, also governed the optimum depth of the ditches, which were commonly between 1.2 and 2.7 metres deep. It is often hard to estimate the original depth as, in many cases, the top has been destroyed by subsequent ploughing and later occupation of the site, leaving only the base. Sometimes ditches were artificially deepened by the addition of a bank consisting of either material from the ditch digging which had proved surplus to the requirements of the rampart, or piles of silty debris derived from regular ditch cleaning.[8]

The fort may have been surrounded by a single, double or multiple ditch system, and the number may even have varied on different sides of the same fort, whilst upon a steep slope the ditches may have been dispensed with altogether. The ditches of a double-ditch system varied in their spacing. They were sometimes dug close together with little or no space between them, or they may have been wider apart—often approximately 3 metres. Multiple ditches were often added to protect particularly weak points in a fort's defences. At Hod Hill, for example, an extra fourth ditch was provided at the vulnerable south-east corner; at Greatchesters or the fortlet at Cappuck, the defences on the sides overlooked by higher ground were reinforced by an extra ditch. At Ardoch, in Scotland, only one ditch was required on the western flank which overlooked a steep slope down to the River Knaick, whilst a series of modifications from the Flavian to the late Antonine periods increased the number of ditches on the north and east to five.[9] Uphill slopes were protected at Birrens, in Scotland, by the digging of six ditches, and Whitley Castle, in northern Britain, had up to seven ditches on one side and either three or four elsewhere.

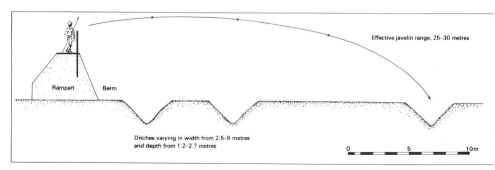

Effective javelin range, 25–30 metres

Rampart   Berm

Ditches varying in width from 2.5–6 metres
and depth from 1.2–2.7 metres

0   5   10m

27. The defensive earthworks of a Roman fort.

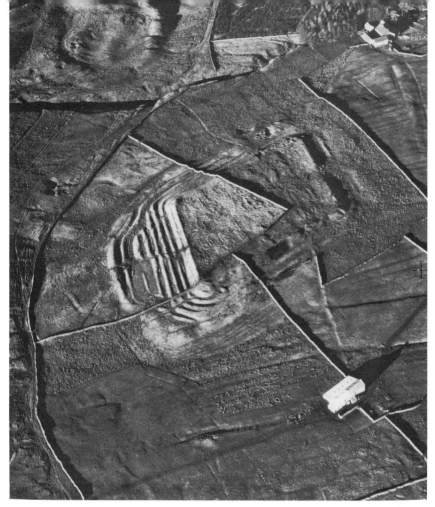

28. An aerial photograph showing the multiple ditches of the fort at Whitley Castle, Northumberland.

The 'depth' of the defences, the space between the rampart face and the outermost ditch, was determined by the maximum range of the garrison's missiles. The effective range for javelins, the weapon used by most auxiliaries, is estimated to have been roughly 25–30 metres, but archers and slingers would have had a much greater range. Artillery, such as spring guns and catapults (*scorpiones* and *ballistae*) were used exclusively by the legions and probably did not figure very prominently in the auxiliary fort's defences until the late second or early third century, when artillery platforms began to be added to fort walls. The depth of defences of a number of Domitianic forts on the North Main frontier in Upper Germany was remarkably constant at 60 Roman feet (17.75 metres).[10] Many British examples are closely comparable, although a few forts with multiple defences such as Cardean, Birrens and Whitley Castle, extended as far as 46 metres beyond the rampart. Examination of the defensive ranges of first-century forts in

49

Britain has suggested two groups, with respective depths of 18–21 metres and 27–30 metres, which may reflect the use of two distinct types of weapons with different ranges.[11]

Two devices were occasionally employed to prevent a direct attack upon a gateway, the *titulum* and the *clavicula*. The *titulum*, according to Hyginus, consisted of a short length of ditch with an accompanying bank, with a length similar to that of the gateway, but placed in front of it at a distance of 60 Roman feet.[12] *Tituli* outside fort gateways were never common, and seem to range widely in date from the Claudian fort at Hod Hill in southern England, to the Severan marching camp at Stracathro in Scotland. Alternatively, sometimes one side of the rampart at a gateway was extended and curved internally or externally to form a defended passageway, a *clavicula*, which meant that a would–be attacker would have access to the gate only with his right sword arm exposed and his shield useless. Such *claviculae* are illustrated upon Trajan's Column and have been found at a number of Flavian marching camps in northern Britain and forts in Scotland.[13]

29. Scene from Trajan's Column showing a tented enclosure with a gateway defended by a *clavicula*. (Scene CXXVIII)

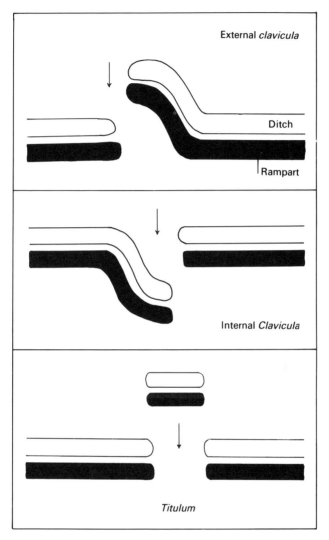

30. Entrances defended by the *clavicula* and *titulum*.

The ditches may have been continuous around the fort with timber bridges in front of the gates, or they may have either terminated in butt-ends or have been looped together to provide an earthen causeway. Combinations of these possibilities can often be seen at the same fort as, for example, at Bar Hill on the Antonine Wall, where the western gate was fronted by a continuous ditch, whilst the ditches were broken at the other entrances. At Oberstimm, in Raetia, the inner ditch was continuous, whilst the outer was broken at the gateways on three sides. Traces of timber bridges spanning the ditches have been detected at Gelligaer, where ledges cut into the ditch scarps in front of the south-west gate are presumed to be supports for a bridge. At Theilenhofen, in Raetia, the actual beams of such a bridge were found *in situ* in front of the rear gate.[14]

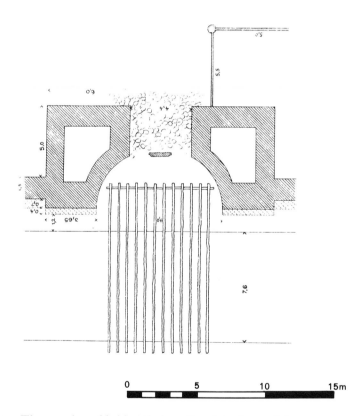

31. The remains of bridge timbers found in front of the rear gate at Theilenhofen in Raetia.

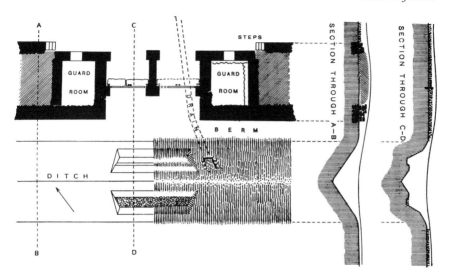

32. Foundation slots within the ditch at Gelligaer, south Wales, to support a timber bridge in front of the south-west gate.

Obstacles

Further obstacles may have been incorporated within the defences both in, between and beyond the ditches, which were designed to hinder an attacker within missile range in much the same way as modern barbed wire.[15] They would have consisted of thorn hedges, stakes, spears or entanglements of branches; features which would normally leave little or no archaeological trace. Caesar described a variety of obstacles employed by the Roman army in the siege of Alesia in Gaul in 52 BC:

> Accordingly tree trunks or very stout boughs were cut, and their tops stripped of bark and sharpened; they were then fixed in long trenches dug five feet deep, with their lower ends made fast to one another to prevent their being pulled up, and the branches projecting. There were five rows in each trench, touching one another and interlaced, and anyone who went among them was likely to impale himself on the sharp points. The soldiers called them *cippi*.[16]

W-shaped ditches found at Hofheim, in Upper Germany, were thought to have contained such branches projecting outwards and upright pointed stakes were fixed in the bottom of the ditches at Wall, Coelbren and Alphen-Zwammerdam. Stakeholes found on the berm between the ditches may have derived from a palisade or from thorn entanglements, and shallow foundation trenches such as those discovered at Trawscoed, in Wales, probably fulfilled a similar function.

53

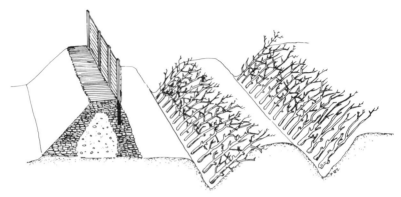

33. The use of thorn branches as obstacles in the fort ditches.

34. Defensive traps (*lilia*) found in front of the northern defences of the Antonine Wall fort at Rough Castle, in 1904.

In addition to the *cippi* Caesar also describes the provision of other obstacles at the siege of Alesia:

> In front of them arranged in diagonal rows in a quincunx pattern, were pits three feet deep, tapering gradually towards the bottom, in which were embedded smooth logs as thick as a man's thigh, with the ends sharpened and charred, and projecting only three inches above ground. To keep the logs firmly in position, earth was thrown into the pits and trodden down to a depth of one foot, the rest of the cavity being filled with twigs and brushwood to hide the trap. These were planted in groups, each containing eight rows three feet apart, and they were nicknamed lilies (*lilia*) from their resemblance to that flower.[17]

These lethal traps have been found arranged in ten parallel rows some 27 metres beyond the northern defences of the Antonine Wall fort at Rough Castle. Each pit was 2.1 × 0.9 × 0.8 metres deep, with the rows arranged in a quincunx pattern. Between two ditches at the south-east angle of the Antonine fort at Glenlochar, also in Scotland, lay nineteen large pits, which probably also once contained sharp stakes.

In all these examples which have hinted at various types of obstacles, none of the sites has been excavated in sufficient detail over a wide enough area to establish whether such features occurred all the way round the circuit of the defences, or only at particularly vulnerable points.

The Berm

To ensure stability a clear space (berm) was usually left between the front of the rampart or defensive wall and the lip of the inner ditch. This served as a precaution both against the rampart slipping forward into the ditch and its being undermined by any excessive erosion of the ditch sides. The berm width varied considerably from as little as 0.3 metres to over 6 metres, although most commonly it was 1.5–2 metres wide, in both earth-and-timber and stone forts; such a width would provide some structural stability and would also allow access to the front of the rampart for maintenance and repair work. The estimation of the original width of the berm can be hampered by later periods of construction, for when repairs were undertaken and a new rampart front added the original inner ditch was often infilled and a replacement dug further out or, as at Tomen-y-Mur in Wales, dug into the former berm itself and so removing it completely.

Evidence has been found at several forts to show that the berm was gravelled or cobbled, and at Arzbach in Germany the ground on the steep north-west side fell so sharply down to the river that no ditch was necessary, and the berm had to be revetted with a drystone wall 2.3 metres high to give stability.[18]

The Rampart (*Vallum*)

The temporary camp was defended, according to Vegetius, by an encircling bank surmounted by a row of wooden stakes forming a palisade. Ideally turf was cut into blocks and piled up, but if the soil was too loose to permit the cutting of turves a trench was dug to provide enough soil for a bank. The main defensive barrier around the permanent fort was provided by the rampart. In his description of a city's defences Vegetius outlines its main constructional principles:

> A rampart to have sufficient strength and solidity should be thus constructed. Two parallel walls are built at a distance of 20 [Roman] feet from each other; and the earth taken out of the ditches thrown into the intermediate space and well rammed down. The inner wall should be lower than the outer, to allow an easy and gradual ascent from the level of the city to the top of the rampart. A ram cannot destroy a wall thus supported by earth, and in case the stonework should by accident be demolished, the mass of earth within would resist its violence as effectively.[19]

The fabric of the rampart had to be fireproof and capable of withstanding both the battering ram and mining operations, with an external face as vertical as possible to prevent an attacker from scaling it easily.

The surviving traces of fort ramparts show a close conformity to these recommendations although it was more common, especially in the first century AD, to use revetments of piled turves, clay or timber at the front, and often at the rear also, rather than stone; the rampart core was composed of the upcast of earth, clay or stone rubble from the ditches. By the end of the first century these ramparts were being repaired and improved, often by the addition of a stone wall at the front, and increasingly during the second century stone defensive walls were built, with usually a clay or earthen bank at the rear.

As ramparts rarely survive today more than a foot or two high, questions relating to their original height or profile are largely conjectural. Fortunately illustrations on Trajan's Column can provide valuable information about the appearance and superstructure of earth and turf ramparts, and recent reconstructions of replicas have begun to resolve many of the practical problems concerning the methods and time taken in construction, weathering, and repair. From a combination of these sources together with information gleaned from archaeological excavation it is possible to imagine the appearance of the fort rampart. The front would have presented either a vertical timber-boarded face, or may have had the appearance of a sloping grassy bank, perhaps three and a half metres high, with a crenellated timber breastwork on top, giving protection to soldiers upon a fighting platform behind. Defensive towers or platforms were spaced at regular intervals around the circuit, standing at least one storey above the rampart walk. Access was provided at the rear of the bank by means of staircases or ramps (*ascensi*).

Foundations

To prevent the body of the rampart from slipping forward a foundation of either timber or stone was often provided. Hyginus suggested that in soft ground, where turves were likely to break and the ditch sides collapse, the turf of the rampart should be founded upon branches (*cervoli*).[20]

Waterlogged conditions at several fort sites have preserved traces of logs set closely together to form a corduroy, and laid as a foundation across part or the whole width of the rampart. The southern rampart and all four angles at Coelbren, in Wales, for example, were founded upon a corduroy of substantial close-set oak logs, fanning out to follow the curve at the angles, and pinned down securely into the subsoil by timber stakes. The ramparts on the other sides were founded upon layers of brushwood, and brushwood or branches have been found in the rampart foundations at other sites, such as Corbridge in northern Britain, or Caermote and Llandovery in Wales. A similar timber corduroy was also preserved at Valkenburg, in Lower Germany, and at Altenstadt and Butzbach in Upper Germany. It is not known how extensive the use of this type of log corduroy was. It may have been employed only on particularly boggy ground, but may have been used far more extensively to provide stable foundations, the evidence only being preserved in waterlogged ground.

The rampart builders at Chesterholm, just south of Hadrian's Wall, faced difficulties when they reached a particularly marshy area of the circuit, but solved the problem by laying down a timber raft packed with stones and debris to consolidate the area before building the stone base of the rampart. Stone was commonly used in rampart foundations from the Flavian period onwards, as can be seen in the cobbled rampart foundations of several Welsh forts of the early Flavian period.[21] The stone may have underlain the whole structure, as in the Antonine Wall forts in Scotland, or only the front toe of the rampart, as in the Scottish fort at Newstead. A graphic demonstration of the need for this type of rampart foundation was given during the construction of an all-turf replica rampart at Chesterholm for, owing to the uneven drying of the turf, part of the rampart collapsed and had to be stabilised by the addition of a stone foundation and the introduction of timber lacing within the rampart body to help secure the turves more firmly.[22]

Timber lacing

Vegetius refers to the use of timbers within the body of the rampart of a permanent camp: 'they construct a rampart with fascines or branches of trees well fastened together with pickets, so that the earth may be better supported'.[23] Timber lacing to provide more stability to the turf or earth bank, in the form of either branches and brushwood or more substantial timbers, has often been detected. Recent excavations at Carlisle have revealed traces of timber strapping within the turf rampart of the Flavian fort, which had been extremely well preserved by waterlogging. Layers of brushwood were frequently incorporated within the body of a clay or turf rampart as seen, for example, at Brough by Bainbridge, and occasionally traces of stouter transverse or longitudinal timbers have been found, as at Caersŵs and at Rottweil in Upper Germany, where transverse timbers were regularly spaced throughout the rampart body at vertical intervals of approximately half a metre.

Width and height

The width of the rampart was dependent upon several factors: the type of revetments used and whether they provided a vertical or sloping face, the desired height, the width required at walkway level, and the type of material used in the rampart core, as some were more stable and cohesive than others. The rampart had to be wide enough at rampart-walk level for two soldiers to pass each other.[24] If it was vertically revetted at the front with timber or stone a narrower width at foundation level was possible than when the front sloped.

The narrowest ramparts have been found in the British turf-revetted examples of the Claudian period at Hod Hill and Wigston Parva in southern England, which were both 3 metres wide, whilst the vertical-fronted timber box ramparts which are mainly known from the German provinces ranged from 3 to 4 metres in width. Other examples of turf, earth or clay ramparts in both Britain and Germany were generally wider, ranging between 4.5 and 9 metres, with a concentration around 5.5 to 7.5 metres.[25] At Baginton, in the Midlands, it has proved possible to reconstruct a rampart 3.6 metres high to the walkway upon such a 5.5 metre base, with a turf-revetted front sloping with a batter of 65°. A striking exception to the norm is seen at Newstead, where the rampart was extended from 7 to 17 metres in width in the late Flavian period, possibly designed to provide an extra fighting-platform.[26]

From the surviving remains it is difficult to judge the original height of the fort rampart. But, given the evidence for the angle at which most rampart fronts sloped, the need for a fighting-platform approximately 2 metres wide, and the usual height of stone walls, a height of approximately 3.5 metres up to the rampart walkway seems likely, with a parapet almost 2 metres high. If all the earth removed from the fort ditches and foundation trenches of the internal buildings was incorporated into the bank it has been estimated that the rampart of the fort at Gelligaer would have stood 3.35 metres high to the rampart walk, with a total height of 4.9 metres to the top of the parapet.[27] However, application of this simple equation does not necessarily work for other sites, and work on the reconstructed rampart at Baginton has highlighted some of the difficulties. Here it was found that the spoil removed from both ditches would be sufficient to provide the core for a rampart only one third of the 3.6 metres estimated height.[28]

Rampart revetments

The most common method of rampart revetment was with turf (*murus caespiticius*). Before construction began it would have been stripped from the projected line of the defences and probably from the interior of the fort as well for use in the rampart. Trajan's Column shows scenes in which soldiers are engaged upon building a turf rampart and are transporting the turves upon their backs, steadying them with lengths of rope.

Vegetius describes the optimum size and shape of the turves: 'If the earth is held strongly together by the roots of the grass they are cut in the form of a brick half a foot high, a foot broad and a foot and a half long' i.e. 15 × 30 × 44 cm.[29] Although remains of such turves occur often as no more than thin dark streaks in the soil it is occasionally possible to determine their original sizes as, for example, at Rottweil where they measured 25–45 cm long × 20–35 cm broad, or at Bearsden in Scotland, which were 45 × 30 cm and reduced to a thickness of approximately 10 cm. The army may not have stuck rigidly to a standard size, for the quality of the turf at individual sites, the time of year at which it was cut, and even the weather conditions at the time were probably more important in selecting appropriately sized turves.[30]

Turf was used frequently in rampart construction in Britain from the earliest days of the conquest, and its use was far more widespread here than in the German provinces. The rampart may have been constructed wholly of turf, or have had a revetment at the front only (single), or at both the front and rear (double). When a double revetment enclosed an earthen core it was normal for the width of each component to be equal, each having one third of the total width.[31] Single turf revetments appear to have been most widely used in the Flavian period. The double turf revetment was probably the most common, at least until the Trajanic period, although it is often difficult to distinguish between the various types in early excavation reports, as excavators tended to be extremely vague in their descriptions.

A variation of the double turf rampart was discovered at the early Flavian fort at Rottweil, in which the rampart was also timber framed and laced. Two parallel rows of timbers spaced 4 metres apart were laid around the circuit of the rampart, and within the front row was found a line of substantial postholes dug 1.3 metres beneath the Roman ground surface and spaced 3.2 metres apart, probably to support the timber breastwork; no postholes were found at the rear of the rampart. Overlying these timbers a corduroy of logs was laid transversely across the width of the rampart, and then turf revetments overlay the corduroy at the front and rear, with up to five or six layers of turf remaining *in situ*. Half a metre above the lower corduroy lay another, with exactly the same arrangement, whilst the rampart core between consisted of clay, gravelly earth and turves. The height was estimated to have been 3 metres up to the fighting-platform. An earthen ramp against the back of the rampart showed that the rear revetment had also been vertical. Several other German forts had ramparts of similar construction, with a foundation corduroy, double turf revetments and perhaps a front and rear palisade trench, but none has revealed evidence for

35. Scene from Trajan's Column showing legionaries building in turf. The turves are being carried on their backs in a rope sling. (Scene LX)

the longitudinal timbers which secured the corduroy at Rottweil, or for the regular timber layers above.[32]

Several important results have emerged from the reconstruction of portions of ramparts at Baginton and Chesterholm, the former with a double revetment and the latter entirely turf-built. At Baginton it was found that the standard-size turf blocks weighed 32–34 kg, and that turf would need to

36. Types of rampart construction in cross-section.

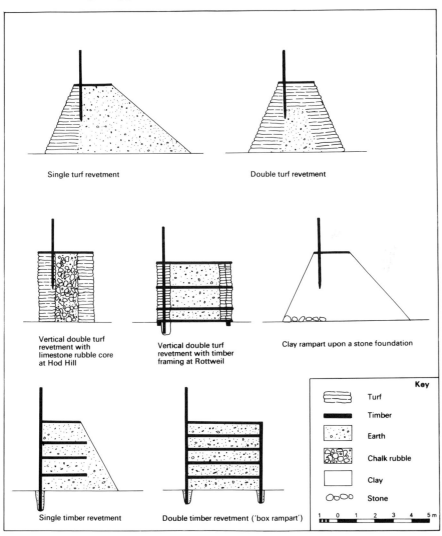

Single turf revetment

Double turf revetment

Vertical double turf revetment with limestone rubble core at Hod Hill

Vertical double turf revetment with timber framing at Rottweil

Clay rampart upon a stone foundation

Single timber revetment

Double timber revetment ('box rampart')

Key

Turf

Timber

Earth

Chalk rubble

Clay

Stone

be stripped at least 38 metres from the back of the rampart to provide sufficient material for a bank 5.5 metres wide and 3.6 metres high.[33] This replica had a batter at the front of 65°, similar to that found at Fendoch, in Scotland, with a low vertical rear revetment and a slope up to the rampart walkway of $42\frac{1}{2}$–45°. A width of 2 metres was allowed for the fighting-platform. It was calculated that to build the total length of rampart at Baginton, a circuit measuring some 283 metres, with one third earth fill, would require 138 000 individual turf blocks, and that with a labour force of 210–300 men (working ten hours per day) under good weather conditions the rampart and double ditch system could be completed in nine to twelve days. The work would have been best carried out in spring or late autumn, when the warmer weather would make the turf easier to cut and transport.[34]

Many ramparts in Britain, particularly from the Flavian period onwards, were constructed entirely of clay. They may have been laid upon a stone foundation base, as at Newstead, or have been strengthened by timber lacing, as at Leintwardine, or a combination of both. Revetments of clay blocks were also used (those found at Brough on Humber measured 30 × 23 × 10 cm) but there are difficulties in distinguishing between these and decayed turves, especially in the older excavation reports.

Alternatively the rampart may have been revetted with timber, having uprights set in either trenches or individual postholes, with a timber planked cladding (known in German as *Holzerdmauer*). The uprights stood generally 3 metres apart, and would presumably have extended to the top of the parapet. There may have been either a single revetment at the front of the rampart mortised into horizontal timbers which were bedded into the earth or clay core, as at Hesselbach or Künzing, or a double revetment, at front and rear, linked by horizontal timbers through the body of the rampart. The latter could be seen at Künzing in its second period or at Rödgen; this double revetment is usually known as a 'box rampart'. The faces of the box rampart may have risen vertically to the height of the rampart walk at both front and rear, with a parapet added at the front; this arrangement has been suggested at several forts in which the timber trenches or postholes supporting the rear revetment were as substantial as those at the front, as at Künzing 2, Rödgen and Oberstimm.[35] Alternatively, where the rear revetment was less substantial it may have remained low with a sloping bank up to the fighting-platform, an arrangement which is thought to have existed at the legionary fortress of Lincoln.

The 'box rampart' was constructed in the Rhineland from the Augustan period, continued in popularity until the end of the first century AD, and proved to be the predominant type of rampart in the German provinces. Its popularity does not seem to have been shared in Britain, where the turf or clay rampart was far more common, and only a handful of timber revetments have been found.[36] It is difficult to explain this divergence of styles. There appears to have been no chronological significance, as both types cover a similar date range, and continue in use until the Antonine period. The difference may reflect some difficulty in obtaining materials in Britain at the time of the conquest, although the supposed lack of seasoned timber for British forts at this time may now be discounted.[37] It has also been suggested that timber was only added to earth or clay ramparts at British forts which had proved unstable and needed repair.

The differences in materials and methods of construction between the British and German examples are probably more apparent than real. Most of our information for German box rampart construction derives from forts which have been dug extensively in recent years, using techniques whereby large open areas have been examined. This has produced conditions which are more conducive to the discovery of rampart postholes spaced up to 3 metres apart than the narrow, often machine-dug, trenches which were frequently employed in Britain until recently. In addition, many of the earth-and-timber forts of the Flavian period in Britain were subsequently rebuilt or refurbished, a process which often entailed the cutting away of the original rampart front and the insertion of a new wall foundation; in circumstances like these traces of an earlier timber revetment may so easily have been destroyed.[38]

External appearance

Trajan's Column provides the principal source of information for the appearance of the turf rampart, although it is here depicted by the sculptor more like a regularly coursed stone or brick wall than a turf bank. Upon the top of the bank were laid longitudinal timbers, and overlying them can be seen the ends of logs placed across the width of the rampart to form the fighting-platform, which was in turn surmounted by a crenellated breastwork. Vegetius records also that the ramparts of both the permanent fort and the city were defended by a parapet with battlements.[39] The parapet must have been supported upon vertical timbers placed deep within the body of the rampart to ensure stability. In the reconstructed rampart at Baginton these timbers were embedded to a depth of 1.5 metres (at Chesterholm 1.83 metres), and were braced in a triangular arrangement to increase their rigidity. However, experience at Chesterholm has shown that the timbers would have been much more stable had they been driven through the turf and into the subsoil. Where timber revetments were constructed the uprights could have easily been extended vertically to support the parapet. The distance between the battlements, or merlons, is difficult to assess from the examples on Trajan's Column, where individual features are not shown to scale, but it is believed to have been at least 1.2 metres.[40]

37. Scene from Trajan's Column showing a turf rampart surmounted by a log walkway. (Scene XI)

38. A portion of the experimental turf rampart and ditch reconstructed in 1966 at The Lunt, Baginton, Warwickshire.

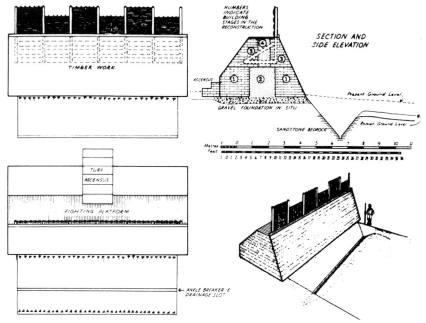

39. Detail of the construction of the experimental turf rampart and ditch at The Lunt, Baginton, Warwickshire.

Timber revetments may have been clad with timber boards or wicker-work panels. Traces of a horizontally-planked rampart front have actually survived in waterlogged conditions at Valkenburg, and these planks were probably extended to include the parapet. Alternatively wickerwork, as described by Caesar,[41] may have been preferred. It has been suggested that the rampart face of the earth-and-timber fort at Heidenheim, in Raetia, consisted of timber uprights with panels of wattlework in between, which were plastered with daub to provide a stable, resilient and fireproof barrier.[42]

The rear of the bank may have sloped from the ground up to the level of the rampart-walk, as at Pen Llystyn in Wales, or it may have risen vertically for perhaps a metre above ground level, retained by timber planks or piles of turves. The remainder of the bank would then have sloped up to the walkway at an angle of 40 or 45°. Drainage gullies were often provided at the rear of the rampart.

Ascensi

Access to the rampart-walkway was provided by ramps or staircases at the rear (*ascensi valli*), constructed in turf, stone or timber, or a combination of these materials. Hyginus recommended that if danger threatened the camp should be provided with double *ascensi* in large numbers to enable the soldiers to reach their stations on top of the rampart with minimum delay.[43]

At Hod Hill narrow turf ramps lay parallel with the rampart and were attached to the rear, on either side of the south gate, and similar turf *ascensi* have been found at the Scottish forts of Strageath and Lyne; the foundation of the latter was revetted with a stone kerb. At Rottweil a ramp was situated next to one of the main gates and consisted of a timber-laced turf extension of the rampart. Cobbled foundations on either side of the east gate at Baginton probably formed the bases for staircases, and were reconstructed with timber steps 0.5 metres high, an arrangement which required a 1.2 metre wide extension at the rear of the rampart.

At the Saalburg, on the Upper German *limes*, twenty-four long narrow stone-built ramps lay parallel with the timber and stone fort wall, secured into the fort wall with timber beams. They were approximately 10 metres long × 1 metre broad and were spaced regularly around the rear of the rampart, on either side of the gates and at the angles, with an intermediate ramp between. Lengths of stone walling attached to the gates of the German forts of Pfünz and Oberflorstadt may also have supported the timber steps of *ascensi*.[44] At the rear of the rampart at Birrens, in Scotland, was discovered a foundation of flat stone slabs approximately 0.6 metres square, the edges of which were notched, probably to support the framework and rails of a timber staircase.

Stone-built Defences

In AD 201 the garrison of the fort at Bumbesti in Moesia, the *cohors I Aurelia Brittonum Antoniniana*, had to replace in stone the turf ramparts which had fallen down because of old age.[45] The general Arrian describes a similar rebuilding programme at a fort on the Phasis (the southern Black Sea coast): 'Formerly the rampart was of earth, and the towers planted upon it were of wood. Now both ramparts and towers are made of brick'.[46] In his address to the troops at the legionary fortress of Lambaesis in North Africa in AD 128, the emperor Hadrian praised their speed and efficiency in camp construction, and contrasted the effort and methods used in both turf and stone construction: 'you build a difficult wall, fit for permanent quarters, in not much longer than it takes to build one of turf. Turf is cut to uniform size, is easy to carry and handle, and not so hard to lay, being naturally soft and even. But you used big, heavy stones of odd sizes, hard to carry, lift and set'.[47]

The life expectancy of a turf, earth or clay rampart is unknown, although observation of weathering at experimental earthworks and rampart reconstructions will ultimately provide a valuable guide.[48] Structural timbers in contact with the ground would have needed replacement after twenty-five or thirty years, and probably even sooner, depending upon the durability of the timber used.[49] Many fort ramparts show signs of repair, with the

40. Staircases
    (*ascensi*) on either
    side of the
    reconstructed
    gate at The
    Lunt, Baginton,
    Warwickshire.

addition perhaps of new turf or clay cheeks, the underpinning of the front of
the rampart with a stone base to prevent collapse, or the insertion at the
front of a stone retaining wall. Walls added in this manner served essentially
as stone revetments to an earthwork, rather than independent free-standing
curtain walls. The front of the existing rampart would normally have been
cut back and a foundation trench and wall built, with soil probably added to
heighten the bank behind, whilst the position of the rampart-walkway and
the rear of the rampart often remained unchanged. The builders at Urspring
in Raetia, however, made no attempt to dismantle the decaying timber
rampart front when the new stone wall was added. Instead it was simply
placed in front, incorporating the old timbers within it. As the timbers
rotted they left voids in the masonry, which were detected during excavation
as slots spaced at regular intervals and extending vertically from the ground
level to the top of the surviving walling.[50]

By the early second century AD, in the reigns of Trajan and Hadrian, the
earth-and-timber forts constructed during the Flavian pacification of Wales
and northern England, and those built by Domitian along the frontiers of
Upper Germany, had begun to decay and required substantial repairs and
refurbishment. The policy of facing the ramparts with a stone wall, which
began under Trajan, and the construction of entirely new stone-built forts
under Hadrian reflects a change in attitude of the Roman army. They had
come to accept a permanent military presence in these frontier regions and
took up a policy of consolidation. Building in more durable materials would
prove more economical in the long run.

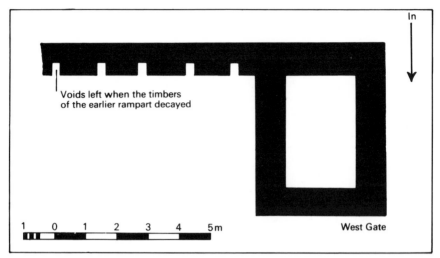

41. Part of the curtain wall and west gate at Urspring in Raetia, showing the facing in stone of the earlier timber framed rampart.

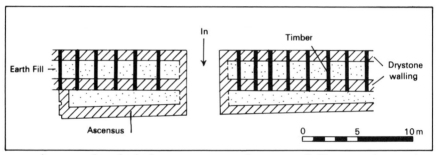

42. An unusual method of rampart construction, *murus Gallicus*, seen here at the north gate at the Saalburg in Upper Germany, c. AD 135.

The change to stone, however, represents only a general trend, and not strictly a chronological development in fort defences, for turf ramparts were still being constructed and repaired alongside stone-built forts, and rebuilding in stone was often itself a piecemeal operation. For example, no signs of any modifications to the turf rampart at Corbridge on the northern frontier were detected which, despite its stone-built neighbours, appears to have remained in commission throughout the life of the fort (from c. AD 90–160). Similarly at Ilkley and Slack, in Yorkshire, there was no evidence for rampart renewal during their fifty years' occupation, although it must be remembered that refurbishment and repair may have been carried out upon the fabric and superstructure without leaving any archaeological trace at the surviving foundation level. At the same time that many forts along the German and Raetian frontiers were rebuilt in stone, under Antoninus Pius, a major new frontier barrier, together with the defences of several auxiliary forts, was being erected, mainly in earth and turf in Scotland (see Chapter 8, p. 274).

The defensive wall of the new Trajanic fort at Gelligaer in Wales consisted of a double stone revetment, with a front wall 0.9–1.2 metres wide, and a narrower rear wall enclosing an earth core, a method of construction very reminiscent of the double turf revetment or the timber box rampart. A similar method was used at the Hadrianic fortlet of Hesselbach in Upper Germany, which had an outer wall 1.5 metres wide, with a slightly narrower inner wall, and still retained traces of a log corduroy within the body of the rampart. As there was no turf available at this site the excavator, Dr D. Baatz, has concluded that this use of freestone instead of turf shows a typical adaptation to local conditions by the Roman engineers.[51]

At the Saalburg, in c. AD 135, the new garrison (*cohors II Raetorum c.R.*) built a defensive wall of unusual construction. It too consisted of two drystone retaining walls, which in this case were both 0.8 metres wide and 2.3 metres apart, but they were anchored together transversely at distances of 1.8 metres (6 Roman feet) by timber beams, which had a cross-section of 20 × 50 cm. The intervening rampart core was infilled with earth and building debris, giving a total width of some 4 metres. The external wall face, with the ends of the timbers visible at regular intervals, presented a chequer-board appearance similar to the native defences which Julius Caesar encountered and described during his campaigns against the Gauls in 52 BC: 'the masonry protects it from fire, the timber from destruction by the battering-ram, which cannot either pierce or knock to pieces a structure braced internally by beams'.[52] This type of wall was known as a *murus Gallicus*.

The stone defensive wall usually presented an ashlar face, and had a mortared rubble core. If added to an existing bank the rear of the wall would not have been faced but left rough and uneven. If newly constructed, both the front and rear would have been faced and provided with offsets, having a clay or earth bank added subsequently at the rear. This backing may have been removed at a later period to enable extra buildings to be crowded into the fort; this is seen, for example, at High Rochester in northern Britain, and at Miltenberg in Upper Germany. The presence of two masonry piers on the inner face of the fort wall at Gnotzheim, in Raetia, and regularly spaced buttresses against the inner wall faces at several Upper German forts may either imply that the wall was constructed before the rampart backing was added, thus requiring temporary supports, or that the walls were here designed to be free-standing.[53]

Fort walls varied in width from 1 to 2 metres above the foundation level. The increased weight of the stone wall demanded a wider berm than an earth or turf rampart to prevent it from slipping forward into the ditch, a factor which is demonstrated clearly upon the Hadrianic frontier in Britain. There the stone Wall needed a berm of 6.1 metres wide, whilst that in front of the turf Wall was only 1.83 metres wide.[54] If a wall was added to existing defences the inner ditch was often infilled and a new one dug further from the wall face to prevent any possibility of collapse.

External appearance

At two points around the defensive circuit at Wörth, on the Odenwald frontier in Upper Germany, portions of the entire fort wall had fallen forward into the ditch, preserving details of its construction and enabling its original height to be calculated.[55] The foundations consisted of sandstone chippings in mortar, partly laid in herringbone fashion, 0.6 metres deep. Above foundation level the wall was 1 metre wide, built with thirty-two courses of faced sandstone blocks, enclosing a mortared rubble core. The height from ground level to the top of the rampart-walkway varied from 4.2 metres (14 Roman feet) to 4.8 metres (16 Roman feet). There was a chamfered course at the level of the rampart-walk, which projected slightly beyond the face of the wall and above this stood a narrower parapet 1.6 metres (5.4 Roman feet) high; worked stones from the parapet and merlons were found in the ditch in front of the front gate (*porta praetoria*). Comparison with surviving fortifications in Rome has suggested that the merlons may have been between 1 and 2 metres broad, separated by openings of anything between 1.5 and 3 metres.[56]

There is evidence from several German forts that the defensive wall, and probably also some of the internal buildings, were plastered externally with white mortar upon which were painted red joint-lines depicting regularly coursed stonework.[57] The quality of masonry used in fort walls was usually high, with well-dressed blocks in regular courses, not random-built, and

43. Part of the fort wall at Wörth which had collapsed into the ditch.

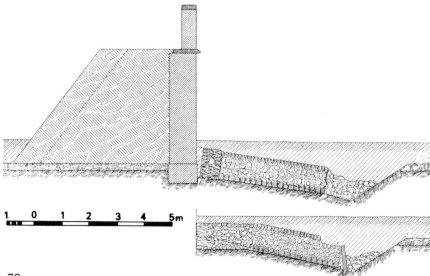

with perhaps a chamfered plinth at the base. The blocks tended to be square. The building stone employed depended largely on local resources; at Risingham, for example, in the Severan period the wall was built in a particularly fine-grained sandstone which was well suited for monumental building. Here large blocks were used, with their external faces tooled, and built above a plinth.[58] At Kapersburg, in the Taunus region of Upper Germany, on the other hand, where such fine stone was not available, the main body of the wall was built from irregular quartzite, with sandstone blocks used only for the quoins and the inner faces of the gate arches.

Construction work

Work on a replica section of Hadrian's Wall at Chesterholm, based upon the dimensions of the Broad Wall, has emphasised the amount of labour needed to build such a structure. The work included the quarrying of facing stones, stone cutting and dressing, the collection of stone chippings and fragments for the wall core, the procuring of vast quantities of lime mortar, and water for mixing it (the mason rebuilding a 14 metre long stretch of wall at Chesterholm required 800 gallons, or 3637 litres, of water per day to mix the mortar), obtaining timber for scaffolding — together with the transport of all these materials to the site.[59] It has been estimated that for every ten men actually involved in the construction of the wall another ninety were needed to obtain and supply the raw materials; and a similar expenditure of time, labour and materials would have been necessary when building a fort's stone defences. The speed and efficiency of the Roman army in such projects is commented upon by Josephus: 'The camp and all that is in it is encompassed with a wall round about, and that sooner than one would imagine, and this by the multitude and skill of the labourers'.[60]

During the construction of the ditch and rampart Vegetius tells us that the 'centurions measure the work with rods ten feet long (*decempedae*) and examine whether each one has properly completed the proportion assigned to him'.[61] Three inscribed stones from the Hadrian's Wall fort at Carvoran

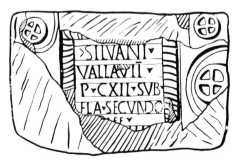

44. Centurial building stone from Carvoran on Hadrian's Wall (*RIB* 1820), c. AD 136–8. It reads:

> *c(enturia) Silvani vallavit p(edes) CXII sub Fla(vio) Secundo [pr]aef(ecto)*
> 'The century of Silvanus built 112 feet of rampart under the command of the prefect, Flavius Secundus.'

record the work of individual centuries of *cohors I Hamiorum*, who were engaged upon rampart construction and were responsible for lengths of 100 or 112 Roman feet.[62] So too, in the construction of the stone defences, each century appears to have been responsible for a particular length of walling, or perhaps a tower or gate—other centurial building stones from Carvoran record various lengths of walling completed (19, 20 and 30½ feet respectively) which probably derived from the gates or towers.[63] A corner stone found near a gate at Chesters, also on Hadrian's Wall, was inscribed on two faces, which suggests that it had been set into a tower where both faces would have been visible. An inscription on one side records that a length of walling had been built, and on the other the name of the group responsible, either a century or a *turma*.[64]

Angle and Interval Towers

In his description of the defences of a temporary camp, written towards the end of the first century AD, Josephus remarks that 'the outward circumference has the resemblance to a wall, and is adorned with towers at regular distances'.[65] Excavations at many auxiliary forts have revealed the presence of such towers at each of the four angles, and spaced at intervals between the angles and the gates; they were probably originally provided in most forts. Both angle and interval towers standing at least one storey above the rampart-walkway are depicted upon Trajan's Column. One scene shows them as wooden platforms open to the sky and surrounded by a timber rail, whilst another shows an angle tower with a gabled roof; it was probably timber, for no masonry joints are shown. A stone-built interval tower is also illustrated. No roof is visible, but it may have been a pent-roof, sloping from the front to the rear.

The timber towers were supported within the body of the rampart, with posts driven into the subsoil, and rose above the rampart-walkway to provide look-out towers, roofed strongpoints, or platforms from which missiles could be discharged and artillery fired.[66] There were difficulties in fitting the rectilinear timber tower within the rounded angle of the fort and various different solutions were tried. In the Claudian forts of Hod Hill and Valkenburg three posts at the front and three at the rear were arranged in a chevron pattern in order to follow the curve as closely as possible. A rectangular tower constructed upon six posts was used in the pre-Flavian fort of Jay Lane, and square towers at Rottweil some twenty years later. Perhaps the best solution is seen in the Flavian forts of Künzing in Raetia and Pen Llystyn in Wales, where a wedge-shape was adopted, with three posts at the front and two at the rear.

Interval towers were usually placed equidistant between the angle and the gate. They were square, with their width corresponding to that of the rampart or slightly smaller. The use of larger timbers for the angle towers at Pen Llystyn (36 cm square at the angle and 15 cm square at the intervals) has prompted the suggestion that the towers at the angles may have stood higher than the interval towers.[67]

The provision of angle and (probably) interval towers was also standard in stone-built forts. Towers may have been constructed entirely of stone or, as is probably the case at Gelligaer, where the walls of the interval towers were of markedly slighter construction than the gatetowers, with timber superstructures above a stone base. At the corner the front wall of the tower was normally formed by the curving fort wall, whilst its sides enclosed either a square chamber whose width corresponded to that of the rampart, or a wedge-shaped tower tapering towards the rear of the building. At the forts of Holzhausen and Wiesbaden in Upper Germany the back walls of the angle towers were actually curved, reflecting the rounded angle of the external wall face. At Caerhun in Wales the angle towers of the Antonine

45. A selection of towers and gates illustrated on Trajan's Column.

46. The foundations of the curtain wall and the south-east angle tower at Unterböbingen in Raetia.

47. The replica stone tower and section of wall at Chesterholm-Vindolanda, Northumberland.

48. Replica towers in timber and stone constructed at Chesterholm-Vindolanda, Northumberland.

49. Foundations of the curtain wall and an interval tower at Unterböbingen in Raetia.

75

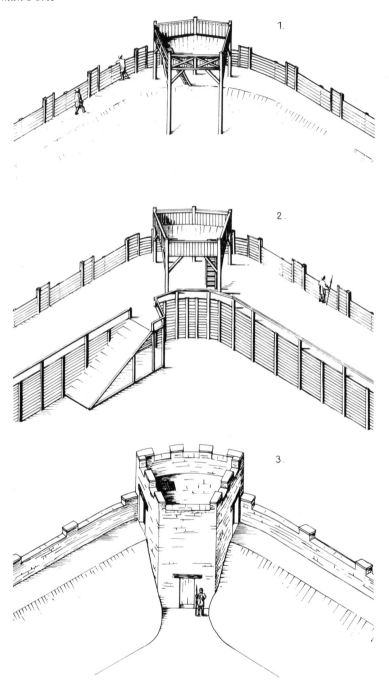

50. The suggested reconstruction of successive towers at the south-east angle of the fort at Künzing in Raetia.

fort were detached completely from the fort wall and stood independently within the core of the rampart. This fact, together with the displacement of a guard chamber at the rear gate some 0.7 metres behind the line of the fort wall, implies that they were erected prior to the defensive wall, which subsequently failed to link them.[68]

Stone interval towers were usually square, their size being governed by the rampart width. The replacement of timber towers, which had their timber supports embedded within the rampart, by stone towers meant that basements were now provided at street level. Stone towers may have contained ladders to give access to the rampart-walkway, but their ground floors often seem to have been used to house ovens or hearths, although they do not seem to have been particularly important. At Housesteads, on Hadrian's Wall, for instance, during reconstruction of the water supply to the latrine, access to the base of the south-east angle tower was first restricted and then prevented altogether by the building of water tanks against the doorway. The towers may have sheltered the guards on watch. In this connection Vegetius describes how, in the city 'Fierce dogs kept in the towers have proved useful in discovering the approach of an enemy by their scent, and giving notice thereof by barking'.[69]

The towers of most first and second century auxiliary forts were built against the rear of the defensive wall and did not project beyond it. By the late second and early third centuries however, the need was increasingly felt for more defensive fort architecture, characterised by solid projecting towers at the gates and spaced at regular intervals along the curtain wall. These towers are seen first at the Upper German fort of Niederbieber in c. AD 185; the design was fully developed in the later third and fourth centuries in the externally projecting bastions of the forts of the Saxon Shore.[70]

The Gates (*Portae*)

The auxiliary fort normally possessed four gateways. The front and rear gates (*porta praetoria* and *porta decumana*) lay in the centre of their respective sides, whilst the *portae principales* lay not in the centre, but displaced towards the front of the fort, at either end of the principal street. Occasionally further gates were added (for example at the forts which lay astride Hadrian's Wall) with the front part of the fort, the *praetentura*, projecting beyond it. In these cases all three principal gates opened upon the northern side of the frontier, and so additional single-portalled gates were provided at each end of the *via quintana* to give better access behind the Wall. On the other hand, a few forts and fortlets were laid out without the customary *retentura*, and therefore no rear gate was provided.

The groundplan of the fort gateway, whether constructed in timber or stone, was basically the same. A single or double portal was usually, although not always, flanked by square or rectangular towers. The entrance passageway was bridged at rampart-walk level and the space above either left open with a parapet, or roofed to form a more substantial gatehouse. The towers may have provided guard chambers on the ground floor, with staircases internally up to the rampart top. The height of the gate passage must have been at least 3 metres in order to accommodate wheeled traffic and riders, and the gatetowers at least 2.5 or 3 metres above the rampart-walkway to allow free access beneath for defenders.[71]

The entrance was commonly recessed a little from the front of the rampart or wall as a defensive precaution, so that it could be overlooked from above. Double-leaved doors were pivoted, rather than hinged, on either side of the passageway, closing against a raised threshold or doorstop. Fragments of iron binding discovered at the north gate of the timber fort at Fendoch probably derived from a door of stout oak reinforced with iron plates and sheathing like those described by Vegetius, who recommended that 'to secure the gates of a city from fire, they should be covered with raw hides and plates of iron'.[72] Underground drains or water conduits often passed through the gate portals beneath the road metalling.

Timber gates[73]

Bridge The simplest form of timber gateway consisted of four or six uprights arranged in pairs on either side of the opening. Behind these uprights timber boards were secured to revet the ends of the rampart. The uprights supported a timber bridge over the gate at the same level as the rampart-walkway, and probably provided the framework for a tower above, although this is not certain. Trajan's Column usually, though not invariably, depicts the gateways surmounted by towers, and it does seem unlikely that towers should have been built elsewhere around the defensive circuit, at the angles and intervals, and not be provided to protect the gates. The double-leaved gates would have been set on the outside of the gate passage so that they lay flush with the line of the rampart externally and could be easily observed from the rampart-walkway above.[74] The gates were not hinged but socketed into a timber lintel above and a timber threshold beneath. It is possible that in cases where three or four pairs of posts flanked the entranceway the gates were hung not at the very outside of the gate passage, but were slightly recessed and placed in the centre, with only the rear of the gate passage bridged and supporting a tower.

Several variations of this 'bridge' type have been detected, single portals which were flanked by either two, three or even four pairs of posts, and double portals. Single portals with two pairs of posts occur at Hod Hill and Great Casterton in the Claudian period, and were still in use in the Antonine

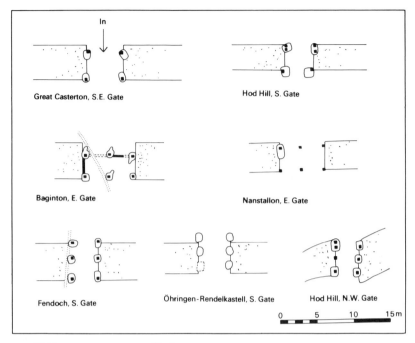

In

Great Casterton, S.E. Gate

Hod Hill, S. Gate

Baginton, E. Gate

Nanstallon, E. Gate

Fendoch, S. Gate

Öhringen-Rendelkastell, S. Gate

Hod Hill, N.W. Gate

0   5   10   15 m

51. Bridge-type gateways. Scale 1:500

Wall forts of Old Kilpatrick and Cadder. Three pairs of posts were used in another gate at Hod Hill, at the Flavian fort of Fendoch, and the south gate of Rendelkastell Öhringen, in Upper Germany, where in the mid-second century a timber revetted passage with a timber bridge provided access through a stone defensive wall. This type was further used in the gateways of milecastles in the turf section of Hadrian's Wall, and in a few Antonine Wall forts, where up to four pairs of uprights were used.[75] Double portals are known only from three forts, at Baginton and Nanstallon in the Neronian period and early Flavian Brough on Humber; it has been suggested that this type was Neronian in origin. A modern reconstruction has been made of this type of gate building at Baginton (see p. 85).

Towers flush with the rampart   This gate type comprised square towers, which may or may not have housed guardchambers, flanking either a single or double portal, and lying flush within the line of the rampart. Single portals flanked by four-post towers have been found at Jay Lane in Herefordshire and Crawford in Scotland, both dating to the Flavian period. Another gate at Jay Lane, and one at the neighbouring fort of Buckton, had towers constructed with four uprights flanking a double carriageway. Central posts were added to support the superstructure, at the outside of which were hung the gates. A similar arrangement was used at Oakwood in Scotland. Here the discovery of metalling between the posts shows that they

79

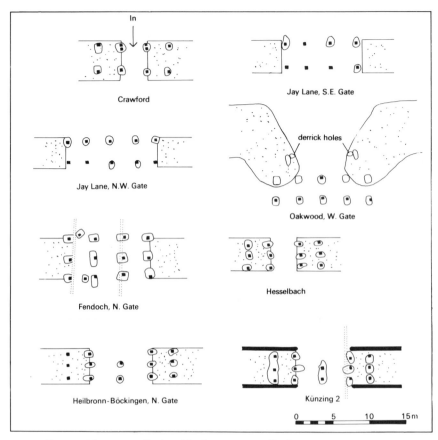

52. Gates with towers flush with the rampart. Scale 1:500

were open frameworks supporting towers or platforms; it must be pointed out, though, that the association between rampart and gates at this fort is atypical, with inturned ramparts abutting the fronts of the towers. At another Scottish fort of the same date, Crawford, the rampart apparently enclosed the timber uprights of the towers, which were filled up solidly to the gate passageway.

Towers built flush within the rampart but supported upon six or more posts probably had recessed gates placed halfway down the gate passage, with a bridge constructed only above the rear of the portal. They flanked single carriageways at Fendoch, in the Upper German forts of Echzell and Hesselbach, and also at the Raetian fort of Oberstimm where, unusually, the towers had eight posts. There are other examples with a similar plan, but with a double portal in which central posts defined a recessed entrance; at Künzing and Heilbronn-Böckingen these were flanked by six post towers— at Corbridge by ten post towers. A reconstructed drawing of this type of gate plan at Künzing (Ill. 55) in the first two periods of occupation (c. AD 90–135) shows towers on either side of the carriageway, their uprights supported within the body of the rampart, a bridge over the gate and a breastwork at the height of the rampart-walk. It remains uncertain whether the towers were generally filled from ground level with rampart material, providing platforms only above the rampart-walkway as found at Künzing or Oberstimm, or whether at some forts they were left hollow, with guard-chambers at ground level, providing access by a ladder inside to the rampart top. Certainly the excavators of the gatetowers at Echzell and Fendoch believed that they had been hollow at the base, either remaining open at ground level, or possibly being clad with timber boards to provide guardchambers.[76]

Gates with internal towers The third principal type of gate plan consisted of gatetowers projecting internally on either side of a single or, more commonly, a double portal, with the gates themselves recessed far down the gate passage to create a deep 'courtyard' in front of the entrance which could be commanded by the defenders. This method of gate construction had a long history, for it was employed, built with drystone walling, in the north-west gate of a camp at Renieblas in Spain in c. 153 BC and is believed to occur even earlier at the town of Pompeii.[77]

An important group of deeply-recessed timber gateways occurs in the Augustan camps and forts of the Rhineland (Ill. 53). At Oberaden and Beckinghausen, for example, built c. 11 BC, the flanking towers were supported upon ten posts, and at Haltern upon eight, whilst a more common six-post structure was found at Rödgen. Other gates of the same date had a similar depth but were further extended to incorporate the rampart ends to form L-shaped towers, which are seen at Haltern and Rödgen.

After the Augustan period although the use of the internal flanking gate tower became common, the deeply recessed gateways became much shallower, with the gates set halfway down the gate passage, usually in line with the back of the rampart. Such gateways have been found in the Claudian period at Hod Hill and Valkenburg, and continued throughout the Flavian period at, for example, Pen Llystyn, Rottweil or Heilbronn-Böckingen. At Rottweil and Valkenburg they flanked single entrances, although double portals were more common, especially in Britain. It is probable that the front half of the gateway towers was in fact an extension of the rampart, filled with earth and turf, which would give solidity to withstand a battering ram. The rear half of the tower may have been open, as shown in the reconstruction of the gate at Rottweil (Ill. 57) or it may have been boarded with timber to provide a guardchamber. Alternatively the entire space may have been filled with rampart material to provide extra support and solidity for the towers and walkway above, as depicted in the reconstruction of the gate at Rödgen (Ill. 55).

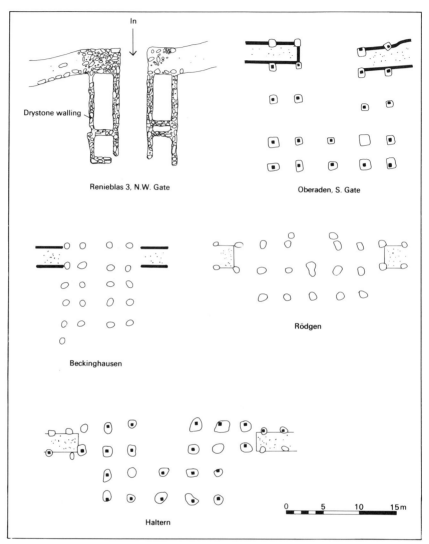

In

Drystone walling

Renieblas 3, N.W. Gate

Oberaden, S. Gate

Beckinghausen

Rödgen

Haltern

0   5   10   15m

53. The distinctive groundplans of some Republican and Augustan gates. Scale
1:500

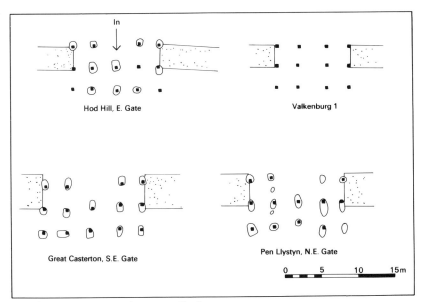

54. Gates with internal towers. Scale 1:500

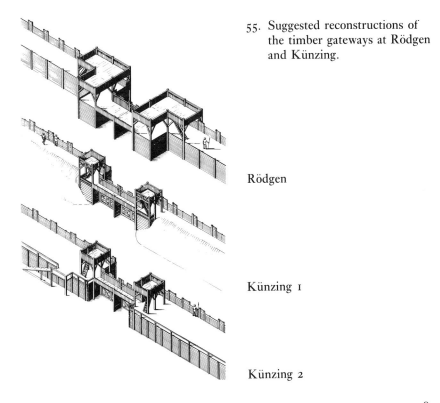

55. Suggested reconstructions of
the timber gateways at Rödgen
and Künzing.

Rödgen

Künzing 1

Künzing 2

56. View through a gate portal of Flavian fort at Carlisle showing threshold beams with door sockets, cart ruts, gate posts and timber-lined drains. In the right foreground is a slot for the pre-gate drain and an unrelated stone well.

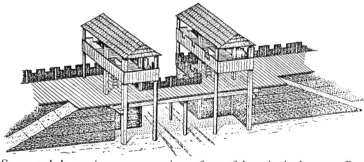

57. Suggested alternative reconstructions of one of the principal gates at Rottweil in Upper Germany.

Dating   All three major types of timber gateway were built over a long period of time, although certain chronological developments can be seen. The simple bridge gate continued in use throughout the first and second centuries AD and was used in smaller forts such as Nanstallon in Cornwall or the fortlet at Old Burrow in Devon. It was also used for the less important gates of a fort, such as the postern gate at Hod Hill, or the gates leading to annexes at Fendoch and Great Casterton. The distinctive group of recessed gateways seen in the Augustan forts of the Rhineland were replaced from the reign of Claudius, both in Britain and Germany, by a much shallower internal tower, which continued in use well into the Flavian period, but was gradually replaced by the simpler type with flanking towers set within the width of the rampart; it was this type which gained increasing popularity and later became translated into stone. Double portalled gates were usually provided at the main entrances, whilst less important gates were often single. This can be seen, for instance, at Rottweil, where the principal gates were double, whilst the rear gate had only a single carriageway.

Reconstruction   In September 1970 a party of Royal Engineers rebuilt the east gate of the fort at Baginton.[78] The excavated ground plan showed the six large post pits, set within the width of the rampart, of a double-portalled gate, with no guardchambers. The form and superstructure were based on illustrations from Trajan's Column, although here single rather

58.   Royal Engineers erecting a reconstruction of the timber east gate at The Lunt, Baginton, Warwickshire in 1970.

59. The completed gateway at The Lunt, Baginton, seen from outside the fort.

60. Scene from Trajan's Column showing a camp with timber gate and angle towers. (Scene LI)

than double passageway gates are usually depicted, with a gatetower rising above the rampart top forming an open platform with a lattice-work parapet around it. Access to the top of the rampart from ground level was provided at each side of the gate by timber staircases.

As timber gateways usually show such uniformity in overall dimensions and the sizes of timbers used it is generally assumed that they were largely prefabricated in the legionary workshop and then assembled on site; so too with this reconstruction, which was prepared in modern army workshops and erected on the site using no modern equipment.[79] The reconstruction work has demonstrated that ten men using a single pole with pulleys and guylines could haul the individual sections into place with ease, and the whole gateway was completed within three days. The original excavations at Baginton had found construction ramps in front of several of the gateposts, and at Oakwood possible derrick holes used when hoisting the gatepost timbers into place were detected in front of the east and west gates.[80]

Stone gates

The stone gateway[81] usually comprised a double portal which was arched and vaulted, flanked by square or rectangular gatetowers set within the width of the rampart, and open at ground level to provide guardchambers. The passageways were either completely separate and divided by a solid wall, or provided with an arched access between, supported on stone piers at the front and rear; the central partition is known as the *spina*. The entrance was frequently slightly recessed from the outer face of the

61. Foundations of the curtain wall and south gate at Buch, in Raetia, during the excavations of 1972.

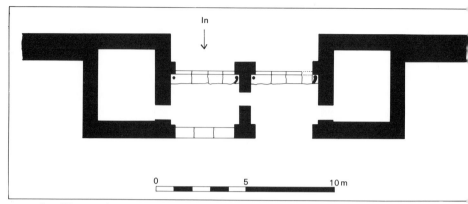

62. The south gate at Chesters on Hadrian's Wall, showing the stone threshold with channels to locate the door pivots.

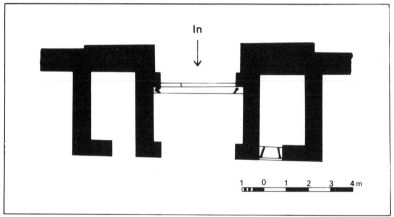

63. The south-east gate at Hesselbach in Upper Germany, with channels to locate the door pivots in the gate threshold and guardroom doorway.

defensive wall and towers. The gates themselves were placed at the front of the arched openings, often set behind stone projections in the central pier and side walls to mask and protect their edges.

The gates closed against a raised stone threshold or doorstop. The thresholds of several gates of forts on Hadrian's Wall are very well preserved[82] and provide evidence for the outer raised rim against which the doors were secured, sockets for the collars of the door pivots, and bolt holes. Additional strength was provided by metal or timber bars slotted across the back of the doors. At the south and east gates at Chesters, and the south-east gate at the fortlet of Hesselbach, grooves were cut on each side of the threshold to allow the initial positioning of the gates; these grooves were then infilled with lead so that should it be necessary to remove the gates at any time the lead could be easily melted.

The carriageways were flanked by stone towers, which were entered either from the gate passages or from the rear. The average width of a gateway including both towers and the carriageways was approximately 15–18 metres, and the depth ranged from 5 to 6 metres. The largest stone gateway which has been excavated in a British auxiliary fort was discovered at Buckton in Wales (c. 22 × 5.8 metres overall). Its unusual width may be explained by the provision of stone-founded internal staircases within the guardchambers, a feature which has not been detected within other auxiliary gatehouses. It seems certain, though, that timber staircases, or at least ladders, must usually have been provided to give access from the guardchamber to the top of the fighting-platform.

External appearance   It is possible to draw a tolerably clear picture of the stone-built gateway, as the remains on the ground are more substantial, and the mouldings, voussoirs, window and door heads and other architectural fragments are often preserved. More indications are provided by Trajan's Column and the well preserved remains of one of the gates of the Severan fort at Bu Njem in Libya. An illustration of its north gate, made by G. F. Lyon in 1819, shows the original single-portalled entrance flanked by square gate towers still standing to first floor level, with later masonry additions above.[83]

64. The well preserved remains of the north gate of the Severan fort at Bu Njem in Libya, illustrated by G. F. Lyon in 1819.

65. Decorative door-head with central bull's head motif from a gatetower at Hesselbach.

66. Detail of a mosaic found near Orange, and now in the museum at Avignon. It depicts the gateway of a Roman town which, although probably more elaborate, would have been broadly similar in appearance to a fort gateway.

The towers must have stood at least two storeys high, rising high above the rampart walkway. They may have had pitched roofs or flat roofs with crenellated parapets, covered with either tiles or wooden shingles. Trajan's Column shows a gatetower with a pitched roof and small round-headed windows in the upper storey. Two similar windows were preserved in the front walls of the towers at Bu Njem, placed at the level of the rampart walk. Semi-circular door and window heads have often been found amongst the debris of fort gates; notable are the many examples from Birdoswald on Hadrian's Wall, and a door head from Hesselbach which bore a bull's head relief.

At Bu Njem the space above the entrance arch, between the towers, was left open with a crenellated parapet, and it is probable that the tops of the towers were also originally treated in this way. The gates of many Roman forts may well have been similar, although in less amenable climates the area between the towers may have been provided with windows and roofed to give a chamber above the gate. A mosaic from Orange depicts a gateway of a Roman town which is important when considering the form and appearance of fort gateways. The gate shown here has a double arched entrance, and a chamber above with three small windows, flanked by gatetowers three storeys high, with round headed windows and battlements.[84] A similar gatehouse has been suggested in the reconstruction of the gates at Hesselbach.

Externally there is evidence for some architectural embellishment and elaboration at the gateways. The vaulted arches provided impressive

a

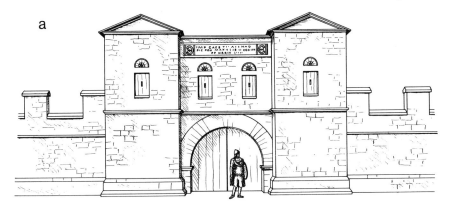

b

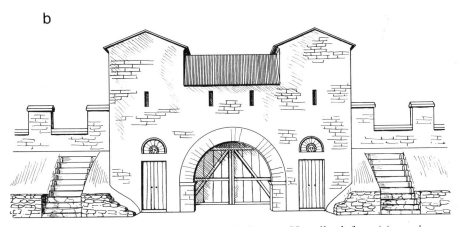

67. Suggested reconstruction of the principal gate at Hesselbach from (a) exterior
    (b) interior.

entrances, which were further emphasised by the stone mouldings and
decorated window-heads. Evidence for the plastering in white of external
fort walls with the joint lines of the stones picked out in red mortar or paint
has been found at some German forts; plaster from Arnsburg shows that
here the gateways were treated in a similar manner. Inscriptions recording
the date at which the gate was erected, and the unit responsible, were
originally placed above the centre of the gateway; one was still in position at
Bu Njem in 1819 and a similar inscription was recorded at the east gate at
Chesters.[85] The dedication would have been either inscribed upon stone
with the letters picked out in red paint, or have consisted of individual
bronze or gilded letters applied to a stone tablet; such letters have been
found in front of the principal gates of several German forts.[86]

The most important gateway of the fort, providing access to the *principia*
and the other central buildings, was the *porta praetoria*, and this gate often
received particular attention. At Ambleside in the Lake District, for

68. The east gate at Birdoswald on Hadrian's Wall, seen from the inside of the fort.

69. Detail of the east gate at Birdoswald showing the springer stone for one of the arches.

example, this was the only gate with a double portal and gatetowers; the other three were single with no towers at all. At Brecon Gaer in Wales it was the *porta praetoria* which was selected for rebuilding in a new style in the Antonine period, the first of its kind known in Britain, in which the gatetowers projected well in front of the defensive wall, with a recessed double entrance. Single portals, as with timber examples, tended to be used for the less important entrances, especially the rear gate, and simple single carriageway gates without towers were used as posterns occasionally, or as *portae quintanae* in those Hadrian's Wall forts which projected to the north of the frontier.

Changing styles[87]   Gatetowers projecting in front of the defensive wall appear in the reign of Antoninus Pius, and from this period onwards a more general trend can be seen towards a highly defensible auxiliary gateway, whose entrances could be enfiladed from the ramparts. This style developed in the early third century into projecting semi-circular towers, and later into the rounded bastions of the Saxon Shore forts. Projecting rectangular gatetowers were added to several auxiliary forts in the Antonine period, at Brecon Gaer in Wales and a number of German examples. The brand new fort built c. AD 185 at Niederbieber in Upper Germany had such gateways, and the style continued in use in the Severan period at South Shields and Valkenburg.

Semi-circular projecting towers appear generally from the beginning of the third century onwards, although earlier examples occur occasionally in the mid-second century at Castell Collen in Wales or the legionary fortress of Lambaesis in North Africa.[88] Another style of gate appeared at the same

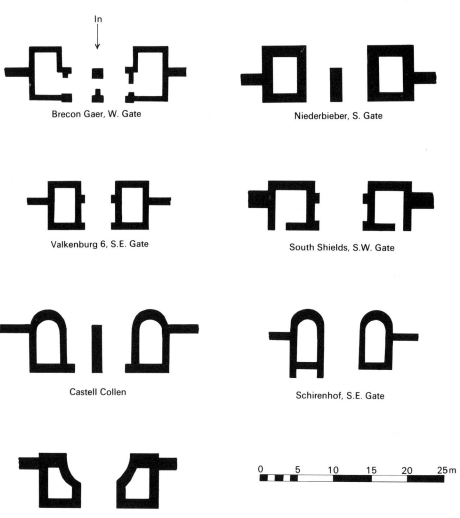

In

Brecon Gaer, W. Gate

Niederbieber, S. Gate

Valkenburg 6, S.E. Gate

South Shields, S.W. Gate

Castell Collen

Schirenhof, S.E. Gate

Theilenhofen, S. Gate

0   5   10   15   20   25m

70. Gatetowers which projected in front of the curtain wall, usually second century or later in date. Scale 1:500

time, with projecting gatetowers with straight front walls, but with sides which curved or tapered inwards to provide a funnel-shaped approach to the gates. This plan was adopted in three of the gates at Bu Njem, the legionary fortresses of Lambaesis and Carnuntum, and the auxiliary fort of Theilenhofen in Raetia.

Catapult Platforms (*Ballistaria*)

The presence of artillery pieces within legionary camps is amply confirmed by Classical authorities. Vegetius records each legionary century having charge of an *onager*, a large catapult discharging stone missiles, which is described in action at the Siege of Jerusalem by Josephus, and later by Ammianus.[89] Each century also had smaller artillery pieces such as *scorpiones* or *ballistae* which, working on the cross-bow principle, discharged metal bolts; these weapons too are described by Vegetius and Vitruvius and depicted in the charge of legionaries upon Trajan's Column.[90] But the use of these catapults to defend permanent auxiliary forts of the first and second centuries is attested neither by epigraphic nor literary sources, and it seems that they were not normally used by auxiliaries, at least in the first century.[91]

An exception may be seen at Hod Hill, where a mixed unit of legionaries and auxiliaries bombarded the native hillfort in AD 43–4 and erected a fort of their own within its ramparts. At least two artillery platforms (*ballistaria*) were provided behind the rampart, one on the east and the other on the south side, both next to gates. The platforms were of chalk rubble 6.7 × 6.1 metres, rising with a batter of 26° at the rear which, if continued, would probably have reached the level of the rampart-walkway at a height of 3 metres. The sides of the platforms were probably revetted with timber, and further tied into the rampart body with timbers. Turf staircases (*ascensi*) were provided at each side. The platforms are thought to have been wide enough to accommodate two machines.

Masonry platforms have been found at the rear of the defensive wall in several stone-built forts, and they are generally considered to be third-century additions to the defences. They are difficult to date because to prevent structural damage from the recoil of the *onager* (so-called because its action was likened to the kick of a wild ass) the platform upon which it was mounted was not bonded in with the rear of the fort wall. It is often difficult, therefore, to assess whether the two were contemporary or whether the platform was a later addition. Only at High Rochester, in northern Britain, can an excavated platform be linked with dated inscriptions. Here dedication slabs record the construction of a *ballistarium* in AD 220, and the restoration of this or another similar platform in AD 225–35.[92] Against the back of the northern rampart of the Severan fort a large platform, extending 9.8 metres behind the wall, had been built. It was faced with large ashlar blocks upon a plinth enclosing a core of rubble bedded in clay, designed to absorb the recoil of the catapult; several stone missiles were also found within the fort, many weighing approximately 50 kg.

71. An inscription from High Rochester, Northumberland (*RIB* 1281) recording the restoration of an artillery platform (*ballistarium*) in AD 225–235. It reads:

Imp(eratori) Caes[(ari) M(arco) Aur(elio) Seve]ro Alex[andr]o P(io) F(elici) [Aug(usto) . . . matr(i)] i[mp(eratoris) Caes(aris) et ca]s(trorum) coh(ors) I F(ida) Vard(ullorum) m(illiaria) S(everiana) A(lexandriana) ballis(tarium) a solo re[sti]t(uit) sub c(ura) Cl(audi) Apellini le[g(ati)] Aug(ustorum) instante Aur(elio) Quinto tr(ibuno)

'For the Emperor Caesar Marcus Aurelius Severus Alexander Pius Felix Augustus . . . and for . . ., mother of the army, the First Loyal Cohort of Vardulli, one thousand strong, *Severiana Alexandriana*, restored this artillery platform from ground level, under the charge of Claudius Apellinus, imperial legate, and under the supervision of the tribune, Aurelius Quintus'

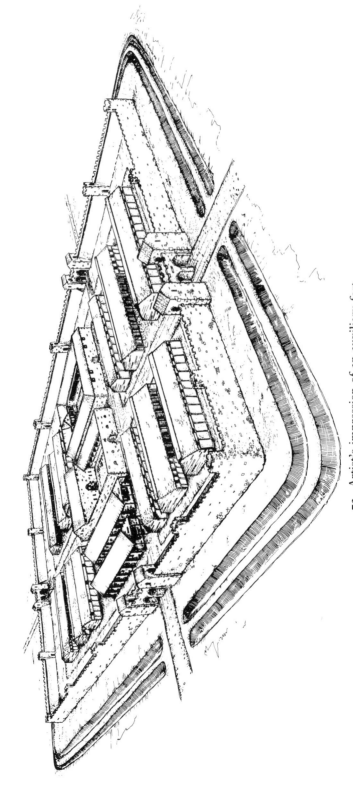

72. Artist's impression of an auxiliary fort.

5 The Internal Buildings

The internal buildings of the first-century auxiliary fort were normally constructed in timber and, like the defences, were often eventually rebuilt in stone. The rebuilding process was frequently a rather piecemeal operation, starting with the headquarters building and the granaries, extending to the commander's house and any other buildings in the central range, and only then moving on to include the barracks and ancillary buildings. The stages in the transition from a timber to a completely stone-built fort can be seen in the developments at Corbridge between c. AD 90 and the middle of the second century (Ill. 73). In many cases the stone rebuilding programme was never completed and the barracks, and sometimes also the commander's house, continued to be renewed and repaired in timber throughout the life of the fort.

Most of our information about the internal buildings comes from the excavation of structures in the central range of the fort. This is mainly because, especially during excavations in the last century, attention has been concentrated upon the centre of the fort, particularly on the site of the headquarters building (*principia*). Here the buildings were most likely to have been stone-built and therefore more substantial, and were more easily recognisable from their distinctive groundplans. In forts excavated before the introduction of modern techniques, the postholes and foundation trenches of timber buildings such as barracks and stables were often overlooked and only the stone structures were recorded. An increasing number of both earth-and-timber and stone forts have subsequently been excavated in considerable detail, and in a few cases virtually the entire layout of the internal buildings has been revealed. There are still problems, though, in distinguishing between buildings which are similar in groundplan and have no distinctive features. These are thought to have served a variety of different functions, perhaps as stables, storebuildings, or workshops.

Building methods

Timber uprights were either set in foundation trenches, in individual postholes, or into sleeper beams or sills let into the ground. The most common construction method, and probably also the most convenient, was

97

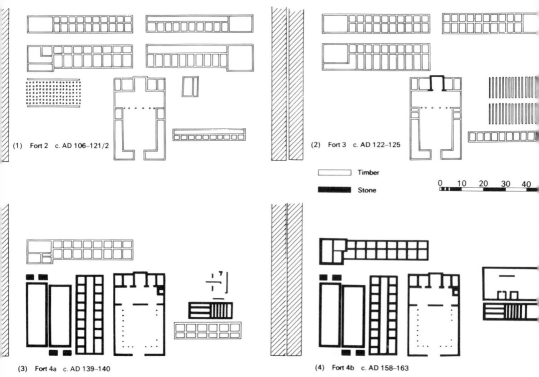

(1) Fort 2 c. AD 106–121/2

(2) Fort 3 c. AD 122–125

Timber

Stone

0   10   20   30   40

(3) Fort 4a c. AD 139–140

(4) Fort 4b c. AD 158–163

73. Successive stages in the rebuilding of the fort at Corbridge, showing the gradual transition from a timber to a completely stone-built fort.

to dig a trench along the projected wall line of the building in which the individual uprights, or a prefabricated framework of timbers, could be aligned and positioned with ease, with the backfill rammed down and consolidated around them. Posts set in individual pits occur frequently as load-bearing posts or columns supporting verandahs or porticoes around courtyards, or as aisle posts in the crosshall or forehall of the *principia*; the posts were often placed against one edge of the posthole, or stone packing was used, to give greater stability. Sleeper beams were set into the ground and the uprights were then mortised into them, a method which required very accurate carpentry. Traces of this type of construction are often recognisable as narrow vertical-sided trenches cut into the subsoil.

Between the uprights timber-framed walls were constructed with either woven wattle panels plastered with daub, or horizontal overlapping timber planks, as illustrated on Trajan's Column. It is usually impossible to determine which method of walling was used, although occasionally the discovery of burnt daub fragments which have fallen into the top of the foundation trenches may give a clue. Exceptionally, the remains of the actual wattlework panels may survive in waterlogged conditions, as at Valkenburg, where the panels were supported on posts set in continuous trenches, or with a timber sill. Here also were preserved *in situ* the timber thresholds of doorways, sleeper beams still retaining the bases of uprights, roadways laid on log corduroys, and timber-lined drains.

The external walls were plastered and whitewashed, as demonstrated by finds of plaster from several forts, both from the vicinity of the central buildings and also the barracks. Evidence of even finer plaster from the walls of timber barracks at the Upper German forts of Butzbach and Echzell shows that here the walls were not only plastered but also painted internally. The roofs were clad normally in timber shingles[1] or, occasionally, tiles; they are unlikely to have been thatched, as it would have been too great a fire risk. Window glass has often been found in the debris of the *principia* and the commander's house and sometimes from the barrack blocks. All the fort buildings would have been constructed in this manner, except the granaries, which were usually provided with a raised floor and clad with weatherproof boards (see p. 153).

A considerable amount of timber was needed to construct the internal buildings of an average-sized auxiliary fort. Estimates suggest that a fort covering an area of approximately 1.6 hectares would require some 184 cubic metres of structural timbers, excluding cladding and infilling, with a further 283 cubic metres for the roof trusses and rafters.[2] Oak would have been the most suitable wood, and has been found at many fort sites, but

74. Opposite: the timber foundations, well preserved in waterlogged conditions, of part of the courtyard-plan workshop in the Claudian fort of Valkenburg, in Lower Germany. (The well at the top of the photograph is modern.)

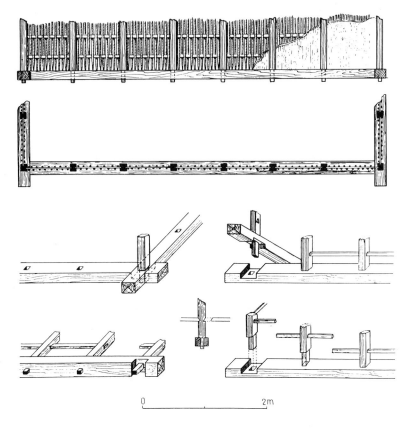

75. Detail of timber construction techniques revealed at Valkenburg, in Lower Germany.

where it was not available other timbers were substituted; at Valkenburg, for example, a great deal of local alder was used.

It is probable that an oak post with a cross-section of 10 cm, if in contact with the ground, would have had a life of perhaps thirty years, whilst other species were much less durable. Emphasis has frequently been placed upon the need for large quantities of seasoned timber for the construction of Roman forts and their internal buildings. From his excavations at Fendoch in Scotland, in 1936–7, Professor Ian Richmond concluded that the Roman army had military stockyards in which timber was kept to season, cut into standard lengths, and prefabricated into building sections for transport to a new fort site. Sound timbers which had been dismantled from forts elsewhere were returned to these stockyards for re-use.[3] This conclusion was based upon a number of factors. The absence of oak from the pollen sequences at Fendoch implied that suitable timber was not available locally and had to be transported to the site which, if it was to be well seasoned before construction began, must have been in store for some time beforehand. In addition, the uniform-sized timbers suggested that they had been cut and shaped according to a standardised pattern. More recent work by W. S. Hanson, however, has shown that there was no need to season timber at all, and that local trees could be felled and utilised straight away.[4] The evidence for standard lengths of timbers is unsatisfactory, as excavators tended to publish generalised sizes and spacing for timbers. On examination of the evidence the spacing of uprights shows little uniformity.[5] The fact that the timbers conform to roughly consistent dimensions is hardly surprising as the buildings were designed by the Roman military for similar purposes and for optimum efficiency.

The shell of the old timber building was not always demolished when rebuilding in stone, as examples have been found in which the old timbers were encased in stone and incorporated into the new structure. This can be seen in the principal buildings of the central range at Urspring, in Raetia, where the timbers had rotted leaving tell-tale voids in the masonry which accurately reflected the shape of the vertical notched timber posts of the earlier building, spaced at one metre intervals. The walls of the new buildings had been plastered internally and externally to mask the timbers. Only the granary and the shrine of the headquarters building had been rebuilt entirely in stone. A similar technique was also used at Corbridge, where the timber uprights of the headquarters shrine were encased within the stone building of a later period.

Buildings with stone foundations need not necessarily have stood to their full height in stone; it is possible that they were just provided with stone sleeper walls upon which stood a timber-framed superstructure. The wall thickness may give a guide here, as the average width for a wholly stone-built wall appears to be in the region of 0.8–1.0 metres, or more. The dearth of stone debris at a number of fort sites has often led excavators to conjecture that half-timbered buildings were constructed, although this may also be a result of extensive stone robbing in a later period.

Occasionally stone and timber were combined. At Caerhun and Corbridge, for example, stone-built shrines were added to otherwise timber headquarters buildings, and in several forts in the Taunus section of the Upper German *limes* only the shrine and perhaps the rear range of the *principia* were ever constructed in stone, whilst the main body of the building remained timber; in several other German forts timber halls were added to the front of stone-built *principia*.[6] In some German forts, such as Niederbieber and the Saalburg apparently isolated hypocausted rooms, or suites of rooms, have been found which seem to have been the heated, and therefore stone-built, rooms of otherwise timber buildings. These were

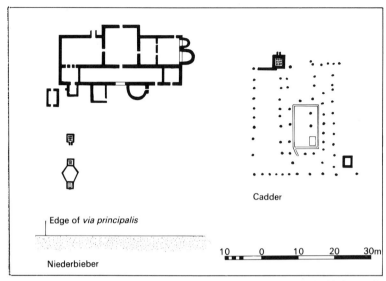

76. Commanders' houses at Niederbieber and Cadder. At Niederbieber only the stone walls have been recorded, the rest of the building was probably timber. At Cadder only a small heated room and a short length of wall were in stone, whilst most of the house was timber-built. Scale 1:1000

probably commanders' houses, whose timber foundation trenches or postholes were overlooked in nineteenth- and early twentieth-century excavations. The type of information which may have been missed can be glimpsed at Cadder, on the Antonine Wall, where only one hypocausted room and a neighbouring wall were built in stone, and the outline of the four wings of the commander's house, with its central courtyard, during several periods of occupation was delineated by rows of postholes. More recently stone bathhouses with timber changing rooms have been excavated at Walldürn in Upper Germany and Bearsden on the Antonine Wall.

The stone buildings of several low-lying forts in the Rhine delta were founded upon rammed timber stakes to minimise movement or sinkage into the subsoil.[7] At Alphen-Zwammerdam, for example, the foundations of the stone *principia* consisted of a 2 metre broad and 0.5 metre deep packing of gravel which rested upon a mass of timber stakes set very close together and rammed into the sandy subsoil. These stakes were 2 metres long and 0.1 metres in diameter, and were spaced with a density of approximately 28 per square metre; a minimum of 10 000 were used under this building alone.

The stone walls usually consisted of ashlar blocks with a mortared rubble core. A few clues about the decoration of some of the fort buildings, especially the headquarters, can be seen in the surviving column capitals and bases from the porticoes, the sculptured keystones from arches, statues and reliefs, fragments from decorated panels or pediments, and the wealth of

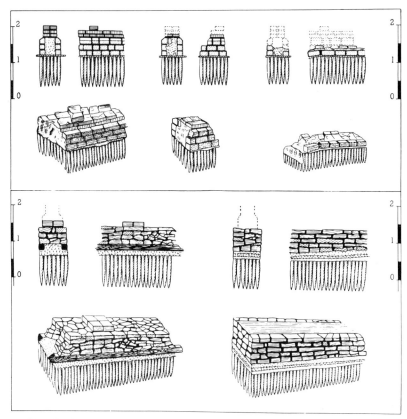

77. Detail of wall foundations laid upon timber piling at Valkenburg, a method which was used at several other low lying forts in the Rhine delta.

inscriptions and sculptures which were set up inside. Many of the internal walls were both plastered and painted, and the windows glazed or provided with wooden screens. The roofing consisted mainly of tiles or wooden shingles, although evidence for lead sheeting has been found in the debris of several headquarters buildings.

The Headquarters Building (*Principia*)

The administrative and religious focus of the fort was the headquarters building, the *principia*. It was distinguished by its size and its imposing architecture, and was positioned centrally, opposite the junction of the two principal streets, facing towards the front gate. Its tripartite plan with a courtyard surrounded by colonnaded ambulatories, a lofty aisled cross-hall and rear range of rooms housing the regimental shrine, strongroom and offices, closely resembled the *forum* and *basilica* of civilian architecture, and combined many of the same functions.

Auxiliary *principia* ranged considerably in size, from c. 60 × 45 metres in the milliary *ala* forts of Aalen and Heidenheim down to c. 14 × 11 metres at the *numerus* fortlet of Hesselbach, with an average of some 30 × 25 metres.

Terminology Polybius tells us that within the Republican marching camp the open space in front of the general's tent, which extended to the centre of the main street, was termed the *principia*, and we are told by several other Classical authors that the entire area occupied by the general's quarters, including this space in front, was called the *praetorium*.[8] It was this name therefore which was applied to the headquarters building of the Roman forts excavated during the last century. It was not until 1899, after extensive work along the Upper German *limes* and at the legionary fortress of Lambaesis in North Africa that a German scholar, von Domaszewski, concluded that there was no reason to term the central fort building the *praetorium* as it demonstrably did not provide sufficient living accommodation for the commanding officer.[9]

The discovery of several inscriptions from British forts provided important new evidence. From the central building at Rough Castle, on the Antonine Wall, in 1903 came an inscription which mentioned the *principia* specifically for the first time, and in 1929 an inscription was found at Birdoswald, on Hadrian's Wall, which showed conclusively that the *principia* and *praetorium* were quite independent structures.[10] Taken in conjunction with altars from a house within the central range at Chesterholm dedicated to the 'Genio praetorii' it became clear that in the

78. Section drawn through a typical *principia* showing its principal features.

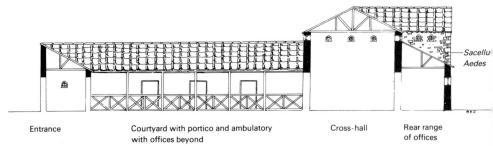

Entrance
Courtyard with portico and ambulatory with offices beyond
Cross-hall
Rear range of offices

Sacellu Aedes

auxiliary fort the central headquarters building was termed the *principia* and the residence of the commanding officer the *praetorium*.[11]

The entrance

The *principia* was often fronted by a portico or, occasionally, a forehall, a long hall which spanned the whole width of the *via principalis*, a feature which will be discussed in more detail below (p. 120). The portico columns may have been set in postholes, founded upon stone bases at ground level, or supported upon low sleeper walls. There was generally a single arched gateway in the centre of the outside wall. Unusually, in the German forts of Alphen-Zwammerdam and Hofheim, the front wall of the *principia* consisted of a single row of posts, which may have provided a series of doorways, and the design of the entrance to the *principia* at Nanstallon, in Cornwall, with a recessed entrance fronted with eight timber posts, is unique.

Fragments of painted wall plaster from the front wall of the *principia* at Niederbieber, in Upper Germany, show that it was painted white, with the outlines of squared stones picked out in red mortar. Above the entrance an inscription was probably placed recording the construction of the building, and it has been suggested that this outside wall was the appropriate place for the fort sundial.[12] An inscription recording the repair of a sundial has been found at Remagen, in Lower Germany. In AD 218 the commander of the *cohors I Flavia*, Petronius Athenodorus, set up this inscription recording that he had repaired at his own expense the sundial (clock) which did not show the correct time and had broken down through old age.[13] Water clocks (*clepsydrae*) were also used by the Roman army to measure the duration of the four watches (*vigilae*) of the night, and it is probable that these clocks were also housed within the *principia*, as it was here that the guards of the various watches were assembled and the orders were given.

79. An inscription from the Lower German fort of Remagen which records the repair of the fort clock in AD 218. It reads:
.... *Petronius Athenodorus Prae(fectus) coh(ortis) I Fl(aviae) horolegium ab horis intermissum et vetustate colabsum suis impendis restituit ...*
'Petronius Athenodorus, prefect of the First Cohort Flavia restored at his own expense the sundial which did not show the correct time, and had broken down through old age.'

The courtyard

The main entrance from the *via principalis* led into a paved or metalled open courtyard, which was surrounded on three or four sides by a portico of timber or stone columns, with ambulatories beyond. The presence often of a gutter running around the perimeter of the courtyard shows that the ambulatories had pent-roofs, sloping inwards towards the centre (Ill. 81). This part of the *principia* probably served as a meeting place, and notice boards may have been displayed here. The courtyards of individual *principia* varied considerably in size and proportions. Sometimes they occupied, with their surrounding ambulatories, the whole width of the building; others were smaller, being surrounded not only by an ambulatory but also on the two longer sides by narrow ranges of rooms which may have provided weapon stores or offices.

Excavations at Bar Hill, on the Antonine Wall, have recovered the remains of a large number of column shafts, capitals and bases from the portico which had been thrown into the courtyard well when the *principia* was demolished.[14] The fragments included column bases with a double torus moulding and capitals with acanthus leaf or chevron decoration. It has been estimated from these remains that the portico must have been at least 2.4 metres high.[15] The discovery on two of the bases of small circular holes, 50–60 mm in diameter, on one side of the shaft above the upper torus, together with similar holes near the bottom of another two broken shafts suggests that a horizontal iron or timber bar must have originally run between the columns about 0.25 metres above the ground. At Ribchester the column bases of the courtyard portico had deep grooves cut into the sides into which timber panels or screens had probably been slotted.[16] Two of the shafts from Bar Hill had corbels in the shape of bulls' heads (*bucrania*), which may have supported an inscribed panel either at the entrance to the *principia* itself or to the cross-hall.

Wells were frequently provided in one corner of the courtyard both to ensure a reserve water supply in an emergency, and for use in sacrifices during religious ceremonies. In forts where the water table was too deep, or where the bedrock was too hard to sink a well, storage tanks were used instead. Within the courtyard at Benwell on Hadrian's Wall, for example, an elaborate conduit and filtering system was constructed consisting of at least five stone water tanks, whilst at the Scottish fort of Lyne water was conveyed in a channel which crossed the courtyard and discharged into a rectangular stone tank built against the front wall of the *principia*. Timber or clay-lined tanks which have been found within the courtyard or under the front portico of headquarters buildings in several earth-and-timber forts probably fulfilled the same function.

In addition to two wells, a small stone-built structure some 5 metres square was discovered in the courtyard at the Saalburg, thought to have

82. A keystone, with
    a sculptured
    bull's head,
    found in the
    courtyard, close
    to the cross-hall
    wall, in the
    principia at South
    Shields.

80. Column bases, capitals and shafts from
    the courtyard portico of the *principia* at
    Bar Hill on the Antonine Wall, which
    had been thrown down the well in the
    courtyard when the building was
    demolished.

81. The courtyard of the reconstructed
    principia at the Saalburg, looking from
    the forehall towards the rear range, with
    the shrine (*sacellum*) in the centre.

contained a hearth in one corner. This was believed by its excavator to have been a shrine to a military deity, although other functions have been suggested, including that of a guardhouse.[17] Similar square foundations have been found in other *principia* courtyards, such as Brecon Gaer in Wales and Arnsburg in Germany. At Rottweil, in Upper Germany, a stone foundation measuring c. 1.8 × 1.6 metres lay in the centre of the courtyard, which probably provided the base for a statue or an altar; a similar foundation was also found at the Lower German fort of Valkenburg.

Weapon stores (*Armamentaria*)

Long unpartitioned halls or ranges of small rooms often flanked the courtyard on its two longer sides. These rooms closely correspond to the single or double ranges of rooms on either side of the courtyard of legionary *principia*, which are usually interpreted as armouries (*armamentaria*) or storerooms.[18] The association between the headquarters building and the armoury is suggested by an inscription from Lanchester in northern Britain, which records the reconstruction of the *principia* and *armamentaria* which had fallen down through old age.[19] The relationship is far from clear, however, as another inscription from Leiden-Roomburg in Lower Germany commemorates the rebuilding solely of an *armamentarium*, which implies that it was an independent structure.[20]

Finds of weapons and military equipment from several legionary and auxiliary headquarters buildings add weight to the conclusion that the armouries were generally housed in what must have been the most securely guarded building in the fort. At the legionary fortress of Lambaesis in North Africa, for instance, a large quantity of military stores was found in rooms adjoining the courtyard of the *principia*. In one were found 6000 terracotta sling bolts, together with some 300 other missiles, whilst in others were found altars dedicated by an armourer (*custos armorum*) and the man in charge of the armoury (*curator operis armamentarii*), who probably had offices next to the weapon stores.[21] Similar finds have occasionally been made within auxiliary headquarters: a quantity of weapons, iron harness fittings and armour were found at Niederbieber, a number of unpolished spearheads at Stockstadt, 800 arrowheads at Housesteads, and several tuffstone *ballista* balls and arrowheads at Niederberg. All were discovered in side halls flanking the *principia* courtyard. Indirect evidence also comes from Künzing in Raetia, where fragments of bronze parade armour and horse fittings were buried just outside the west *armamentarium* of the early third-century *principia*, whilst on the other side of the building, buried in a shallow pit, was discovered a hoard of iron weapons and tools weighing a total of 82 kg; nails, tent pegs, axes, mattocks, chains and handcuffs were also found, which may have derived from an arms and equipment store within the *principia*.[22] At the Antonine Wall fort of Old Kilpatrick a similar store close to the courtyard has been inferred from the presence of hundreds of slingstones, which had been used to infill the postholes of the original *principia* portico.

The *armamentaria* were occasionally divided into small square rooms, but often appear as long unpartitioned halls, although it is possible that in many cases they were originally subdivided by timber partitions which have left no trace at foundation level. Not every *principia* possessed an *armamentarium*; they were absent in many forts, both large and small, where arms must have been housed in a separate building altogether (see p. 190).

The cross-hall

Beyond the open courtyard a cross-hall extended across the whole width of the *principia*; an inscription from Reculver, on the south-east coast of England, shows that this part of the building was termed the *basilica*.[23] The majority of the earliest known headquarters buildings comprised simply a colonnaded courtyard with a rear range of offices behind, and the cross-hall makes its first appearance in the Augustan-early Claudian period at Soissons in Gaul, and again a decade later at Valkenburg in Lower Germany, whilst the earliest example known from Britain is seen at the Agricolan fort of Fendoch.

There has been some doubt amongst excavators in the past as to whether the cross-hall was roofed or not. As a result of his excavations at the Saalburg the German scholar L. Jacobi concluded that it had remained open, and so when the building was reconstructed on the site at the turn of the century it consisted of an unroofed inner court divided by a porticus from the outer courtyard.[24] The cross-hall of the legionary *principia* at Vindonissa in Switzerland, which was built c. AD 45, appears almost certainly to have remained an open courtyard, although this is an exception. An increasing volume of evidence from both legionary and auxiliary cross-halls, of clay flooring and roofing debris (as found at Ambleside or Niederberg) or collapsed oak rafters scattered across the cross-hall floor at Croy Hill, make it clear that this part of the headquarters was normally roofed to provide a lofty and spacious hall.

As this hall was situated towards the rear of the building, adequate lighting could only have been provided by clerestory windows set in one or two rows above the level of the roofs of the courtyard portico and the rear range. Its walls must therefore have stood higher than its neighbours, with the probable exception of the shrine in the rear range; evidence from South Shields shows that the front wall of the cross-hall was at least 9 metres high. The largest fragment of cross-hall walling to be recorded is known from the legionary fortress of Burnum in Dalmatia (modern Yugoslavia), which consisted of a central arched entrance flanked by at least two smaller ones on each side. An illustration made in 1774 shows it still standing some 9 metres high from ground level to the top of the principal arch.[25] Some

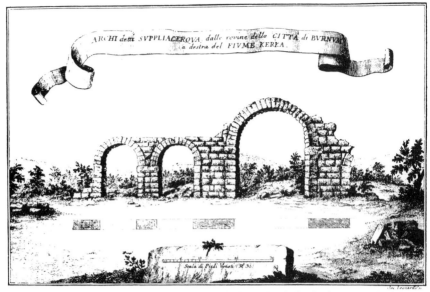

83. The surviving portion of the cross-hall wall of the legionary *principia* at Burnum (in modern Yugoslavia), recorded in 1774.

principia, although not all, seem to have had more substantial foundations for the front cross-hall wall than the rest of the building. At the earth-and-timber fort of Hesselbach, for example, the post trenches were deeper and broader at this point and the wall posts were strengthened at the corners. At Fendoch, similarly, larger timbers were used to support this wall, whilst in stone-built examples thicker walls or more massive piers have often been noted in this position.

Where this type of strengthening has been observed, we might expect a corresponding massiveness in the rear wall of the cross-hall, which would then have formed the front wall of the rear range and have provided additional structural strength to help bear the weight of the roof. This does not seem to have been the case, however, for although the central shrine (*sacellum*) was usually well built the front walls of the rooms on either side were often insubstantial. This suggests that the front wall of the *basilica* was in many cases strongly built so that it could be extensively pierced by arched entrances with a clerestory above, as with the structure at Burnum. Extra width may also have been needed in the front wall at a lower level to help support the roof timbers of the rear portico of the courtyard, which were largely supported by the main external walls of the building on the other three sides.

There were probably stout gates, and perhaps a guard posted, at the entrances to the cross-hall to give security to the shrine and the regimental treasury and offices beyond. In several cases there were one or two additional entrances to the cross-hall at either side of the building behind the cross-hall wall, with the opposite side of the passageway delineated by a row of columns to support the roof.

At one end of the cross-hall, usually on the right-hand side, facing towards the rear of the building, stood a rectangular platform or dais, the *tribunal*, from which the commander might address his officers and men, issue orders, and perform military or religious ceremonies.

Altars or statues probably stood in the cross-hall. Part of a sculpture was found *in situ* in front of the shrine at Stockstadt in Germany, and statue bases flanked the *sacellum* entrance at Brough-by-Bainbridge, and the cross-hall doorway in the Constantinian *principia* at Risingham.

A small group of *principia* had ranges of small rooms not only at the rear, but also at each end of the cross-hall.[26] At the legionary fortress of Lambaesis inscriptions were found in the rooms surrounding the cross-hall which linked them with the *scholae*, the meeting rooms and clubs of the officers of the legionary garrison.[27] No comparable evidence has been found within an auxiliary fort, but it is quite probable that *scholae* were provided in the *principia* in rooms either flanking the cross-hall or the courtyard.[28]

The obvious parallels with civilian *basilicae* suggest that the *principia* cross-hall combined a variety of ceremonial, religious, administrative and judicial functions carried out by the commander of the garrison who, as the local magistrate, was responsible not only for these military duties but also for dispensing civil justice and order. Whatever its precise function, by the late third century AD the cross-hall appears to have lost some of its importance, as, from this period onwards, an increasing number were subdivided into smaller rooms to provide more office and storage space for the administrative staff.[29]

The rear range

Behind the cross-hall lay a rear range of rooms, usually five in number.[30] The central room had a special significance, as it is identified as the regimental shrine (*sacellum* or *aedes*).[31] Its importance is emphasised by its position upon the longitudinal axis of the *principia*. The façade of the shrine was visible from the *via principalis* and provided the main focus of the building.

A papyrus from the archives of *cohors XX Palmyrenorum*, which was stationed at Dura Europos, dating to the reign of Severus Alexander (c. AD 225–7), provides a list of selected military festivals which were observed by the army (known as the *Feriale Duranum*), which would have been issued to every garrison in the empire.[32] This papyrus, although incomplete, gives the dates of the religious festivals and details the nature of the observances and sacrifices required. Three types of ceremony are included: the rites of the gods, the imperial cult (including the annual oath of allegiance to the emperor), and other military festivals such as the birthday of the unit and the cult of the *signa* (the veneration of the standards). The particular importance of the cult of the emperor is reflected in this document—it is mentioned twenty-seven times in the extant forty-one entries.

Tacitus records that imperial images were kept in the headquarters building,[33] and fragments of imperial statues have been found in several fort shrines; at the Saalburg fragments of a bronze statuette of the emperor Antoninus Pius were discovered, and a similar figure was also found at Theilenhofen. An index finger from a larger-than-life bronze statue came from the shrine at Marköbel, whilst a statue of an emperor in the guise of Hercules had once stood in the *principia* at Brough-by-Bainbridge. A description of a religious ceremony held within the headquarters of *cohors I Flavia Cilicum equitata*, stationed at Syrene, to celebrate the birthday of the emperor Severus Alexander in AD 232, has been preserved upon a papyrus:

> Upon the occasion of the celebration of the birthday of Caesar M. A. Severus, the commander together with the tribune of the cohort stationed in Syrene, the centurions, the *beneficiarii*, the *principales* and the men carried out in the *principia* and the imperial shrine the offerings to the gods, which have all been merciful. Then after the distribution of the usual gifts he worshipped upon his knees our master and emperor M. Aurelius Severus Alexander and our empress Julia Mamaea, the *mater Augusti et castrorum* and delivered a speech to the cohort followed by a parade inspection by the *praefecti praetorio*, *Praefectus Aegypti* and commander Maximinus and his son. Afterwards the commander remained with the tribune during a march past of the troops. Close to the imperial shrine a banquet was set up, to which the *principales* were also invited.[34]

Within the *sacellum*, in addition to the statues of the imperial deity, were kept the *signa*,[35] the emblems and standards of the garrison together with the *vexilla*, the flags of the individual centuries or cavalry troops, and the garrison's altars. A bronze military standard in the form of a prancing horse has recently been discovered within a civilian house outside the fort of Chesterholm; it is the only example known from Britain. It would originally have been mounted upon a wooden pole and housed in the *sacellum*. Unfortunately the garrison which it represented is unknown.[36] Part of a statue base which must originally have stood in the shrine was found at Birdoswald on Hadrian's Wall, and was dedicated 'to the standards and to the deity of the emperor'.[37] Tacitus appears to refer to the standards being raised on a dais in the *sacellum*,[38] and at Castell Collen in Wales they were ranged upon a stone revetted platform which ran round three sides of the room. At Risingham, in northern Britain, there was originally a dais approached by two steps in the *sacellum*. The *Feriale Duranum* mentions the celebration of two festivals which were associated with the cult of the *signa*. The first was the *Rosaliae Signorum*, where the garrison was assembled in

84. Bronze military standard from
Chesterholm-Vindolanda,
Northumberland.

the courtyard of the *principia*; the standards were brought out and decorated with crowns of roses, then followed by a thanksgiving (*supplicatio*). The second, the festival of *natalis signorum*, was also held exclusively in their honour, although in all the other religious and military ceremonies the standards played an important role.[39]

Several *sacella* have yielded altars dedicated to the gods or to the *genius* (guardian spirit) of the garrison; an altar and figure of Jupiter was found in the cellar beneath the shrine at Murrhardt, a *genius* figure at Kapersburg, parts of a bronze statue at Theilenhofen, and larger-than-life fragments from a Hercules sculpture were found at Köngen. Statues also often flanked the entrance to the shrine. Two inscriptions from the legionary fortress of Caerleon in Wales record dedications made by *legio II Augusta* in the years AD 234 and 244, both on the 23rd of September, the birthday of the emperor Augustus from whom the legion took its name.[40] Another military festival, the *Armilustrium* (associated with Mars), celebrated on October 19–20th and connected with the dedication of arms at the conclusion of a campaigning season, was commemorated on two inscriptions found at the auxiliary fort of Papcastle in Cumbria, which may have come from the garrison's shrine.[41]

The *sacellum* also housed the regimental treasury, holding the military funds, pay-chest and also the savings of individual soldiers. Vegetius tells us that each soldier was obliged to deposit half of every imperial donative with the standards (*ad signa*), in the treasury at the *sacellum*, for 'the soldier who knows that all his fortune is deposited at his colours entertains no thoughts of desertion, conceives a better affection for them, and fights with better intrepidity in their defence'.[42] The pay accounts of several soldiers have survived upon papyri; they show that after the usual deductions for food,

85. Key to a *signifer's* paychest, found in the legionary fortress at Neuss. Engraved on one side: ≡BASS CLAUDI FABI SIG and, on the other: >BAS. (The key was broken in antiquity)

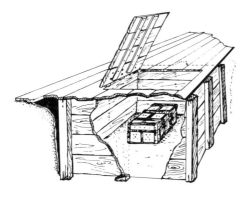

86. The regimental treasury was sometimes located in a lined pit beneath the floor of the shrine.

clothing, boots and, probably, bedding, and possible contributions to a burial club or regimental dinner, a balance was left in credit.[43] From the reign of Domitian a limit of 1000 *sesterces* was placed upon the amount which an individual might save in this way, a measure which was intended to prevent a recurrence of the revolt of Saturninus in AD 89, when the seizure of the savings of the two legions stationed at the fortress of Mainz in Upper Germany proved sufficient to finance the rebellion.[44]

Vegetius also records that the garrison's finances were administered by the standard bearers (*signiferi*), who placed the money in bags or baskets, and kept the appropriate records.[45] A key to a chest found in a barrack at the legionary fortress of Neuss, and now in the museum at Mainz, belonged to such a *signifer*.[46] The money was probably kept safe within the *sacellum* in an iron-bound wooden chest. In most earth-and-timber forts of the first century AD this paychest probably stood directly upon the *sacellum* floor, although very occasionally it was placed, for greater security, in a timber or stone-lined pit underneath, which could be reached only through a trapdoor in the wooden floor. (Early examples of timber-lined pits have been found at the Neronian fort of Baginton, and the pre-Flavian fort at Oberstimm on the Danube, whilst at Brough-by-Bainbridge in Yorkshire there was a concrete-lined pit within the timber *principia* of the Flavian-Trajanic fort.) In many cases where there was no sunken pit at all in the *sacellum*, or only a very shallow one, the timber floor may have been raised and approached by a staircase from the cross-hall, giving sufficient space beneath for a secure strongroom without digging a pit. At the Raetian fort of Künzing, for example, in the middle of the second century AD, the *sacellum* floor was probably raised some 1.5–2 metres high, providing a cellar beneath, whilst the shrine itself was entered by a staircase at the front.[47] A number of *sacella* had stone-built antechambers, a feature seen clearly at Echzell, Neckarburken-West or Osterburken, which may represent the foundations for staircases up to a raised floor.[48] The *sacellum* was often the most solidly constructed of the rear rooms, and in several cases only the *sacellum* and perhaps part or all of the rear range was constructed in stone in an otherwise timber building. Moreover, the foundations were often exceptionally strong, which suggests that it may have been intended to stand to a greater height than adjacent rooms. In the *principia* with a cross-hall it seems probable that the roof of the *sacellum* was at the same height as that of the cross-hall, giving two storeys, with a strongroom at ground level and shrine upon the first floor.

By the Severan period the simple pit within the shrine, which had become increasingly common during the second century AD, had developed in many cases into a sunken strongroom reached by a flight of steps. This transition can be seen clearly during the four periods of occupation of the earth-and-timber fort at Künzing. In its two earliest phases, from c. AD 90–135, a rectangular pit in one of the rooms adjoining the shrine probably housed the paychest, whilst in the middle of the second century the floor was raised to provide a cellar beneath. In its final occupation, in the early to mid-third century, a rectangular stone-built cellar with a vaulted ceiling was constructed, some 1.6 metres deep, which was entered down a flight of stone steps (probably numbering five).

Sometimes the strongroom lay not under the *sacellum* but, as at Chesters or Benwell, under one of the flanking rooms, with access permitted only from the shrine itself. Stone steps led down to the strongroom entrance which may have been secured by a stout timber door or, as at High Rochester, by a large stone slab which slid into a recess at the side upon a pair of iron wheels.[49] When the strongroom at Chesters was investigated in 1840 the excavators found traces of the oak door still in place; the door was reinforced with iron studs and bindings, but unfortunately it soon disintegrated upon contact with the air.[50] The floor was usually stone flagged and the roof vaulted with ribs, perhaps arched, bridged by stone slabs, as seen at Chesters and Greatchesters, or with a barrel vaulted tile ceiling, similar to that found at Künzing. Occasionally traces of windows

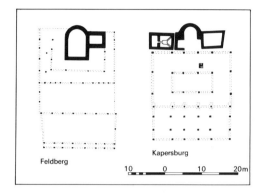

87. Headquarters with part-stone and part-timber construction. Scale 1:1000

88. Successive designs of the *principia* at Künzing in Raetia.

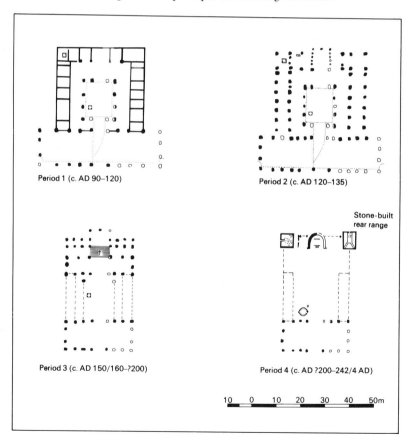

89. The strongroom beneath one of the rear rooms in the *principia* at Chesters, on Hadrian's Wall.

have been preserved within these cellars; at Benwell a window was set low down in the external wall of a room next to the *sacellum* in which the strongroom lay, and at South Shields a three-barred window admitted light from the cross-hall. The strongroom of the Severan *principia* at Brough-by-Bainbridge lay 1.7 metres beneath the floor of the *sacellum* and its entrance stood directly beneath the threshold of the shrine above. Access was provided by a flight of steps down from the cross-hall with a passage almost 2 metres long to provide the necessary headroom; presumably the steps were covered by a trapdoor when not in use.

An inscription from the legionary base at Aquincum records the rebuilding of a guardroom for soldiers guarding the standards.[51] It is clear from a papyrus of the cohort stationed at Dura Europos detailing the various guard duties that a guard was normally posted outside the *sacellum* (the author Tertullian discusses the spiritual dilemma of the Christian soldier who was forced to stand guard outside the pagan shrine)[52] but whether an actual guardroom was provided either at the entrance to the *sacellum* or in the cross-hall of the auxiliary *principia* remains uncertain.

Vegetius describes the huge amount of paperwork involved in the administration of the legion and recommends that legionary recruits should be selected for their proficiency in reading, writing and accounts.[53] A lot of paperwork was also necessary in the administration of an auxiliary fort and its garrison, and papyri provide important evidence for the wide range of documents kept in the fort. Especially instructive are the files of *cohors XX Palmyrenorum* from Dura Europos, which include fragments of rosters showing details of the strength of the garrison from day to day, individual service and pay records, guard duties, special leave, records of secondment, promotions, transfers, requisitions and receipts.[54]

The office in which all these records were kept was the *tabularium*, which was supervised by the senior clerk (*cornicularius*) assisted by his deputy (*actuarius*) and often by office clerks (*librarii*). The offices of the *cornicularius*

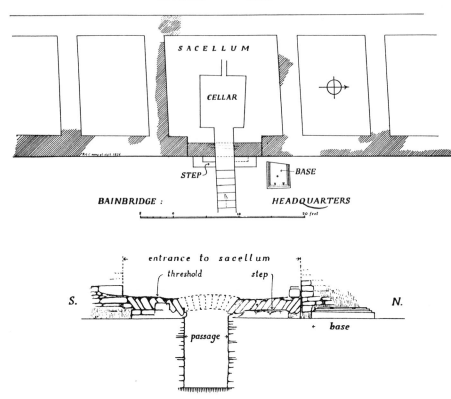

90. The strongroom of the Severan *principia* at Brough by Bainbridge, North Yorkshire.

were housed in the rear range of the *principia* to one side of the shrine, and usually comprised at least two rooms. The corner room was sometimes smaller and frequently not entered directly from the cross-hall but from its neighbour, suggesting that it may have been used as a file and document store. At the German fort of Niederbieber an inscription was found within an end room in the rear range, dedicated by a *librarius* to the Genius of the *tabularium* of the garrison,[55] the *numerus Brittonum Antoniniorum*; in a neighbouring room were found various metal fittings from locks and documents. The bronze lid of a *capsa*, a box in which documents and scrolls were kept, was found in a room adjacent to the shrine at Chesterholm, and the large quantity of writing tablets belonging to an earlier fort on the same site may well have derived also from the *tabularium*. Officials responsible for the administrative paperwork are mentioned upon inscriptions from auxiliary forts: a *cornicularius* is known from Greatchesters, *actuarii* from

Ebchester, Ambleside and Caernarfon, and a *librarius* from Corbridge and Schirenhof.[56]

The offices of the standard bearers (*signiferi*), who were responsible for the financial affairs of the garrison, lay on the other side of the *sacellum*. At Niederbieber in Upper Germany a room adjoining the *sacellum* was identified as the office of the *signifer* by the discovery inside of a sandstone statue dedicated by a *signifer* and an *imaginifer* (image bearer).[57] All the financial records, accounts and receipts would have been stored here, and the standard bearers were directly responsible also for the treasury and the strongroom in the *sacellum* next door. Cashiers' counters comprising stone screens with grilles in the top at which payments were transacted have been discovered at Housesteads and Chesterholm. In the rear rooms at Rottweil were found timber slots which may represent the remains of built-in cupboards to house the files and records, and similar traces have been found at Fendoch and Caerhun.

91. Sandstone statue from one of the rear rooms of the *principia* at Niederbieber in Upper Germany. The base bears an inscription dedicated by the standard and image bearers, dated AD 239. It reads:

In h(onorem) d(omus) d(ivinae) Genio vexillariorum et imaginif(erorum) Attianus Coresi f(ilius) vexillarius Fortionius Constitutus im(a)g(inifer) signum cum aedicula et tabul(am) m(a)rmoream dono dederunt dedicaverunt im(peratore) d(omino) n(ostro) Gordi(a)n(o) Aug(usto) et Aviola consulibus

'In honour of the Imperial House the standard-bearer Attianus, son of Coresus, and Fortionius Constitutus, image-bearer, donated and dedicated the likeness of a small temple and a marble tablet to the Genius of the standard-bearers and image-bearers, in the consulship of our emperor Gordianus Augustus and Aviola'

Variations in the arrangement of the rear range occur occasionally, as in the Augustan fort and supply base at Rödgen in Upper Germany, where the offices and dwelling of the commander may have been combined, and at Claudian Hod Hill, where two units are believed to have shared the same headquarters building (Ills. 97/98). The plan of the rear range here consisted of small rooms at each end with a larger room between, which have been interpreted as shrines for each of the different units in garrison, with an unpartitioned cross-hall between them.[58] Similarly, in the Claudio-Neronian fortress of Xanten in Lower Germany two legions shared the same headquarters and are thought to have had separate shrines at either end of a common cross-hall.[59]

The forehall

Several *principia* had an additional component, a long hall which was attached to the front of the building and extended across the whole width of the *via principalis*. This forehall often projected beyond the width of the rest of the building on one or both sides, and in many forts it was linked with neighbouring buildings within a unified architectural scheme.[60] Although the provision of a forehall was quite common in the German provinces and in Raetia (where it is known as an 'exerzierhalle') there are only a handful of examples known in Britain.[61]

Parallels have been drawn between the development of the forehall in military architecture and civilian fashions, when streets were often provided with porticoes and monumental arches.[62] Several legionary fortresses had colonnades alongside their principal streets, which at Lambaesis connected with a monumental arch (*quadrapylon*) built at the entrance to the *principia*. Similar gateways to the *principia* are known from Dura Europos and Lauriacum, but the *principia* forehall seen in auxiliary forts is largely unknown in legionary fortresses.[63] Timber colonnades ran alongside the principal streets and fronted the *principia* at several first-century earth-and-timber forts and, although it did actually span the *via principalis*, the forehall of the *numerus* fort at Hesselbach was not much wider than these porticoes. For this reason it has been suggested that the porticoes found in front of these first-century headquarters buildings may represent the forerunners of the auxiliary forehall.[64] The earliest example of a forehall comes from the first timber fort at Künzing, which was built c. AD 90.

Timber forehalls were provided for the part-timber and part-stone *principia* at Kapersburg and Feldberg on the Wetterau *limes*, and they also fronted wholly stone-built *principia* at Zugmantel, Stockstadt and Urspring. From the assymetrical arrangement of the stone *principia* and forehall at Brecon Gaer in Wales it appears that the two were not built contemporaneously and that the stone forehall may have originally fronted a timber headquarters building.[65] Stone forehalls are known predominantly

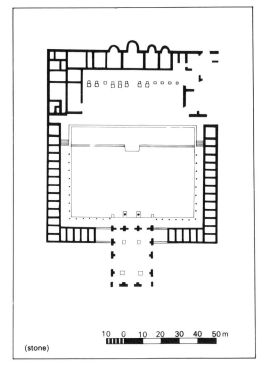

92. The *principia* of the legionary fortress at Lambaesis in North Africa. Scale 1:2000

10 0 10 20 30 40 50 m

(stone)

from the Antonine period onwards, and they increased in architectural elaboration throughout the second and third centuries, as can be seen in the Severan examples at Haltonchesters or Ribchester.

The forehall normally had wide entrances in the shorter sides and either one principal doorway, which might have been embellished by the addition of a porch as at Eining or Weissenburg, or several arches, as seen as Gnotzheim or Buch. The outer wall in the forehall of the latest *principia* at Valkenburg consisted solely of columns. The side entrances at Theilenhofen had buttressed supports on either side of the 4.6 metre wide entrances. The excavator suggested that, judging from the depth of the foundations and the massive ashlar superstructure, the entrances here may have formed triumphal arches.[66]

The discovery of aisle posts and roofing debris from several forehalls confirms that they were roofed. At Zugmantel, for instance, internal post rows divided the hall into a nave 4.5 metres wide with aisles of 3.3 metres, and two rows of timber aisle posts were also detected at Kapersburg. Four of the original eight stone columns which formed one aisle at Ribchester were found in position, their double torus mouldings and fillets giving some hints of former architectural elaboration. Debris including pillar bases, roof tiles and nails were found in the vicinity of the forehall at Gnotzheim, and roof tiles also lay around all three sides at Weissenburg which, in conjunction

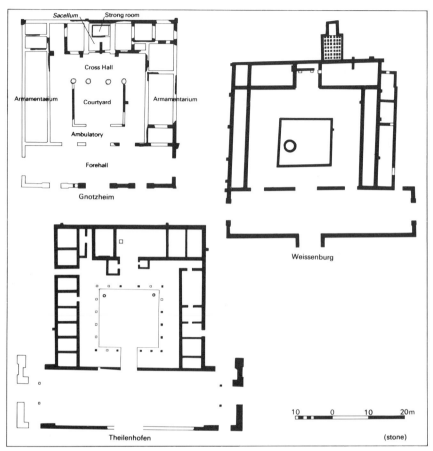

93. *Principia* forehalls with elaborate entrances. Scale 1:1000

with a large quantity of nails and internal wall plaster, leaves no doubt that these halls were roofed. The buttressing of the walls at the Saalburg and Butzbach implies that they stood to a considerable height and carried a substantial roof weight, and so the forehall which has been reconstructed at the Saalburg consists of a tall and spacious hall 11.5 metres wide without aisles, with a clerestory to provide sufficient light. A central entrance in the outer wall is protected by a porch, and there are five arches leading from the forehall into the *principia* courtyard, with further doorways at each end of the hall.

The absence of roof-tile debris and either postholes or column bases from the forehall at Niederbieber, combined with its considerable breadth, led its excavator to conclude that the building had never been roofed.[67] The span of 21 metres at Niederbieber is the largest excavated so far, but would not have been impossible to roof. The excavators at Niederbieber generally

94. The interior of the reconstructed forehall of the *principia* at the Saalburg, Upper Germany.

located few traces of timber-buildings, and it is quite possible that rows of timber columns either set in postholes or standing upon stone bases originally supported the roof, but may have been overlooked during excavation.

Doubts have been cast on whether the forehall at Brecon Gaer was roofed, because here a gutter ran alongside an internal wall, and a drain apparently discharged through one of the side entrances.[68] However, the presence of drainage trenches here, and also at Künzing and Urspring, does not necessarily mean that these structures were unroofed; covered drains may well have passed under the floor of a roofed forehall just as they ran under other buildings. In many cases the forehall was a later addition to the main building, as at Newstead or Weissenburg, for example. In that event, the forehall would have enclosed an area in front of the *principia* which had previously consisted of a metalled roadway with flanking drains, which may or may not have continued in use and so it is difficult to establish contemporary features within some excavated forehalls.

Excavations at the *numerus* fort of Hesselbach have shown a contrast between the individual trimmed timbers of 25–30 cm cross-section set in postholes which supported the forehall, and the post-in-trench construction of the rest of the building. From this evidence it has been suggested that the forehall may have remained open all-round, with perhaps only the upper part weather-boarded, the rest of the *principia* being constructed with smaller uprights supporting screen walls of wattle and daub.[69] This

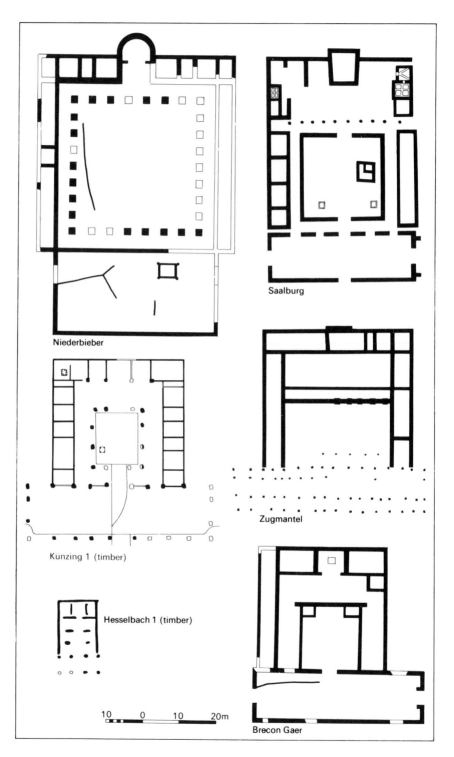

Niederbieber

Saalburg

Künzing 1 (timber)

Zugmantel

Hesselbach 1 (timber)

Brecon Gaer

10   0   10   20m

difference in constructional techniques between the forehall and the remainder of the building is also seen at Künzing. It is not clear, however, what the significance of these differences is for in the Hadrianic period it was replaced by a building consisting entirely of posts in individual postholes, which must have been boarded or infilled with wattle and daub panels. It seems probable that where greater structural stability was needed in the forehall to carry the roof over the *via principalis* deep individual post settings were preferred, whilst elsewhere adequate support for the wattle and daub walls would have been provided by uprights set in a trench. Timber planking or panels of wattle and daub were probably inserted between the posts of the forehall from ground level to provide an enclosed hall.

The function of the forehall is still far from clear. They do not occur in every fort and they were far more common in Germany and Raetia than in Britain. They were not confined to a particular date range, as they occur in c. AD 90 at Künzing on the Danube and were still being constructed in the Severan period at Haltonchesters on Hadrian's Wall. German excavators have interpreted them as 'Exerzierhalle', or drill halls.[70] In his discussion of the forehall at Brecon Gaer Sir Mortimer Wheeler linked it with the cavalry drill hall (*basilica equestris exercitatoria*) mentioned upon an inscription from Netherby, built in AD 222 by *cohors I Aelia Hispanorum milliaria equitata*.[71] He cited two further inscriptions which refer to a *basilica* erected by cavalry units, at Lancaster and Assuouan on the Nile, although emphasising that the term *basilica* did not always necessarily refer to the same type of building.[72] Of the thirty-one forehalls known over half can be shown to have been connected with cavalry units, either *alae* or *cohortes equitatae*, and five with *numeri*. Of the remainder, one, at Murrhardt, was associated with a *cohors quingenaria* assumed to be *peditata* (*cohors XXIV Voluntariorum c.R.*), and the other eight examples have yielded no information at all concerning their garrisons.[73]

The absence of internal partitioning and structures, with the exception of aisle supports, shows that the forehall was designed essentially to be open inside and points to its being used as an assembly or drill hall. Vegetius describes the provision of drill facilities for both cavalry and infantry soldiers: 'To continue this drill without interruption during the winter they erected for the cavalry porticoes or riding halls covered with tiles or shingles, and if they were not to be procured, with reeds, rushes or thatch. Large open halls were likewise constructed in the same manner for the use of the infantry. By these means the troops were provided with places of drill sheltered from bad weather'.[74] He further observes that 'as far as the health of the troops is concerned, daily exercises with arms is of greater benefit than doctors. Accordingly they wished the infantry to be exercised under cover without interruption from rain or snow and on other days in the open'.[75]

95. Opposite: *principia* with forehalls. Scale 1:1000

Each forehall would have provided sufficient standing room for every member of the garrison to gather on special occasions, to take part in religious ceremonies and to hear speeches and orders. Built in the only available space in a densely populated fort at the junction of the two main wide principal streets, it seems probable that the forehall was designed to give drill and assembly facilities in bad weather for both cavalry and infantry troops.[76]

Evolution and development

The plans of a large number of headquarters buildings are known from auxiliary forts which enables a very broad pattern of chronological, and sometimes regional, changes to be detected.

The commander's tent in both the Republican legionary marching camp of Polybius and the model camp of Hyginus was situated at the junction of the two major streets and in the open space in front of his quarters stood an altar for religious sacrifice. This was the spot on which the auguries were taken (*auguratorium*), and a *tribunal* from which orders and speeches could have been delivered. The earliest reasonably complete plans of Roman military headquarters come from the Republican camps of Castillejo and Peña Redonda, which were built in 134–3 BC by Scipio to besiege the native stronghold of Numantia in Spain (see Chapter 8, p. 225). Although not strictly one-night marching camps they nevertheless retained the essential elements described by Polybius. Both headquarters had a courtyard entered from the principal street and surrounded by ranges of rooms on three sides; at Peña Redonda the outer court was separated from an inner by a pair of projecting wing-rooms. Both these examples combined the living quarters of the commanding officer with the administrative and judicial functions of his command.[77] A similar plan is seen also at another siege camp, at Masada in Palestine, which was constructed in AD 72–3.

96. The headquarters of Republican camps. Scale 1:1000

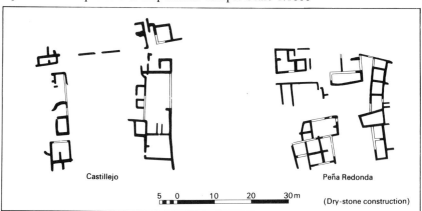

Castillejo   Peña Redonda

5   0   10   20   30 m

(Dry-stone construction)

There are no further clues available upon the form and development of the headquarters building until the permanent legionary fortresses at Neuss and Haltern were built in the Rhineland during the reign of Augustus. The earliest *principia* at Neuss consisted of a large courtyard flanked on at least one side by long narrow rooms with other small rooms projecting into the courtyard, with traces of a further range of small rooms at the rear. Unfortunately the traces are very fragmentary and the full extent of these rooms remains unknown. In its second period this building comprised a courtyard surrounded by a colonnaded ambulatory, presumably on all four sides, with a rear range of rooms, the layout of which is largely unknown. At Haltern a colonnaded courtyard led into a hall with its roof supported upon ten columns, whilst the rear range beyond had a central passageway.

The army when on campaign, constructing a temporary camp after a day's march, carried only the basic essentials of equipment, supplies and administrative paraphernalia. When in permanent garrison, on the other hand, much more space was needed to house not only arms, supplies and equipment, but also the records and files of the clerical staff. This expansion of administrative requirements dictated that the commanding officer, who in peacetime was often accompanied by his family, should occupy a residence completely detached from his military headquarters. Already in the Augustan period at Haltern there was apparently no room available in the *principia* for the commander's quarters, and during its second period the building was considerably enlarged and a dwelling for the commander provided at the rear, separated from the rest of the building by an alley; there is insufficient evidence to indicate where the commander was accommodated at Neuss at this time.

Only two auxiliary forts seem to have retained a combined *principia* and *praetorium*, although it continued in use in the marching camp, as can be seen at Masada in AD 72–3. The Augustan fort and supply base at Rödgen in Upper Germany had a central building of assymetrical plan, set within an irregular defensive line, which may have incorporated the residence of the commanding officer in one of the groups of small rooms which flanked the colonnaded courtyard on two sides. The *principia* of the earliest fort at Valkenburg in Lower Germany, which was built c. AD 40, was thought by its excavator to have incorporated a dwelling in one of the two ranges of rear rooms which were separated by a narrow corridor, whilst small rooms grouped on either side of the main entrance into the courtyard have been interpreted as further officers' quarters. However, this assumption has been recently challenged because of the discovery of what is believed to have been a separate *praetorium* for the commander sited in the *praetentura*; so the question must remain unsolved.[78]

The headquarters buildings of the Claudian forts at Hofheim, Hod Hill and Oberstimm are very similar to each other in groundplan, each comprising a courtyard with a portico on four sides with a range of small

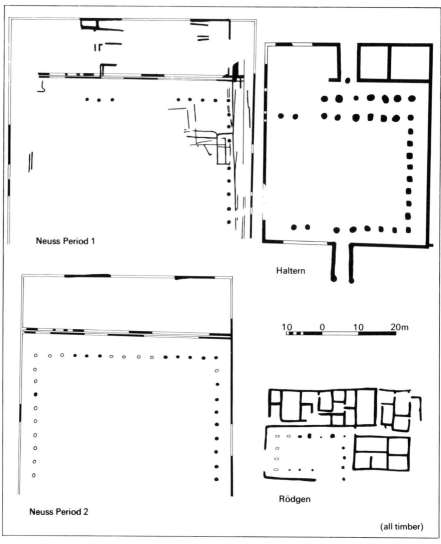

Neuss Period 1

Haltern

Neuss Period 2

Rödgen

10   0   10   20m

(all timber)

97. The headquarters of Augustan forts. Scale 1:1000

98. Opposite: developments in the *principia* plan: Claudian, Neronian, Late Flavian. Scale 1:1000

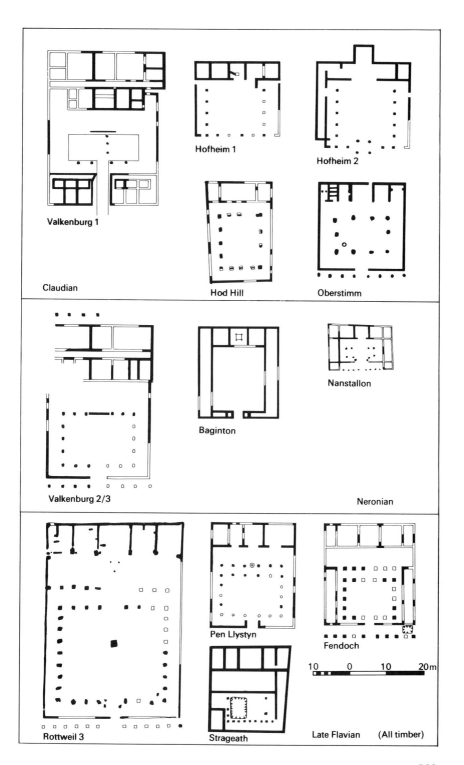

Valkenburg 1

Hofheim 1

Hofheim 2

Claudian

Hod Hill

Oberstimm

Valkenburg 2/3

Baginton

Nanstallon

Neronian

Rottweil 3

Pen Llystyn

Fendoch

Strageath

Late Flavian   (All timber)

10   0   10   20m

rooms at the rear; all were timber-built. Variations on this plan occur at Claudian Valkenburg, which had additional ranges of rooms both at the rear and flanking the entrance, and in the Neronian forts of Baginton and Nanstallon, where long narrow halls were added on two sides of the courtyard portico; Baginton also had a sunken pit in the *sacellum*, and the recessed entrance at Nanstallon is a unique feature. At both Nanstallon and Valkenburg the distance between the rear of the courtyard portico and the rear range is significantly greater than on the sides, which suggests that this area was used for the same functions which elsewhere required a roofed cross-hall. This type of *principia* without a cross-hall was still being built in AD 185 at Niederbieber, where it was provided with flanking *armamentaria*, and it survived into the Severan period at Eining on the Danube, although it was never common; less than two dozen examples are known altogether. This type of *principia* occurs contemporaneously with those which have cross-halls, and there appears to be little chronological significance in the design chosen.

The majority of excavated *principia* consisted of a courtyard with an ambulatory on two, three or four sides, sometimes flanked with *armamentaria* and sometimes not, with a roofed cross-hall and rear range. This type is seen first in the Augustan legionary base at Haltern and in the Augustan or early Claudian fort at Soissons in Gaul, and it provided the prototype of a groundplan which was used extensively in both legionary fortresses and auxiliary forts well into the third and fourth centuries AD.

A group of timber-built *principia* of the Flavian period show great similarities in their plans, with a double row of posts separating the courtyard from the rear range. They are seen at Echzell and Rottweil in Germany, and Fendoch and Pen Llystyn in Britain: their construction dates span the period AD 80–100. Other timber *principia* of this date had a continuous post trench construction for the cross-hall wall, as at Strageath, or a single line of posts, as seen at Corbridge and Valkenburg. The earliest known forehall was also built at this date at Künzing in Raetia.

From the reign of Domitian *principia* appear more often built in stone, or with stone foundations for a timber superstructure. The courtyard portico may have been supported on stone bases, as at Wiesbaden, or upon low masonry walls. A cross-hall was usually, although not invariably, provided, and stone-built forehalls, such as that seen at Heidenheim in Raetia, appear at this date. The reign of Trajan saw the majority of new headquarters buildings constructed in stone; they were occasionally still built in timber until the Hadrianic period, as at Künzing and Echzell, but these examples are rare.

Several stone-built *principia* of Hadrian's Wall forts show the same basic plan, for example at Rudchester, Chesters, Benwell and Housesteads, which all had colonnaded ambulatories and an extra row of columns supporting the roof of the cross-hall. In all four cases the structural remains show a high

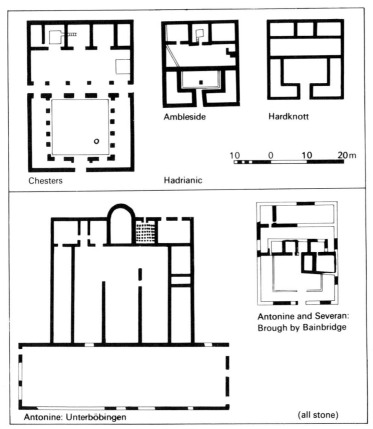

99. Developments in the *principia* plan: Hadrianic, Antonine, Severan. Scale 1:1000

degree of architectural elaboration. At Chesters and Rudchester, and perhaps Housesteads also, a passageway ran behind the cross-hall wall. Other Hadrianic examples were similar, with the courtyard surrounded on three sides often by wall foundations forming either L-shaped rooms, or representing sleeper walls which carried the columns to support pent-roofs; good examples of this type are seen at Ambleside, Hardknott and Melandra Castle.

Most of the excavated *principia* belong to the Antonine period. Apsidal *sacella* were added at a number of German forts at this date, but not in Britain, although in several cases the rear wall of the *sacellum* did project beyond the rear wall of the building; the reason for this difference in styles is unknown. A particularly unusual layout is seen at the Antonine fort of Brough-by-Bainbridge where, instead of a cross-hall a range of four offices was provided which were entered from the courtyard, and two small rooms were also inserted in the courtyard itself.

131

In the late second and third centuries the headquarters show much rebuilding and alteration. Forehalls were added at the British forts of Newstead in Scotland and Haltonchesters on Hadrian's Wall, and there was an increasing use of *armamentaria*, apsidal *sacella* in Germany, and the insertion of stone-built strongrooms beneath the *sacellum* floor. There are many examples of alterations to the existing accommodation; especially noticeable is the addition of hypocausted rooms and perhaps latrines in the rear range and the partitioning of cross-halls and *armamentaria* to provide extra space for offices, stores, and even living accommodation. At Housesteads, for example, in the middle of the fourth century the ambulatories were blocked off to form rooms, whilst hearths were laid in the cross-hall. In the same period at Chesterholm drastic alterations were taking place, with the courtyard porticoes turned into storerooms with raised floors, and the side rooms of the rear range converted into living quarters.

The Commander's House (*Praetorium*)

The commanding officer of the garrison and his household were accommodated in a spacious and private residence, which was usually situated in the central range. The general's tent in the marching camp was known as the *praetorium* and when, in the permanent fort, the living quarters of the commander were separated from the administrative offices of the garrison, this term was retained for the commander's dwelling, whilst the headquarters was called the *principia*.[79]

It is difficult to estimate the size of the average household, although presumably it included the commander's immediate family and their domestic servants. Members of his personal staff may perhaps have had offices and even living quarters on the premises also. In addition, guest rooms were probably provided for visiting officials, although they may have lodged in a guest house (*mansio*) outside the fort. Inscriptions found at Birdoswald on Hadrian's Wall provide rare evidence for the presence of the commander's family within the fort. One commemorates the construction of a new granary dedicated by the tribune of the garrison, Aurelius Julianus, whilst the other, this time a tombstone, sadly records the death of his infant son, Aurelius Concordius, aged only one year and five days.[80] Further evidence for the commander's family within the fort comes from the occasional discovery of women's and children's leather shoes within waterlogged deposits at the bottom of rubbish pits or fort ditches.[81]

Ground plan and architecture

The house comprised four ranges of rooms grouped around a central courtyard, which would have allowed sufficient accommodation for the family, service quarters and rooms for guests. Its plan closely resembled

100. A tombstone from Birdoswald (*RIB* 1919) recording the death of the infant son of the garrison commander. It reads: *D(is) M(anibus) Aureli Concordi vixit ann(um) unum d(ies) V fil(ius) Aurel(i) Iuliani trib(uni)* 'To the spirits of the departed, Aurelius Concordius, who lived one year, five days, the son of the tribune Aurelius Julianus'

civilian counterparts, and parallels can be found in the courtyard plan of many provincial town and country houses.[82] The courtyard groundplan was developed in the warmer Mediterranean climate to provide welcome shade, but in British and German forts it served more probably to give seclusion and privacy. Yards, gardens, domestic service quarters, stables and occasionally bathhouses may have been added to one side of the main building. The courtyard *praetorium* plan continued in use from the Claudian period at Hofheim, into the fourth century at Caernarfon; an exception has been found at Templeborough in Yorkshire, which had an aisled dwelling.

Because it was essentially a private dwelling the *praetorium* tended to be less stereotyped in its internal arrangements than other fort buildings, and so evidence for the function of individual rooms or suites is often rather scanty. Stone structures may sometimes retain traces of an underfloor heating system or bath, and occasionally drains or latrines survive, but in many cases floor levels and partition walls have been ploughed away, or the stone robbed, leaving ranges of rooms without any distinguishing features. Taking the available archaeological evidence in conjunction with descriptions given by the architect Vitruvius of the typical Roman house it may be possible in some instances, to suggest the uses to which the various ranges of rooms were put.[83]

The entrance to the building from the main street into the vestibule or entrance hall was often flanked by small rooms which may have served as reception rooms, or have housed a porter. At Fendoch three different colonnaded entrances gave access to the various parts of the house, which are thought to have been the private family quarters, the service wing and a reception hall. Directly opposite the main entrance there often lay a large room, which was approached across the open courtyard, a feature which can be clearly recognised at Fendoch and Oberstimm. This is usually identified as the principal dining room, the *triclinium*.[84]

The rest of the house comprised for the most part ranges of small rooms, often of indeterminate function. At Fendoch a water tank in the south-west corner of the south wing may have been a plunge bath in the family's private rooms; the north wing is believed to have housed the kitchens and servants' rooms, leaving the west wing for the reception of guests and official functions, with possibly some additional administrative offices. Kitchens have occasionally been identified from the presence of an oven, as at Housesteads, or from the discovery of kitchen refuse. The position of the kitchen in the *praetorium* at Hod Hill, for example, was indicated by a dump of oyster shells against an external wall, and similarly the kitchen area at Hofheim was identified from the pits dug outside which were filled with animal bones and oyster shells. The living rooms often had hypocausts to provide underfloor heating, or occasionally as part of an integral bath-suite for the commander's personal use. Although small plunge baths were frequently provided, more elaborate baths within the commander's house are rare until the latter half of the second century, and invariably represent later additions to the house, as seen at Chesters on Hadrian's Wall. The *praetorium* of the second period fort at Mumrills on the Antonine Wall had such a large and complex bathhouse added that it seems unlikely to have been intended solely for the commander's household, and was probably designed for more general use. Traces of painted wall plaster, the remains of hard cement (*opus signinum*) floors, the quantity of window glass, and even a fragment of moulded *verde antico* marble from the *praetorium* at Bewcastle, give occasional glimpses of the comfort and luxury which was enjoyed by the commanding officer of the fort in his own residence.

Recent excavation and re-interpretation of the commander's house at Housesteads has considerably extended our knowledge of both the internal arrangements and the structural history of the building.[85] It was originally an L-shaped structure with its north and west wings built upon a steep slope. Subsequently two more wings were added to produce the familiar courtyard layout; the time lapse between these two phases of construction was very short. The building remained in commission with basically the same plan from the Hadrianic period into the fourth century, with a period of rebuilding attested during the reign of Severus. The north and west ranges, which contained hypocausted rooms, a latrine and a plunge bath, probably served the commander and his family; this was the most secluded part of the building as it was farthest away from the service range and the

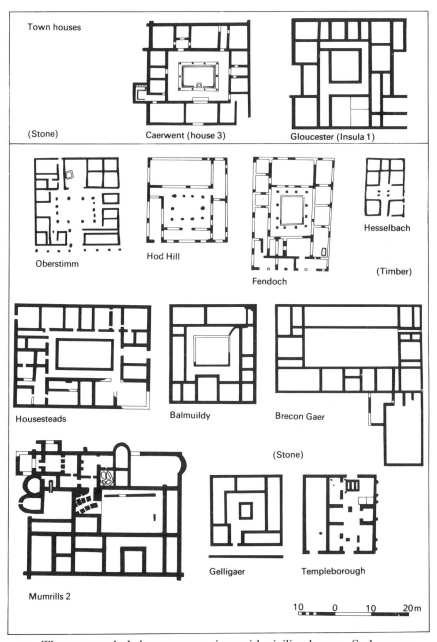

Town houses

(Stone) Caerwent (house 3) Gloucester (Insula 1)

Oberstimm Hod Hill Hesselbach

Fendoch (Timber)

Housesteads Balmuildy Brecon Gaer

(Stone)

Mumrills 2 Gelligaer Templeborough

10 0 10 20m

101. The commander's house: comparison with civilian houses. Scale 1:1000

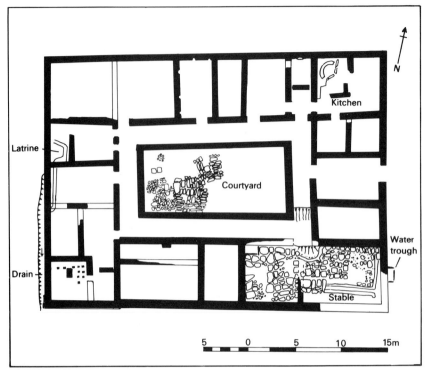

102. Groundplan of the commander's house at Housesteads, on Hadrian's Wall.

general noise and bustle of the fort. The east range, which lay adjacent to the *via principalis*, had a central entrance hall with perhaps a small reception room next door. At the north-east end of this wing lay a kitchen with an oven in one corner, and next to it a small room which may have been used for the preparation or storage of food. Two rooms at the south-east corner of the south range had stone flagged floors, and one also had a flagged rock-cut drain, which identifies them most probably as stables; a water trough was placed against one of the outer walls.

The ground upon which this house was built sloped so steeply from north to south that the individual wings stood at various levels terraced into the hillside. To provide a level courtyard it had been necessary to build a retaining wall on the south (lower) side and infill the space within with stone and clay to obtain the required height. The northern range lay at the highest part of the site and must have been reached from the front door on the east side by a flight of steps set within the courtyard ambulatory. A similar staircase led from the lowest part of the building, at the south-east corner, up to the west wing. The differences in levels was so great that the south range, and perhaps part of the east side also, probably had two storeys, which would have provided extra accommodation for servants or stores above the stable wing.

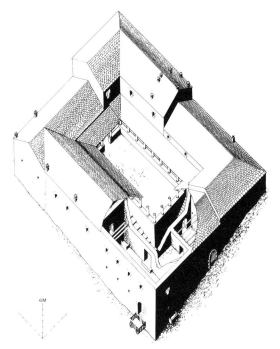

103. Reconstruction drawing of the commander's house at Housesteads.

Yards, compounds and gardens

A small number of *praetoria* had yards or compounds attached to the main house with various sheds and outbuildings grouped around them. The earliest example, at Hofheim, had a yard to the north of the house, defined by timber trenches, which enclosed a large timber-lined water tank and several pits. Sheds and working areas in lean-to structures are believed to have lain around the perimeter of this open yard, and additional rooms on its western side have been tentatively interpreted as the dwelling of a porter and stabling for the commander's horses.

The compound adjoining the *praetorium* at Nanstallon was defined by a timber fence, and the yard surface was lightly metalled. A drain ran from a latrine in the north-east corner and discharged into the *via principalis*, and postholes within the enclosure suggest the presence of lean-to sheds. It has been suggested that this compound was used as an ablutions block and a walled yard in the central range at Gelligaer between the *principia* and a granary which also had a latrine in one corner, may have fulfilled a similar role, although it was not actually attached to the *praetorium*. Within the compound on the north-west side of the *praetorium* at Pen Llystyn were located the foundations of several small rooms with a corridor down the centre, and an even larger compound lay behind the *praetorium* at Rottweil; despite poor preservation the foundation trenches of some internal rooms were detected, together with a drain. The yard at Caernarfon was also roughly the same size as the house, and had two rooms on one side. The plan of another Welsh example, at Caerhun, seems confused, but probably also represents a house with an adjacent yard. The house proper probably consisted of four ranges of rooms around a courtyard, together with a yard, outbuildings and perhaps a garden on one side. The enclosing walls appear to be contemporary and so the plan of this building, if it is of one period, is unusual and the *praetorium* considerably larger than the majority of excavated examples.

The function of these yards or compounds is uncertain and may have varied at different sites. They may sometimes have provided stabling for the commander's horses, as suggested at Hofheim, or they may have been used to supplement the service quarters of the main house. Alternatively, although attached to the *praetorium* they may have been independent structures providing washroom or workshop facilities for the garrison. In

104. Commanders' houses with adjoining compounds. Scale 1:1000

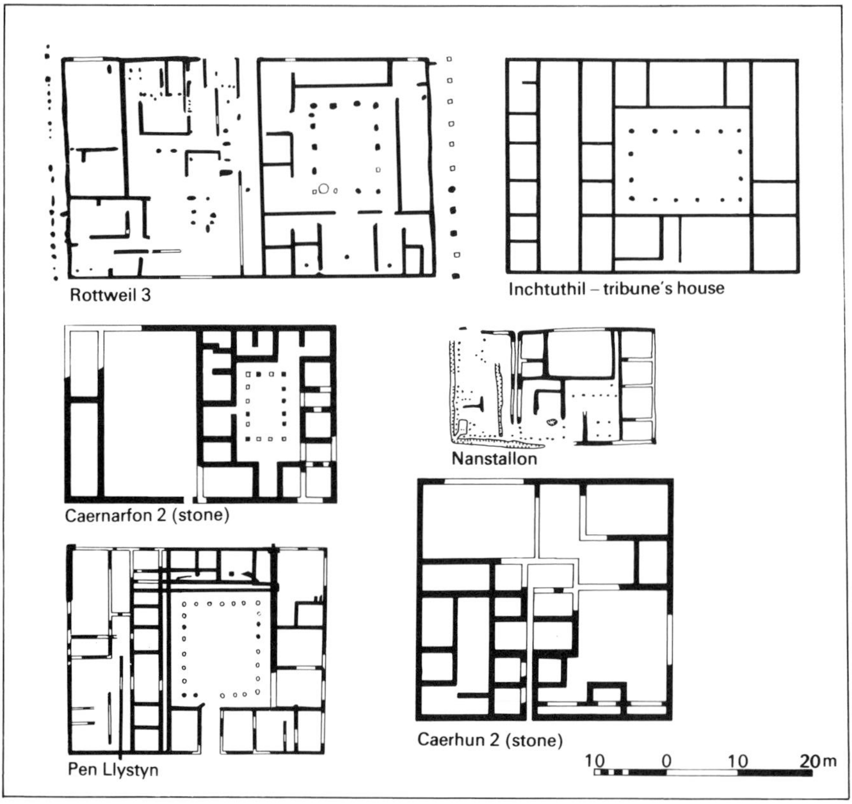

Rottweil 3

Inchtuthil – tribune's house

Caernarfon 2 (stone)

Nanstallon

Pen Llystyn

Caerhun 2 (stone)

10   0   10   20m

general a wide range of functions was probably served from the storage of provisions and fuel to stables, workshops, kitchens, washrooms and even private gardens.

Siting

The *praetorium* lay usually in the central range next to the *principia*, and was frequently placed to the south-east or south-west of this taller adjacent building to gain the maximum amount of sunlight for the dwelling. The house might occupy the whole of the space available between the headquarters and the side gate, or may have shared the area with another building, often a granary. Most had a common frontage along the *via principalis* with the other central buildings, extending back as far as the *via quintana*. Exceptions can be seen in the Claudian forts of Hod Hill, Oberstimm and the late first-century fortlet at Hesselbach, where the *praetorium* lay immediately behind the headquarters and both buildings were flanked by barracks or stables, an arrangement which is often seen within legionary fortresses. In several German forts the commander's house lay in the *praetentura*. Often, as at the Saalburg or Kapersburg, in the Taunus mountains, isolated hypocausted rooms which probably represent the only stone-built features of otherwise timber houses, have been discovered in this position.

Once a site had been selected for the house there is plenty of evidence from a number of forts that it was subsequently rebuilt and remodelled upon the same site. At Mumrills, for example, the original timber dwelling was first rebuilt in stone and then had an elaborate bath building added. At Corbridge, on the other hand, the position of the *praetorium* on one side of the *principia* and granaries on the other was reversed several times during the various stages of fort rebuilding (see Ill. 73). A probable explanation for these changes is that during the transition stages of rebuilding, the granaries of the previous fort were kept in commission to preserve the garrison's food supply whilst new granaries were erected on the opposite side of the *principia*, on the site of the former commander's house. Upon completion of the building work the grain could easily be transferred and the old granaries demolished to make way for the new residence.[86]

Additional *praetoria*

As well as the house in the central range, a handful of forts had a second and larger courtyard building, which was often sited in the *praetentura*. Either or both of these, could be identified from their groundplan as commanders' houses. At Hod Hill one courtyard house lay in the left *praetentura* and another behind the *principia* (Ill. 182). A mixed garrison of legionaries and auxiliary cavalry is believed to have been stationed here and so the extra, more spacious, house has been interpreted as the dwelling of the cavalry commander (*praefectus equitum*), whose superior rank and status would have required more elaborate accommodation than the other commander, who would have been a legionary centurion.[87] At Baginton also an extra *praetorium* has been located in the left *praetentura*. It was more extensive than its counterpart in the central range and is thought to have been the residence of a senior officer who may have been in command of specialist cavalry training at the fort.[88]

The early Flavian fort at Rottweil had courtyard-plan buildings on either side of the *principia*. (See Ill. 189.) One had four ranges of similar-sized rooms grouped around a large open courtyard with a drain running down the long axis of the building (Building B). The second (Building C) had two distinct parts: the western half which fronted onto the main street, with four wings and a colonnaded internal courtyard, and the eastern part which, although badly preserved, showed the partition walls of several small rooms of various shapes and sizes, with an internal drain. The barrack accommodation, which was examined in the *retentura*, when taken together with estimates of space available in the rest of the fort, has suggested that (as at Hod Hill) a legionary detachment was in garrison here, probably in conjunction with an auxiliary unit. Two *praetoria* would therefore have been necessary.[89]

However, the identification of the buildings as officers' dwellings is based solely upon their courtyard plan and their sheer size. In one or two cases where two courtyard buildings have been found within the same fort, as at Oberstimm and Wiesbaden, sufficient evidence has survived, in the form of a massive central water tank with a water course and the presence of hearths, crucibles and bronze and iron slag, to show that they were workshops (*fabricae*) rather than dwellings. This interpretation also seems the most likely for similar buildings found at Valkenburg and Caernarfon (Ill. 140 and see p. 186). It is impossible to be sure whether the extra courtyard buildings at Hod Hill and Baginton had a similar function, or whether they did in fact provide extra accommodation. There are doubts about the identification of Building B at Rottweil as an additional *praetorium* because of the water course which ran down the centre of the building; this may originally have supplied a central water tank like the one found at Oberstimm. Unfortunately the centre of the courtyard was destroyed so that the presence of such a tank could not be tested.

The rank of the commander

The auxiliary commander was a man of equestrian rank whose career would normally follow a well-established pattern.[90] The first step in his career, the *militia prima*, was the command of a quingenary cohort (*praefectus cohortis quingenariae*), and the second (*militia secunda*) could either be as a legionary tribune (*tribunus angusticlavius*) or having an independent command as the tribune of a milliary cohort (*tribunus cohortis milliariae*). Promotion might follow into the *militia tertia* as the prefect of a quingenary *ala* (*praefectus alae quingenariae*), and ultimately in the *militia quarta* to the command of a milliary *ala*. He might then proceed, perhaps, to even higher office in the imperial service. At every stage up the promotion ladder the number of hopeful candidates greatly exceeded the opportunities available; in the second half of the second century AD, for example, the number of quingenary *alae* outnumbered the milliary *alae* by nine to one, so that at every stage the less able and dedicated dropped out as the available posts diminished.[91]

It seems reasonable to suppose that the commanding officer was given accommodation appropriate to his rank and status. If this were the case then it should be possible to infer the size and type of the fort's garrison from studying the plan and dimensions of its *praetorium*. Unfortunately in practice there are many variables and uncertainties, which make it difficult to judge the rank of the commander and the importance of his command from the size of the house; the equation is by no means straightforward. It is often difficult, when dealing with the groundplan of a house which has so often been recovered only at foundation level, to distinguish between the family's living rooms, servants' quarters, courtyards and gardens, and although it is easy enough to compare the generosity of space allocated with *praetoria* in other forts it is far more difficult to assess the comfort and facilities afforded within individual houses. Nor is it possible to gauge the influence of individual commanders upon the layout and size of the dwelling, or how far modifications reflect personal tastes. Even in the very few forts which are known from inscriptions to have had similar garrisons a comparison between their *praetoria* only emphasises the considerable variations between them, both in size and internal arrangements.

The legionary tribune and the auxiliary commander of a milliary cohort held the same rank in the *militia secunda*, and it is not surprising that the plans of several tribunes' houses, especially in the fortresses of Inchtuthil, Vindonissa and Vetera, provide close parallels with many auxiliary *praetoria*; particularly closely matched in both plan and dimensions are the houses at Inchtuthil with those at Pen Llystyn, Caernarfon, Hod Hill and Rottweil (Ill. 104). Unfortunately we do not know the garrisons of any of these auxiliary forts for certain—probably two or even three of the four did not house milliary cohorts. Therefore comparison of the auxiliary commander's house with the tribunes' houses is misleading, as although there are general similarities, these cannot point to specific garrisons.

The majority of *praetoria* were sited in the central range of buildings and were allotted usually between 20–30 per cent of the available space, although this was very much dependent upon the requirements of the other central buildings such as granaries, workshops and, possibly, the hospital. If there was sufficient room the *praetorium* may have been allowed extra space, although it does not seem to have exerted a major influence upon the planning and layout of the fort. In fact this building may often have been the last to be built in the central range; at the legionary fortress of Inchtuthil work on the *praetorium* had not even begun when the decision to abandon the site was taken. Similarly, when rebuilding in stone the commander's house followed the *principia* and the granaries, and in many forts it was never totally rebuilt in stone.

The Granaries (*Horrea*)

The granaries were usually situated in the central range of the fort close to the *principia*. Their distinctive groundplan, with a raised floor designed to provide maximum ventilation for the grain and other foodstuffs stored inside, makes them easily recognisable, and those built in stone are often so substantially constructed that they remain the best-preserved structures within the fort.

A building stone found within the granary at Kapersburg, on the Upper German frontier, positively identifies it as a *horreum*, and an inscription from the entrance of the west granary in the military depot at Corbridge records the 'officer in charge of the granaries at the time of the most successful expedition to Britain', believed to refer to the Scottish campaigns of the emperor Severus in AD 209–11.[92]

Principles and problems of grain storage

To store grain successfully it is necessary to minimise germination and insect infestation and to prevent contamination and destruction by rodents and birds. Grain continues to respire, taking in oxygen and giving off heat, carbon dioxide and water long after it has been harvested, and so to preserve it in storage these processes must be slowed down as much as possible by reducing the temperature, moisture content and the amount of oxygen available.[93]

Grain will remain dormant as long as the temperature and moisture content are low, but if stored whilst too hot or too wet it will begin to germinate and the dampness will encourage the activity of bacteria in the air, causing the growth of moulds and fungi which will eventually rot it. Infestation by insects damages the grain directly by eating or contaminating the cereal grains, and indirectly by inducing heating which, if unchecked, will soon make it unfit for either flour or malting. The most troublesome insects and mites in modern granaries are the saw-toothed grain beetle, the grain weevil, the rust red grain beetle and the flour mite. Until recently it had generally been believed that the saw-toothed grain beetle was a relatively modern introduction to Britain, which had arrived as a result of the increase in commercial traffic from abroad, but analysis of insect fauna from several sites has revealed that it was also a pest in granaries in Roman Britain.[94] Again, the most effective method of controlling the spread of these insects, and also moulds and bacteria, is to reduce the moisture content and temperature of the grain.

Bulk grain in storage also poses certain structural problems, for it is not only weighty but acts as a 'semi-fluid', exerting a lateral thrust against the walls of the bins in which it is stored and against the external walls of the store building.[95]

To counteract these problems the Roman granary was designed with a raised floor to allow a good circulation of air underneath, and was solidly constructed to withstand the pressures of the grain inside, whilst at the same time providing sufficient openings and ventilators to maintain the low temperature necessary. The granaries would have been thoroughly water-proofed, with a sound roof, and probably overhanging eaves to ensure that rainwater was conveyed away from the building and into drains around the perimeter.

Classical references to grain storage

Classical authors provide some information about the conditions which were thought necessary for the storage of grain and perishable foodstuffs in the Roman world. Marcus Cato, writing in c. 160 BC, recommended that a mixture of chaff and the residue of crushed olives (*amurca*) should be smeared over the interior of the granary to prevent damage to the grain by weevils or mice, and Varro (in 37 BC) also advocated that the walls and floor of the granary should be coated, either with marble cement or clay mixed with chaff and *amurca*.[96] Columella, in AD 60, described a method of storage in which the granary, with a vaulted ceiling, had its earthen floor first soaked with lees of oil, then rammed down firmly like *opus signinum*, and finally overlain by tiles set in a cement whose lime and sand had been mixed together with oil lees instead of water. The walls were plastered with clay and oil lees mixed with the dried leaves of the wild olive, and any joint between the floor and walls was well sealed to prevent the harbouring of insects in the cracks.[97] According to Varro other measures taken by farmers to prevent deterioration included the sprinkling of *amurca* over the wheat, or alternatively using Chalcidian chalk or wormwood.[98] If it was intended to store the grain for a long period Columella suggests that it should be threshed twice to discourage weevils.[99] However, if the grain should become infested Varro suggests an unlikely cure: the grain should be taken outside into the sunshine and bowls of water then placed around it, in the hope that 'the weevils will congregate at these and drown themselves'.[100]

Varro says that wheat should be stored in granaries raised above ground level (*sublimia*) and open to the draught on the north and east sides in order to prevent dampness. He describes also examples in Hither Spain and Apulia where granaries were built above ground in such a way that the wind could cool them, both at the sides by means of windows and from underneath.[101] Vitruvius, writing in the early 20s AD agreed that granaries should have a north or north-east aspect and concrete floors, for if they were not kept cool the grain would be damaged by weevils and rodents.[102] In his *Naturalis Historia*, written in AD 77, Pliny summarises the main methods of grain storage, and the controversies between the different authorities on the subject. Some preferred brick granaries with walls a yard thick without any ventilators or windows, whilst others, such as Vitruvius, favoured windows. Some granaries were built of timber and supported upon pillars to provide ventilation, but there were those who believed that grain shrinks in bulk if the floor is raised. Pliny also records the antics of those who thought that they could best preserve the grain by hanging up a toad by one of its longer legs at the entrance of the granary before the corn was stored. He himself thought that the most important factor was to place the grain in storage at the appropriate time, as it was useless to store it if it was insufficiently ripened or too hot, for both conditions encouraged pests to breed. In addition, he advocated storing grain on the ear as the method in which it was least likely to suffer damage.[103]

The design of military granaries

The principal type of granary found in the auxiliary forts of Britain and Germany consists of a long, narrow structure usually with a raised floor, which in timber granaries was supported upon wooden posts and in stone-built examples either upon low walls or pillars.[104] Stone granaries were generally buttressed and had ventilators pierced in the outside walls beneath floor level. The granaries were commonly paired, often flanking the *principia* or placed side by side within the central range. Occasionally stone granaries were double-size, with two adjacent buildings linked together either sharing a common central wall, as at Benwell and the Saalburg, or flanking a central yard, as seen at Caerhun and Ambleside; very occasionally they were built end to end, as at Birrens. The choice between single or double granaries seems to have been governed by convenience of access for loading and unloading at individual sites.

Sizes and proportions Granary sizes varied considerably. Timber examples ranged in size from 35 × 10 metres at Loudon Hill in Scotland to as small as 8 × 6 metres at Abergavenny in Wales; their average length is 17–24 metres, and they were normally from 8 to 9 metres wide. Their width was governed, to a large extent, by the maximum practical roof span available. There is a noticeable difference in the sizes and proportions of the stone granaries found in Britain and Germany. British examples ranged from 20 to 30 metres in length and 6 to 10 metres in width. (The largest auxiliary granary at Haltonchesters measured 41 × 10 metres and the smallest at Croy Hill 14 × 5 metres.) In German *horrea* the average length was similarly 20 to 30 metres, but their width was generally greater, between 10 and 14 metres. (The largest German examples, from Niederbieber, were

53 × 16 metres, even larger than the legionary granaries at Chester, and the smallest, at Kapersburg, 16 × 9 metres.)

Floor supports and flooring The raised floors of most military granaries provided ventilation under the building, which maintained the best conditions for grain storage.

In the timber granary[105] a grid of evenly spaced posts, which were often circular in cross-section and stood perhaps 0.8–1 metre high, supported the platform of the floor, upon which the superstructure of the building was erected.[106] These posts were placed either in individual postholes, in continuous foundation trenches or, unusually, were rammed directly into the ground with a pile driver. There appears to have been no exclusiveness in date between the various techniques. Individual postholes occur in the Augustan period at Haltern, in Claudian contexts at the supply base at Fishbourne, in the auxiliary forts of Hofheim and Hod Hill, and this method was still being used in the latest timber granaries known, which were constructed in the Antonine period at Old Kilpatrick and Brough-on-Noe. The post-in-trench granaries at Corbridge were replaced in the early second century AD by a granary supported on posts in individual postholes, but in a later reconstruction at the same fort the builders reverted to the former method of floor support.

The post trenches may have been laid out either longitudinally or transversely across the building. The longitudinal trenches occur first in the military supply bases of Rödgen, in the Augustan period, then at Richborough and Fishbourne, and the auxiliary fort at Wall, under Claudius. In one granary at Richborough a longitudinal system was replaced by transverse trenches. Transverse trenches occur at Claudian Oberstimm, and proved to be the most common arrangement within the timber granaries of the first century AD, surviving into the middle of the second century at Valkenburg. The spacing between the trenches, measuring from centre to centre, and between the posts set in them, where they survive, is generally uniform and often 1.5 metres (5 Roman feet). Even in examples where the trenches appear to have been rather irregularly laid out, the spacing of the remaining posts was nevertheless very even.[107]

Three different methods of supporting the floors of stone-built granaries[108] were employed: by means of either transverse walls, longitudinal walls or pillars, although sometimes the floor was not raised at all.

Transverse sleeper walls were usually built some 0.6 metres wide and stood 0.7–0.9 metres apart; they vary in number from six at Gelligaer to seventeen at Castell Collen. This type of floor support was first used in the stone granaries of Trajanic forts in Wales, and the style seems to reflect a direct translation into stone of the transverse post trench commonly used in timber counterparts.[109] Later examples appear at Gnotzheim in the middle of the second century AD and in the Antonine granaries at Lyne and Unterböbingen, but they were not common. Some transverse walls had a

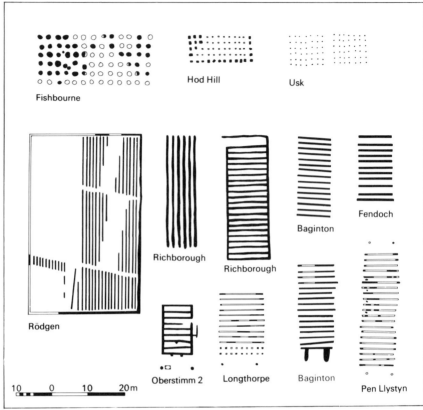

Fishbourne

Hod Hill

Usk

Rödgen

Richborough

Richborough

Baginton

Fendoch

Oberstimm 2

Longthorpe

Baginton

Pen Llystyn

10   0   10   20m

105. Types of timber granaries. Scale 1:1000

central break, probably to ensure a good circulation of air, whilst others were continuous. At Penydarren, though, a mixture of the two was used. The discovery of nails in the debris between floor supports at Gelligaer and Penydarren suggests that the floors were timber-boarded, and this combination of transverse sleeper walls supporting a timber floor represents the earliest type of stone-built granary found in Britain, dating to the Trajanic-Hadrianic period.

The most common method of floor support in British granaries was the longitudinal sleeper wall, although only a handful of German examples are known.[110] The actual number of walls used varied from four to eight; they were sometimes continuous, but many had breaks at regular intervals which corresponded with the position of ventilators in the external walls. The date range of this type extends possibly from the late Flavian period into the reign of Severus.[111] A variation of this type can be seen at Old Church, Brampton and Ribchester, where there was only a single continuous sleeper wall running down the centre of the building. Either timber floorboards or

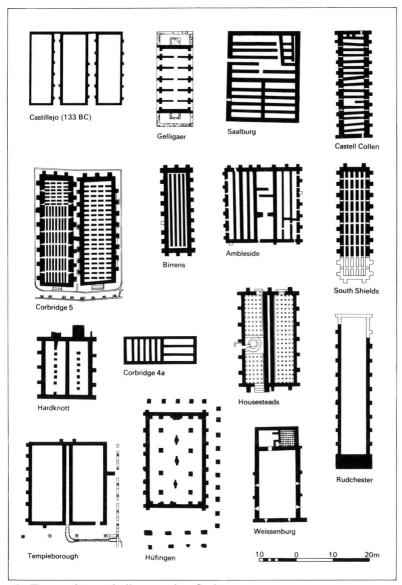

106. Types of stone-built granaries. Scale 1:1000

stone flagstones were used; what little evidence there is suggests that the stone flagging of a raised floor may be more characteristic of the Antonine or Severan periods.

Occasionally granary floors were supported upon stone pillars arranged in parallel rows. Only a few examples of this method have been found in British forts and just one in Upper Germany, although this technique was

147

107. Longitudinal sleeper walls supporting the flagged floor of the granary at Corbridge, Northumberland.

108. The granary at Housesteads on Hadrian's Wall. The floor was supported upon rows of stone pillars.

used there in the legionary granaries of Bonn and Neuss.[112] The well preserved granary at Housesteads shows evidence for square sockets in the long walls with a ledge underneath to locate the timber floor joists, and ventilators beneath the floor level set at regular intervals in the long external walls corresponded with gaps between the rows of squared stone pillars (Ill. 108).

The various methods of floor support were not exclusive to a particular date, nor even a particular site. The Hadrianic granary at Haltonchesters, for example, contained transverse sleeper walls in one half of the building and had longitudinal walls at the other end, whilst a granary at Corbridge had two longitudinal walls in the western part and six transverse walls in the east. In the Antonine fort at Lyne the single granary on one side of the *principia* had transverse walling; a double granary on the other side had longitudinal supports. These variations can also be seen at Ribchester, where one side of the double granary had longitudinal walls and the other had stone pillars.

A number of stone granaries had floors laid directly upon the ground and were not provided with elaborate ventilation systems. Some had flagged floors laid upon the natural subsoil, and others had floors of beaten clay; the granary floor at Caerhun still retained a 3–7 cm thick layer of decomposed cement, which is reminiscent of the floor described by Columella (see page 143). It is not always possible to be sure, however, whether the granary was originally designed to have a flagged or clay floor at ground level, or whether it represents the subsequent modification of a former granary for another purpose, in which a raised floor was no longer necessary. There would have been no real need to have a raised stone floor as flagging, unlike a timber floor, would have been quite sufficient to counteract rising damp. Whether or not the floor was raised, the combination of stone walling and flagging must have contributed significantly to the refrigeration effect which would have preserved not only grain but other foodstuffs in cold storage. Even on a waterproof floor, though, there would still have been problems with dampness, the bottom layer of grain being chilled through contact with the floor, and it would therefore probably have been necessary to store the grain on wooden gratings or pallets to prevent this.

Stone walls and buttresses   The most characteristic feature of the Roman military stone granary is its substantial construction. The walls varied in thickness from 0.8 to as much as 1.3 metres, and the majority had buttresses along their long external walls and often at their ends (averaging 1 metre square) well bonded with the walls. They were usually regularly spaced and, where sufficient evidence survives, it appears that they were paired across the width of the building. A small number of stone granaries had no buttresses and it is possible that these examples were not wholly stone-built but half-timbered, founded upon low masonry walls, with timber clad roofs rather than heavy tiles.[113]

The foundations consisted predominantly of rubble or clay-packed foundation trenches which closely followed the line of the walls and their projecting buttresses. Several British granaries show particularly distinctive foundations, with broad stone-flagged rafts overlying rammed clay and cobbles. Three examples of this type from Hadrian's Wall forts, at Benwell, Haltonchesters and Rudchester, display such similarity in construction, each founded upon a massive concrete raft, that they may all have been built by the same unit—a detachment of the British fleet which is attested on an inscription from the granary at Benwell.[114]

Ventilators   Ventilators, usually placed between each pair of buttresses, pierced the external walls of many stone granaries beneath floor level, and gaps were often left in the longitudinal walls supporting the floor to coincide with the position of the ventilators and to ensure a good circulation of cool air. The width of the ventilator openings varied from 0.3–0.8 metres and as such large apertures could not have excluded rodents and other small animals from entering the basement beneath the floor, attracted by spillage of grain through cracks in the floor, they must have been screened with a wooden or iron grille. Excavations at several British forts have detected deposits of burnt material alongside the outer walls of the granaries, notably at Cadder, Castlecary and Slack, and at Castell Collen particularly strong signs of burning were recorded outside one the ventilators. It has been suggested that these layers represent attempts to smoke out vermin from beneath the granary floor.[115]

109. The granary at Corbridge, Northumberland, showing detail of an underfloor ventilator with a central mullion.

110. The granary at Corbridge, Northumberland, showing the loading platform, portico column and drain.

Loading platforms and access   Almost invariably access was provided at the end of the granary and loading platforms, which would have made it easier to transfer large quantities of grain from carts to the interior of the building have occasionally been found against one or both of the end walls. In some cases the roof may have been carried over a loading area in front of the granary and supported upon posts or columns to form a portico, which would have given extra shelter when loading and unloading. Alternatively flights of steps up to the front of the building may have been preferred, such as those surviving at Housesteads and Benwell, or reconstructed at the Saalburg.

Evidence for loading platforms has rarely been found outside timber granaries. Only at Baginton, where two timber slots projected in front of one of the granaries, and at Oberstimm, where two extra posts jutted out from the front wall, can such platforms be suggested (Ill. 105). It seems probable that a loading platform was created in timber granaries not by adding it to the front of the building but by setting back the main body of the granary from the edge of the raised floor, enabling carts to drive up to the front, and providing steps for pedestrian access at the side. This arrangement has been reconstructed at Baginton. Although it is extremely difficult to verify this assumption from the archaeological remains of posts and trenches beneath floor level, structural differences in the layout of the grid of posts and trenches have been noted at Fendoch and Longthorpe, which may imply that a lighter load was anticipated at one end of the floor, perhaps because it was used solely for loading purposes.[116]

Well preserved loading platforms have, however, been recorded in front of a number of stone-built granaries, notably at Hardknott, Ribchester, Rudchester, Rough Castle and Corbridge. They were constructed of solid masonry, and projected from 2–3 metres beyond the end of the building. There are also less substantial examples, as at Castlecary or South Shields, where one of the end walls was doubled in thickness to produce a platform. Loading platforms were built at each end of the granaries at Gelligaer, and extended across the full width of the buildings. They comprised an outer framework built with well-dressed stone enclosing a rubble infill, with the whole platform flagged over; an examination of worn and unworn flagstones hinted that a portico may originally have been constructed on their perimeter.[117] Most stone granaries do not seem to have had such platforms. It is possible that some may have been served by timber platforms whose foundations have not been discovered, or that foundations of platforms which were not as substantially built as the rest of the building have been destroyed by stone robbing or ploughing. It is clear, however, that in some cases it was necessary to utilise all the space allotted to the granary in the central range between the two lateral streets, leaving insufficient room for a projecting loading platform.

The postholes of porticoes have been found in front of the timber granaries of Pen Llystyn and Oberstimm, whilst column bases have been discovered in front of the stone granaries at Benwell, Newstead, South Shields and Corbridge, on two sides at Templeborough and three at Hüfingen. It is quite probable that many more porticoes originally existed, but early excavators who were merely following the walls of the building were unlikely to have found the traces of a portico built some metres away from it.

Siting

The granaries had to be readily accessible for unloading supplies but sited so that the coming and going of carts would cause as little obstruction as possible to the daily routine of the fort. Most were situated within the central range and close to a gate, standing either singly, with one on either side of the *principia*, or paired to one side of it. More unusually, as at Beckfoot or Bearsden for example, one granary lay in the central range whilst its partner lay on the other side of the *via principalis*; at Birrens a double granary lay on the opposite side of the street to two singles which flanked the *principia*. The single granary at Hod Hill was placed not in the central range but in the *praetentura*, next to the east gate, a position which was preferred in the legionary fortresses. Several forts, especially in Germany, have also revealed granaries in the *praetentura*, but it is not always certain, where the fort has not been completely excavated, whether they are the only granaries in the fort or whether they supplemented more centrally positioned ones. Less frequently granaries have been found in the *retentura*. At Baginton, for example, one granary was conventionally placed in the central range and another lay at the rear of the *retentura*. In its second period the fort had two granaries built on an irregular alignment at the rear of the *retentura*, and granaries have also been found in this position at Oberstimm and Theilenhofen.

A striking variation in the siting of granaries can be seen at South Shields. In the Hadrianic period a double granary stood in the central range next to the south-west gate, but in preparation for the Scottish campaigns of the emperor Severus (AD 208–11) the fort was converted into a supply depot. Eighteen single granaries were added (two more are inferred), which were built in three parallel rows occupying the *retentura*, the central range and half the *praetentura*.

Possible reconstruction of the granary

Timber Although the excavated groundplan of timber granaries shows quite clearly that the floor platform was supported by a grid of posts we know nothing of how the building was constructed above floor level, and any reconstruction must be hypothetical. Some of the timbers in the grid may have been carried up into the body of the building as structural members, or the whole superstructure could have been erected quite independently on top of a rigid timber platform.[118] The walls would have consisted either of panels of wattle and daub or overlapping timber planks, probably the latter, for it has been noted in one or two recent excavations that the burnt daub debris which covered most of the fort buildings was absent in the vicinity of the granaries.[119] Louvred ventilators may have been placed in the top of the walls beneath the eaves. The absence of roofing tiles from the debris of timber granaries suggests that the roofs were probably covered with timber planks or shingles.

Reconstruction of a timber granary was undertaken in 1973 at Baginton by a team of Royal Engineers. The granary was erected exactly upon the Roman groundplan; it measures 21 × 9 metres and stands 9 metres high to the apex of the roof. The floor was laid upon a grid of circular posts which were spaced c. 1.5 metres apart. At each end the body of the granary was set back from the edge of the raised floor, forming a loading platform for carts, with steps at each side. A painting by Alan Sorrell gives a vivid impression of carts unloading at such a platform (Ill. 112). The side walls of the building stood to a height of 3 metres and were clad with overlapping planks. There were regularly spaced louvred openings placed under the eaves and the roof was clad with timber shingles.[120]

Stone It has often been assumed that the thickly buttressed walls of the stone granary were needed because of the considerable lateral thrust exerted by the loose grain stored inside.[121] But the pressures exerted on the external walls would have been no greater than those imposed upon the timber bins inside, or upon the walls of timber granaries, and the stone walls were generally strong enough to withstand the pressures of grain stacked to a height of at least 3 metres.[122] It is more probable that the granaries were strongly buttressed not to resist the thrust of the grain but rather to support

111. The granary at
The Lunt,
Baginton,
Warwickshire,
reconstructed
by Royal
Engineers in
1973.

112. Reconstruction drawing of the timber granary at
The Lunt, Baginton, Warwickshire, by Alan
Sorrell.

113. A pair of stone granaries reconstructed at the Saalburg, in Upper Germany.

the considerable weight of a tiled roof with its complex of timber beams. Quantities of roofing tiles are often found during the excavation of stone granaries. At Okarben, in Upper Germany, for example, burnt debris from the granary which included numerous stamped tiles of *legio XXI* appears to represent a complete tiled roof which had collapsed after a fire; both slate and stone roofing slabs have also been found at granary sites. Other stone buildings within the fort, notably the *principia* and *praetorium*, also had tiled roofs but few exhibit the buttresses which are so characteristic of the granaries. This is probably because the basic courtyard plan of these buildings, incorporating as it did many more load-bearing partitions, presented smaller expanses to be continuously roofed, and would have produced fewer practical problems. In the stone granary the buttresses acted as a series of strong masonry piers which supported the bulk of the roof weight and the thrust of the grain, as the intermediate stretches of walling were structurally weakened by the insertion of ventilators both beneath the floor and at a higher level.[123]

The walls of a granary which was discovered within the *classis Britannica* fort at Dover were still standing 2.75 metres high. The discovery of various timber slots in the walls have led the excavator to suggest that the building had a second storey.[124] No other granaries have survived to this height and so the question as to whether they normally had two floors remains open, although patches of cobbling which are occasionally found against an outer wall may represent the foundations of staircases leading to an upper floor.

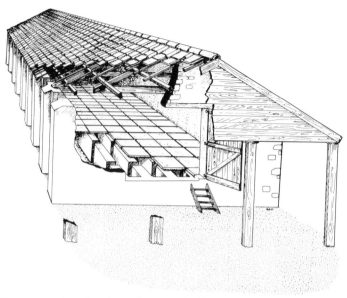

114. Reconstruction drawing of a stone-built granary.

The interior Unfortunately there is no evidence at all for the internal arrangements of the granary. It is generally supposed that the grain was stored in timber bins which lined the full length of the granary, with a corridor down the centre, and on this assumption various calculations have been made to assess the capacity of individual granaries and to compare it with the presumed garrison of the fort.[125] It is far from certain, however, whether bins of this sort were used. Their sides would have had to withstand the same lateral thrust as the external walls and so they must have been keyed into the floors and walls of the building to prevent them from slipping forward under the weight of the grain. Although the timber floors which may have provided this evidence have long since perished, we should expect to find the sockets or slots into which they had been placed in surviving stone-flagged floors, such as those in the military depot at Corbridge, but no traces have been found.

It is feasible that bulk grain was stored loose on the floor, although this method presents problems as it would have been difficult to separate fresh grain from old stock, which would have made handling and distribution difficult. The most practical and convenient method of storage and handling would have been the use of containers such as wicker baskets or, more probably, sacks such as those shown on a wall painting of a grain ship from Ostia.[126] The use of sacks would have made the rotation of stock and its distribution to the garrison much easier: it is hard to imagine any other

115. A grain ship depicted on a wall painting from Ostia, showing the use of sacks.

system of storage being practicable, particularly in the case of supply depots, such as South Shields, which must have had a frequent turnover of grain.

Whereas the main emphasis was on the storage of cereals, other foods would also have been stored in the granary; the low temperature and good ventilation would have preserved a variety of foodstuffs, and the massive construction of the building would have provided a secure store for the entire garrison's supplies. There may even have been some provision for the hanging of carcasses from the rafters in much the same manner as a modern cold store. Several Classical authors describe the use of a *carnarium*, which was a frame suspended from the ceiling comprising a series of hooks upon which provisions were hung, normally used in the kitchen and the tavern; similar devices may have been used in military granaries.[127] The reconstruction of the timber granary at Baginton demonstrated that there was considerable extra space available in the roof, which may have housed extra provisions. Small chambers, which were sometimes hypocausted, have been found at the rear of several stone granaries, mainly in Germany.[128] They may have provided offices for the granary clerks (*librarii horreorum*), or may have been drying rooms for grain which might otherwise have been spoilt.

The Hospital (*Valetudinarium*)

The promotion of physical fitness and good health was of paramount importance to the Roman army. Vegetius placed great importance upon a careful choice of camp site, a pure water supply, medicine and exercise to ensure good health, and favoured frequent changes of encampment to minimise the risk of disease from 'pollution of the air or water'. These considerations are reflected in the careful siting of permanent forts and the provision of a fresh water supply either from wells, storage tanks, pipelines

116. Scene from Trajan's Column showing a soldier receiving medical attention on the battlefield. (Scene XL)

or aqueducts. Careful attention was paid also to the arrangement of proper drainage and adequate sanitation, often with flushing latrines, and hot baths were usually available outside the fort.

Daily exercise and training helped to maintain the strength and morale of the soldiers for, as Vegetius recognised, 'health in the camp and victory in the field depend on them'.[129] Regular drills on the parade ground, in the amphitheatre, and training further afield on route marches or manoeuvres kept the troops at a peak of physical fitness, and drill halls were often built to provide training facilities in bad weather (see page 125). Recruits had to pass a medical examination upon entry to the service, and they were further weeded out during their basic training if found to be unsatisfactory.[130] However, if soldiers were wounded or fell ill Vegetius tells us that: 'It is the duty of the officers of the legion, of the tribunes and the commander in chief himself to take care that the sick soldiers are supplied with a suitable diet and diligently attended by the doctors.' Periodic health checks were made and if found unfit a soldier might be invalided out of the service (*missio causaria*).[131]

Many military doctors, like their civilian counterparts, were of Greek origin. Medical skills were highly developed in the Roman world, and doctors were well trained in their profession and highly respected. Several treatises on medical practice have survived, notably those of Celsus, Galen and Paul of Aegina, which give detailed accounts of surgical techniques, the extraction of missiles, anatomy, general treatments and pharmacy; it was these works which formed the basis of medical knowledge and practice well into the Middle Ages.[132]

The medical services of the legions are fairly well documented from a combination of literary, epigraphic and archaeological sources but, in contrast, there is little information about the provision and scale of medical care afforded to auxiliary troops. It is worthwhile therefore to summarise the evidence for the existence of legionary hospitals and medical staff to give a clearer idea of the extent of medical care available in the Roman army,[133] which was also extended to the auxiliaries, either in their own fort hospitals or at the nearby legionary base.

The legions

The overall responsibility for organisation and medical supplies lay with the *praefectus castrorum*, while the hospital was run by the *optio valetudinarii*.[134] The title *medicus*, which appears upon many inscriptions, embraced a whole range of different ranks from the chief medical officer (*medicus ordinarius*) whose status was broadly comparable with a centurion, down to the *miles medicus*, a medical orderly, who was an ordinary soldier exempted from general duties in order to work in the hospital.[135] Dressings were carried out by *capsarii*, men of similar rank to the orderlies, so-called from the cylindrical bandage box (*capsa*) which they carried. The work of such men upon the battlefield is clearly depicted upon Trajan's Column, which shows a field dressing station where a wounded cavalry trooper is having his thigh bandaged, and a legionary soldier is being examined by the medical orderlies. The medical staff were fully trained, as is shown by an inscription from the legionary fortress of Lambaesis which mentions trainee dressers (*discentes capsariorum*).[136] In addition, some units had doctors who specialised in the treatment of particular ailments—for example an inscription reveals that *cohors IV praetoria* had both a surgeon and a specialist in internal complaints, and the British fleet had its own oculist.[137]

In his model marching camp Hyginus placed the tents of the hospital (*valetudinarium*) in the *praetentura*, in a position where the patients would be least disturbed by noise.[138] Where hospitals are known within legionary fortresses they are usually situated with the central range of buildings at the rear of the *principia*.[139] The groundplan of the legionary hospital consisted normally of a courtyard surrounded on all sides by double ranges of small rooms or wards. A central corridor ran between the ranges and, additionally, each group of two or three wards was separated from its neighbours by a short transverse corridor, which was designed to provide as much ventilation and light as possible. The best preserved example, at Vetera, had a courtyard surrounded on three sides by double ranges of small wards, with a large aisled reception hall on its fourth side, and perhaps an operating theatre beyond. To one side of this hall lay a kitchen range and on the other a suite of baths with latrines. It is believed that there may have been sixty wards within such a legionary hospital which would correspond with the

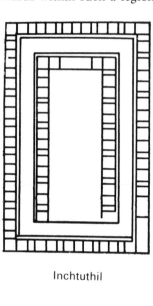

Inchtuthil

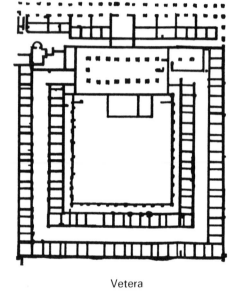

Vetera

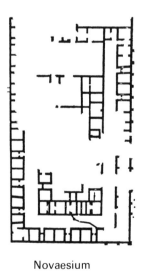

Novaesium

Vindonissa

117. Groundplans of legionary hospitals. Scale 1:1500

sixty *centuriae* of the garrison, with each ward capable of holding ten beds. This arrangement would allow up to 10 percent of the legion sick or wounded.[140]

The positive identification of these legionary buildings as hospitals is based principally upon the discovery within them, notably at Neuss, of large numbers of surgical and medical instruments, which included scalpels, spatulae, probes, clips, tweezers, spoons and mixing bowls.[141] The remains of medical supplies have also been found in several fortresses. A lead stopper from what may have been a medicine jar was found in the *principia* at Haltern and bore the inscription 'Ex Radice Britanica', which refers probably to the *radix Britannica*, a form of broad-leaved dock. It was described by the Elder Pliny as a cure for scurvy, which the army of Germanicus had learned from the Frisians.[142] An amphora fragment from Carpow in Scotland bore a graffito identifying its contents as wine flavoured with horehound, a remedy described by the physician Dioscurides for the relief of chest complaints.[143] Evidence for medicated wine has also been found at Aquincum, where barrels which had been re-used as linings for wells bore the stamp: 'immune in r(ationem) val (etudinarii) leg(ionis) II Adi(utricis)', wine destined for the legionary hospital which had been exempted from customs duty.[144]

The auxiliaries

A few auxiliary medical officers are known from inscriptions, such as the *medicus* of the *ala Vettonum* who dedicated an altar at Binchester, the *medicus ordinarius* recorded upon a tombstone at Housesteads, and the *medicus ordinarius* and *capsarii* who are known from Niederbieber.[145] Medical instruments have often occurred as stray finds within auxiliary forts, but have nowhere been associated with a particular building which could be identified as a hospital.[146] In an annual strength report (*pridianum*) of an auxiliary cohort stationed at Stobi in Macedonia (in AD 105) we are told the

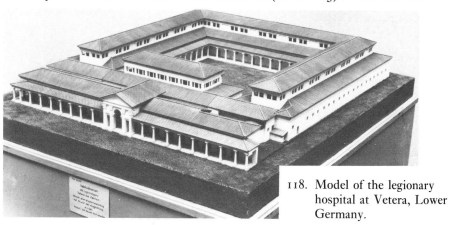

118. Model of the legionary hospital at Vetera, Lower Germany.

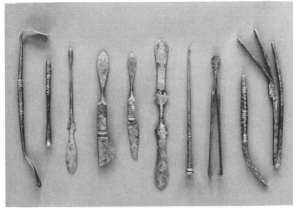

119. Surgical instruments from a doctor's grave at Bingen in Upper Germany.

120. Lead stopper from a medicine jar found at Haltern, bearing the inscription: 'Ex Radice Britanica', referring probably to the *radix Britannica*, used as a cure for scurvy.

number of soldiers who had reported sick (*aegri*), but unfortunately the document gives no indication as to where they were cared for.[147]

There are two distinct types of buildings which, from their groundplan, have been interpreted as hospitals in auxiliary forts. One is a courtyard building, which is seen at Housesteads and appears to be a scaled-down version of the legionary hospital, and the second is a corridor building, with two ranges of small rooms flanking a corridor, as seen at Oberstimm. Only a handful of examples of either type are known. Within the central range at Housesteads, behind the *principia*, lay a stone building consisting of four ranges of small rooms grouped around a central courtyard, including a larger room which is thought to have been an operating theatre, a latrine, and possibly a plunge bath.[148] Its position was secluded, with the wards ranged around the private courtyard, which may perhaps have contained a garden for medicinal herbs.[149] Similar courtyard buildings which have been found in the central range at Benwell and Wallsend and in the *praetentura* at Hod Hill are believed to have been hospitals of this type.[150]

The corridor type is known from a small number of forts and has also been generally identified as a hospital. A classic example is seen at Fendoch, where a central corridor was flanked on one side by eight almost square

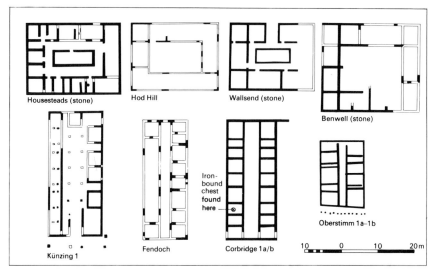

121. Possible hospitals within auxiliary forts. Scale 1:1000

small rooms and on the other by a long unpartitioned hall with small rooms at each end. Here each of the ten small rooms is thought to have been a ward allocated to a century of the milliary cohort presumed to have been in garrison, with the larger hall perhaps serving as an operating theatre or reception hall.[151] In some examples the flanking rooms were equal-sized and arranged symmetrically on both sides of the corridor, as at Corbridge; in others one or two small rooms alternated with narrow corridors, as at Künzing, a feature which is reminiscent of legionary hospital wards.

No archaeological evidence has yet been found which would allow us to describe any of these buildings conclusively as hospitals, and comparison with a similar structure recently excavated within a military depot near Corbridge (at Beaufront Red House) has in fact suggested an alternative identification.[152] Just outside this corridor building within a fenced compound to the west lay several workpits, reddened by intense burning and filled with charcoal, which had been used for metalworking. The close association between this building and the metalworking hearths and pits identifies it most probably as a workshop (*fabrica*) rather than a hospital.[153] Beneath the floor of the corridor 'hospital' at the fort of Corbridge was found the remains of a small iron-bound wooden chest which contained scrap metal, nails, spearheads, masons' and carpenters' tools, iron armour plates (*lorica segmenta*), a bronze scabbard with fastenings, writing tablets, a wooden mug, leather fragments and glass gaming counters.[154] Its presence under the floor of a hospital ward has always been rather difficult to explain, and it seems more probable that it was a scrap hoard buried within a workshop or store.[155]

Another clue to the probable identification of these corridor buildings not as hospitals but as stores or workshops, is given by comparison with the groundplans of civilian granaries and storebuildings (*horrea*) in the port of Ostia, near Rome.[156] Here two types of *horrea* are known, a courtyard and a corridor type, the latter with two rows of small rooms separated by a central corridor, with more small rooms on the third, shorter side. Examples are similar in size (c. 25 × 15 metres) to those found in British and German auxiliary forts. Fragments of a huge plan of Rome which was inscribed upon 151 rectangular marble slabs during the reign of Septimius Severus (AD 203–11) also show the two distinctive plans of Roman storebuildings.[157] Only one building is actually labelled as a store, the *Horrea Lolliana*, which consisted of two large colonnaded courtyards surrounded on all sides by equal-sized storerooms, but other storebuildings illustrated on this plan bear a marked resemblance to the corridor 'hospitals' of auxiliary forts.

To summarise, at present it is difficult to identify hospitals within auxiliary forts, or to be even sure that they were provided at all. Miniature versions of the well known legionary courtyard examples may have existed in the Hadrian's Wall forts of Housesteads, Benwell and Wallsend, although none has yielded any medical or surgical instruments to reinforce this identification. From the evidence available the corridor building, which has often been regarded in the past as a hospital, is best identified as a workshop or store. We are aware of the high standards of medical care in the Roman army and have some evidence that the auxiliary units had their own medical staffs, but where the sick and wounded were cared for in most auxiliary forts remains a mystery. Routine sickness and minor injury amongst the soldiers would have been dealt with by the garrison's own medical officers. They may well have been treated in a hospital whose groundplan today is not distinctive enough to be recognised during archaeological excavation, or alternatively perhaps one of the extra rooms usually provided in each barrack block was used as a sick room. Undoubtedly the more severe cases could have been transferred to the nearest legionary fortress for more specialist care, as its hospital would normally have provided sufficient accommodation for auxiliary soldiers.

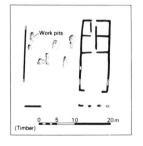

122. The corridor-plan building, associated with metalworking, found at Beaufront Red House, near Corbridge. Scale 1:1000

123. Fragments of the marble plan of Rome showing the commercial sector close to the Aventine Hill. The plan almost certainly depicts storebuildings.

124. Details of storebuildings depicted on the marble plan of Rome.

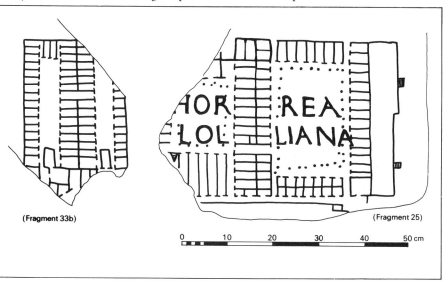

(Fragment 33b)

(Fragment 25)

0   10   20   30   40   50 cm

Barracks (*Centuriae*)

The origins of the permanent barrack block can be seen in the tented accommodation of the marching camp in which, according to Hyginus, each legionary century occupied eight leather tents (*papiliones*),[158] which were pitched in a long line (*hemistrigium*). Each tent measured 10 Roman feet square (c. 3 × 3 metres) and housed a tent group (*contubernium*) of eight men; only eight tents were needed per century as a group of sixteen men was constantly posted on guard duty. A space equivalent to two tents was allocated to the centurion at the end of the tent row. Two lines of tents were drawn up facing one another across an open space 28 Roman feet wide, allowing enough room in front of each row for the piling up of arms and equipment (*arma*) and the tethering of baggage animals (*iumenta*). Between the tents narrow passages were left for the guylines.[159]

The barracks of both the legionary fortress and the permanent auxiliary fort were laid out in much the same way as the tent rows of the marching camp, although the accommodation which they provided was normally more spacious. The barrack was L-shaped, with the wider part of the building, which was usually adjacent to the *intervallum* and the defences,

125. Scene from Trajan's Column showing tents within a fortified enclosure. (Scene XXI)

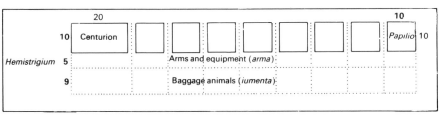

126. The arrangement of the century's tents within the marching camp, according to Hyginus. (Measurements are in Roman feet.)

127. A typical auxiliary barrack block.

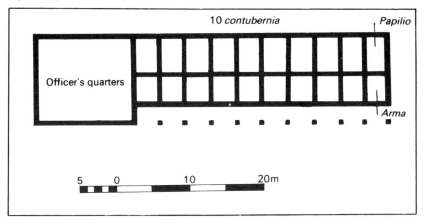

occupied by the officers' quarters and the remainder divided into a range of equal-sized pairs of rooms for the men, fronted by a verandah. The barrack blocks (*centuriae*)[160] often lay in pairs, facing each other across a metalled street. The average dimensions of an auxiliary barrack are approximately 10 metres wide and 40–50 metres long. They were sited generally in the *praetentura* and the *retentura*, with the central range reserved solely for administrative and specialist buildings. (Exceptions can be seen at the Claudian forts of Hod Hill and Valkenburg where there was no *retentura* and the *principia* was flanked by barracks, and at Oberstimm, where the *retentura* was filled with workshops and other specialist buildings.)

The infantry barrack consisted of not less than ten pairs of rooms (*contubernia*) to house the eighty men of each century and included quarters for the centurion and his subordinate officers (the *signifer*, *optio* and *tesserarius*). The cavalry barrack had essentially the same plan and was probably designed to house sixty-four men (2 *turmae*), with eight men accommodated in at least eight rooms; there were also quarters for the officers of each *turma* (the *decurio*, *duplicarius* and *sesquiplicarius*). Extra rooms were often provided within the barrack which may have served as living quarters for junior officers, additional storage space, or perhaps common rooms or sick bays for the soldiers.

The centurion or decurion occupied spacious quarters in a self-contained suite of rooms at one end of the barrack, which extended across the full width of the building. Occasionally the officers' accommodation was completely detached from the rest of the building, separated from the men's rooms by a narrow passage. Excavations of the barracks at Valkenburg in Lower Germany have uncovered a detailed picture of the internal arrangements of the officers' quarters. Here many of the timber walls and partitions have been preserved in waterlogged ground and reveal a suite of six or seven rooms grouped around a central corridor. Each lodging possessed a hearth and a latrine, with timber-lined drainage channels leading to a soakaway outside the building.[161] The spaciousness of the accommodation together with hearths, washing facilities and latrines emphasises the relative comfort in which the officers lived. This is further highlighted by the discovery within one of the officers' rooms of a barrack at Echzell of a large quantity of fine painted wall plaster showing a high standard of workmanship, which had adorned the wattle and daub walls of the timber building. Fortunately the fragments of plaster had fallen into a timber-lined pit beneath the floor and had been preserved when the barrack was

129. Opposite: comparative plans of auxiliary barracks. Scale 1:1000

128. Pair of reconstructed timber barracks on stone foundations at the Saalburg in Upper Germany.

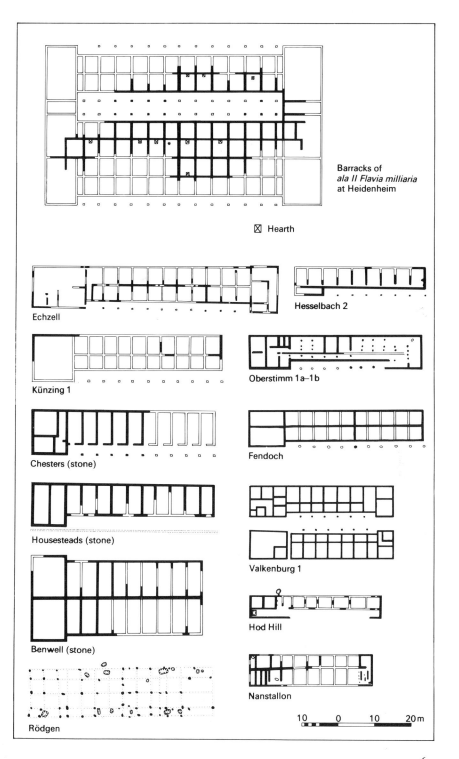

Barracks of
ala II Flavia milliaria
at Heidenheim

⊠ Hearth

Echzell

Hesselbach 2

Künzing 1

Oberstimm 1a–1b

Chesters (stone)

Fendoch

Housesteads (stone)

Valkenburg 1

Benwell (stone)

Hod Hill

Nanstallon

Rödgen

10   0   10   20m

130. A panel of
 painted wall
 plaster, depicting
 Fortuna and
 Hercules, found
 in an officer's
 rooms in a timber
 barrack at
 Echzell, in Upper
 Germany.

demolished.[162] Small pits were often dug beneath the floors, and they may
have originally contained wooden boxes in which personal documents or
valuables were kept; one example from Great Casterton contained the studs
and a bronze binding from just such a box.[163] It is not clear how many
people were actually housed within the officers' quarters. They may have
been designed to accommodate not only the centurion or decurion but also
their subordinate officers. They may alternatively have been intended
solely for the senior officer, his servants or slaves and possibly even his
family.[164]

Within the legionary camp described by Hyginus the tents of the senior
legion lay on the right-hand side, and similarly in the permanent single-
legion fortress the accommodation of the double-strength first cohort lay to
the right of the *principia*.[165] On this basis it has been suggested that in the
auxiliary fort the same principles were followed; the barrack which housed
the most senior centurion or decurion lying on the right-hand side, and that
in any pair of barracks the senior of the officers occupied the right-hand
building, looking towards the officers' end of the barracks.[166] There are
certainly examples which seem to support this supposition, in which more
spacious accommodation was provided for the officer in the right-hand
barrack, but there are an equal number in which the lodgings on the left-

hand side are larger, and many forts do not appear to show any marked differences in size between the officers' quarters at all.[167]

Accommodation for each *contubernium* of eight men in an auxiliary barrack consisted usually of two rooms, one at the rear (*papilio*) for sleeping, and another at the front for the storage of equipment and personal possessions (*arma*), with a verandah running in front of the building. Hearths are commonly found, placed usually in the rear room, and consisting either of a stone or tile setting with probably a semi-circular stone or tile flue. The floors were often of trampled earth, although traces of joists for timber floor boards have occasionally been detected. The discovery of fragments of window glass amongst barrack debris at several sites shows that at least some of the windows were glazed, although timber shutters or louvres may also have been used.

Much valuable information showing the internal layout and fittings within the *contubernium* has been provided by the excavations of the milliary *ala* fort at Heidenheim in Raetia.[168] Here hearths lay in the rear rooms set against the partition walls separating the front and rear rooms; they were constructed with semi-circular or rectangular tile settings which probably originally had a chimney flue above. The floors were of pounded clay mixed with tile fragments, and the outlines of the trenches in which the wattle and daub panels of the partition walls had stood were clearly visible. A rectangular arrangement of four post-holes was found in one of the rear rooms, placed in front of the fireplace, which may represent the supports for a table or bench upon which the soldiers dined and drank and played board games; a number of gaming pieces were found amongst the debris of these barracks. On three sides of this room small postholes defined areas of some 200 × 80 cm, probably the remains of bedsteads for bunk beds which originally lay opposite the fireplace and along the side walls.[169] The front room of the *contubernium* (the *arma*) may have been the same size as the sleeping room, but was often much smaller. It was not usually heated, and was probably furnished with lockers and shelves to store the weapons and the wide range of military and personal kit belonging to the eight roommates.[170] Personal possessions would have included clothing and valuables, weapons, tools and cooking utensils, and there may also have been a communal store for the *contubernium*'s own grinding mill, cooking pots and crockery (see page 199). It was here that the soldiers cleaned and polished their arms and armour, and probably also where their food was prepared. Small pits were often dug beneath the barrack floor in both the front and rear rooms, and sometimes in front of the entrance to the building under the verandah porticus. Occasionally they contained iron or bronze nails showing that they had been either originally timber-lined, or housed small wooden boxes, like the pits found in the officers' rooms, and had probably contained valuables or personal possessions. The pits dug in the entranceway or under the verandah must have been covered with timber

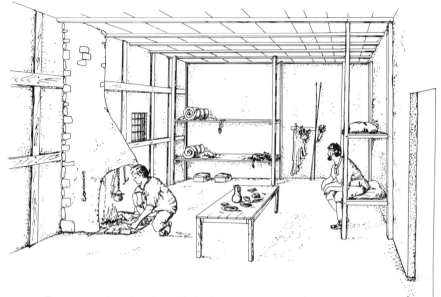

131. Reconstruction drawing of the interior of a barrack room, based on the evidence found at Heidenheim, in Raetia.

trapdoors, and probably served a different function, as they lay in too vulnerable a position to have housed anything valuable.

Two barracks were often placed back to back in a double block, leaving only a narrow space between the rear walls of each building. When two buildings were paired in this way there was no window to illuminate the rear sleeping quarters, and light must have been provided either by a skylight in the roof, or by raising the roof of the rear rooms higher than that of the front rooms, and allowing a clerestory between them. At Carrawburgh the wall foundations of the partition walls between each pair of barrack rooms had been strengthened, suggesting that this wall had stood to a greater height than the front wall to provide such a clerestory.[171]

The number of *contubernia* within the barrack block varied according to the type of unit which was in garrison. The eighty men of an infantry century are presumed to have been housed in ten *contubernia*, whilst two *turmae*, each with thirty-two men, occupied a cavalry barrack, requiring at least eight rooms. Frequently, however, additional rooms were provided which makes it often extremely difficult to identify and distinguish between infantry and cavalry barracks solely from the number of *contubernia*. At Chesters on Hadrian's Wall, for example, one of the few sites where a cavalry garrison is known and can be compared with the barrack accommodation, the barracks had ten *contubernia*; and at several other sites which are presumed to have been cavalry forts the number of barrack rooms ranged from six to ten.[172] Occasionally barracks have been found with even more *contubernia*, as in the Augustan supply depot at Rödgen, which had from eleven to sixteen irregularly partitioned rooms in each barrack block, and at the Flavian fort of Rottweil, which had thirteen rooms. In these cases it is probable that the forts were not designed specifically for an auxiliary garrison, but housed detachments of legionaries, sometimes brigaded together with auxiliaries, a practice which was especially common in the Augustan and Claudian periods.

In the marching camp Hyginus allotted two and a half times more space to the trooper with his equipment than the foot soldier.[173] In the permanent fort where the horse was stabled separately there was probably no reason why the trooper should have needed so much extra space. He may still have been required to keep his saddle, harness and grooming equipment in his own lodging, although harness rooms may have been provided in the stables. Nevertheless higher rank and status demanded that his quarters should be more spacious and comfortable than those of the infantryman, which is generally reflected in the larger *contubernia* found in known cavalry forts. Differences between the rank and status of the successive occupants of the barracks at Valkenburg may be seen in the enlargement of the accommodation. Here the number of rooms was reduced from seven to six and the *arma* nearly doubled in size until it almost equalled the *papilio*. These changes are presumed to represent the replacement of the infantry contingent of a *cohors equitata* by part of an *ala*.[174] Similarly, throughout its history a barrack in the *retentura* at Corbridge alternated between eight and ten *contubernia*, implying a change in rank of its occupants from cavalry to infantry (Ill. 73). In early British forts such as Claudian Hod Hill and Neronian Baginton the *contubernia* were very cramped and had only one room, and it is possible that in these early examples we may be seeing the minimum requirements deemed necessary by a garrison building permanent quarters for the first time and adapting from the restrictions of the marching camp.[175] As time passed the barracks tended to become more spacious. At Valkenburg, for example, during three periods of rebuilding, the barrack rooms of the *cohors IIII Thracum quingenaria equitata* were gradually increased in size, probably reflecting an improvement in living standards during the life of the fort.[176]

In some barrack blocks additional accommodation was provided. Between the officers' quarters and the first *contubernium* at Echzell lay a room with irregular internal partitions, and similar rooms are known in the legionary barracks at Neuss. Their function is unknown, although it has been argued that this room may have been allocated to lower ranking officers next door to the quarters of the centurion or decurion.[177] In other cases 'end rooms' or 'end buildings' have been discovered at the opposite end of the building to the officers' suite. Sometimes they simply formed a continuation of the barrack rooms and were fronted by the verandah, as at Rottweil, and in other examples they projected beyond the front wall of the adjacent *contubernia*, as seen at Oberstimm or Valkenburg; again their function is uncertain.

Normally the barrack housed an entire century or two *turmae* in one long building, but occasionally lack of space may have made it necessary to divide the barrack into two halves. This may be seen at Valkenburg where, in the Claudian period, four pairs of barracks lay in the combined central range and *retentura*, flanking the *principia* (Ill. 132). Four of the buildings had projecting officers' quarters lying close to the rampart, whilst their opposite numbers consisted of large rectangular buildings, often detached from the rest of the block, which contained treadmills for grinding grain, hearths, and storage platforms. Here each pair of barracks is seen as an entity, a centurial barrack split into two, providing officers' accommodation, fourteen *contubernia*, two 'end rooms' and the century's workshop and storehouse (*fabricula*), an arrangement which may also be seen at Hod Hill (Ill. 182).[178] The reason for such an unusual layout may simply be the lack of space available for fitting four full-length barrack blocks of the normal 50 metres

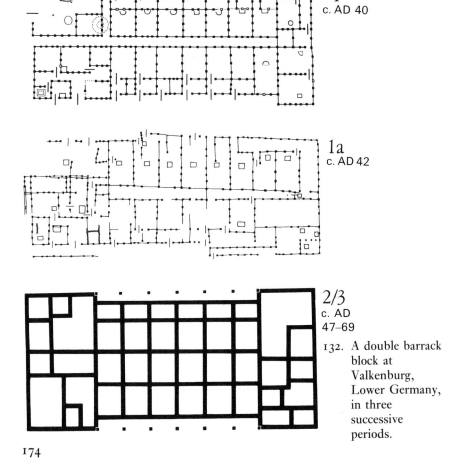

1
c. AD 40

1a
c. AD 42

2/3
c. AD
47–69

132. A double barrack block at Valkenburg, Lower Germany, in three successive periods.

length into the shallow (39 metres) combined central range and *retentura*, so common in forts of the early Claudian period.

The number of excavated forts in which the barrack accommodation can be matched with an *ala* or a part-mounted garrison is small. The only examples of barracks built for a cavalry unit 1000-strong are the three barracks of the *ala II Flavia milliaria*, which were uncovered recently at Heidenheim in Raetia.[179] The blocks (c. 76 × 10 metres) consisted of projecting decurions' quarters at each end of the buildings, with twelve equal-sized *contubernia* between them. They were divided by a slightly thicker partition wall in the centre, giving the impression of two small barrack blocks placed end to end, each housing one *turma*. Where cavalry units of 500 men are known to have been in garrison, as for instance at Chesters and Newstead, the numbers of *contubernia* varied considerably (see

133. An aerial photograph of the excavations at Heidenheim in 1965, showing the foundation trenches of the timber barracks in the north-west corner of the fort.

page 295 and note 20). There is little close correspondence either between the barracks of known *cohortes quingenaria equitatae*; at Künzing the barracks had probably ten *contubernia* whilst a similar unit at Valkenburg occupied nine or ten barrack rooms. The sizes of the rooms at these forts differed considerably, however, with those at Künzing providing up to one third more floor space. No epigraphic evidence has yet been found to link any excavated barracks conclusively with an infantry unit, but the discovery of ten barrack blocks at both Fendoch and Housesteads, each with ten *contubernia*, indicates that both were probably designed to house the ten centuries of a *cohors milliaria peditata*. The dimensions of the living rooms of both forts are closely comparable, and more cramped than the cavalry examples.[180] Barracks thought to have been occupied by a *numerus* have been excavated at Hesselbach. Each of the four barracks probably provided accommodation for a century of thirty or thirty-two men in its varying number of barrack rooms.

Stables

Hundreds of horses would have been needed by the various auxiliary cavalry units and every garrison, whether infantry or cavalry, had its own pack animals, yet very little is known about stables within Roman forts.[181] Fragmentary traces have been found at only a handful of sites, and nowhere has there been found sufficient evidence to show the complete layout of a fort's stable accommodation. The problem may be primarily one of identification, for the few stable blocks which have been positively recognised were long narrow buildings which could only be distinguished from neighbouring structures with identical ground plans because they had been provided with a stable drain. But a drain was not essential and without one, or any environmental evidence for the presence of horses, there is no way of differentiating from their ground plan alone between stables and similar buildings which may have served as stores or workshops. Perhaps we should not expect to find stables within the fort at all, as in many cases the cavalry mounts and pack animals may well have been coralled outside.[182]

What little evidence we do have for Roman horses and military stables can be briefly summarised. The Roman cavalry horse was generally smaller than the modern horse. Examination of equine skeletons from the fort of Newstead, in Scotland, has shown that the horses ranged in size from the native bred 'Celtic ponies' of 11–12 hands, and other ponies of 12–13 hands up to horses of 15 hands, although the majority lay just below 14 hands.[183] Similar evidence from other Roman forts shows that the cavalry horses usually attained a height of perhaps 13–14 hands (c. 1.4 metres to the shoulder) compared with the larger standard size of some 14–15 hands for late nineteenth- and early twentieth-century cavalry mounts; smaller ponies and mules would have been used as pack animals.[184] Judging from the few excavated examples, and from the practice laid down by cavalry manuals written at the turn of this century, the most efficient stable layout would be to tether the horses in long rows within narrow rectangular stable blocks, leaving a longitudinal corridor, and perhaps a drain, at the rear for access and cleaning. The animals may have been separated from each other by swinging wooden bails suspended by ropes, or have had individual timber-built stalls which, if they were stabled for long periods, would have been spacious enough to allow them to lie down.[185] Looseboxes would have been needed for the isolation and treatment of sick horses. The stable may have housed a single row of horses with a corridor behind, or two rows with a corridor between them.[186]

In the absence of organic remains of dung, bedding or fodder, the most convincing evidence for the identification of Roman stables comes from the discovery of internal drains, which were often provided at the rear of the stall to keep the floor dry. Xenophon, writing in the early second century AD, advised that a sound, well-drained floor should always be laid in the stable:

> Now damp and slippery floors ruin even well-formed hooves. In order that they may not be damp, the floors should have a slope to carry off the wet, and that they may not be slippery, they should be paved all over with stones, each one about the size of the hoof. Such floors, indeed, have another advantage because they harden the feet of the horses standing on them.[187]

Fragments of stone-built stables with drains running down the interior have been found in the forts of Ilkley and Brough-on-Noe. At Ilkley a double stable lay in the *praetentura* of the Severan fort. Each half of the building was served by a central longitudinal stone-built drain which, at least on one side, was flushed by water conveyed from the eavesdrip surrounding the building through a conduit under the stable wall. In the infilling of this drain was found a bronze strigil (which would normally have been used in the bathhouse to scrape clean a bather's body). The blade had been broken in antiquity and had then probably been relegated to the stables for grooming the horses.[188] Two troughs stood upon the thick gravel and cobblestone floor, and postholes thought to have been for tethering posts were also found. At the late third–early fourth-century fort at Brough-on-Noe one side of a barrack appears to have provided a stable, as it had a stone drain set in the cobbled floor, which ran parallel and one metre away from the external wall. It turned at right-angles and ran under the wall of the building, beneath the adjacent rampart street and out of the fort; a few horses' teeth were found in the infilling. At neither fort was the full length of the building excavated, nor were the arrangements of the internal partitions discovered.

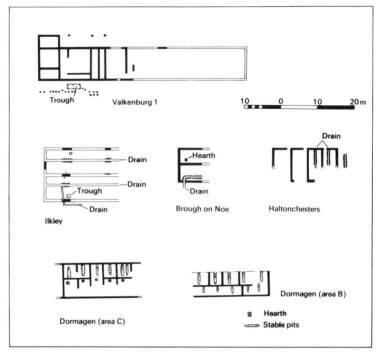

134. Stables found in auxiliary forts. Scale 1:1000

More internal details were preserved in the timber stable of the Claudian fort at Valkenburg, which lay in the left *praetentura*, facing a barrack block. Here two large rooms were excavated, flanked by narrow passages, with an internal drain. Outside the building lay a sunken horse trough into which had been dropped a small pottery lamp in the form of a horse's head. The horses were probably tethered to a row of deeply set posts which ran parallel with the external wall of the building. An open space (14 metres wide) was left between the stable and the rampart, which may have been used for exercising and grooming, and for the assembly of pack animals; a similar metalled yard was provided at Ilkley between the stable and the *via principalis*. A completely different stable layout is seen in the Severan fort of Haltonchesters, where a series of five detached rooms each had an open drain running down the central long axis.

An internal drain was not essential in the stable. Traces of at least four timber-built stables have recently been excavated at Dormagen (which housed the quingenary *ala Noricorum*), situated on the left bank of the Rhine in Lower Germany.[189] Here soakaway pits had been dug into the well-drained gravel subsoil in each stable room. Three of the stables lay partly in the central range and partly in the shallow *retentura*; a fourth had been built at right-angles to them at the rear of the *retentura* and adjacent to the rampart street. The best preserved example, close to the southern rampart, had a

135. Part of a small pottery lamp in the form of a horse's head found at Valkenburg in Lower Germany.

groundplan similar to a barrack block, and apparently housed both men and their horses, each in similar-sized rooms on either side of the longitudinal partition wall. Only five pairs of rooms could be investigated, and the overall length of the building is, unfortunately, unknown. The rooms of the southern wing probably served as living quarters, as each had a simple hearth set in front of the central partition wall. Running across the centre of each room in the northern range were long pits up to a metre wide and dug at least half a metre deep into the sandy clay and gravel subsoil. These pits had sloping sides and round bases, and their infilling included traces of lime, whilst the surrounding ground had been stained and reduced by their strong phosphate content. The pits were probably originally covered with timber boards. Analysis of the discoloured soil helped to confirm this building as a stable, an identification which was further reinforced by the discovery of carbonised plant remains from the horses' hay and fodder.[190] This stable was destroyed by fire in AD 120–40, and was replaced by a new one with soakaway pits arranged on a slightly different line; no traces of the partition walls of this structure had survived. A similar building on the opposite side of a metalled street also accommodated both men and horses within the same block. Next to the western rampart street lay a building which had been used solely as a stable. Although its internal partitions had been largely destroyed the stable pits remained, showing that it had been subdivided into stalls approximately 3–4 metres wide. A fourth stable lay on the opposite side of the *principia*.

In the absence of drains or soakaways sufficient bedding would have been provided to absorb the excreta, and the stables would have been cleaned out regularly, preferably, according to Xenophon, daily.[191] The Great Roster of AD 222 from Dura Europos records a trooper, J. Maximus, engaged upon such a task, 'rast [rum]', mucking out the stables.[192] Soiled straw and bedding must have been removed regularly to a convenient storage area away from the stables.

The stables at Hod Hill were not served by drains, but were identified by their excavator, Sir Ian Richmond, from the patches of wear in the floor which had been caused by the trampling and pounding of horses' hooves. The stables lay to the left of the *principia* in the central range, and consisted of a group of six long narrow buildings. The complete arrangement of the internal partitions was traced only in Building II, which contained a total of eleven compartments, with five large central rooms and three smaller ones at each end. In one of the rooms in Building I the chalk subsoil had been trampled in two distinct rows running parallel with one of the transverse partition walls, and the ground was heavily stained and darkened. This disturbance is thought to have been caused by the front and rear hooves of horses tethered not against the long walls, but to the partitions. It has been estimated that two rows of three horses could be accommodated like this in each room, separated by a corridor 1.8 metres wide, with quarters for grooms, together with fodder stores and harness rooms, probably provided in the rooms at either end of the stable block.[193] However, the distance between the two patches of disturbance was only 0.9 metres, and if they did represent the positions of the front and rear hooves they imply a very small horse of not more than 10 hands (c. 1.1 metres to the shoulder), which is smaller than a modern child's pony, rather than a cavalry horse of 14 hands.[194] If the buildings at Hod Hill were stables they probably housed pack animals rather than cavalry mounts.

At the earth-and-timber fort of Künzing, on the Danube, limited trial trenching has enabled the complete layout of the barracks and stables of the first fort (occupied c. AD 90–120, probably by the *cohors III Thracum quingenaria equitata*) to be conjectured. Four long narrow buildings in the *retentura* have been identified as stables. They varied in width and groundplan; two were narrow blocks and behind them lay a wider building which had two longitudinal partitions. On the opposite side of the *via decumana* the fourth building had a single longitudinal division. However, the investigation was carried out only in limited trenches and few internal partitions were discovered, so that their identification as stables and the restoration of their internal arrangements remains hypothetical.[195] Until the complete excavation of a cavalry fort has been undertaken and all the stables positively identified all the problems and questions concerning military stables—whether all the horses were accommodated inside the fort, the numbers of animals involved and how the stabling of cavalry mounts and pack animals differed—must remain unanswered.

Sufficient space was also needed either in the stable itself or within an adjacent building to store fodder, bedding, harness and other equipment. Polybius, writing c. 140 BC, recorded the monthly rations of an auxiliary

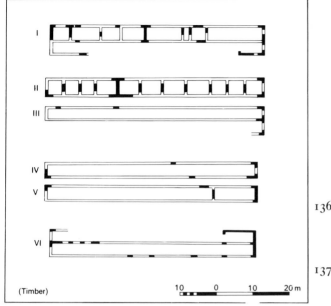

136. Stables at Hod Hill. Scale 1:1000

137. Possible stables at Künzing, Raetia. Scale 1:1000

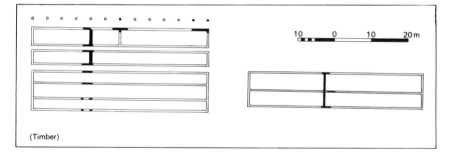

cavalryman in the Republican army, which amounted daily to c. 1.9 kilograms of wheat for himself and 6.1 kilograms of barley for his horse.[196] Several documents surviving upon papyrus refer to the receipt of barley (*hordeum*) by cavalry troopers. From Egypt, for example, a papyrus dated AD 185 records the annual requisition for the quingenary *ala Heracliana* as 20 000 *artaba*, an Egyptian measure which would amount to less than half the ration suggested by Polybius.[197] Nevertheless this quantity of grain would have been quite sufficient for a Roman cavalry horse if complemented by up to 4.5 kilograms per day of hay and green forage.[198]

Part of a receipt book for hay (*faenarium*), belonging to the *ala Veterana Gallica* has been preserved upon papyrus. It contained sixty-seven receipts covering the period from 9th January to 10th April AD 179.[199] A typical entry was dated January 16th:

Iulius Serenus, cavalryman of the ala Gallica, turma of Herodianus, and Iulius Nepotianus, same turma, and Pathernouthis Orsenuphis, turma of Pactumaius Serenus, to Iulius Serenus, summus curator. We have received from you our hay allowance for the 19th year, each of us 25 denarii. Year 19 of the Aureli Antontinus and Commodus the Lords Augusti, Tybi 21. I, Sossius Eudaemon, signifer of the turma of Herodianus, have written for them on request because of their not knowing how to write.

Other receipts and documents also mention loads of hay for the cavalry, although it is impossible to assess the quantitites involved in modern terms.[200]

Hay lofts may have been provided above the stable stalls to give dry and well ventilated storage, and fodder stores must have been built to house the considerable quantities of barley, probably with much the same design as the granary for the soldiers' grain; it is thought that a buttressed store building situated next to the rear gate at Caernarfon in Wales may have been a store of this type.[201]

Classical writers, such as Josephus, Vegetius and Varro, all acknowledged the importance of providing grazing for horses, and cavalry and pack animals may well have been allowed to graze extensively within the *territorium* of the fort.[202] A plentiful supply of bedding, either straw, bracken, leaves or peat moss, would also have been required to provide dry and warm insulation and prevent injury from the hard stable floor.[203] A constant water supply was important, and many water troughs would have been needed in the stables, as each horse required between 35 and 55 litres daily.[204]

Harness and parade armour may have been hung upon the walls of the stable itself, or have been aired and cleaned in an adjoining harness room, or even hung up in the troopers' barrack rooms. Vegetius tells us that it was the duty of the decurion to encourage his men 'to keep their armour, lances and helmets always bright and in good order. The splendour of the arms has no inconsiderable effect in striking terror into an enemy'.[205]

Veterinarium   In the camp described by Hyginus the *veterinarium* for sick horses was placed in the *praetentura* next to the men's hospital.[206] The soldiers who attended the legionary cavalry mounts and baggage animals, and who were also responsible for the animals used in sacrifices, were known as *veterinarii* and *pecuarii*.[207] The provision of care for the horses in auxiliary forts is, however, largely unknown, although a horse doctor (*hippiatros*) assigned to the *cohors I Thebaeorum equitata* is recorded.[208]

The Workshop (*Fabrica*)

The Roman army included within its ranks a wide range of skilled craftsmen and technicians. Vegetius provides a list of legionary *immunes*, men employed upon specialist tasks who were exempted from general duties, which is further amplified by Tarruntenus Paternus to include 'ditch diggers, farriers, master builders, pilots, shipwrights, *ballista* makers, glaziers, smiths, arrow makers, coppersmiths, helmet makers, wagon makers, roof-tile makers, swordcutlers, water engineers, trumpet makers, horn makers, bow makers, plumbers, blacksmiths, masons, limeburners, woodcutters, charcoal burners, butchers, huntsmen, keepers of sacrificial animals . . . grooms and tanners . . .'[209] All these craftsmen were under the overall command of the *optio fabricae*. Vegetius also mentions the workshops where shields, helmets, armour, spears and weapons of all kinds were manufactured, for 'the ancients made it their chief care to have everything for the service of the army within the camp'.[210] In the temporary camp of Hyginus the workshop (*fabrica*) stood in the *praetentura* as far away as possible from the hospital so that the noise would not disturb the patients.[211]

Fabricae have been identified within several legionary fortresses, primarily from their association with ovens, smelting hearths or metal slag and debris which bears witness to metalworking. The excavated legionary examples fall broadly into three categories, according to their ground-plan (Ill. 138).[212] The majority consisted of a long rectangular hall, with perhaps a central corridor or verandah, containing rooms of various sizes. A second group had a U-shaped plan, with ranges of rooms or aisled halls forming three sides of a square. Perhaps the best example of this type is seen at Inchtuthil where, in the *retentura*, stood a large building comprising three double-aisled halls, with a further range of larger rooms making the fourth side of the square. The remains of a blacksmith's forge, together with ashes and debris attest its function as a *fabrica*. Beneath the floor were found almost a million unused nails of different sizes, weighing almost twelve tons together with ten iron wheel-tyres, belonging to the stores.[213] At both Vindonissa and Lambaesis similar *fabricae*, only with three wings rather than four, were raised upon a podium to facilitate the loading and unloading of materials. The third *fabrica* type was a large square or rectangular building which contained numerous rooms of various sizes grouped around a central courtyard.

It is not certain how far Paternus' list of legionary specialists can be extended to the auxiliaries, but it is clear that craftsmen with many of the same ranges of skills would have been needed. Brand new tools, weapons and equipment may not have been made within the auxiliary fort, but requisitioned from a nearby legionary fortress or supply depot. Nevertheless the routine upkeep of fort buildings, the maintenance of the water

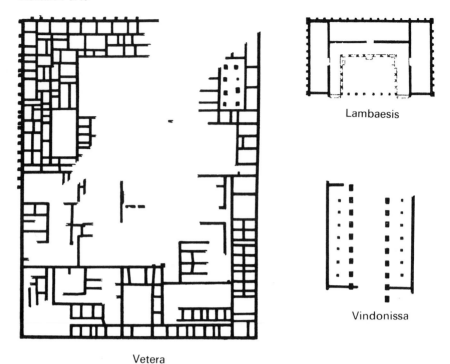

Lambaesis

Vindonissa

Vetera

138. Workshops (*fabricae*) in legionary fortresses. Scale 1:1500

139. The workshop (*fabrica*) of the legionary fortress of Inchtuthil, Scotland. Scale 1:1000

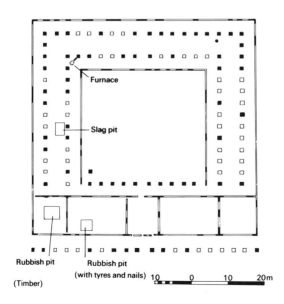

Furnace

Slag pit

Rubbish pit

Rubbish pit
(with tyres and nails)

(Timber)

supply and drainage, together with the repair of wagons, weapons, tools, personal kit and artillery pieces required trained craftsmen with the appropriate workshop facilities, and stores for raw materials and both finished and partly finished articles. Such workshops have been recognised in auxiliary forts, within a variety of different types of building.

The most complete plan of an auxiliary workshop has been discovered at Oberstimm, on the Danube.[214] This timber building with a courtyard plan was constructed in the Claudian or Neronian period. It occupied the whole of the right *retentura*, almost encroaching upon the back of the rampart. The internal courtyard was surrounded by a porticus and in the centre lay a timber-lined water tank, supplied with fresh water by a timber-lined aqueduct, which entered the fort under the rear gate. A particularly large room lay in the north wing, which had an entrance onto the *via decumana*, with a well in one corner. The north-west corner of the building consisted of three rooms, in one of which was found a tile-built hearth. The adjacent room is of particular importance and interest, for within it lay a rectangular chamber, 4.4×3 metres, whose floor and walls had been constructed with clay bricks; the floor level of this chamber was sunk over a metre below the general ground surface. A fire had been lit in a depression in the centre of the floor, which had burnt the clay tiles here bright red. The excavator believed that this fire had been intended to dry or smoke rather than to burn fiercely, and the room is thought to have been a smoking room in which meat and fish could be preserved.[215] None of the other rooms retained any special characteristics. Evidence for ironworking on the site came from dozens of fragments of iron slag; the working of bronze, copper, tin and zinc on the premises is inferred from finds of crucibles, metal slag, and various small metal objects. The unusually large size of the *fabrica*, combined with the fact that the smoking room could preserve far more meat than could be consumed by the garrison of the fort alone, suggests that it may have been responsible for supplying preserved food, and probably also a large range of tools and equipment, to the garrisons of neighbouring forts further along the Danube.[216]

Workshops with similar groundplans are known from Wiesbaden in Upper Germany and Valkenburg in Lower Germany. At Wiesbaden a stone building with a courtyard plan occupied the whole of the space to the left of the *principia* in the central range. The courtyard had a massive water tank in the centre, 7.5×3 metres, and steps led down to the bottom, which was 2 metres deep; the walls were clay-lined and the floor was of *opus signinum*. A drainage trench led from the tank, under the building, and out through the nearest gate. Numerous rooms of many different sizes surrounded the courtyard; two of them retained traces of hypocausts, and in one was found a free-standing stone-built hearth, together with a layer of ash and charcoal, slag, crucible fragments and a lump of bronze, which identify it as a bronze workshop.[217] Similar in many respects is the timber courtyard building in

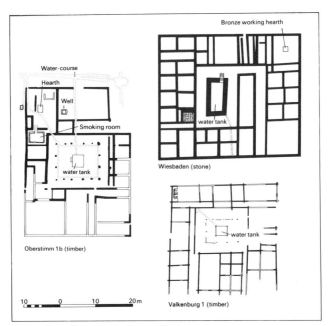

Bronze working hearth

Water-course

Hearth

Well

Smoking room

water tank

Oberstimm 1b (timber)

water tank

Wiesbaden (stone)

water tank

10   0   10   20m

Valkenburg 1 (timber)

140. Auxiliary workshops. Scale 1:1000

the right *praetentura* in the Claudian fort at Valkenburg.[218] Here too, in the centre of the courtyard, lay a timber-lined water tank, and in some of the small surrounding rooms were found traces of iron slag and hearths. A workshop of this type, with a water cistern in the courtyard is known from the Augustan legionary fortress at Haltern, and the discovery of several large timber-lined tanks within a courtyard building and its adjoining yard at the early first-century fort of Hofheim also points to an industrial function. Similar workshops may also have been found at Rottweil, Caernarfon, Baginton and Hod Hill.

In some forts long rectangular buildings have provided evidence for industrial activity and may also be identified as *fabricae*. At Benwell a stone building in the central range, next to the west gate, contained sweepings from a blacksmith's forge which were heaped against the wall, and a pile a coal which must have provided the fuel. A long narrow building at the Scottish fort of Crawford, sited next to the north-east gate, contained the remains of a stone-built hearth associated with a deep layer of wood ash and ironworking slag, and both iron slag and burnt clay debris were discovered in a similar building in the central range at Housesteads. Traces of a series of four buildings have been found at the Welsh fort of Pumsaint, whose actual plans and dimensions are unknown, which contained a total of six bowl furnaces. At Chesterholm only one corner of a possible workshop has been excavated, but the presence upon the floor of bracken and straw together with domestic and industrial waste suggests that it may have been a *fabrica*.

The waterlogged conditions of this site favoured the survival of organic material, and traces of urine and excreta found on the floor may indicate that tanning was carried out on the premises.

The U-shaped groundplan which has been detected amongst legionary workshops is known from only three auxiliary forts, at Gelligaer, Bearsden and South Shields, but unfortunately no evidence for industrial activity has been found within them and their precise function remains uncertain. Industrial activities may also have been carried out in less substantial buildings, often perhaps cut into the back of the rampart and sheltered by a lean-to roof. Behind the rampart at Pen Llystyn, on one side of the rear gate, lay a clay-lined tank, whilst in the vicinity an area of some 9 × 3 metres was covered in iron slag to a depth of at least 0.2 metres; its exact extent was not determined. No furnaces were found here, but there is a strong possibility that iron smelting was carried out, perhaps in a lean-to shed.

Of all the craftsmen employed in the military *fabrica* it is the activities of the blacksmith and the metalworker which are most likely to leave archaeological evidence, in the form of hearths, furnaces, water tanks, industrial waste, charcoal and finished products. Finds of iron and bronze objects from many sites, which are particularly numerous at Künzing and Newstead, show a wide variety and range: bronze studs and rivets, belt fittings, sheet vessels, straps and fastenings, helmets, armour, iron tools and weapons, hinges and bindings for gates and doors, window grilles, chains, bucket loops, padlocks and keys, horse bits and harness, wagon fittings, wheel tyres, etc., which may have been made, or at least repaired, in the *fabrica*.

Although more evidence of metalworking has been preserved, it was not the sole activity within the workshop, nor even necessarily the most important. Crafts and industrial processes which have left less tangible results on the ground can only be glimpsed fleetingly and imperfectly. The detection, for example, of what may be a meat smoking room at Oberstimm hints at the possibility that the preservation of much of the garrison's food within the *fabrica*, by smoking, salting or pickling, was more widespread than has previously been imagined.

In both stone and timber forts the carpenters and joiners would have been kept busy in the routine maintenance and repair of the gates and defences, the fort buildings with their internal fixtures and furniture and looking after the timber channels or pipes which often carried the water supply. The occasional discovery of wooden objects in waterlogged conditions, especially the finds from Bar Hill, Valkenburg, the Saalburg and Newstead, remind us of the wide range of objects which may have been constructed or repaired in the fort's workshops: they include wagon wheels and hubs, oak barrels and buckets, gates, pulley blocks and winding gear, and a variety of wooden handles for weapons and tools. The actual furniture of a carpenter's shop would have consisted mainly of timber saw benches and trestles, which do not survive, although woodworking is amply confirmed by the finding in many forts of iron tools including hammers, chisels, adzes, wedges, saws, knives and planes.

Leather was needed for a wide range of military equipment such as tents, waterproof sheets, shield coverings and horse harness as well as clothing and boots. Even when in permanent garrison the auxiliary unit took part in training manoeuvres in the field and therefore still required tents; fragments of leather tent panels have been found at Birdoswald, Valkenburg and Bar Hill, whilst iron tent pegs are known from Künzing. The forty-eight fragments of tenting from Bar Hill, on the Antonine Wall, did not represent the remains of just one or two tents which had been discarded, but many were offcuts showing secondary use and appear to be serviceable leather pieces suitable for patching which had been salvaged from larger worn panels; such scraps may well have been collected together in a *fabrica* store.[219] A considerable number of shoes and boots for men, women and children have been recovered from the ditches and pits of this fort, together with shield coverings, a leather satchel, and many other unidentified scraps.[220]

There is evidence for tanners within the legionary ranks, but whether tanning was actually carried out in the auxiliary forts is unknown.[221] The process would have required tanks to contain the tanning agents, drying racks for the hides, and a plentiful supply of water. Organic deposits found on the floor of the presumed *fabrica* at Chesterholm, which were preserved under a thick layer of clay, yielded thousands of leather objects, both complete and fragmentary. They were mostly ox hide, although there were a few items of deer or pigskin. The presence of urine and excreta within this deposit suggests that tanning was carried out here, and this possibility is reinforced by the discovery of several half-moon scrapers and combs which still retained strands of cattle hair.[222] Outside this *fabrica*, on the edge of the rampart street, lay an old wooden gate which may have served as the base for a tanning tank.

It is clear from the discovery of leatherworking tools such as awls, knives and scrapers that leatherworking and repairs were carried out within the auxiliary fort. It appears, though, that supplies of leather requisitioned from legionary stores, together with offcuts and pieces cut from unserviceable equipment (such as the bundle of tent leather from Bar Hill) may usually have provided sufficient stocks for the auxiliary leatherworker without his actually tanning hides on the premises.

Storebuildings

Extensive storage facilities would have been required within the fort to accommodate the wide range of the garrison's equipment and provisions, but these buildings are extremely difficult to identify on the ground.

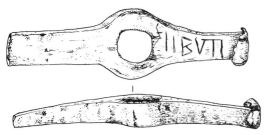

141. Hammerhead from Bar Hill, on the Antonine Wall, engraved >IIBVTI, 'belonging to the century of Ebutius'

Vegetius tells us that 'the magazines must be stored with iron, steel and coals, to make arms, together with wood proper for spears and arrows',[223] and storage space for these raw materials must have been allocated either within the *fabrica* itself, or in a separate building. It seems probable that some at least of the numerous small rooms within the large courtyard *fabricae* would have served as stores for both raw materials and finished items. Whether all the necessary equipment was housed inside the fort or whether more bulky items such as building materials, firewood, food and bedding for cavalry mounts and baggage animals etc., was stored outside, either in the adjacent civilian settlements or within defended annexes, is unknown.

Secure locked stores would have been needed inside the fort for weapons and tools. A hammerhead found at Bar Hill was engraved with the inscription >IIBVTI, 'belonging to the century of Ebutius', which suggests that the century may have been responsible for the security and storage of its own equipment and tools, perhaps in the barrack block, or in a specific area allocated within a larger store building.[224] At the Claudian fort of Valkenburg a detached building was appended to each centurial barrack, apparently providing the workshops and storage facilities (*fabriculae*) for each century (Ill. 132).[225] Two of these buildings housed treadmill tracks, and in the corner of another were found three rows of posts, which probably supported a raised floor for the storage of grain and other foodstuffs. Fire pits rather than hearths were provided, and the doorways were particularly wide to enable wagons to be driven in.

Storebuildings have occasionally been identified from finds made within them. At Hod Hill a tool store was recognised in the *praetentura* from the tools, still in good condition, found inside and at Pen Llystyn the recovery of three samian vessels, which had been broken *in situ*, from a rectangular timber building in the *praetentura* suggested to the excavator that they may have been part of a consignment of pottery in storage there.[226] Generally, however, it is necessary to rely on the groundplan of the building to give a clue to its function, a method which is particularly difficult when dealing with stores. A building with a distinctive groundplan consisting of two rows of equal-sized rooms flanking a central corridor, has been found in the central range at several forts, and has usually been interpreted as a hospital, but comparison with the plans of storebuildings in both Ostia and Rome and

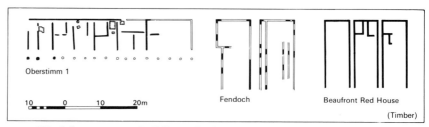

Oberstimm 1

10   0   10   20m

Fendoch

Beaufront Red House

(Timber)

142. Workshops or storebuildings. Scale 1:1000

the evidence from one example which was associated with metalworking, suggests that they were probably workshops or stores. Within this type of building each century or *turma* may have had an equal amount of storage space allocated, although not necessarily a room each.

Narrow timber sheds with no front wall, which may either have been completely open or closed by wide gates, are known at Fendoch, Birdoswald and the works or supply depot at Red House, Corbridge. At Oberstimm an open-fronted building lay in the *praetentura* fronting the *via principalis*, with a portico alongside it. It contained at least eight rooms, all apparently open to the street, which were subdivided at the rear; large pits were found in several of these rear rooms. These open-fronted buildings are usually identified as either workshops, stores or wagon sheds. The Oberstimm example is similar in many respects to the long rows of small square rooms which often lined the main streets of legionary fortresses. These were known as *tabernae*, and are thought to have fulfilled a similar function, as baggage stores or wagon sheds, or possibly accommodation for legionary cavalry.[227]

Storebuildings of a different type lay in the central range at Old Kilpatrick, with their floors raised above ground upon individual postholes, similar to granaries, to keep the contents dry. At Caernarfon a buttressed stone building, resembling a stone granary but without a raised floor or ventilators, was partially excavated next to the rear gate, and was considered to have been used as a store for weapons, artillery or perhaps animal fodder. In some forts the weapon store (*armamentarium*) was housed in rooms flanking the courtyard in the *principia*, and in others a separate building was provided. At Buch, in Raetia, an *armamentarium* may have been situated behind the north rampart, for here were found over 800 spearheads, associated with a fragmentary stone wall which ran parallel with and seven metres behind the defensive wall. It is probable that many of the long rectangular buildings which frequently flanked the main streets, in both the front and rear sections of the fort, were storebuildings also, although their internal arrangements are usually so fragmentary and their groundplans so unremarkable that a precise identification is impossible.

Other Internal Buildings

Gyrus—vivarium?

The eastern defences of the Neronian fort at Baginton were forced to follow an unusually sinuous course in order to enclose a circular timber-fenced arena within the *retentura*, a structure which is quite unique within an auxiliary fort. The arena was 34 metres in diameter and its floor, which had been cut into the gravel subsoil to a depth of some 0.8 metres, had been carefully excavated to provide an almost completely level surface. Around the perimeter ran a palisade trench, and behind it was spaced at regular intervals a row of fifty semi-circular uprights, which were recessed into the gravel subsoil. These timbers would have supported a horizontal timber frame clad with vertical planks, whose bases were located in the palisade trench. The stockade fence is estimated to have stood 2.3 metres high above the internal floor level. The entrance lay on the north-west side, close to the rear of the *principia*, and consisted of a single gate which was approached from the outside by a timber-lined passage, terminating in a second gateway; the floor of the passage sloped gradually, providing a ramp up to ground level. Within the arena all that remained of the original floor surface was a patch of gravel in the centre. In the north-east sector were found six clay pads, defining a rectangular area of some 6×3 metres, which may represent the bases of free-standing posts. There was no evidence for any internal roof supports and so the area is assumed to have been open.

As no comparable structure has ever been found within a Roman fort its purpose remains uncertain. The circular shape suggests a training ring for cavalry (*gyrus*), and probably also for men, such as those described by Classical authors, including Arrian and Xenophon.[228] On the other hand, the provision of an entrance passage with gates at both ends suggests that security, and perhaps a close control of animals was desired. This has prompted alternative interpretations, that the arena was perhaps a *vivarium* where wild animals were collected for the amphitheatre, or a stockade to

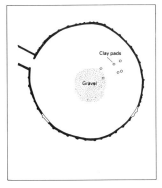

143. Plan of the *gyrus-vivarium* at The Lunt, Baginton, Warwickshire. Scale 1:1000

144. The *gyrus-vivarium* at The Lunt, Baginton, excavated in 1971. The recesses for timber posts are visible around the perimeter, with the entrance on the left.

house prisoners of war or hostages. Trajan's Column shows several circular structures built in turf and timber which may provide parallels, one of which contained buildings or tents, but no traces of internal buildings were found in the Baginton arena. On present evidence it seems most probable that it served as a *gyrus* for the training of horses, and probably their riders also.[229]

Special accommodation

In the central range at Corbridge, Pen Llystyn and Housesteads stood long rectangular buildings, with regular internal partitions, which closely resemble barrack blocks. At Pen Llystyn there were ten equal-sized rooms fronted by a verandah, with a larger room at one end; burnt patches on the floors of two of the rooms probably indicate the positions of hearths. At Corbridge only a few partition walls survived, but judging from their spacing there would have been ten rooms here also, and at Housesteads the few rooms examined were of similar size, but their exact number is unknown. Their similarity to barrack blocks, and the presence of hearths at Pen Llystyn, suggests that they provided residential accommodation, although prisons or hospitals have also been proposed. The term 'administrative block' has been used to describe them, on the assumption that they probably housed men working nearby, administrative clerks from the *principia* or the granary, members of the commander's private staff, or possibly hospital orderlies.[230]

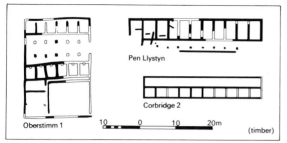

145. Miscellaneous internal buildings. Scale 1:1000

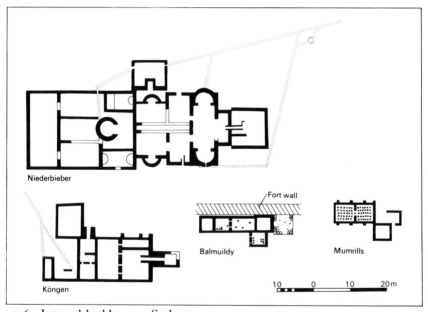

146. Internal bathhouses. Scale 1:1000

Other special accommodation may be seen at Oberstimm in the Claudian period, where a timber building in the *retentura* provided two ranges of six small rooms flanking a colonnaded courtyard. Several of the rooms had well preserved hearths, and therefore appear to have been used as living rooms. To the south side of the building was attached a complex of three large rooms with a courtyard beyond. This accommodation may have housed the various craftsmen and workers who were employed in the nearby *fabrica*.

Internal bathhouses

Whilst it was customary to build legionary baths (*thermae*) inside the fortress the auxiliary bathhouse was normally sited outside the fort, and only exceptionally were internal baths provided. They were often simple three- or four-roomed structures comprising the basic cold, warm and hot rooms with a latrine, built against the back of the rampart, as in the Antonine Wall forts of Bar Hill and Balmuildy, or standing independently, as at Cadder or Mumrills. These Scottish examples were often supplemented by a more extensive bathhouse in an adjoining defended annexe. Occasionally they were built on a much grander scale, as seen in the German Antonine forts of Köngen and Welzheim-West, or the elaborate bathing establishment at the late second-century fort of Niederbieber. Internal baths have also been discovered in the *praetentura* of the Welsh auxiliary forts of Brecon Gaer and Caernarfon. In both these cases they were not original, but are believed to have been added for the convenience of a caretaker force when the garrison was reduced, and built in part of the fort where barrack space was no longer required.

6   Food and the Water Supply

The Military Diet

One of the basic constituents of the military diet was corn (*frumentum*).
Polybius, writing in c. 140 BC, gives details of the grain allowances of both
legionary and auxiliary soldiers, and actual receipts for supplies which
specify the monthly grain ration of individual soldiers have occasionally
survived, preserved upon papyri and *ostraca*, mainly from Egypt and Syria.
These sources suggest that the daily grain ration for each man was
approximately 1 kilogram.[1] Large quantities of charred wheat and barley
have been discovered in several fort granaries.[2] Barley (*hordeum*) was
normally fed only to horses, or issued in place of wheat as a punishment,[3]
but on a stores list preserved on writing tablets from Chesterholm it is
mentioned several times. (This list was written in the month of June, and
may reflect an unusual situation at the end of the season where wheat was
not yet available and so the garrison was forced to eat barley.)[4] The grain
was milled and then baked into bread or made into pasta or porridge dishes;
a recipe for the type of wholemeal bread baked by the troops is given by
Cato.[5] On campaign a form of iron rations made from corn, known as
buccellatum, was issued.

The grain supply was secured mainly by requisition from civilian sources
and from land owned, or leased, by the army itself. Each legion had land
allocated to it around the fortress, often extending for several miles (known
as the *territorium* or *prata*), but how it was organised is unknown. The
military may have taken part in growing crops or raising animals there or
leased it to tenant farmers in return for a proportion of the crop. The
auxiliaries also had their own lands, as is shown by a fragmentary
inscription, dated AD 216, from Chester-le-Street in Co. Durham, which
mentions the *territorium* of an unnamed *ala*, although we have no further
information about their extent or organisation.[6]

Despite the impression given by Julius Caesar that the army subsisted
solely upon corn and ate meat only in emergencies, it is clear from both
documentary and archaeological evidence that the military diet was much
more varied and included a wide range of meat and vegetables.[7] Vegetius
recommended that the troops 'should have corn, wine, vinegar and even

salt, in plenty at all times', and a document from Pselcis acknowledges the receipt by a cavalryman of a *cohors equitata* of 'lentils, salt and vinegar'.[8] In the permanent fort the basic diet probably included corn, bacon, cheese, lard, vegetables, sour wine, salt and olive oil, and it was for these commodities presumably that fixed amounts were deducted (*ad victum*) from the soldiers' pay.[9] These basic rations could be supplemented either by buying extras or by writing home with requests for particular items. Upon the stores list found at Chesterholm some of the entries had the words *per privatum* against them, suggesting that some foods had been ordered specially by individuals to supplement their rations, and letters, written on *ostraca*, thanking relatives for parcels of food have been found at Wâdi Faŵakhir in Egypt.[10]

Vegetius details the provisions to be taken inside the city or fort in times of siege:

> Hogs and all other animals that cannot be kept alive within the place, are to be salted, that the bread may hold out longer by the distribution of the flesh. All sorts of poultry may be kept without any great expense, and are very necessary for the use of the sick . . . Wine, vinegar, grain and fruits of all kinds must be provided in abundance.[11]

Analysis of animal bones from fort sites gives a clear indication of the quantity of meat eaten, the types of animals, and the joints preferred.[12] The stores list from Chesterholm gives details of items which were dispensed in a period of only eight days, and amongst the meat issued was mutton, pork, beef, goat, young pig, ham and venison. A possible meat smoking room found in the workshop at Oberstimm shows that meat may often have been preserved in this way, a process which is also confirmed by an examination of the bones found at Valkenburg.[13]

Other items on the Chesterholm list were fish sauce, pork fat, spices, salt, vintage wine (*vinum*), sour wine (*acetum*) and Celtic beer (*cervesa*); the quantities of wine involved were often very large—for example on June 22nd 73 *modii* (146 gallons) were dispensed to the garrison.[14] Sour wine was commonly drunk by soldiers, who often watered it down to form a drink known as *posca*. An amphora from Newstead had the word *vinum* scratched on the handle to identify its contents, and graffiti on amphorae from Chester record wine 'spiced and flavoured, vintage; for store cupboard . . .' and from Mumrills 'sweet wine', whilst a flagon from Wallsend had contained 'honey sweetened wine'.[15] Amphora fragments are commonly found within forts, although they did not all necessarily contain wine; an amphora at the legionary fortress at Vindonissa had contained honey and another beans, and an example from Brough-on-Noe had probably been filled with plums.[16] Oil and fish sauces were also transported and stored in amphorae. Olive oil or oil of radishes were mainly used for cooking, but other oils were used extensively for lighting, and as an equivalent of soap in the bathhouse. A

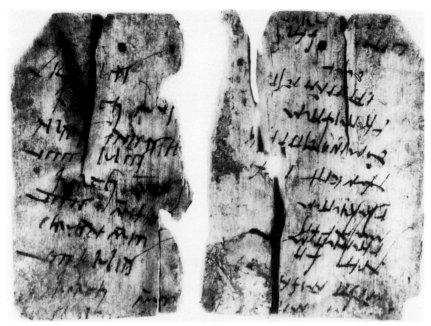

147. A stores list preserved on a wooden writing tablet, from Chesterholm-
Vindolanda, in Northumberland. (Vindolanda writing tablet, no. 33)

large variety of fruits and nuts were represented from pips and kernels
discovered at Vindonissa and the Saalburg, and fish bones, abundant oyster
shells and vegetable remains have been recorded from a large number of
Roman military sites.[17]

Preparation and Cooking

Documents, inscriptions and archaeological finds provide little information
about the organisation of the catering and cooking for a garrison of 500 to
1000 men. Neither Paternus nor Vegetius include cooks or kitchen orderlies
among their lists of legionary *immunes*, and kitchen duties are not mentioned
in any of the surviving duty rosters.[18] The official military personnel
responsible for the acquisition of grain and other provisions and the
paperwork involved in such transactions are, however, recorded in many
receipts and lists, as are receipts for grain signed by individual soldiers, but
there is no clear evidence as to where the grain was milled, the rations
prepared and cooked, or where they were eaten.

Catering for the entire garrison would have required a central millhouse,
bakery, kitchen and dining facilities, each presumably with their own staffs.
Only one example of a general purpose, large-scale bakehouse and kitchen

149. Suggested reconstruction of a corn mill from Zugmantel, housed in the Saalburg Museum. (Only the millstones, vertical drive shaft and pinion were found, the rest is conjectural.)

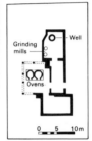

148. The bakehouse a Stockstadt, in U Germany. Scale

has so far been discovered in an auxiliary fort, at Stockstadt in Upper Germany. It stood in the left *retentura* bordering the rampart street. Three of the rooms were stone-built, and the fourth was enclosed by timber posts which had supported wattle and daub walls. This room contained a stone foundation on which stood two circular ovens built with red tiles; many were stamped by the garrison, the *cohors III Aquitanorum*. An adjacent room still retained patches of its paved floor, and was littered with wall plaster, roof tiles and numerous pottery sherds. At the opposite end of the building lay what is thought to have been the mill room; here stood a stone foundation supporting the bases of two hand grinding mills, and a stone-lined well had been dug in one corner.

Herodian, describing the emperor Caracalla in camp, states that 'He ate the bread that was available; with his own hand he would grind his personal ration of corn, make it into a loaf, bake it in the ashes, and eat it',[19] and if every soldier acted similarly we should perhaps be looking not for a central mill and bakehouse, but rather a large number of small grinding querns and ovens. It seems more probable, however, that in the permanent fort each century, rather than each individual, was responsible for grinding its own grain and for its own baking ovens. Classical references and surviving receipts do refer to a 'daily' or 'monthly' grain ration per man, but this may have been a purely theoretical allocation; it is extremely unlikely that 500 or 1000 men had to queue up outside the granary daily, or even monthly, to receive his ration. It would have been far more convenient for a measured quantity appropriate to a century, or a smaller unit, to be collected by one or two men either daily, weekly or monthly, to be distributed amongst their fellow soldiers upon their return to the barracks. If the grain was collected in sacks or baskets of 50 kilograms weight (a convenient lifting and handling size for a grain sack), eleven or twelve sacks per week would suffice for each century.

Evidence for the allocation of supplies to specific centuries has been found at Nanstallon, where part of the handle of an amphora, found in a barrack block, was incised with the graffito]XIIII〉A, meaning '14: Century of A...'[20] This amphora may have contained wine, oil, or perhaps fish sauce for the century. The involvement of the century as a unit with its own cooking activities may be seen in the discovery of a bronze saucepan (*patera*) handle found at Saham Toney in Norfolk, which carries the inscription: ⊃PRIMI, 'the century of Primus'.[21] Each century would have required storage space for cooking and baking utensils, and stores for provisions, perhaps within the barrack block or in a separate storebuilding. Evidence for the milling, drying and storage of grain within centurial barracks has come from the detached 'end buildings' of the barracks at Valkenburg, and three parallel wall trenches in an end room in a barrack at Oberstimm may have supported a raised floor for the storage of foodstuffs.[22]

Millstones which bear the inscriptions of individual centuries are known from the forts of Greatchesters, Wiesbaden and Straubing, and the legionary fortress of Mainz.[23] At the Saalburg a reconstruction has been made of the type of mill from which these stones may have come.[24] In this type, known as a 'slave' mill, a large handle on a horizontal axis was turned to drive geared millstones on a vertical axis at a higher speed, similar in principle to the water mill described by Vitruvius.[25] With this machine four or six men could grind the 100 kilograms of grain needed daily by a century in one hour.[26] Alternatively, an animal may have been used to drive a vertical shaft, connected at a higher level to the geared mill.[27] Traces of possible millhouses have been found at the base of the northern rampart of the Antonine fort at Chesterholm. A row of four circular stone structures opened onto an alley, and there was a similar building opposite. The floors were flagged, and debris inside showed that their roofs had been tiled.[28]

The forts of Newstead and the Saalburg have both yielded large and small millstones. Amongst the hundred stones found at the Saalburg were large stones (diameter 66–81 cm) thought to have belonged to centurial mills, and smaller examples (diameter 35–43 cm), one of which bore the inscription: 'Con (tubernium) Brittonis',[29] which confirms that they were issued to each *contubernium*. Preparing bread flour for the military loaf (*panis militaris*) is a long and relatively specialised process, whilst simple cereal foods such as porridge are quick and easy, and so it seems quite probable that part of the grain ration was allocated to the *contubernia* for this purpose, and the remainder allotted to the centurial mill and bakery which prepared bread for the whole century.

Within the legion each century was responsible for the preparation and baking of its own loaves, which is shown by a bread stamp found at Mainz. This bore the name of the legion and also the name of a particular century

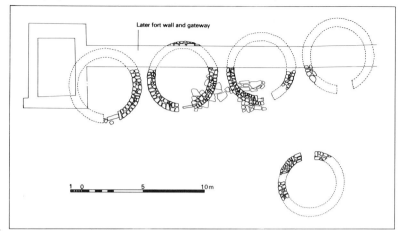

150. Circular structures, possibly millhouses, found close to the north rampart at Chesterholm-Vindolanda, in Northumberland.

151. Small millstone found at the Saalburg, bearing the inscription: Con (tubernium) Brittonis. (*CIL* XIII 11954a.)

and three individuals, probably the bakers, together with the number five, which may have been the number of the oven used.[30] Similarly, the discovery in the auxiliary fort at Fendoch of five ovens, set into the back of the rampart, each at the end of a barrack block, suggests that each oven served one century; the excavator supposed that every *contubernium* took turns on a rota to cook the daily rations.[31] The best preserved oven here consisted of a circular stone-paved floor surrounded by a low stone wall, which had originally been roofed with a dome of rough stones packed with clay; at other sites they may have been of clay fired over a wickerwork former. A small hob lay in front of two of the ovens. They were heated by placing burning fuel inside. When the required temperature was reached the ashes were raked out, the bread was inserted, and the door tightly closed until cooked.[32] A long handled wooden shovel for placing loaves into an oven is preserved in the Saalburg museum.

Ovens similar in construction, sited either in the *intervallum* or actually cut into the back of the rampart have been found at many forts. At Birrens, in the Antonine period, a well preserved oven of the same size as the Fendoch examples was discovered behind the eastern rampart. Its stone walls survived over half a metre high, and part of the original clay dome had collapsed and fallen onto the floor. A stone wall revetted the rampart at this point, creating what was perhaps an enclosed oven yard.[33]

At Pen Llystyn a space of some three metres in width between the base of the rampart and the edge of the rampart street had been raised slightly above the road level with two or three layers of clay and gravel, capped with clay. Upon this 'platform', which ran all around the perimeter of the fort, lay several ovens and a few small pits. At the west angle stood a group of three larger ovens, each with a stone base; a mass of clay had fallen from their domes. Between these ovens and the rear of the rampart ran a timber slot showing that there had originally been an associated timber structure, perhaps no more than a lean-to shed or a windbreak. Two other types of oven were found at this fort: some with large cobbled platforms and others, smaller in size, with clay bases. It is probable that the three large well-built ovens served as an 'official' bakery for the century, with the smaller ovens perhaps catering for individuals or small groups.[34]

Occasionally single ovens or groups were enclosed with timber or stone walls. These 'cookhouses' have been found at the legionary fortress of Caerleon, and at the Saalburg, where at least fifty ovens had been cut into the rampart of the mid second-century fort; one of the groups was enclosed by a row of timber posts running along the front, which may have supported an open shed with a pent-roof. At Caerhun also, rectangular stone buildings,

152. A well preserved stone-built oven, found at the rear of the east rampart at the Antonine fort of Birrens, Dumfries and Galloway.

or fragments of stone walling, found at the back of the rampart in association with ovens may have been cookhouses.[35]

Josephus says that 'Each man does not have the right to have his dinner or breakfast at whatever time he wishes, but they all eat together',[36] but it is uncertain whether the meals were taken communally in a large refectory, or in smaller groups. No fort building has ever been described as a dining room, and it would be virtually impossible to identify such a building from the archaeological remains. On present evidence therefore, it seems that each *contubernium* probably dined together in their own quarters, as each appears to have had its own crockery and mess utensils. For example, a *mortarium* waster from the Neronian fortress of Usk had a graffito scratched on its rim showing that it was the 'mixing bowl for the *contubernium* of Messor', and fragments of two samian dishes, found at Valkenburg and Utrecht, bore graffiti referring to a *contubernium*.[37]

The Water Supply

A plentiful and pure water supply was a prime consideration in the choice of a fort site. Vegetius advised that 'The water must be wholesome and not marshy. Bad water is a kind of poison and the cause of epidemic distempers'.[38] The garrison required a considerable quantity of fresh water, for it has been calculated that 2.5 litres were needed per man each day for drinking and cooking. In addition, supplies were necessary for the cavalry mounts and baggage animals, and for the supply of the bathhouse, latrines, workshops and the commander's house.[39] The risk of fire to closely spaced buildings, especially in a timber fort, would also have demanded that an adequate water supply should be at hand.

Ideally a fort would have incorporated a spring within its defences for, as Vegetius observed, 'perpetual springs within the walls are of the utmost advantage' but 'where Nature has denied this convenience, wells must be sunk, however deep, till you come to water, which must be drawn up by ropes', and the architect Vitruvius also describes the need to dig wells in the absence of running water.[40] Wells have been found in most forts where the water table was reasonably close to the surface, and a well was a common feature in the courtyard of the *principia*. Three principal methods of well construction were used: they were either rock-cut, timber-lined, or revetted with mortared or drystone walling. At the Saalburg at least ninety-nine wells were dug inside the fort and its adjacent civilian settlement, and here all three types of well were represented, although timber-lined examples were the most common. The waterlogged conditions at the bottom of some of these wells have preserved not only information about the methods of construction and the timbers used in the linings, but also examples of the buckets, the rollers from the wooden winding gear, and even fragments of

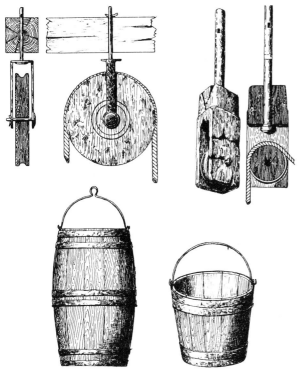

153. Buckets and
winding gear
preserved in
wells at the
Saalburg, Upper
Germany.

the hemp ropes which had drawn the buckets to the surface.[41] From these
finds it has been possible to reconstruct a drawing well at this site.

Another method of lifting water, which may have been used where the
water table was high, was the *tolleno*, a device described by the poet Martial
in the first century AD for watering his garden, in which a bucket on one end
of a pivoting pole was lowered into the well. This pole would normally have
been a pine tree or tapering tree trunk which gave sufficient elasticity and
counterbalance weight to lift the bucket when full and return it to the
surface.[42] A crane described by Vegetius to lift men onto the top of a wall
during an attack is of similar design: 'The crane is a large post fixed firmly in
the ground, with a long transverse beam on top so exactly poised that one
end sinking the other rises of course'.[43] The only evidence for such an
arrangement which would be preserved on the ground would be the
postholes of the two upright timbers supporting the beam, placed at some
distance from the well itself. Alternatively it is possible that pumps, such as
those found at Silchester and Sablon, Metz, were used.[44]

Waterlogged conditions at the Saalburg and Krefeld-Gellep have
preserved details of their timber well linings which show a variety of
constructional techniques. Shafts were dug with either square or rectangular planked linings, usually of oak, which varied in internal width

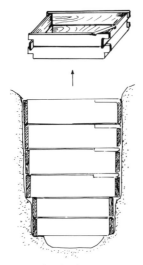

154. Timber well construction: a common type of well lining, based on an example found at the Saalburg.

from 0.8 metres at both sites up to 2.2 metres at the Saalburg.[45] Here several wells still retained the timbers of a square box-like lining of planks stacked on top of one another, with each plank notched and locked into its neighbours at the ends. Rigidity was provided by one or more internal diagonal timber braces, which also served as a ladder for repair and inspection purposes. The upper part of a well at Krefeld-Gellep had a square framework of horizontal oak planks, with their ends mitred to fit each other exactly; they were secured vertically by a pair of grooves and tenons in the upper and lower sides of each plank. The lower part of this well was lined with a barrel, its eighteen vertical oak staves fixed by pegs and external iron bands; this transition from an upper square to a lower circular barrel shaft has often been found elsewhere.

Another method of well construction at Krefeld-Gellep had a square timber upright at each corner of the shaft into which was mortised a framework of timber strengtheners at regular intervals. Upon the outside of this framework oak planks were fixed. Similar wells were also found at Künzing and Oberstimm. At both these sites the timbers had decayed, but the impressions of the four corner posts and the lines of planking behind were detected from the presence of darker soil which had fallen from above into the voids left in the ground when the timbers rotted. Stone-lined wells, with either mortared or drystone construction, are known from many sites, and occur often in the *principia* courtyard, such as at Bar Hill or Birrens.

In forts built upon impenetrable bedrock, or where a shallow water-table prevented the sinking of wells, water was supplied either by an aqueduct or pipeline from an external source, or by the collection and storage of rainwater in tanks. Recent excavations have contributed a great deal of information about the water supply to the fort at Oberstimm, on the

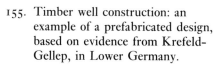

155. Timber well construction: an example of a prefabricated design, based on evidence from Krefeld-Gellep, in Lower Germany.

156. The impression of postholes and timbers commonly found in wells where the well timbers themselves have disappeared.

Danube. Surprisingly, despite its low-lying situation, the fort obtained its water originally not from wells, as was the case in a later period of occupation, but from a timber-lined aqueduct. Water was channelled in a timber walled and roofed conduit set in a clay-packed trench c. 0.6 metres deep and up to 1 metre broad. The supply was laid on from the very beginning of the site's occupation, preceding the construction of most of the principal buildings, and was probably required to provide water to mix daub for the timber-framed structures. By the time the fort was operational this channel had been replaced by another similar one, which ran from the rear gate up the centre of the *via decumana* and from here distributed the supply all over the fort: branches were provided on either side of the commander's house, and another fed a timber-lined water cistern in the courtyard of the workshop (*fabrica*). A pit almost 3 metres square, which was found in the *via quintana* probably represents a distribution chamber to provide access for cleaning and inspection. In the Roman period the nearest source of water was the stream known as the Brautlach, which lay approximately 70 metres from the rear gate. To obtain a supply of running water it would have been necessary to channel it from this stream, but to supply the timber aqueduct over this distance the water would have to have been raised some 3 metres. As this would have presented difficulties, the use of a water wheel (*antlia*), similar to the example described by Vitruvius, has been suggested.[46] This wheel would have been turned by the motion of the current, having jars or buckets attached which filled with water when immersed at the lowest point of the wheel's travel, and emptied at the top, into the aqueduct.

The provision or restoration of the fort aqueduct is often recorded by an inscription; most date to the first quarter of the third century, a period which saw an increase in such projects. At Caernarfon the aqueduct was restored in AD 198–209 for the *cohors I Suniciorum*, and a new water supply was provided at Chester-le-Street in AD 216, at South Shields in AD 222, and at Chesters probably at the same time.[47] Three inscriptions from altars dedicated to the nymphs of the aqueduct, found in the commander's house at Burgkastell, Öhringen, chart the fortunes of the fort aqueduct.[48] The first in the sequence, dated AD 187, records the construction of the aqueduct by a centurion of *legio VIII Augusta Commoda* 'quod aqua non esset' (because there was no water available). On July 23rd AD 231 the commander of the garrison, *cohors I Belgarum*, celebrated the inauguration of a new aqueduct, and only a decade later it was rebuilt 'multo tempore intermissum' (after it had been interrupted for some), possibly by the incursions of the Alamanni across the frontier in AD 233. The commanding officer at this time (December 4th AD 241) stated that he had restored the aqueduct 5907 Roman feet in length because he wished to supply running water to the *praetorium* and the bathhouse.

The aqueduct which supplied the fort of Greatchesters carried water from the Haltwhistle Burn two and a quarter miles away in a channel 1 metre deep. In order to maintain the correct levels it had to be cut into the sides of several hills, and was forced to travel a circuitous route of six miles; how the water was distributed when it reached the fort is unknown.[49] A section of the aqueduct supplying the fort of the British fleet (*Classis Britannica*) at Dover, at the north-west corner, comprised an open channel which distributed water in both timber and clay pipes.[50] The supply usually entered the fort beneath the road metalling of a gate portal, and may have flowed into a distribution or delivery chamber before being piped or channelled into the interior. At Brough-on-Noe the aqueduct, which entered under the rear gate, led to a stone trough, carved from a single block of millstone grit, lying immediately inside the gateway. This trough had two outlets, one to a stone-built conduit, and the other with a circular hole, probably for a lead-piped supply; unfortunately all remains of the water system beyond this point had been destroyed. Branches from the main supply would have fed the *fabrica*, the *praetorium*, the latrines, and perhaps a water tank in the *principia*, and occasionally water tanks and troughs have been found amongst the barracks and stables.

Vitruvius describes three methods of conveying water, by masonry channels (*per canales stuctiles*), lead pipes (*fistulis plumbeis*), or earthenware pipes (*tubulis fictilibus*), and Pliny mentions also water pipes made from leather or hollowed from tree trunks, especially pine, fir or alder.[51]

Examples of all these methods, with the exception of leather pipes, are known within auxiliary forts. Legionary fortresses were usually supplied by lead water mains, and in auxiliary forts also lead pipes served the bathhouses at the Saalburg, Kapersburg and Zugmantel, and pipes from Wiesbaden were stamped by *legio XIIII Gem Mart V*.[52] The dangers of lead poisoning were well known to Classical authors, however, and earthen pipes were considered to be more healthy. Pliny gives the optimum thickness of such a pipe as 2 digits (c. 38 mm) and recommends that the joints between them should have a large overlap and be well cemented; clay pipes such as these are known from Dover, Jagsthausen and Marköbel.[53]

At Zugmantel part of a timber pipeline was preserved in waterlogged ground. It was constructed in two halves from hollowed-out tree trunks and the sides were supported with wooden posts and boards. On both the east and west sides of the fort at Feldberg, at a distance on each side of approximately 18 metres was a timber-lined spring which fed a timber pipeline (the pipes were 2 metres long, 20 cm thick and 12 cm wide); their junctions were bound with iron rings, and similar iron rings mark the original course of a timber pipeline at Kapersburg. A short length of wooden water pipe was

157. One of three inscriptions found at Ohringen, in Upper Germany, which refer to the fort aqueduct. Dated December 4th AD 241 it reads:

Nymphis perennibus aquam Gordianam coh(ors) I Sep(timia) Belg(arum) Gordi[ana]e multo tempor[e intermi]ssam sub cu[ra ... ani consularis] C. Jul(ius) Rog[atianus eques Romanus] praef(ectus) coh(ortis) ei[(usdem) novo aqu] ae d [ucto] pe[r pe] des VDCC[CCVII quod] alere in[stituit iuges puteos] in prae[(torii) ...]s et in bal[(ineo)] dedicata pr(idie) non(as) dec(embres) imp(eratore) d(omino) n(ostro) Gordiano Aug(usto) II et Pompeiano co(n)s(ulibus)

'To the everlasting nymphs, the Roman knight Caius Julius Rogatianus, prefect of the First Cohort of Belgians, bearing the titles Septimiana Gordiana, under the command of the governor ... anus, has rebuilt the Gordian aqueduct, after it had been in disrepair for some time, through a new aqueduct over a distance of 5.907 feet, because he wanted to feed the flowing waters into the commander's house and to the baths. It was dedicated on December 4th in the second consulship of the Emperor, our Lord, Gordianus Augustus, and of Pompeianus'

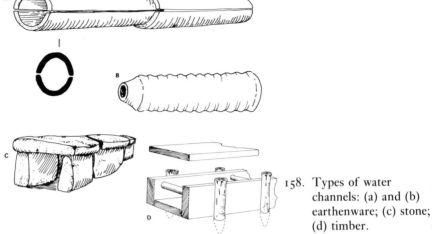

158. Types of water channels: (a) and (b) earthenware; (c) stone; (d) timber.

also discovered in the *via praetoria* at Pen Llystyn. The pipe was square in section, and was set in a construction trench which had been backfilled with gravel; the top was covered by road metalling. At distances of approximately 8 metres the trench was enlarged by rectangular pits (1.2 × 0.9 metres) which probably represent the junctions of pipes or inspection chambers (Ill. 190). Timber-lined channels, similar to those found at Oberstimm, are also known from Zugmantel, where they consisted of oak planks set upon their sides and strengthened externally with timber stakes and internally with regularly spaced cross timbers. These prevented the walls from collapsing and supported the timber-planked roof. The channels were placed in trenches and covered either by timber planks, or by additional layers of metalling where they underlay roads or the walls of buildings. Stone-built channels were also often used, roofed with flat stone slabs, as seen at Birrens or High Rochester.

Vitruvius describes a process of filtering water by passing it through a succession of settling tanks:

> If the cisterns are double or treble, so that they can be charged by percolation, they will make the supply of water much more wholesome. For when the sediment has a place to settle in, the water will be more limpid and will keep a flavour unaccompanied by smell. If not, salt must be added to purify it.[54]

This method of filtration was used at Benwell, where part of a massive masonry tank was discovered in the *principia* courtyard. It was 3.1 metres wide internally and 0.6 metres deep, with an excavated length of 7.6 metres, and contained at least five settling chambers (Ill. 159). The water overflowed from one settling tank to another and then into a distribution chamber, where it was aerated by being passed through circular ducts in the

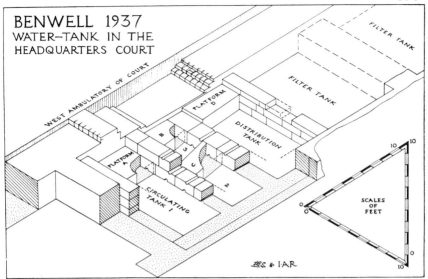

BENWELL 1937
WATER–TANK IN THE
HEADQUARTERS COURT

FILTER TANK

WEST AMBULATORY OF COURT

PLATFORM D

FILTER TANK

DISTRIBUTION TANK

PLATFORM A

B

3

C

2

CIRCULATING TANK 1

SCALES OF FEET

10   10

0   0

10

J.B.S. & I.A.R.

159. The water-settling tank in the courtyard of the *principia* at Benwell, on Hadrian's Wall.

walls, which were placed at three different heights; platforms were built in the last three chambers to enable water to be drawn off. It was by this process that the water, which had travelled at least three miles by way of a rather sluggish gradient, was aerated and regained its sparkle.[55]

Water tanks have often been found standing quite independently, seemingly without any water conduit. Some may have been intended to collect rainwater from the roofs of adjacent buildings, which was recommended by several Classical authors; they would have provided extra water for washing, fire fighting and drinking troughs for animals.[56] It is unlikely that any fort relied solely upon the collection of rainwater in storage tanks to provide the necessary water, even in Britain. Where a number of stone tanks is known, as for example at Housesteads, there is evidence that they were fed by a constant running water supply, either in stone channels or pipes. Three tanks (associated with an adjacent latrine) lay in the south-east corner of the fort, another was built against the rear of a gatetower at the north gate, and a fifth lay in the north-east *intervallum*. The latrine was flushed regularly by means of outlets and overflows from the nearby water cisterns, and it is clear that these tanks, at least, cannot have been completely dependent on rainfall to refill them. Indirect evidence for an alternative method of water supply to these tanks is given by the fact that the rainwater gutters serving the barrack roofs in the left *praetentura* did not connect with a water cistern, which would be expected if rainwater was the only source of supply, but drained directly out of the fort at its north-east corner. Confirmation comes from the discovery here of fragments of a sculptured relief (showing Neptune with a trident on one part, and his feet with two attendant nymphs on the other) in which a central hole provided for the connection of a lead pipe to a fountain, which would have demanded a constant supply for sufficient water pressure.[57] No aqueduct or water channels have yet been found here, although judging by the levels the west gate is the most probable point of entry. It seems likely that the principal function of so many tanks at Housesteads was to slow down and regulate the water supply as it flowed down the steep interior of the fort; an alternative view, expressed by one of the workmen digging here in the last century, was that they were used by the Romans 'for washing their Scotch prisoners in'.[58]

Most legionary fortresses and auxiliary forts lay near a river, from which they could be supplied. A scene on Trajan's Column shows a party of legionaries upon a timber-revetted stage on a river bank filling waterskins— at Hod Hill supplies would have been obtained in this way, as there was no water available within the fort and all water had either to be carried up from the River Stour at the bottom of the hill, or collected from rainwater. It was probably stored in collection tanks within the fort; one such timber-lined tank was found, which had an estimated capacity of 5500–6800 litres (1200–1500 gallons).[59]

Drainage

Rainwater ran from the roofs of the internal buildings into small encircling gutters which conveyed it into the main drains running under or alongside the principal streets and along the *intervallum*. The courtyards of the *principia* and *praetorium* had gutters around their perimeters which transported the surface water under or through the front wall of the building into the *via principalis* drain. At Housesteads a shallow channel was cut into the stone paving around the *principia*. courtyard and the water ran off into an underground drain at the south-east corner. At the junction of the gutter with this drain was a square pit, which may originally have been covered by a pierced stone drain cover found within the fort, which is of similar stone flagging to the rest of the *principia* courtyard.

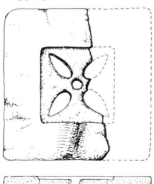

160. Stone drain cover from Housesteads, on Hadrian's Wall.

The main drains discharged at the lowest part of the fort, either through a channel cut in the rampart or defensive wall, or beneath the road metalling of a gateway portal, into the fort ditch. Private latrines in the *praetorium* and officers' quarters in the barracks linked with them, whilst the latrine for the garrison was sited in the *intervallum* at the lowest part of the fort, so that it could be flushed by the waste water before passing out of the fort. The construction of the drains was, on the whole, identical with that of the timber-lined or masonry-built water courses which brought fresh water into the fort. The routine maintenance and cleaning of the fort drains is recorded on a duty roster which records a soldier called C. Iulius Val[e]ns 'ad cunic', (on drainage fatigues).[60]

161. The latrine at Housesteads.

Latrines

Although private latrines are often found in the commander's residence or in the officers' barrack accommodation, less than twenty forts have yielded any evidence for the soldiers' latrines. Most excavated examples consisted of a rectangular stone building situated in the *intervallum* at the lowest corner of the site where several fort drains converged and could be channelled to flush the latrine before discharging from the fort.

A very well preserved latrine has been discovered at Housesteads.[61] This stone building abutted the south wall of the fort, close to the south-east angle tower. In its first (Hadrianic) period a door was provided in the east wall and around the other three sides the seating was arranged over a sewer which had stone side walls and a flagged base. The front of the timber seats

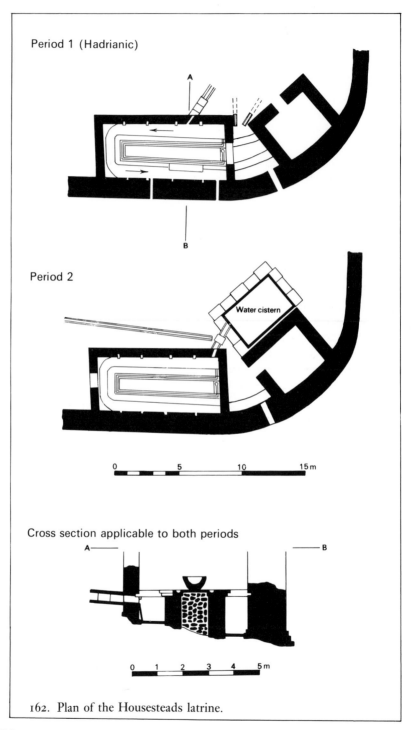

Period 1 (Hadrianic)

Period 2

Water cistern

0   5   10   15 m

Cross section applicable to both periods

A———   ———B

0 1 2 3 4 5 m

162. Plan of the Housesteads latrine.

were socketed into holes in the edges of the flagged floor, and the rear supported upon a series of stone corbels in the outer walls. The sewer became steeper, as it passed from the north-east corner, alongside the fort wall, under the east wall of the building and out through the rampart, close to the south-east angle tower. Water for flushing it entered the building on the north-east side and was conveyed in a stone-built channel. Subsequently the doorway in the south-east angle tower was blocked up to enable the construction of a large water tank against it. The tank consisted of ten large stone slabs which were grooved and sealed with lead, with dovetailed iron cramps to secure their tops, and holes for iron support bars in the sides and base; two coping stones remained *in situ*. An outlet at the base of the tank supplied water to the north side of the latrine, and the previous stone channel was abandoned.

The paved floor of the latrine was bordered by a stone gutter where the sponges which were used instead of toilet paper were washed and rinsed.[62] A gradual fall from the south-east to the north-east enabled this gutter to be flushed adequately, with the waste water emptying into the sewer beneath. Upon the paved floor stood two stone hand basins, with inlet and outlet holes for lead pipes, although how they were actually supplied with water is unknown. Whether the sponge channel and hand basins belonged to the second period of alterations or to subsequent layouts is uncertain. Eventually the south wall of the fort collapsed and had to be rebuilt, which resulted in the original doorway of the latrine being blocked: a new entrance with a porch was then provided at the opposite end, together with a new outfall sewer, an extra water tank, and a complex of new stone channels to supply water to the sponge channel and to flush the sewer. The remains of similar stone-built latrines have been discovered at Castlecary, Chesterholm, Neath and Piercebridge, and at Binchester and Ribchester the septic tanks into which the latrine drains discharged have been found, although the buildings themselves have not been investigated.

The latrine at Bar Hill was incorporated within the internal bathhouse. It lay at the lowest part of the fort and was flushed with waste water from the bathhouse, and latrines were also generally found in the external military bathhouses. At both Nanstallon and Gelligaer latrines were provided within enclosed yards in the central range. Many pits at Künzing are thought to have been latrine pits, dug beneath the clay subsoil and into the gravel terrace of the River Danube,[63] and two timber-built latrines are known from Usk. In the absence of a water supply at Hod Hill for flushing latrines, tubs or buckets were provided which could be regularly emptied. Situated next to the south gate, in the *praetentura*, lay a timber building comprising a row of ten open-fronted cubicles with a passage in front, entered from the main street. Beyond the passage lay two large rooms, an arrangement which suggests that there was probably a row of latrines, with removable tubs, together with an adjoining ablutions block. Similar closets with removable

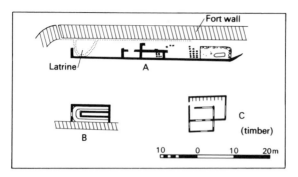

A Bar Hill
B Housesteads
C Hod Hill

163. Latrines in auxiliary forts. Scale 1:1000

buckets may have been provided in the officers' quarters of barracks where there was no real water supply. The latrines at Valkenburg consisted of slit trenches with wooden covers, which also had removable tubs.[64] A duty roster from an Egyptian legion for October 2nd AD 87 shows that M. Longinus A . . . was 'ad stercus', (on latrine duties).[65]

7 External Structures

The Parade Ground (*Campus*)

Adjacent to each auxiliary fort lay a parade ground, used for weapon training and military drill, and where the entire garrison could be mustered for inspections or parades on ceremonial occasions.[1] The importance of regular drills and training exercises was recognised by Vegetius: 'Hence we may perceive the importance and necessity of a strict observance of the military exercises in an army, since health in the camp and victory in the field depend on them'.[2] Such exercises would not only have maintained physical fitness but were also thought to occupy the soldiers' minds and discourage idleness and mutiny, so that 'even in winter, if it did not rain or snow, they were obliged to perform their drills in the field lest an intermission of discipline should affect both the courage and constitution of the soldier'.[3] Training was undergone by both recruits and veterans, on the parade ground when it was fine, and in a covered drill hall in bad weather.[4]

Vegetius listed marching, running, jumping and swimming as necessary parts of the training of new recruits. Arms exercise was naturally important too: a target mounted on a post (*palus*) was attacked using dummy swords and shields.[5] Javelin throwing and the use of the bow and arrow were also taught, and part of the exercise and training of cavalry mounts and riders was undertaken on the parade ground. Writing in the middle of the second century AD Arrian described the preparation of a parade ground for cavalry training. Roman cavalry horses were not shod, so they required a soft unmetalled surface: 'They choose a site where the exercises are to be held that is level and they work on it in addition. From the whole field they demarcate the area in front of the platform into the shape of a square and dig the middle to an equal depth and break up the clods to obtain softness and springiness'.[6] The circular stockaded enclosure found within the fort at Baginton may have been designed as a *gyrus*, for the breaking in and drilling of cavalry mounts (see page 191). Training was also carried out further afield by infantry on regular marches and manoeuvres, and by cavalry in crossing difficult and uneven terrain 'to prepare them for all kinds of accidents and familiarise them with the different manoeuvres that the various situations of the country may require'.[7] Training was given in the construction of camps

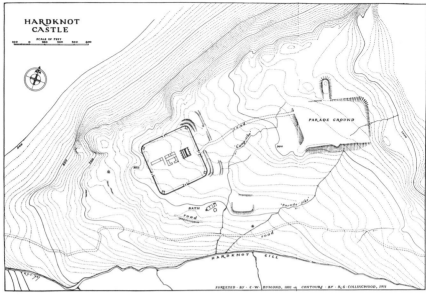

164. Plan of the fort and adjacent parade ground at Hardknott, Cumbria.

165. Aerial photograph of the Roman fort at Hardknott, Cumbria. Beyond the fort lies a flat area terraced into the hillside, which served as the parade ground.

and forts, and groups of practice earthworks have been found in the vicinity of a number of auxiliary forts, especially in Wales.[8] Tertullian summarised the principal elements of military training: 'even in peace-time soldiers still learned to inure themselves to warfare by toil and trouble, by route-marches in battle kit, by manoeuvres on the parade ground, by constructing ditches, and by forming the "tortoise" '.[9]

Parade grounds have been found outside several auxiliary forts.[10] At Hardknott, a level area of some 1.3 hectares had been terraced into the hillside on the north-east side of the fort, and was connected with it by a road. In the centre of one side rose a mound of loosely-piled stones standing six metres high, which probably formed the *tribunal*, from which the commander would have reviewed and addressed his troops; access was provided by a ramp. Similar mounds are known at Maryport (a feature known locally as Pudding Pie Hill), Tomen-y-Mur and South Shields.

The garrison would have assembled on the parade ground to participate in many of the religious and ceremonial occasions which were observed in the military calendar.[11] At the end of the last century a series of fourteen altars dedicated to Jupiter Optimus Maximus, and two to Mars Militaris, were found at the site of the parade ground at Maryport.[12] They all bore a standard formula, giving the name of the cohort and its commander, suggesting that they were official dedications, and their unweathered condition implies that they had been buried purposely. This sequence of inscriptions is therefore believed to represent a succession of altars which were dedicated annually when the soldiers renewed their oath of allegiance to the emperor; a time when a new altar may have been erected and

166. An altar from Auchendavy, in Scotland (*RIB* 2177), dedicated to the goddesses of the parade ground (the *Campestres*). It reads:
Marti Minervae Campestribus Herc(u)l(i) Eponae Victoriae M(arcus) Coccei(us) Firmus c(enturio) leg(ionis) II Aug(ustae)
'To Mars, Minerva, the Goddesses of the Parade-ground, Epona, and Victory, Marcus Cocceius Firmus, centurion of the Second Legion Augusta (set this up)'

167. Parade armour from Straubing in Raetia: Bronze face masks.

dedicated, whilst the previous one was ceremonially buried beside the parade ground.[13] A group of altars dedicated to Jupiter Optimus Maximus by *cohors I Dacorum* from Birdoswald probably also derived from the parade ground, and similar altars are known from Auchendavy, where one was dedicated to Jupiter Optimus Maximus and Victorius Victory and the other to Mars, Minerva, Hercules, Epona, Victory and the *Campestres*, (the goddesses of the parade ground). The *Campestres* were worshipped by cavalry troopers rather than infantry soldiers, and further dedications to them have been found at Newstead, Cramond, Castlehill and Benningen.[14] An inscription from Benwell records the reconstruction of a temple from ground level which was dedicated to the *Campestres* and the *Genius* of the regiment; it may have derived from a temple built on or near the parade ground.[15]

Arrian describes the dazzling sight of a cavalry *ala* on parade: many of the higher ranking soldiers and those especially gifted in horsemanship were decked in gilded iron or bronze parade helmets covering their faces completely, with flowing plumes trailing behind. The horses were also provided with armour.[16] Such parade helmets have been found in the forts at Ribchester, Newstead, Echzell and Straubing where several other items of parade armour were discovered, including greaves and protective plates for the horses' faces.[17]

An amphitheatre (*ludus*) for weapon training and assembling the garrison was provided outside each legionary fortress, and examples are also known at the auxiliary forts of Tomen-y-Mur, Dambach and the Saalburg.

168. Opposite and below: parade armour from Straubing, in Raetia: Highly decorated bronze protective plates for the horses' faces.

The Bathhouse

Bathhouses were generally built outside auxiliary forts. They were constructed in stone and tile to minimise the fire risk, and were often sited beneath the fort on a slope down to a nearby river to secure a good water supply. Despite individual variations the principal components of the bathhouse were standard, as described by many Classical authors.[18]

A dressing room (*apodyterium*), often with an adjacent latrine, was provided at the entrance. This unheated part of the building was occasionally built in timber rather than stone, as seen at Bearsden (Ill. 206) and Walldürn. At Chesters the large changing room had seven round-headed recesses along one wall which may have held lockers for clothes, or have housed statues or altars. The *apodyterium* functioned both as a changing room and a meeting place or club where the soldiers could relax after their bath, and the discovery of altars to the goddess Fortune within several bathhouses, together with gaming pieces, suggests that gambling took place here. From the *apodyterium* the bather entered a series of steam baths, similar to a Turkish bath, in which the temperature was gradually increased from the *frigidarium* (cold room) through one or more warm rooms (*tepidaria*) to a hot room (*caldarium*). Once the pores had been opened the body was anointed with oil and the sweat and grime scraped off with a curved metal scraper (*strigil*), after which the bather returned to the *frigidarium* and a cold plunge bath. Dry-heated rooms may also have been provided, similar to the modern sauna, in a *sudatorium* or *laconicum*. Furnaces (*praefurnia*) provided the hot air which circulated in channels under the raised floors supported on tile pillars or stone piers, and through flues in the walls.

The simplest layout of baths may have consisted solely of the minimum number of steam rooms, although a small *sudatorium* was often added, like the detached circular example at Hardknott. Although the basic elements were the same the various fort bathhouses differed widely in the number of rooms provided and in their degree of elaboration.

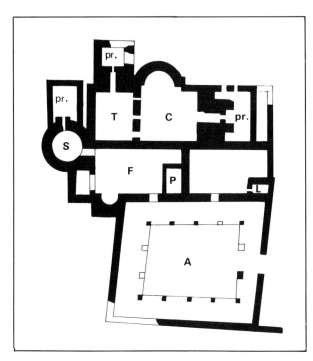

A *apodyterium*
(changing room)
F *frigidarium*
(cold room)
P plunge bath
T *tepidarium*
(warm room)
C *caldarium*
(hot room)
S *sudatorium*
(hot dry room)
L latrine
pr *praefurnium*
(furnace)

169. The principal components of the auxiliary bathhouse, based upon the bathhouse at Red House, Corbridge, Northumberland.

170. The bathhouse at Chesters on Hadrian's Wall, looking from the changing room (*apodyterium*) towards the baths. The stone-built niches on the right may originally have housed timber clothes lockers.

8 The Development of the Fort Plan

The preceding chapters have considered in detail the individual components of the defences and the internal buildings, and in this chapter the fort plan as a whole will be considered and placed into chronological perspective. The development from the earliest temporary marching camps of the Republican period to the permanent stone-built forts of the early third century AD will be traced. During this period the influence of the Roman empire expanded to its maximum extent, was consolidated along permanent frontiers, and subsequently became increasingly vulnerable from hostile barbarian forces gathering beyond its boundaries. These developments are reflected in the design and construction of the auxiliary forts built to defend the empire.

Republican Camps

The tradition of regularly planned Roman fortifications and towns evolved from the adoption and adaptation of many elements from Etruscan and Greek town planning and land division. The earliest examples of Roman military planning are seen in the colonies (*coloniae*), self-governing settlements occupied by citizens, often strategically sited on neighbouring coasts, which were designed to extend Roman influence and protect her interests abroad. Excavations at the port of Ostia, 25 kilometres from Rome, have revealed that the colony founded here in the late fourth century BC was rectangular in plan and defended by a stone wall, with a regular arrangement of streets and building plots inside, whilst other colonies of the same period show a similar plan.[1]

When on campaign in the summer months the Roman army usually constructed a new camp every night. According to Polybius, writing in the middle of the second century BC, these temporary camps (*castra aestiva*) were rectangular or square enclosures defended by a ditch and an earthen bank surmounted by a palisade of wooden stakes, within which the leather tents of the soldiers were laid out in a precisely defined and regulated pattern.[2] In the winter the troops retired to semi-permanent quarters (*castra hibernae*) which, especially towards the end of the Republican era, were provided with more comfortable accommodation, occasionally with stone or turf foundations upon which the tents were erected, and in some camps timber storebuildings may have been built.

Spain

Very few traces of Republican camps have been found, and the most valuable archaeological evidence for this period, broadly contemporary with the writings of Polybius, comes from Spain where a series of fortifications, including both summer and winter camps and a stone-walled circumvallation, was erected during successive attempts to besiege the native stronghold of Numantia. The history of these campaigns was documented by the contemporary Greek historian Appian,[3] and excavations carried out by the German archaeologist Dr Adolf Schulten between 1905 and 1912 have succeeded in identifying each of the sites mentioned by him.[4] The summer camps were, by definition, only intended to give temporary shelter and, apart from the encircling ditch, have provided little evidence for the arrangement of the tents inside. The winter siege camps, on the other hand, had stone-built ramparts and buildings, and at three sites in particular (Renieblas, Castillejo and Peña Redonda) Dr Schulten was able to recover often extensive traces of their internal layout. It must be stressed, though, that the dating and identification of the internal features of individual camps have not always been established conclusively.

The oldest camps were located upon a rolling hilltop at **Renieblas**, some $5\frac{1}{2}$ kilometres from the native fortress. The earliest (Camp I) has been attributed, on scanty evidence, to the Elder Cato's campaign of 195 BC, and subsequently a much larger winter base (Camp III) was built, probably designed for two legions, which is assigned to the campaign of A. Fulvius Nobilior in 153–2 BC. Both camps were irregular in shape, defended by a rampart with an inner and outer stone revetment enclosing a rubble core, which followed a gently curving outline conforming to the contours of the hilltop: no ditch was needed on this naturally well defended and rocky site. One of the gateways of the earlier camp was protected by an additional bank, an early example of a *titulum*, and one of the angles was further defended by an artillery platform (*ballistarium*). Although badly preserved the internal buildings of the first camp were apparently laid out systematically, with the barrack buildings designed to form three sides of a square. The internal layout of its successor conformed broadly with the Polybian model, although here the range of administrative buildings lay immediately adjacent to the northern rampart and there was no space provided behind them for the quarters of the allied troops, who seem to have been housed in a fortified annexe adjoining the main camp. The legionary barracks were arranged in regular lines, but instead of forming rectangular blocks containing the two centuries of each maniple separated from each other by a central narrow passage, as in the Polybian scheme, they were arranged around three sides of

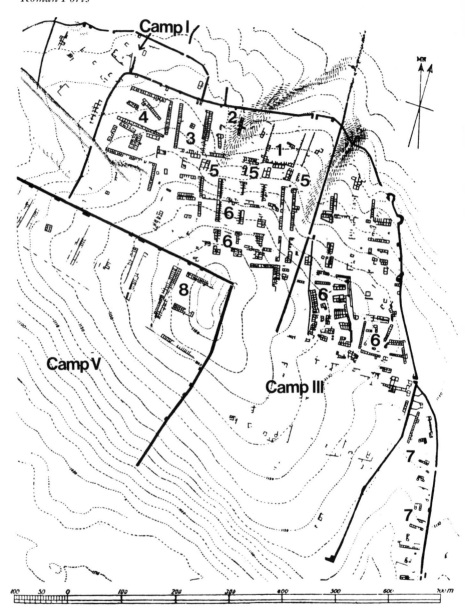

171. Renieblas, Numantia. Camp I—uncertain date. Camp III, assigned to the campaign of 153–152 BC, estimated 40 hectares. With *praetorium* (1), ? barrack (2), *forum* (3), and *quaestorium* (4) and, in front of the administrative buildings, the tribunes' houses (5). The barracks (6) were all built around three sides of a square, with rectangular blocks (*strigae*) in the adjoining annexe (7). Camp V, c. 75–74 BC. The barracks (8) retained the old-style three sided arrangement. Scale 1:6666

a square, with an open space in the centre where pack animals could be tethered. In contrast several of the auxiliary barracks in the annexe were laid out in regular rectangular blocks (*strigae*), a pattern which was to become the norm in forts of the imperial period.

During the campaigns of Scipio in 133 BC the Roman army completely encircled the native stronghold of Numantia with a stone wall, which extended altogether a distance of some 9 kilometres and was reinforced by at least seven siege camps sited upon neighbouring hills. The internal arrangements of the camps at **Castillejo**[5] and **Peña Redonda** have been examined in some detail. As at Renieblas the shape of the hilltops on which they were built dictated an irregular defensive circuit for these camps, in contrast to the rectangle or square recommended by Polybius. Two types of barracks were detected at Castillejo (Camp III), with the infantry apparently accommodated in rectangular blocks paired on either side of a metalled yard. The cavalry barracks retained the older plan, seen at Renieblas, with blocks forming three sides of a square. At Peña Redonda, on the other hand, all the barracks were arranged in rectangular blocks, divided into two-roomed *contubernia*. The three granaries sited near the south-east gate at Castillejo, with their regular buttresses and raised floors supported upon a single central longitudinal sleeper wall, are identical in plan to the stone granaries which are so common in forts of the imperial period.

In contrast to the Numantian hilltop sites, whose irregular outlines were dictated by the terrain, the camp at **Cáceres** in central Spain, believed to date to Metellus' campaign of 79 BC, is the earliest known camp which displays the rectangular layout of the Polybian model camp. It was defended not only by a clay-bonded stone wall, but also with two V-shaped ditches, which were to become common in the camps described by Julius Caesar, and standard features of later fortresses and forts. Although the internal buildings were badly preserved it is clear that the interior was divided into three unequal parts by lateral streets, with the *praetorium* sited in its customary position at the junction of the two main streets.

Closely contemporary are the two later camps at **Renieblas,** which have been ascribed to the campaign of Pompey against Sertorius in 75–4 BC. Both camps had a much more regular rectangular shape than their predecessors. The earlier (Camp IV) was a summer camp with no internal buildings. Its successor (Camp V) was a winter camp which, despite extensive damage from ploughing, yielded traces of two sizes of barracks, both of which retained the old-fashioned arrangement set around three sides of a square, whilst the tribunes' houses and granaries were more closely related to imperial types.

Opposite

173. Peña Redonda, Numantia, c. 133 BC, 11.2 hectares, with *prae-torium* (1), and ? *forum* (2). All the barracks (3) were arranged in rectangular blocks, and tribunes' houses (4) lay close to the east gate. Scale 1:3000

172. Castillejo III, Numantia, c. 133 BC with an area of just over 7 hectares. Of the administrative buildings only the *praetorium* (1) is known in detail, and facing it were two types of barracks, rectangular blocks (2), and the earlier three-sided type (3). The granaries (4) are similar to imperial fort granaries. Scale 1:3000

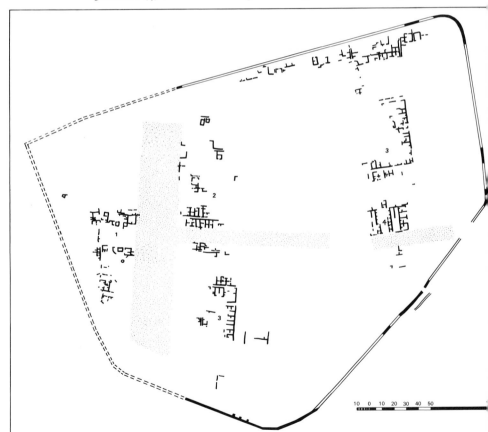

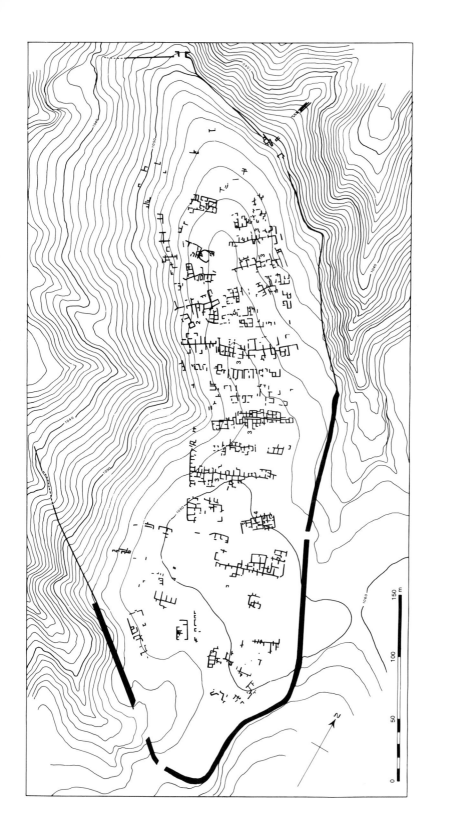

Julius Caesar

Although Julius Caesar made many references to camps and siege works in his commentaries on the Gallic Wars, and provided a wealth of detail about camp construction, organisation, and tactics, very little archaeological evidence for his marching camps or winter quarters has ever been found. The defences of only a handful of camps are known in Gaul, and nowhere have internal buildings been preserved, although recently several new sites have been located by aerial photography which may radically alter this picture.[6] Similarly, no traces of Caesar's activities in Britain (in 55 and 54 BC) or in the Rhineland (in 55 and 53 BC) have yet come to light, so that hardly anything is known about the form and internal arrangements of Roman camps in the first century BC.

On rare occasions it is possible to identify particular sites on the ground with locations mentioned by Caesar, as for example **Alesia** and **Gergovia** in Gaul, both strongholds of the native leader Vercingetorix, which he besieged in 52 BC.[7] The siege works around Alesia, which according to Caesar consisted of a series of ramparts and ditches linked with eight siege camps and displayed a wide range of Roman defensive devices, were investigated at the instigation of Napoleon III in 1861–5.[8] The defences of one of the two camps built to besiege Gergovia have also been examined in detail and found to enclose an almost rectangular camp of some 35 hectares, with a rather sinuous northern side which followed the slope of the ground. A marching camp of 41 hectares at **Mauchamp**, Aisne, was also found to have an almost rectangular outline, with one rounded angle. Each of its five gateways was defended by a *clavicula*, an extension of the rampart which curved inwards at the gate.[9] Aerial photographs have also revealed the characteristic double ditches of a small number of other military sites, presumably of this date, as at Breuteuil-sur-Noye, where the double ditches of a large camp together with a gateway defended by a *titulus* have been observed.[10]

Augustus
(23 BC–AD 14)

Even though Caesar had been the first Roman general to subdue the territory on the west bank of the Rhine, it is not until the campaigns of the emperor Augustus and his generals in c. 16–13 BC that we are able to detect the presence of troops here archaeologically, for it was at about this time that the legions were first posted in permanent quarters along the Rhine. These new bases frequently housed more than one legion, together with auxiliary troops.

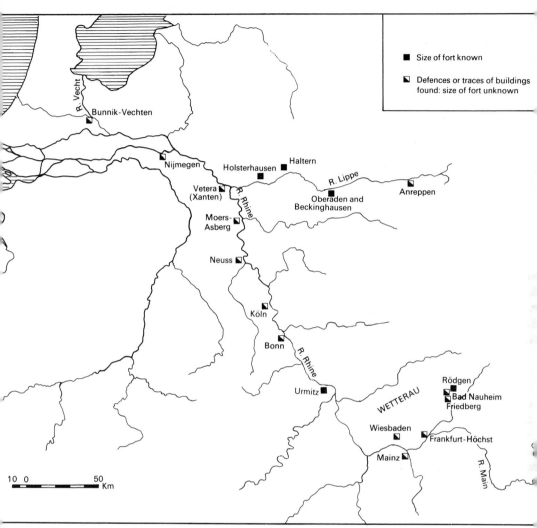

Map 1   Roman bases established in the Rhineland, c. 19 BC–AD 16.

Many of the sites chosen were occupied for a long time by the army, and, after a long period of occupation, their remains often survive only as fragmentary traces. There is little likelihood of their full internal layout ever being revealed, and only a handful of sites of this date, which were abandoned after a relatively short time, are known in any detail. There are also problems in dating them precisely, for although the dates and many details of the campaigns of Augustus' generals in the Rhineland were documented by contemporary historians, it is extremely difficult, in most cases, to assign an exact date to a site solely from an examination of its pottery and coin sequences. This means that the periods of occupation can often be only generally dated to the Augustan or Tiberian period.[11]

At this time the bases were usually polygonal in shape, defended by at least one V-shaped ditch and an earthen rampart revetted with timbers at the front, and sometimes also at the rear; the uprights for these revetments may either have been set in continuous trenches or in individual postholes. They were characterised also by their distinctive timber gateways, with the entrance recessed at the end of a deep passage flanked on either side by long narrow towers (see p. 81 and Ill. 53).

Where they are known the timber internal buildings were laid out in a regular grid pattern, with the principal street running usually down the longitudinal axis of the fortress, rather than the short axis, which was to become customary in fortifications from the Claudian period onwards. The administrative offices and living quarters of the commander may have been combined within the same building, as at Rödgen, or have been split into a separate *principia* and *praetorium*, as was the case at the legionary base of Haltern. Large timber granaries, with raised floors supported on posts set in post-trenches are known at Dangstetten and Rödgen; they are the earliest examples of military timber granaries. From the Augustan period onwards the barracks had a standard groundplan, comprising rectangular blocks which were frequently arranged back-to-back in pairs, with either one or two rooms allocated to each *contubernium*. Differences in the actual number of *contubernia* reflect the fluidity in the composition of the garrisons at this time, which were often composed of a mixture of legionary and auxiliary forces in detachments of varying strengths.

The earliest fortress which can be dated with any certainty from pottery and coin evidence has been found on the right bank of the Rhine at **Dangstetten**, at the mouth of the Wutach valley. Built in c. 15 BC it was probably occupied for no more than five years, and provided an important base during the conquest of the Alps for Drusus and Tiberius, the stepsons of Augustus. The garrison was probably a combination of legionaries and auxiliaries, as a small bronze plate inscribed 'legio 19' has been found here, together with auxiliary cavalry and archery equipment.[12]

It was to his stepson Drusus that Augustus entrusted the command of the advance across the Rhine into the heart of Germany, first to the river Weser and then on to the Elbe, in the campaigns of 12–9 BC.[13] The Roman army followed three major invasion routes, utilising wherever possible navigable waterways to penetrate deep into German territory.

The first route was along the river Vecht, which was canalised probably by Drusus (and known as the *fossa Drusiana*) to give access to the Ijsselmeer and the Frisian coast, and from there to the mouths of the Weser and the Elbe.[14] A small supply and naval base of this period lay on the Vecht at **Bunnik-Vechten**, comprising a rectangular defensive circuit enclosed by a single ditch and an earth-and-timber rampart: no internal buildings have been found.

The second of the bases from which these campaigns were launched lay at **Vetera**, opposite the confluence of the river Lippe with the Rhine, where fragmentary traces of at least seven fortifications, all of pre-Claudian date, have been detected. Upon the Lippe legionary bases probably associated with Drusus have been located and partially excavated at Haltern and at Oberaden, which also had an adjacent auxiliary base (at Beckinghausen). At **Haltern** a complex of military installations has been found, although none are securely dated.[15] Probably the earliest fortification, which may have been established by Drusus, lay on a hill known as the Annaberg, some 1.4 kilometres from the remainder of the fortifications. It was triangular in plan with an area of 7 hectares encompassing the hilltop, defended by a single ditch and an earthen rampart revetted with timbers only at the front: no internal buildings are known. Further to the north-east, underlying a later legionary base, was a temporary marching camp of 36 hectares, roughly rectangular in shape, but with a rounded angle. The rampart was probably of turf, and there was a single ditch. The defences of the fortress at **Oberaden** were also polygonal in shape, with seven sides encircling a hilltop and enclosing an area of 60 hectares, large enough for two legions and also auxiliaries. The small auxiliary fort of **Beckinghausen**, with an internal area of only 1.6 hectares, which lay only 2 kilometres from Oberaden, on the bank of the river Lippe, probably guarded an important river crossing. The internal layouts of both sites remain largely unexplored.

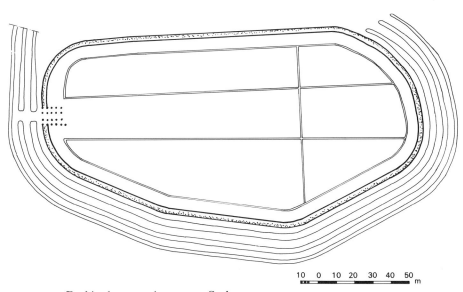

10 0 10 20 30 40 50
m

174. Beckinghausen. Augustan. Scale 1:2000

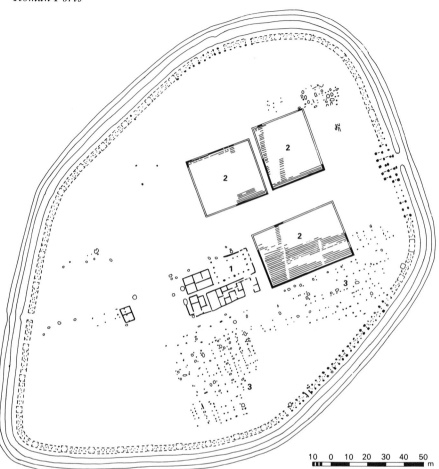

175. Rödgen. Augustan, (timber). With *praetorium* (1), granaries (2), and barracks (3). Scale 1:2000

The third invasion route ran from Mainz, opposite the mouth of the river Main, into the region of the Wetterau.

Instead of imposing upon the local native population the responsibility for supplying and feeding the army, as Caesar and his predecessors had done, the logistics and organisation of supplies was established on a completely new basis by Augustus and for the first time supply depots were built. Such a depot, dating from this period, has been found on the east bank of the river Wetter, a tributary of the Main, at **Rödgen**. Founded in c. 10 BC it provided a supply base of c. 3.2 hectares in an area for troops operating further north. All these sites, like Dangstetten, were probably abandoned shortly after the death of Drusus in 9 BC.[16]

Drusus was succeeded by his brother Tiberius, who completed the conquest of Germany and presumably reached the Elbe in his campaigns of

0 20 40 60 80 100 120 140 160 180 200
m

176. Haltern. Augustan, (timber). Legionary base with *principia* (1), *praetorium* (2), workshop/stores (*fabrica*) (3), hospital (4), tribunes' houses (5) and barracks (6). Scale 1:4000

8–7 BC. Hardly any traces of marching camps or fortifications of this period have been discovered, the only exception being probably the legionary base with its attendant stores depots and riverside fort at **Haltern**. The legionary base was almost rectangular with rounded corners, enclosing 18 hectares; it was later extended on one side to include a further 2 hectares. The timber internal buildings showed signs of repair and reconstruction before being destroyed by fire, apparently after the defeat inflicted by the Germans in AD 9. Within the headquarters the commander's residence and offices had become separate by this time, as an independent *praetorium* was built at the rear of the *principia*. Also in the central range stood the large and distinctive courtyard-plan *fabrica*, and opposite the hospital, with small wards arranged around a central courtyard.

After another short campaign in Germany in AD 4–5 Tiberius was recalled for service elsewhere in the empire, and the task of organising and incorporating the conquered German territories into a new province was

233

given to P. Quinctilius Varus. His subsequent disastrous defeat and loss of three legions in the Teutoberg Forest (in AD 9) at the hands of the German Arminius proved a sudden and dramatic check to Roman expansion, and forced Augustus to postpone and ultimately relinquish any hope of conquest to the east of the Rhine. His advice to his successor Tiberius (AD 14–37) to consolidate what had been gained and not to extend the boundaries of the empire any further[17] was accepted and, apart from punitive campaigns led by Germanicus in AD 12–16 the Rhine and the Danube, for the most part, defined the boundaries of the empire.[18] Many of the forts and fortresses built or reoccupied on the left bank of the Rhine during the reign of Tiberius had so many subsequent periods of rebuilding that little remains to show their original layout. There were no forts at all actually situated on the bank of the Danube until the reign of Claudius and although the Romans presumably controlled the territory up to the riverbank the forts of the Augustan-Tiberian period were sited well back from the river, and were situated rather at the river crossings of its tributaries, the Iller, Lech and Isar.[19]

Claudius
(AD 41–54)

The reign of Claudius was characterised in Germany by a programme of pacification and stabilisation, and in southern Britain by a policy of expansion and conquest.

Forts and fortresses on the left bank of the Rhine became permanent at this time, and during this process of consolidation timber buildings and defences began very gradually to be rebuilt in stone. In the double-legionary fortress at Vetera, for example, the earliest stone building, the hospital, appears at this date, although the bulk of the rebuilding programme in stone was not undertaken until the reign of Nero. The plan of this hospital, with its central courtyard surrounded by a double range of small wards, retained the same basic groundplan, seen first in the Augustan base at Haltern, which was to become common in later fortresses in both Germany and Britain.

The polygonal shaped camps and fortresses in which the defences closely followed the contours of the site are, in general, a feature of Republican and early imperial fortifications, and from the Claudian period fortresses and forts (with the exception of **Vindonissa** and **Hofheim**) usually conformed to either a regular rectangular (playing-card), or sometimes a square, shape. The defences consisted of one or two ditches with a rampart, which was often revetted in timber in German examples, and in turf in British. The gates were frequently flanked by towers which lay either flush within the line of the rampart or projected slightly into the interior, in contrast with the very deep projecting towers of Augustan gates. Internally the *via principalis* still often ran longitudinally down the axis of the fort, dividing the interior

177. Hofheim, Claudian, (timber). (1) *principia*, (2) courtyard building, either the *praetorium* or *fabrica*, (3) stores, (4) barracks. Scale 1:2000

in half to provide a range of administrative buildings flanked by barracks and a *praetentura*, but no *retentura*. The *principia* probably comprised a colonnaded courtyard with a rear range of offices, without a cross-hall and, in the very early examples, may still have included accommodation for the commander within the administrative offices; the earliest example of a *principia* forehall comes from the Claudian legionary fortress of Vindonissa, at Windisch in Switzerland.

The results of extensive excavations at **Valkenburg**, close to the mouth of the Rhine, are particularly important as the earliest fort on the site represents a base constructed just prior to the invasion of Britain. Many of the timber structures here were so well preserved in the waterlogged subsoil that they have provided a wealth of information about military timber

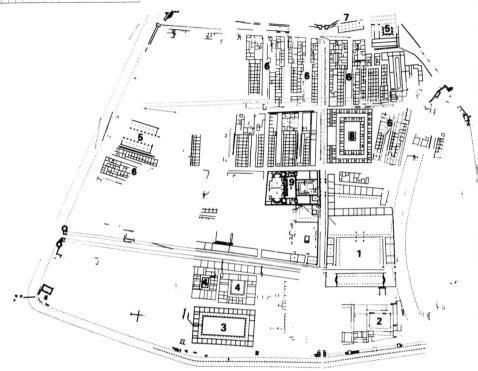

178. Vindonissa. Claudian legionary fortress, stonebuilt. (1) *principia* with forehall, (2) ? *praetorium*, (3) *fabrica* or store, (4) tribunes' houses, (5) *fabrica*, (6) barracks, (7) granary (*horreum*), (8) hospital, (9) baths. Scale 1:5000

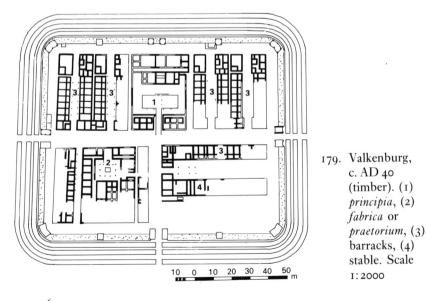

179. Valkenburg, c. AD 40 (timber). (1) *principia*, (2) *fabrica* or *praetorium*, (3) barracks, (4) stable. Scale 1:2000

236

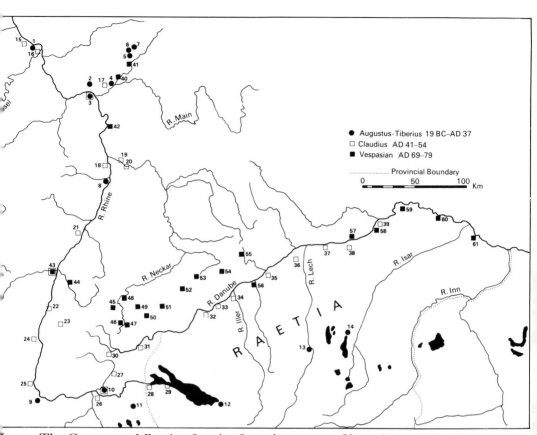

Map 2   The German and Raetian frontier from Augustus to Vespasian, 19 BC–AD 79.

Augustus-Tiberius 19 BC–AD 37

- Urmitz
- Wiesbaden
- Mainz
- Frankfurt-Höchst
- Friedberg
- Bad Nauheim
- Rödgen
- Speyer
- Basel
- Dangstetten
- Oberwinterthur
- Bregenz
- Lorenzberg
- Gauting

Claudius AD 41–54

- Andernach
- Koblenz
- Hofheim
- Rheingönheim

19   Ladenburg
20   Heidelberg-Neuenheim
21   Seltz
22   Sasbach
23   Riegel
24   Kunheim-Oedenbourg
25   Kembs
26   Zurzach
27   Schleitheim
28   Eschenz
29   Konstanz
30   Hüfingen
31   Tuttlingen
32   Emerkingen
33   Risstissen
34   Unterkirchberg
35   Aislingen
36   Burghöfe
37   Neuberg
38   Oberstimm
39   Weltenburg-Frauenberg

Vespasian AD 69–79

40   Frankfurt-Heddernheim
41   Okarben
42   Gernsheim
43   Strasbourg
44   Offenburg
45   Waldmössingen
46   Rottweil-Neckarburken
47   Rottweil Hochmauern
48   Sulz
49   Geislingen a.R
50   Lautlingen
51   Burladingen
52   Gomadingen
53   Donnstetten
54   Urspring
55   Heidenheim
56   Günzberg
57   Kösching
58   Eining
59   Regensburg-Kumpfmühl
60   Straubing
61   Moos

buildings of this period. The headquarters building, with a double range of rooms at the rear, and further small rooms on either side of the entrance, may have housed the commander or perhaps his junior officers; it is uncertain whether a courtyard-plan building located in the right *praetentura* should be identified as the commander's residence or a workshop/*fabrica*. On either side of the *principia* lay two pairs of barracks, with each pair providing officers' accommodation, thirteen barrack rooms and a workshop or store. The garrison is uncertain, although it probably consisted of a detachment from the *cohors III Gallorum quingenaria equitata*, whose name was found inscribed upon two wax tablets.[20]

By the reign of Claudius the new province of Raetia had been established, and in order to ensure its security forts were brought up to the south bank of the Danube for the first time, and in AD 46–7 a road was constructed (the *Via Claudia Augusta*) along the bank of the river Lech as far as the Danube.[21] Although the sites of several of these forts have been located, only at the most easterly of them, at Oberstimm, has the Claudian fort plan been revealed in any detail.

The earth-and-timber fort at **Oberstimm** was occupied from c. AD 40 until AD 69–70. Its internal layout reflects a new departure in fort planning, with the principal street running not down the longitudinal axis dividing the

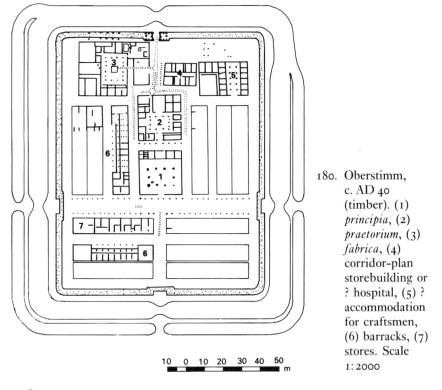

180. Oberstimm, c. AD 40 (timber). (1) *principia*, (2) *praetorium*, (3) *fabrica*, (4) corridor-plan storebuilding or ? hospital, (5) ? accommodation for craftsmen, (6) barracks, (7) stores. Scale 1:2000

10 0 10 20 30 40 50
m

238

interior into two, but rather along the short transverse axis, providing three main divisions (the *praetentura*, central range and *retentura*)—an innovation which quickly became a standard feature of fort design. The commanding officer had his quarters in a courtyard house, which lay immediately behind the *principia*. Both buildings were flanked by barrack blocks, a feature seen commonly in earlier camps and fortresses and which remained customary in permanent legionary bases, but rare in auxiliary forts after this date, as the central range was normally reserved for administrative and official buildings, with the men's barracks confined to the front and rear sections. Unusually the whole of the *retentura* at Oberstimm appears to have been occupied by workshops and storebuildings, where what may have been accommodation for the craftsmen was situated too.

The defences of several contemporary Danubian forts, all rectangular in shape, have also been discovered, but nothing is known about their internal layout.[22] Outside one of them, at Burghöfe, traces of a civilian settlement (*vicus*) have been found, believed to be the earliest example in western Europe.[23]

The invasion of Britain in AD 43 was undertaken by four legions (*legio II Augusta*, *IX Hispana*, *XIV Gemina* and *XX Valeria*) together with a large number of auxiliary troops, under the command of Aulus Plautius. Landing in Kent the invading army crossed the river Medway after a fierce battle and advanced to the Thames, where it was forced to remain for several weeks to await the arrival of the emperor Claudius, who wished to lead his victorious troops and receive the surrender of the native stronghold of *Camulodunum* (modern Colchester) personally. The army was subsequently divided into three and spread out into the Midlands, the south, south-west, and East Anglia to crush all resistance and enforce Roman authority in the new province.

More is known about the advance into the south-west than elsewhere because the legion sent to subdue this area, *legio II Augusta*, was commanded by Titus Flavius Vespasianus, who was later to become emperor himself (in AD 69). His biographer, Suetonius, records that Vespasian fought thirty battles, defeated two hostile tribes, captured 20 *oppida* and the Isle of Wight.[24] Graphic evidence for his campaigns has been found at the Iron Age hillfort of Maiden Castle near Dorchester where, in a war cemetery near the east gate, a skeleton was found to have a legionary artillery *ballista* bolt embedded in its spine.

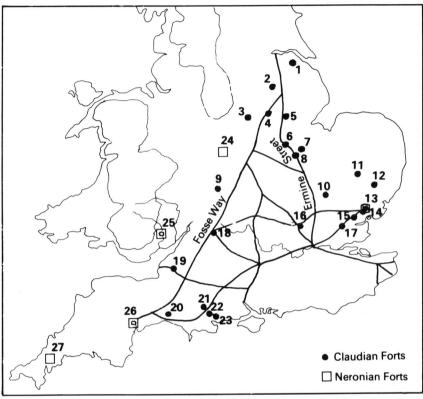

Map 3 The forts of the conquest period in southern England.

Claudian Forts

1   Kirmington
2   Littleborough
3   Broxtowe
4   Thorpe by Newark
5   Ancaster
6   Great Casterton
7   Longthorpe
8   Water Newton
9   Alcester
10 Great Chesterford
11 Ixworth
12 Baylham House
13 Colchester (*Camulodunum*) (legionary fortress)
14 Stanway
15 Kelvedon
16 Verulamium
17 Chelmsford
18 Cirencester
19 Charterhouse
20 Waddon Hill
21 Hod Hill
22 Shapwick
23 Lake Farm

Neronian Forts

24 The Lunt, Baginton
25 Usk (legionary fortress)
26 Exeter (legionary fortress)
27 Nanstallon

At another hillfort, **Hod Hill**, also in Dorset, evidence has also been found for a Roman artillery bombardment, and it is here that extensive excavations in the 1950s have revealed the most detailed plan yet discovered of an earth-and-timber fort of the invasion period. It had been built within one corner of the hillfort, utilising the native defences on two sides. The slope on these sides is particularly steep, making access difficult, and so orthodox gateways were dispensed with, leaving only a narrow postern gate leading down to the river. The unusual shape of the fort was dictated by a strip over 20 metres wide lying immediately behind the native ramparts which contained numerous Iron Age quarry pits. The new Roman defences incorporated a *titulus* and *ballistarium* at both gates. The internal layout was similar to Valkenburg, with the main street running down the longitudinal axis and dividing the fort in half. The garrison is believed to have been a mixed legionary and auxiliary cavalry detachment, judging from the large quantity of military equipment from both types of unit which has been found during ploughing on the hilltop, mainly in the last century;[25] two courtyard buildings, one behind the headquarters and another on the opposite side of the *via principalis*, have been interpreted as the dwellings of the two commanders.[26] The cramped barracks, with only one room provided for sleeping and equipment storage, probably represent the minimum requirements for the invasion army in the field: they were normally much more spacious in later permanent forts.

181. The Roman fort built within the north-west defences of the Iron Age hillfort at Hod Hill, Dorset.

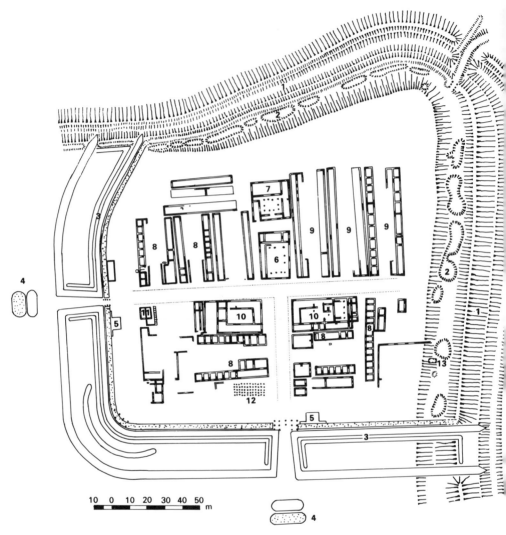

182. Hod Hill, c. AD 43–44, (timber). (1) Defences of the Iron Age hill fort, (2) Iron Age quarry pits, (3) Roman fort defences, (4) *titulus*, (5) artillery platform (*ballistarium*), (6) *principia*, (7) *praetorium*, (8) barracks, (9) stables, (10) courtyard buildings of uncertain function, (11) latrines, (12) granary, (13) water tank. Scale 1:2000

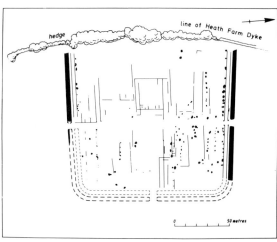

183. Plan of the defences and timber internal buildings of the fort at Stanway plotted from aerial photographs. Scale 1:2000

184. The Roman fort at Stanway, Gosbecks, near *Camulodunum* from the air.

Another Roman fort sited within a native enclosure has recently been located from the air close to the British capital of *Camulodunum*, at **Stanway**. The fort faced the religious sanctuary at Gosbecks, Cheshunt Field, which provided an important focus to the life of the pre-Roman community. Sited within the Colchester Dyke system, its western side may actually have abutted one of the dykes. As no excavation has yet taken place the construction date is uncertain. It probably belongs to the early stages of the conquest, when the army first received the submission of Camulodunum and prior to the establishment of a legionary fortress there, although alternatively it may have been connected with the restoration of Roman authority after the Boudiccan revolt of AD 60. The air photographs have revealed a rectangular ditched enclosure with the principal street running across the short axis, giving a shallow *retentura*. The foundation trenches of the timber *principia* and several rubbish pits are also clearly visible.

The concept of a frontier maintained by a network of small auxiliary forts and backed up by legionary bases in the rear had not fully evolved at this time, and in the early years of the conquest it is common to find both legionary and auxiliary troops brigaded together. This happened both in small forts, such as Hod Hill, and also in much larger bases, ranging in size from 8 to 12 hectares, which were intended probably for only short sporadic periods of occupation as winter quarters or semi-permanent bases during the initial stages of conquest, rather than long-term installations; although some were undoubtedly occupied for longer than was probably intended.

243

Approximately a dozen of these larger bases, generally known as 'vexillation fortresses', which were intermediate in size between the auxiliary fort and the full legionary fortress, have been found in the Midlands and the Welsh Marches.[27]

Only one, at **Longthorpe** near Peterborough, has been excavated. It comprised a double ditched rectangular enclosure with rounded corners, occupying an area (within the ditches) of c. 11 hectares. The *via principalis* ran down the longitudinal axis of the site, as at Hod Hill, but here there was space allocated to the *retentura*. The *principia* was examined, together with two granaries in the *retentura*. The complete plan of only one barrack was uncovered, which had a peculiar irregular tapering groundplan: with a length of over 104 metres it is the longest barrack block known. Finds of military equipment indicate that here too, as at Hod Hill, the garrison was probably a mixed detachment of legionaries and auxiliary cavalry, numbering here perhaps a total of 2800 men. Subsequently a smaller enclosure, perhaps an auxiliary fort, was placed within the defences of its predecessor, making use of part of the southern defences. The dating of both periods of occupation is AD 44/8 until AD 61/2 and it is not possible to refine the construction date of the smaller fort within this time span.[28] A single ditch was dug to enclose only 4.4 hectares, and a new *porta decumana* was built. There was apparently no substantial reorganisation of the internal timber buildings, so that the fortress *principia* and some of the barracks probably continued in use in the reduced fort, although they were not purpose-built for it.

The river valleys from the Humber and the Trent, following the Avon to the Severn and down to the Exe provided a natural boundary to the new province and after the initial military conquest, although no formal rigid frontier was established, the extent of the Roman influence in the reign of Claudius was marked by a network of forts on and behind this line, spaced probably one day's march away from each other, and linked by a major road, the Fosse Way.[29] To the north the client kingdom of Brigantia provided a buffer state, but there was a much more troubled boundary to the west with the Welsh tribes. Behind this boundary the legions were based in fortresses situated at key points in lowland Britain.[30] The positions of several of these conquest-period forts have been located by aerial photography, and the sites of many more suggested from finds of military fittings, or the discovery of portions of ditch systems or timber buildings. Their ditches generally enclosed a regular 'playing-card' layout, but little is known of their internal plans.[31]

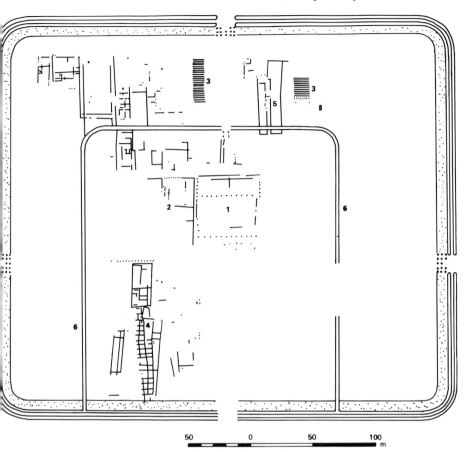

185. Longthorpe vexillation fortress, c. AD 44/8 (timber). (1) *principia*, (2) ?
praetorium, (3) granaries, (4) legionary barrack, (5) auxiliary barrack, (6) the
defences of the reduced fort. Scale 1:3000

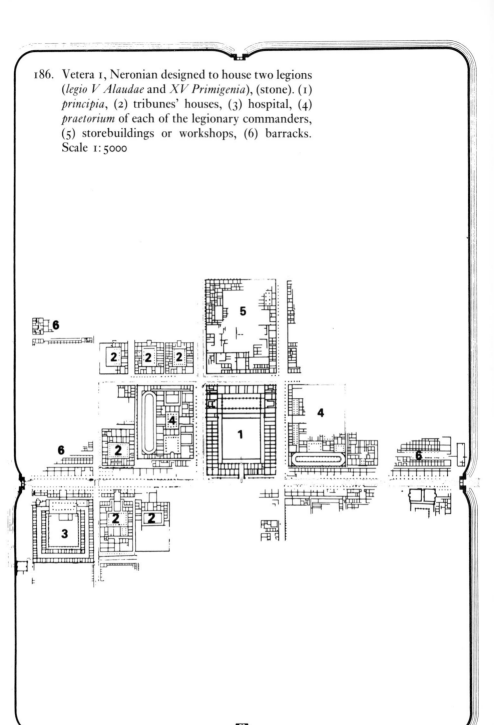

186. Vetera 1, Neronian designed to house two legions
(*legio V Alaudae* and *XV Primigenia*), (stone). (1)
principia, (2) tribunes' houses, (3) hospital, (4)
praetorium of each of the legionary commanders,
(5) storebuildings or workshops, (6) barracks.
Scale 1:5000

0   100   200m

Nero
(AD 54–68)

The accession of Nero in AD 54 saw no major policy changes on the Rhine and Danube frontiers, and Claudius' policy of consolidation was continued. On the lower Rhine the legionary fortress at **Vetera** was probably completely rebuilt in stone at this time. Like most of the fortresses and forts from this period onwards it conformed to the normal rectangular plan with the *via principalis* running down the short axis, and the interior divided into three main divisions. It extended over an area of some 56 hectares, providing duplicate accommodation for two legions, with the elaborate *praetorium* of each legionary commander and the houses of his tribunes sited on either side of the *principia*.

The turbulent Welsh tribes had presented a threat to the new Roman province of Britain from the earliest years of the conquest, and the historian Tacitus records campaigns against individual tribes from AD 48 onwards.[32] The successive appointments of two experienced generals as governors, Q. Veranius (AD 57–8) and C. Suetonius Paulinus (AD 58–61) shows that Nero was determined to solve the recurring problem of the Welsh frontier once and for all, and successful campaigns against several tribes were documented by Tacitus, culminating in the capture of the Druidic stronghold of Anglesey in AD 60. However, the outbreak of the Boudiccan rebellion in East Anglia in the same year, which demanded the immediate withdrawal of troops from Wales, delayed final pacification and consolidation, and in the event it was to take almost another twenty years to complete Paulinus' work.[33] Very little archaeological evidence for this activity has ever been found, with the exception of a few temporary camps, and only at Usk in Gwent, and Exeter in Devon have legionary bases of Neronian date been examined in any detail.

Built in the territory of the Silures in the mid-50s the 19 hectare fortress at **Usk** was occupied for only perhaps ten or fifteen years, being ultimately replaced (in the mid-70s) by a new fortress at Caerleon, situated only 13 kilometres away. Limited excavations have revealed that the interior was regularly planned, with the *via principalis* flanked by stone-lined drains and a timber colonnade. The legionary base at **Exeter**, built at the same time, provides the earliest evidence for a stone military building in Roman Britain, for close to the centre of the fortress, amidst timber barracks, workshops and granaries, stood a large and impressive stone-built bathhouse.

The only two auxiliary forts of Neronian date which have been investigated in any detail both exhibit unusual features. At **Nanstallon**, near Bodmin in Cornwall, part of a small earth-and-timber fort, of 0.8 hectares internally, has been excavated. It is too small to have accommodated a complete auxiliary unit and probably housed a detachment, which may well have been engaged in the supervision of lead and silver

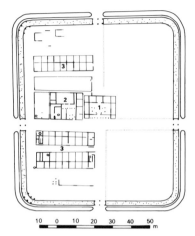

187. Nanstallon, c. AD 60 (timber). (1) *principia*, (2) *praetorium* with adjoining compound, (3) barracks. Scale 1:2000

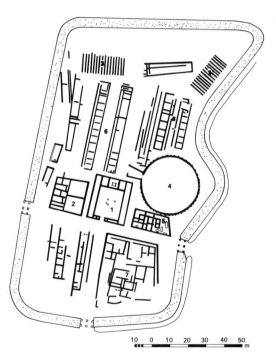

188. Baginton, c. AD 64 (timber). (1) *principia*, (2) ? *praetorium*, (3) granaries, (4) circular stockade (*gyrus-vivarium*), (5) building of unknown function containing several water tanks, (6) barracks, (7) ? residence of a senior officer. Scale 1:2000

extraction in the vicinity.[34] The plan of the *principia* is curious, as it was very wide in proportion to its depth, incorporating long halls (*armamentaria*) on either side of the courtyard, with a recessed entrance and a portico at the front of the building. The barracks consisted of rectangular blocks with no projecting officers' quarters or verandahs, although larger rooms which were presumably for the officers were provided at the end of each block.

The rebellion of the Iceni and their neighbours in East Anglia, led by Boudicca in AD 60, threatened the security of the whole of lowland Britain, and such was the extent of the casualties inflicted and the trail of destruction extending from Colchester to London that Nero may well have seriously considered relinquishing the province. Instead, almost the whole of the next decade was marked by a policy of pacification and reorganisation, with more troops stationed in the Midlands and East Anglia, whilst all thoughts of further conquests in Wales or the north were abandoned. In the aftermath of these troubles a new fort was built at Baginton, near Coventry.

The earliest occupation at **Baginton** dates to c. AD 60, but its original nature and size remain largely unknown, as it extended beyond the defences of the later fort and its defensive circuit was not located. The internal timber buildings included two granaries, and two of the barracks were halved in length by the construction of a circular stockaded arena, believed to have been a *gyrus* for training horses. In c. AD 64 a smaller fort was built on this site. Its defences, which have been located on only two sides and inferred on the others, enclosed an area estimated at approximately 1.2 hectares. Three of the sides probably followed the standard rectangular pattern, but the fourth was forced to curve around the existing *gyrus*, which remained in use, following a sinuous course which is quite unknown in other British or German forts. The provision of an arena or *gyrus*, which is unique within a Roman fort, indicates that this site had a specialist function, probably in the training of cavalry horses and officers, and so much of its internal layout is atypical. The *principia* courtyard was flanked by long rooms on both sides, as at Nanstallon, and the central shrine had a small timber-lined pit dug beneath the floor to house the regimental treasury—the earliest example known in Britain. The barracks, like those at Nanstallon were simply rectangular blocks, with a verandah, but no projecting officers' quarters. The whole of the left *praetentura* was occupied by a large and complex building, thought to have been the residence of a senior officer involved perhaps with cavalry training in the *gyrus*. The garrison was probably a mixed one, as shown by the discovery of several fragments of legionary armour (*lorica segmentata*), together with items of bronze cavalry equipment.

The Flavian Emperors
(Vespasian AD 69–79; Titus AD 79–81; Domitian AD 81–96)

The suicide of Nero in AD 69 resulted in a civil war from which Vespasian eventually emerged the victor. The legacy he inherited was one of chaos and rebellion, for the frontiers along the Rhine and Danube had been depleted of troops to support the four individual contenders for the imperial throne (Galba, Otho, Vitellius and Vespasian). There had been widespread destruction of forts and civilian settlements along the whole length of the frontier, and the Batavians of the lower Rhine, led by Civilis, were in open revolt.[35] In Britain also, although there had been no actual fighting between different factions within the province, troops had been withdrawn to support the claims of Vitellius, and the opportunity was seized in the north by Venutius, consort of Queen Cartimandua of the Brigantes, to expel her from the throne and reject Roman authority over this former client kingdom.[36]

Having crushed the Batavian revolt Vespasian set about the re-organisation of the legionary positions to prevent a recurrence of the recent unrest. The double-legionary site at Vetera was replaced by a new single fortress (Vetera II), which was sited approximately 1.5 kilometres away and closer to the Rhine, and another new fortress was constructed on the Rhine at Nijmegen.[37] The fortresses at Neuss, Bonn and Mainz, which had all been burnt down in the troubles of AD 69–70 were reconstructed in stone. Excavations have revealed virtually the complete layout at Neuss, but far less at Bonn and Mainz. From the Flavian period onwards, and throughout the second century AD, the layout of legionary fortresses, whether built in stone or timber, conformed broadly to a familiar pattern, which is typified by Neuss see p. 31ff and Ill. 17.

Despite the rebuilding of these German legionary bases in stone the auxiliary forts of the Flavian period, both in Britain and Germany, were still of earth-and-timber construction. From this time it is clear that their layouts followed the same basic standardised pattern, albeit with many significant variations in detail. The rampart, which was often timber revetted in Germany and turf revetted in Britain, enclosed a regular 'playing-card' shape, defended by timber towers spaced regularly around the perimeter, and by one or two ditches. The timber gates were flanked by towers which may have projected slightly into the interior of the fort or, more commonly, were set flush within the line of the rampart. The *principia* had a courtyard surrounded by a colonnaded ambulatory and perhaps flanked by *armamentaria*, separated from the rear range of five rooms by a double row of columns. It was flanked on one side by a courtyard-plan *praetorium* and on the other usually by a pair of granaries. The barracks were invariably L-shaped, with verandahs, and were grouped in pairs in the front and rear portions of the fort.

Vespasian's policy was one of reconstruction and gradual expansion. He was responsible for the construction of roads to improve communications between the Rhineland and the Danube. On the Upper Rhine forts were moved onto the right bank for the first time, and were connected by a new road. A milestone[38] records the building of another new road under the supervision of Gn. Pineius Cornelius Clemens in AD 73/4 through the Black Forest. The project was designed to link the legionary fortress of Strasbourg with the province of Raetia and its capital of Augsburg, and to

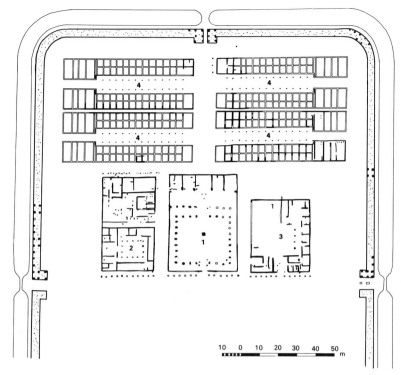

189. Rottweil 3, c. AD 72/3, (timber). (1) *principia*, (2) *praetorium* with adjoining compound, and (3) a larger courtyard building, more probably a *fabrica* than a second *praetorium*, (4) barracks. Scale 1:2000

incorporate the territory between the Upper Rhine and the Danube known as the *agri decumates*.

Several forts were probably brought forward into the Upper Neckar region in conjunction with this advance. At **Rottweil** (Hochmauern)[39] for example, recent excavations have located an earth-and-timber fort of some 3.5 hectares internally, whose construction date is given by a freshly minted coin of Vespasian (dated AD 72–3) found beneath the rampart; it was occupied until c. AD 80. The rampart was of unusual construction, with a double turf-revetted and timber laced rampart founded upon a log corduroy (see p. 60). Only the central range and part of the *retentura* were available for excavation. Each of the barrack blocks located in the *retentura* was unusual in providing thirteen double-roomed *contubernia* for, in general, auxiliary units required less (a minimum of eight, and more often ten or eleven). This fact, together with their particularly large size makes them more readily comparable with legionary barracks, and it seems probable therefore that a legionary detachment rather than a regular auxiliary garrison was stationed here.[40]

251

Elsewhere, on the Upper Danube frontier, building inscriptions from Günzburg (dated AD 77–8) and Kösching (AD 80), taken together with the results of excavations at Risstissen, demonstrate that rebuilding in stone was being undertaken in the latter years of Vespasian's reign, and at the same time a new road was built running along the northern bank of the river and crossing it again at the new fort of Eining, which has yielded an inscription dated AD 79–81.[41]

Vespasian sent the experienced general Petilius Cerialis to deal with the troubled northern border in Britain. Cerialis, who had recently defeated the Batavian rebels on the lower Rhine, brought with him an extra legion, which succeeded in defeating Venutius and led to the absorption of the former client kingdom of Brigantia into the Roman province by his successors. Although the defeat of Venutius is documented by Tacitus, there is little archaeological evidence for the campaigns, except for the fact that the legionary fortress at York was founded at this time.

According to Tacitus the next military governor, Iulius Frontinus (AD 74–8), concentrated upon the conquest of Wales and finally subdued the southern tribe of the Silures. His work was completed by Iulius Agricola (AD 78–84/5) who, in a short time, defeated the Ordovices of central Wales and brought the pacification of Wales to a successful conclusion. The establishment of earth-and-timber auxiliary forts spaced a day's march apart (c. 15–20 kilometres) and connected by a network of good roads imposed control on the native population, backed up by new legionary fortresses sited in the south at Caerleon on the Usk, and in north Wales at Chester on the river Dee. Many of these Flavian forts were subsequently reconstructed in stone and although traces of their defences are often detected, usually insufficient evidence survives to show their internal layout.

Only at **Pen Llystyn**, situated some 19 kilometres south of Caernarfon, has the complete plan of a Flavian fort in Wales been recovered largely undisturbed by later occupation. This almost square fort, enclosing an area of 1.6 hectares, was built c. AD 78–9 and was probably occupied for no more than a decade before being destroyed by fire. Its plan displays all the classic features which were to become the norm throughout the later first and second centuries, apart from the fact that up to twelve barracks each with ten *contubernia* were provided here, which does not seem to fit the requirements of any of the auxiliary units, even the milliary cohorts which had come into being by this time. However, the presence of a gate across the *via decumana* which separated the rear six blocks (five of which appear to have been barracks) from the rest of the fort may give a clue that we may here be dealing with two separate units, probably two quingenary infantry cohorts, housed together within the same fort.[42]

The survival of a biography written by Tacitus of his father-in-law, Iulius Agricola, has given us a great deal more information about his career and achievements than any of his contemporaries. Despite this wealth of

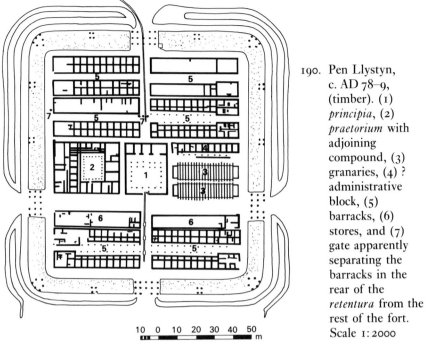

190. Pen Llystyn,
c. AD 78–9,
(timber). (1)
principia, (2)
praetorium with
adjoining
compound, (3)
granaries, (4) ?
administrative
block, (5)
barracks, (6)
stores, and (7)
gate apparently
separating the
barracks in the
rear of the
retentura from the
rest of the fort.
Scale 1:2000

10 0 10 20 30 40 50
m

information he unfortunately provides very few geographical details so that it is necessary to rely upon archaeological research, in locating marching camps and forts from the air, and detecting their defences on the ground, to build up a picture of Agricola's campaigns. A combination of these documentary and archaeological sources reveals that during the two terms of his governorship Iulius Agricola succeeded not only in subduing Wales, but he also advanced into northern England and deep into Scotland as far as Strathmore, culminating in a major success in battle against the Caledonian tribes at Mons Graupius, which may have been fought somewhere near Aberdeen.[43] As he advanced he established a network of auxiliary forts and roads to consolidate his hold on the new territory, and perhaps as many as seventy new forts built in northern England and Scotland can be attributed to his policies.[44]

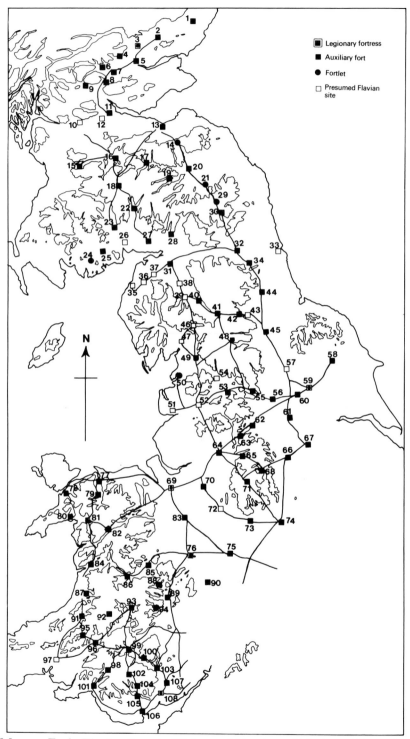

Map 4   Early Flavian forts in Wales and Northern Britain c. AD 74–84.

Legionary fortress
Auxiliary fort
Fortlet
Presumed Flavian site

1	Stracathro	37	Old Carlisle	73	Rocester
2	Cardean	38	Old Penrith	74	Littlechester
3	Inchtuthil	39	Brougham	75	Eaton House
4	Fendoch	40	Kirkby Thore	76	Wroxeter
5	Bertha	41	Brough	77	Caerhun
6	Dalginross	42	Bowes	78	Caernarfon
7	Strageath	43	Greta Bridge	79	Bryn-y-Gefeiliau
8	Ardoch	44	Binchester	80	Pen Llystyn
9	Bochastle	45	Catterick	81	Tomen-y-Mur
10	Cadder	46	Low Borrow Bridge	82	Caer Gai
11	Camelon	47	Watercrook	83	Whitchurch
12	Castlecary	48	Brough by Bainbridge	84	Pennal
13	Inveresk	49	Overborough	85	Forden Gaer
14	Oxton	50	Lancaster	86	Caersŵs
15	Loudon Hill	51	Kirkham	87	Trawscoed
16	Castledykes	52	Ribchester	88	Clun
17	Easter Happrew	53	Elslack	89	Leintwardine
18	Crawford	54	Long Preston	90	Walltown
19	Oakwood	55	Ilkley	91	Llanio
20	Newstead	56	Adel	92	Beulah
21	Cappuck	57	Aldborough	93	Castell Collen
22	Milton	58	Malton	94	Discoed
23	Dalswinton	59	York	95	Pumsaint
24	Gatehouse of Fleet	60	Newton Kyme	96	Llandovery
25	Glenlochar	61	Castleford	97	Carmarthen
26	Ward Law	62	Slack	98	Coelbren
27	Birrens	63	Castleshaw	99	Brecon Gaer
28	Broomholm	64	Manchester	100	Pen-y-Gaer
29	Chew Green	65	Melandra	101	Neath
30	High Rochester	66	Templeborough	102	Penydarren
31	Carlisle	67	Doncaster	103	Abergavenny
32	Red House	68	Brough on Noe	104	Gelligaer
33	South Shields	69	Chester	105	Caerphilly
34	Ebchester	70	Middlewich	106	Cardiff
35	Maryport	71	Buxton	107	Usk
36	Caermote	72	Chesterton	108	Caerleon

In the Highlands of Scotland he did not attempt to overrun the highland massif, but sited forts at the entrances to the glens, in order to control the movements of the natives and to prevent the gathering of hostile forces. This strategy took account of a new legionary base at Inchtuthil, on the river Tay. One of these auxiliary forts has been excavated extensively, at **Fendoch**.[45] This fort of 1.5 hectares internally controlled the entrance to the Sma' Glen near Crieff in Tayside. It was built upon a glacial moraine which imposed a rather elongated rectangular shape. Constructed in the mid-80s AD the timber buildings had just one period of occupation, and were apparently

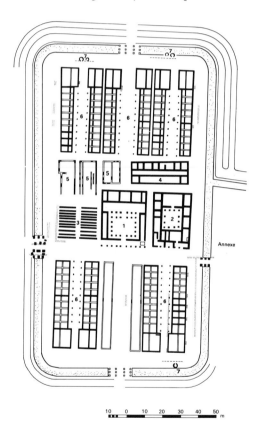

Annexe

191. Fendoch,
c. AD 82–4,
(timber). (1)
principia, (2)
praetorium, (3)
granaries, (4)
corridor-plan ?
storebuilding or
workshop, (5)
miscellaneous
stores, (6)
barracks, (7)
rampart ovens.
Scale 1:2000

10 0 10 20 30 40 50
m

dismantled and the site tidied before evacuation. The number and internal arrangements of the barracks has suggested that the garrison was an infantry cohort nominally one thousand strong (*cohors milliaria peditata*).

The strongpoint in the control of the Highlands lay in the new legionary fortress at **Inchtuthil**. Excavations in the 1950s and 1960s succeeded in recovering almost the whole of its plan. It is unique in north-west Europe as, in contrast to all other legionary fortresses, it has remained free from subsequent disturbance and has revealed the complete one-period layout of a site designed by the Roman army at the height of its expansion and power in Britain. Building work started here in c. AD 83 and after a short occupation, in which there was insufficient time to erect all the internal buildings, it was systematically dismantled and virtually everything of use, including one million unused nails and large quantities of ironwork, were buried to prevent them from falling into enemy hands; the date of this demolition, judging from the discovery of mint coins in the debris was c. AD 86/7. The almost square fortress, enclosing 21.4 hectares was defended originally by a turf rampart, which had subsequently been cut back at the front to allow the insertion of a stone wall. The gate towers were set within the body of the rampart and did not project behind it, a pattern which was followed almost exclusively in stone-built gateways of the second century (see p. 31). The internal buildings were all timber-built. The *principia* was surprisingly small in comparison with other legionary examples, and was set back from the main street. One of the open spaces either to its left or at the rear had presumably been allocated to the commander's house, but the decision was taken to abandon the fortress before construction work had even begun: this was also the case with the tribunes' houses on the opposite side of the *via principalis*, as only four instead of the required six had been completed. Unlike most legionary bases which were equipped with elaborate internal bathhouses, a small stone bathhouse was provided just beyond the southern defences at Inchtuthil.

Other auxiliary forts of this date in Scotland have revealed striking variations to the standard Flavian fort plan. The *principia* of the 1.7 hectares fort at **Strageath**, to the south of Fendoch was rather unusual, as a large water tank had been dug in the courtyard, and on either side were built two rather irregular rooms, although the usual five rear rooms and cross-hall were present. At Cardean, 24 kilometres north-east of Inchtuthil, a combination of aerial photography and limited trial trenching has defined the defences, which formed a parallelogram, whose exact size is still uncertain. At the south gate the rampart on one side of the opening was sharply in-turned, whilst the other curved more gently. The groundplan of the small (0.6 hectare) fortlet at Crawford in Strathclyde is particularly unusual, as the main street ran down the longitudinal axis of the site providing only a central range and *praetentura*, which has more in common with Claudian sites such as Hod Hill or Valkenburg. Although Flavian forts were in general

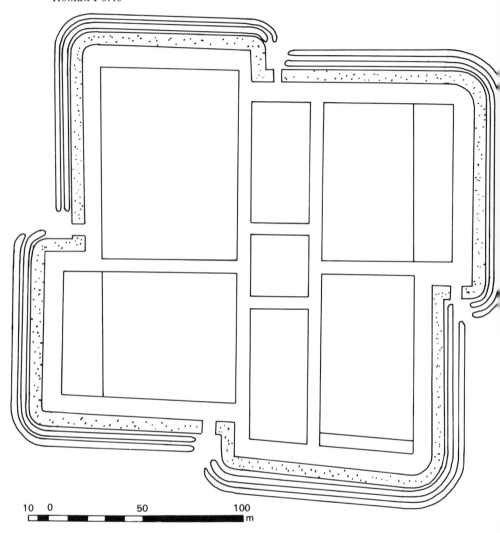

10 0   50   100
                                          m

192. Newstead, c. AD 80. Scale 1:2000

characterised by their regular rectangular or square shape,[46] several striking examples of what appears to be experimentation in the layout of defensive circuits have been discovered. At **Newstead**, for example, a fort was built in c. AD 80 overlooking the crossing of the river Tweed by Dere Street, at Melrose. Basically rectangular in shape the clay rampart and two ditches of each quarter of the circuit were offset and staggered at the gateways to produce an unusual layout (covering 4.3 hectares over the ramparts), which would expose the vulnerable right-hand side of an attacker to fire from the

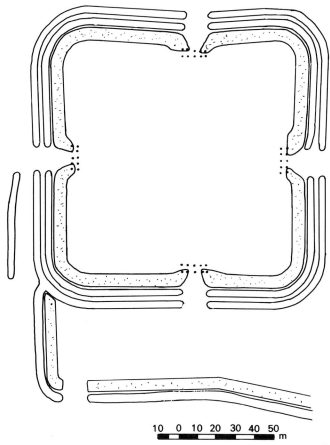

193. Oakwood, c. AD 80. Scale 1:2000

ramparts.[47] Another device was used to enable greater surveillance at the approach to the gateways at Oakwood, in southern Scotland, where the rampart ends were inturned at the openings and the timber gateways set right back from the rampart line.[48]

The departure of Agricola from Britain in AD 84/5, recalled by the new emperor Domitian (who had succeeded his brother Titus in AD 81), marks the limit of Flavian expansion in Britain, and within just a few years the Roman army had abandoned not only its new fortress but also most of its forts north of the Forth–Clyde isthmus: a withdrawal precipitated by events in Germany which urgently demanded the removal of one of Britain's four legions (*legio II Adiutrix*) to fight against the Chatti on the Danube.[49] There was no formal frontier line at this period, but rather a complex of forts spread out over the whole of northern England and southern Scotland which extended, with a few possible exceptions, no farther than this point, defining the extent of Roman interest and influence.

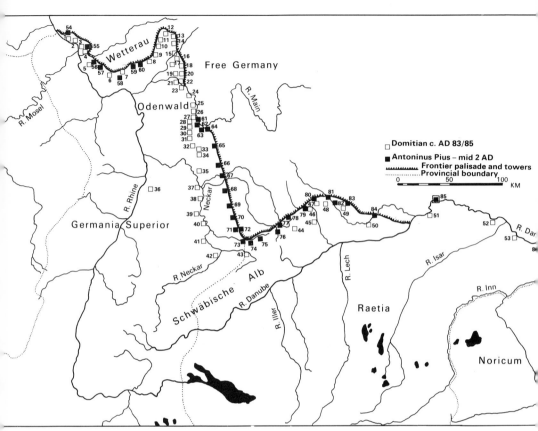

Map 5   The German and Raetian frontier, from Domitian to Antoninus
Pius, AD 81–mid 2nd century AD.

The beginning of Domitian's reign saw expansion in Germany. From
AD 83–85 he fought against the Germanic tribe of the Chatti, whose
territory lay in and beyond the Wetterau plain in the central Rhineland,
between the Taunus and Vogelsberg mountains. Probably shortly after the
conclusion of these campaigns the provinces of Lower Germany (*Germania
Inferior*) and Upper Germany (*Germania Superior*) were officially con-
stituted, with provincial capitals at Cologne and Mainz respectively. The
offensive against free Germany was never fully accomplished, partly as a
result of the withdrawal of troops from the Main area following the
attempted coup of one of the legionary commanders, L. Antonius
Saturninus in AD 88–9, and partly because troubles on the Danube were
increasingly demanding reinforcements.[50] Although never originally intended as such the halt line of this advance, which had thrust deep into the
Wetterau, became the frontier of the empire, at first defined simply by a
pathway cleared through the forest, guarded by timber watchtowers, with
small earth-and-timber forts at the rear.[51]

260

Domitian c. AD 83/85

1	Heddesdorf
2	Bendorf
3	Niederberg
4	Ems
5	Marienfels
6	Kemel
7	Zugmantel
8	Saalburg
9	Kapersburg
10	Langenhain
11	Butzbach
12	Arnsburg
13	Inheiden
14	Echzell
15	Oberflorstadt
16	Altenstadt
17	Heldenbergen
18	Marköbel
19	Hanau-Kesselstadt
20	Rückingen
21	Hainstadt
22	Gross-Krotzenburg
23	Seligenstadt
24	Stockstadt
25	Niedernberg
26	Obernburg
27	Seckmauern
28	Lützelbach
29	Vielbrunn
30	Eulbach
31	Würzberg
32	Hesselbach
33	Schlossau
34	Oberscheidental
35	Neckarburken
36	Wiesental
37	Wimpfen
38	Heilbronn-Böckingen
39	Walheim
40	Benningen
41	Stuttgart-Bad Cannstatt
42	Köngen
43	Eislingen-Salach
44	Oberdorf a.I
45	Munningen
46	Aufkirchen
47	Unterschwaningen
48	Gnotzheim
49	Weissenburg
50	Pfünz
51	Alkofen
52	Steinkirchen
53	Künzing

Antoninus Pius (mid 2nd century AD)

54	Niederbieber
55	Arzbach
56	Hunzel
57	Holzhausen
58	Heidekringen
59	Heftrich
60	Feldberg
61	Wörth
62	Trennfurt
63	Miltenberg-Altstadt
64	Miltenberg-East
65	Walldürn
66	Osterburken
67	Jagsthausen
68	Öhringen
69	Mainhardt
70	Murrhardt
71	Welzheim
72	Welzheim-East
73	Lorch
74	Schirenhof
75	Unterböbingen
76	Aalen
77	Buch
78	Halheim
79	Ruffenhofen
80	Dambach
81	Gunzenhausen
82	Theilenhofen
83	Ellingen
84	Böhming
85	Regensburg
86	Passau

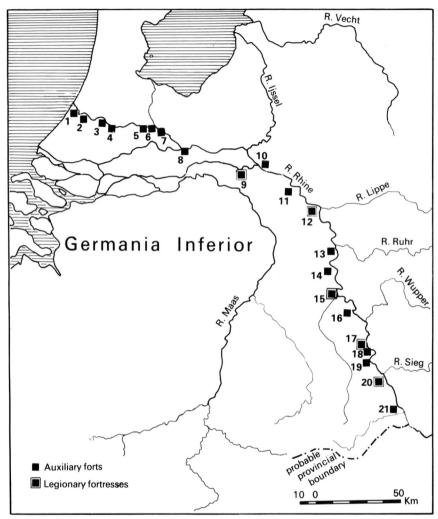

Map 6 The Roman frontier in Lower Germany (Germania Inferior).

1	Valkenburg	12	Xanten (*Vetera*)
2	Leiden-Roomburg	13	Moers-Asberg
3	Alphen	14	Krefeld-Gellep (*Gelduba*)
4	Alphen-Zwammerdam	15	Neuss (*Novaesium*)
5	Vleuten-De Meern	16	Dormagen
6	Utrecht	17	Köln (*Apud Aram Ubiorum*)
7	Bunnik-Vechten	18	Köln-Altenburg
8	Maurik	19	Wesseling
9	Nijmegen (*Noviomagus*)	20	Bonn (*Bonna*)
10	Herwen en Aerdt-de Bijland	21	Remagen
11	Kalkar-Altkalkar		

This frontier (*limes*) was extended on the north-west to include the Neuwied basin, as far as the right bank of the Rhine at the mouth of the Vinxtbach; the frontier of Lower Germany remained unchanged on the left bank of the Rhine. To the south the *limes* followed first the line of the river Main, defended by earth-and-timber forts on its west bank, and then passed through the forests of the Odenwald, where it was defined by a road, watchtowers, and a series of small fortlets. Further south the left bank of the middle Neckar was included, eventually linking up with a line of forts connected by a road, which had been advanced some distance north of the Danube into the Swabian Alb. The frontier then crossed the Danube near the fort of Eining and continued eastwards upon its southern bank. Here, as in so many Flavian forts in Britain, most of the frontier forts were continuously occupied well into the third century AD, and so traces of the earliest earth-and-timber layouts are difficult to find. The most detailed picture of a timber fort constructed c. AD 90 has been recovered from the Danubian fort of Künzing.

Extensive exploratory excavations at **Künzing** have enabled most of the groundplan of this c. 2 hectare fort to be restored. The *principia*, which was examined in detail, was fronted by a forehall; this is the earliest date at which the forehall appears. Four pairs of barracks in the *praetentura* have been interpreted as the accommodation for the attested garrison, *cohors III Thracum c. R. equitata*, with possible stabling located in the *retentura*, together with further accommodation for a small detachment, possibly of frontier scouts.[52]

Similar in date is the fort of **Heidenheim**, built c. AD 90 and occupied until c. AD 150. With an internal area of 4.8 hectares it was the largest auxiliary fort in Raetia, garrisoned by an *ala milliaria* (*ala II Flavia pia fidelis milliaria*). The fort was defended by a stone wall, and fragments of a stone-built *principia* have also survived showing that it too had a forehall. Three timber barracks in the left *praetentura* provide the only evidence available for the accommodation provided for a milliary *ala*; each block provided 12 spacious *contubernia*, with projecting officers' quarters at each end.

Several earth-and-timber forts on the southern fringes of the Wetterau, on the plain of the river Main, were rebuilt in stone round about AD 90, or soon after.[53] The best preserved example is seen at **Wiesbaden**, which was occupied until the Hadrianic reorganisation of this part of the frontier in AD 121–2. A stone wall enclosed an almost square area of c. 2 hectares, giving a broad central range and *praetentura*, but a shallow *retentura*. Most of the buildings in the central range are known, all with stone foundations, but only the street system and fragmentary traces of the rest of the fort layout are known.

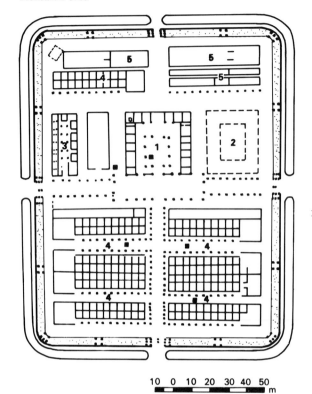

10 0 10 20 30 40 50
m

194. Künzig,
c. AD 90,
(timber).
(1) *principia*,
(2) site of
praetorium,
largely
unexplored,
(3) corridor-plan ?
storebuilding or
workshop,
(4) barracks,
(5) ? stables.
Scale 1:2000

195. Wiesbaden,
c. AD 90,
(stone).
(1) *principia*,
(2) ? *praetorium*,
(3) granaries,
(4) *fabrica*,
(5) barrack.
Scale 1:2000

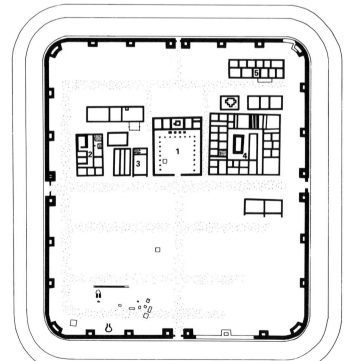

10 0 10 20 30 40 50
m

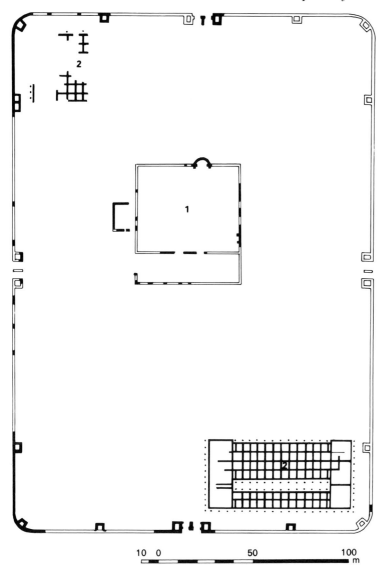

196. Heidenheim, c. AD 90, with stone-built *principia* (1), and timber
barracks (2). Scale 1:2000

Trajan
(AD 98–117)

The attention of the soldier-emperor Trajan was firmly focused upon the Danubian provinces and the East. Having successfully overcome the Dacians, who threatened the security of the middle and lower Danube, in the wars of AD 101–2 and 105–6,[54] he subsequently turned his attention, with less success, to Arabia and the kingdom of Parthia in the East:[55] he was responsible for no new initiatives on either the British or German frontiers.

In Britain his reign saw the final withdrawal of troops from Scotland as far south as the Tyne–Solway isthmus, where an east–west road known as the Stanegate and built by Agricola, linked two important river crossings of major roads into Scotland: Carlisle on the west and Corbridge on the east. The scanty evidence for this period suggests that small forts[56] may have been spaced along it at regular intervals, reinforced by watchtowers, to protect military traffic and allow extensive patrolling of the new border zone, although no actual physical barrier was envisaged until the reign of Hadrian.

After a period of some 20–30 years' service the defences and timber buildings of many Flavian forts and fortresses in Britain were coming to an end of their structural lives, and the most significant feature of military building at the beginning of the second century AD is the change, albeit gradual, from timber to stone construction. The decision to start rebuilding some forts in stone during the Trajanic period reflects a shift in imperial policy towards stability and consolidation within the existing boundaries, and away from territorial expansion. The erection of a stone building or gate was normally commemorated by an inscribed stone slab, and with the increase in the amount of stone building comes a corresponding growth in the number of inscriptions, which can often provide precise details of the date of construction and the name of the garrison involved. Inscriptions record rebuilding in the legionary fortresses of Caerleon (AD 100), Chester (AD 102–17) and York (AD 107–8).[57] Initially the defences only were rebuilt, and the internal buildings followed later in a rather piecemeal fashion, which means that the work may often have taken several decades to complete.[58]

The internal layout of **Caerleon** is the best known, as the site has remained relatively free from subsequent occupation. It had all the same basic elements previously seen at Inchtuthil, although here the bathhouse lay within the *praetentura* and not outside the defences, and an amphitheatre was discovered outside the south-west gate.

A handful of auxiliary forts are also believed to have received a new stone defensive wall at this time.[59] The front of the existing earth or turf rampart was normally cut back to receive the new stone face, and the gates and angle

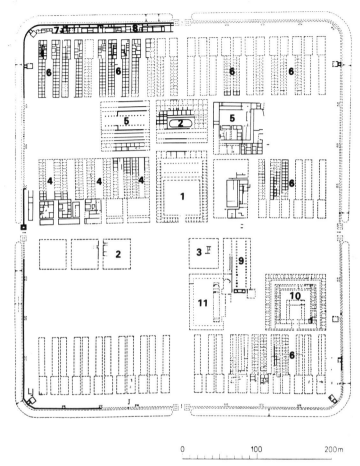

197. Caerleon, legionary fortress, c. AD 100 (stone). (1) *principia*, (2) *praetorium*, (3) tribunes' houses, (4) barracks of the First Cohort, (5) ? storebuildings/workshops, (6) barracks, (7) latrine, (8) workshops, (9) ? *schola* of the First Cohort, (10) hospital, (11) baths. Scale 1:5000

and interval towers were replaced at the same time: as in the legionary examples the reconstruction of the interior tended to be piecemeal, starting with the principal buildings in the central range.

Completely new Trajanic forts were built in London and at **Gelligaer** in South Wales, where extensive excavations at the turn of this century have revealed most of the fort plan. The new fort was built alongside its larger

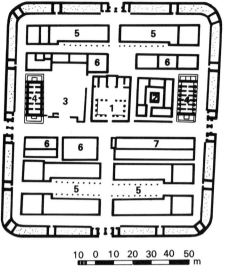

198. Gelligaer,
 c. AD 103–111 (stone).
(1) *principia*, (2)
praetorium, (3) walled
compound with latrine,
(4) granaries, (5)
barracks, (6) unknown
function, (7) ? stable
with water tank
outside. Scale 1:2000

10 0 10 20 30 40 50 m

Flavian predecessor, with the defences enclosing an almost square area of 1.2 hectares. The earthen rampart was faced at the front with a stone wall and had, unusually, a masonry revetment also at the rear. The gates were flanked by square towers set within the width of the rampart, characteristic of the plan of most stone gateways in the second century. The construction date is known from inscriptions found at the principal gateways to have been AD 103–11; the work was carried out by *legio II Augusta*.[60] The internal buildings also had stone foundations, although they may well have had timber superstructures. In their groundplan and arrangement they conformed closely to the general pattern already established in Flavian earth-and-timber forts such as Fendoch or Künzing. To the north-east of the fort lay a roughly paved parade ground, and attached to the south-eastern defences was an annexe also defended by a stone wall (which may not have been built until the third or fourth centuries), enclosing the bathhouse and other stone buildings.

In Germany this period saw the reorganisation of the civilian administration safe behind the new frontier. The pattern of rebuilding Flavian earth-and-timber forts in stone which was seen in Britain also continued here, as can be seen, for example, at Benningen, Stuttgart-Bad Cannstatt or Neckarburken, on the Neckar *limes*.[61] Unfortunately only a very few details of their internal arrangements survive. The new defensive walls incorporated square interval towers and trapezoidal angle towers, and the gates were flanked by square towers which projected slightly beyond the face of the fort wall. At Benningen only fragmentary traces of the *principia* and two granaries on either side of the front gate, have been located. At Bad Cannstatt the *principia*, with an apsidal *sacellum*, lay upon the longitudinal axis of the fort, more reminiscent of first-century layouts. The cohort fort at

Neckarburken had a large *principia*, with an internally apsed *sacellum*. Only 200 metres to the west lay a smaller fort of about one quarter its size, probably designed to house a *numerus*. This fort (Neckarburken-East) was also defended by a stone wall, enclosing a rather irregular shape with rounded corners; no traces of internal buildings were found. In size this fort corresponds closely with the *numerus* forts erected on the Odenwald *limes*.

One of them, at **Hesselbach**, was constructed in earth-and-timber in c. AD 100, and was occupied until AD 115/130, when it was rebuilt with stone defences. The earthen rampart had a timber revetment at the front, mortised into horizontal timbers spaced throughout the body of the rampart. The area enclosed was just 0.6 hectares. Internally the layout comprised a central range and *praetentura* with no separate *retentura*. The tiny *principia* had a forehall. Behind it lay probably a small courtyard-plan *praetorium*, and on either side stretched a pair of barrack blocks.[62]

Hadrian
(AD 117–38)

After making a personal inspection of the British and German provinces in AD 121–2 the emperor Hadrian determined to define the frontiers by means of permanent physical barriers. In Britain a stone wall with a ditch in front was built, 76 Roman miles long, linking the river Tyne with the Solway, which was designed 'to separate the Romans from the barbarians' according to his biographer, who also records the erection of a timber palisade along the entire length of the Upper German and Raetian *limes* at the same time.[63]

Originally only part of Hadrian's Wall was built in stone, comprising the eastern stretch from Newcastle upon Tyne to the river Irthing, and the remainder, as far as Bowness on Solway, was completed in turf. Subsequently this turf sector was rebuilt in stone and the Wall was extended east from Newcastle along the north bank of the Tyne to Wallsend. Spaced at intervals of one Roman mile were fortlets, which provided double gates at the front and rear giving access through the frontier, and also contained barrack blocks to house the guards and soldiers on patrol. Between the milecastles lay two small square turrets, similar to the watchtowers used on the German frontier, although here they were all stone-built. A similar combination of fortlets and turrets was continued beyond Bowness and down the Cumbrian coast for a distance of at least 40 kilometres; but here no wall was necessary.

It had been intended at the start of the project to incorporate the forts of the earlier Stanegate line to back up the new frontier, whilst beyond the Wall, to the north-west, three additional outpost forts were built, probably to secure friendly territory which had been isolated in front of the new barrier.[64]

Map 7   The forts on Hadrian's Wall.

However, the need was soon realised for auxiliary garrisons to be actually stationed on the line of the Wall rather than in the rear, and so fourteen or fifteen new stone-built forts[65] were added, and where parts of the Wall or turrets had already been constructed they were demolished to accommodate the new forts. They were probably all designed to lie astride the Wall initially, with their front and both principal gates opening to the north to permit swift and easy access,[66] although at Housesteads and Bowness the Wall ran upon the top of a scarp with a precipitous slope to the north, which dictated that the forts here should be appended to the rear of the frontier instead. By the time the latest in this series of forts were built (c. AD 128–38) this design feature had been abandoned and the new forts, at Greatchesters, Carrawburgh and Carvoran, all abutted the rear of the Wall. Behind the forts the frontier zone was further defined by the *vallum*, an earthwork consisting of a flat-bottomed ditch with earthen mounds on each side set back c. 10 metres from the lip of the ditch; the whole earthwork being some 36 metres wide.

The Hadrian's Wall forts appear generally to have conformed to the 'standard' layout seen in the earth-and-timber forts of the Flavian period, now translated into a more durable material. Their average size was between 1.4 and 2 hectares, but there were larger forts also such as Stanwix, which is thought to have been the base of a milliary *ala*, and smaller fortlets are known at Drumburgh, and Beckfoot on the Cumbrian coast.[67] All were rectangular with rounded corners and defended by a stone wall with an earthen rampart backing, with square interval and angle towers. The four principal gateways had double carriageways with square or rectangular towers set within the line of the rampart, and in those forts which did project beyond the Wall additional single portal gates were provided (*portae quintanae*) at each end of the *via quintana*. All the Hadrian's Wall forts were occupied on and off well into the fourth century AD and consequently underwent a great deal of rebuilding and modification, so that it is often difficult to detect the original Hadrianic plan beneath the many later levels. In almost all cases, however, it has been possible to trace the circuit of the defences and sometimes recover the groundplan of at least the central buildings, and perhaps one or two barracks.

The fort at **Housesteads** has been extensively explored. The stone defensive wall with a clay backing enclosed an area of 1.7 hectares. Excavations in 1898[68] enabled a very full plan of the internal layout to be made, but although the outlines of the stone internal buildings were uncovered the structural phases were not determined, and it was not until the programme of re-excavation and consolidation undertaken during the last twenty years by the Department of the Environment that detailed information about the original Hadrianic layout has emerged. Much of the Hadrianic groundplan has also been revealed at **Wallsend**, and less at **Benwell**, which were neighbouring forts at the eastern end of the frontier. In all three forts the *principia* was flanked by a double buttressed granary and a courtyard-plan *praetorium*, with a small hospital behind. Very few details of the original plan of other Hadrian's Wall forts have been found, with the exception of the headquarters building,[69] which had the same basic design in each of the forts—five rear rooms, a cross-hall with a row of aisle posts down one side and perhaps a passageway behind, and a colonnaded courtyard beyond, with no forehall or *armamentaria*. The barracks at Housesteads and Benwell were L-shaped, with verandahs, providing ten

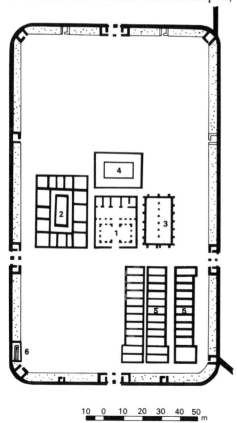

10 0 10 20 30 40 50
━━━━━━━━━━━━━━━━ m

199. Housesteads, Hadrianic (stone). (1) *principia*, (2) *praetorium*, (3) double granary, (4) hospital, (5) barracks, (6) latrine. Scale 1:2000

and nine *contubernia* respectively, whilst those at Wallsend, also with nine barrack rooms, were rectangular with no projecting rooms, still providing officers' accommodation at one end.

Other auxiliary forts built in stone at this date include **Ambleside** and **Hardknott** in Cumbria, which were built to control the road which ran from Ravenglass on the Cumbrian coast over the Wrynose and Hardknott Passes to Ambleside, at the northern end of Lake Windermere. Only the defences and the buildings in the central range have been investigated.

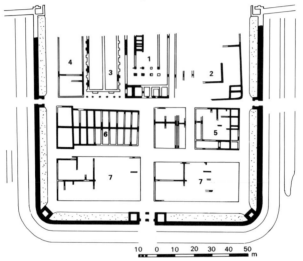

200. Benwell, Hadrianic (stone) (1) *principia* with water-settling tank in the courtyard, (2) traces of the *praetorium*, (3) double granary, (4) workshop, (5) hospital, (6) barracks, (7) ? barracks or stables; the internal arrangements are too fragmentary to be certain. Scale 1:2000

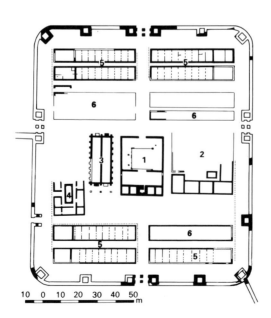

201. Wallsend, Hadrianic (stone). (1) *principia*, (2) *praetorium*, (3) double granary, (4) hospital, (5) barracks, (6) ? stores or stables. Scale 1:2000

Although they had stone foundations it is probable that their superstructures were of timber. Both headquarters buildings had three rear rooms, a cross-hall and a courtyard flanked by L-shaped rooms. The *praetorium* at Hardknott had only one stone-built wing. It is possible that the building was unfinished, but it is more likely that the rest of the house was timber-built. In many forts in northern England and Wales rebuilding was in progress at this time, with stone walls being added to existing earth or turf ramparts.[70]

In Germany Hadrian was responsible not only for the introduction of a timber palisade to demark the frontier, but also for rationalising the siting and organisation of the associated auxiliary forts and *numerus* fortlets,[71] and during his reign a number of small earth-and-timber forts on or near the *limes* were enlarged to hold a full auxiliary garrison.[72] At the **Saalburg**, in the Taunus mountains, for example, between AD 125 and 139 the Flavian fortlet of 0.7 hectares was enlarged to a 3.2 hectare fort for *cohors II Raetorum c.R. (equitata)*. Very little is known about its internal plan at this time, but its defensive wall had an unusual construction, as it consisted not of a single stone wall with an earthen bank behind, which is seen in many contemporary forts in Britain and Germany, but instead had a front and rear stone revetment, enclosing a rubble core, which was strengthened by regularly spaced transverse timbers.[73] The *numerus* fortlet at **Hesselbach**

202. Ambleside, Hadrianic (stone). (1) *principia*, (2) *praetorium*, (3) double granary. Scale 1:2000

203. Hesselbach, Hadrianic (timber). (1) *principia*, (2) *praetorium*, (3) barracks, (4) uncertain function. Scale 1:2000

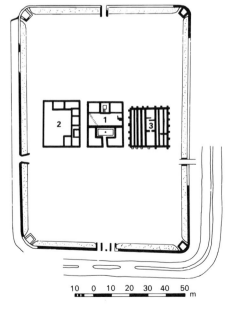

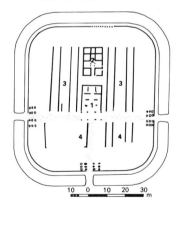

273

was also defended in the Hadrianic period by a wall consisting of a double drystone revetment with an earth core, reminiscent of the fort wall in the Trajanic Welsh fort of Gelligaer.

At other German sites stone defensive walls were added to old ramparts although, as at Hardknott in Cumbria, the internal buildings were not necessarily all renewed in stone, and they often remained a mixture of timber and stone construction. On the eastern side of the Wetterau *limes* the timber fort of Echzell was rebuilt during the reign of Hadrian, with a stone defensive wall, to which the gates and towers were subsequently added, and new timber internal buildings. Elsewhere on this frontier forts such as Butzbach, Kapersburg and Zugmantel all had new stone walls, although most of the internal buildings, with the exception of the *principia*, were of timber.[74]

Antoninus Pius
(AD 138–61)

The Antonine period saw advances in the frontiers of both northern Britain and central Germany, the result being the desertion of Hadrian's Wall and the Odenwald-Neckar *limes*.

Within just twenty years of its conception Hadrian's Wall was abandoned and a new barrier, the Antonine Wall, was constructed 160 kilometres further north, across the Forth–Clyde isthmus. The precise reasons for this change are not clear; it probably followed the suppression of an uprising in the Scottish lowlands at the very beginning of Pius' reign, although few details have survived in the documentary records.[75] The decision for this shift in policy was made and implemented without delay by the new governor, Q. Lollius Urbicus. By AD 139–40 he is named on two inscriptions from Corbridge,[76] which appears to have been reoccupied at this time as a supply base for the advance north. Many of the new forts established by Lollius Urbicus as he advanced along the major routes north into the lowlands of Scotland, in the Forth–Clyde isthmus, and beyond the new frontier in Strathmore, occupied sites which had been chosen originally by Agricola sixty years previously.[77]

The Antonine Wall consisted of a turf rampart upon a cobbled stone foundation, with a ditch in front and a military road running parallel at the rear. It was only half the length of Hadrian's Wall, extending for a distance of 60 kilometres, from Bridgeness on the Firth of Forth to Old Kilpatrick on the Clyde estuary. Like its Hadrianic predecessor the new frontier had forts not only along the line of the Wall, but also on the southern banks of the estuaries to protect its flanks.[78] The new Wall was defended by a total of probably nineteen forts (sixteen are known and three more inferred). Unlike the Hadrianic frontier there were no regularly spaced milecastles, although a

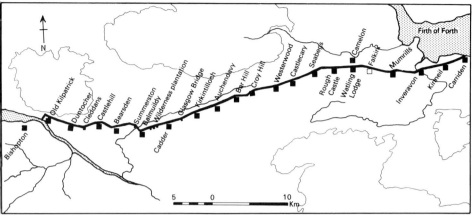

Map 8   The forts on the Antonine Wall.

handful of small fortlets slightly larger than the Hadrian's Wall milecastles have been found between some of the forts. Turrets were not provided either, but six beacon platforms for signalling are known.

Most of the forts abutted the rear of the Wall, with the exception of Bar Hill, which was completely detached. They ranged in size from only 0.2 hectares at Duntocher to 2.6 hectares at Mumrills, with an average of about 1.3 hectares.[79] Several would have been too small to accommodate a full auxiliary garrison. They lay much closer together than the forts on Hadrian's Wall, the average distance between them being only about three kilometres, but their spacing was less regular, with more emphasis placed upon the local topography in the siting of each fort. Like the Antonine Wall itself, most of the fort ramparts were of turf set upon a stone base, with regular drainage channels cut through them to ensure stability. (The only exceptions were at Balmuildy and Castlecary, where stone defensive walls were built.) The number of ditches varied from two to four. Internally the principal buildings were of stone, or were at least stone-founded; the barracks, stables and stores were timber-built. Each fort had an adjoining annexe, often as big as the fort itself, defended by a rampart and ditch. Insufficient excavation has been carried out to reveal a clear picture of their internal arrangements, but they usually contained a stone-built bathhouse and probably a complex of timber storebuildings and sheds for military equipment and wagons. The provision of these annexes appears to be a departure from the Hadrian's Wall forts, although on Hadrian's Wall the military zone demarcated by the *vallum* would have allowed enough space for this type of accommodation in the vicinity of each fort.

The central range normally consisted of the *principia*, flanked on either side by a single buttressed granary. On one side was the commander's house

275

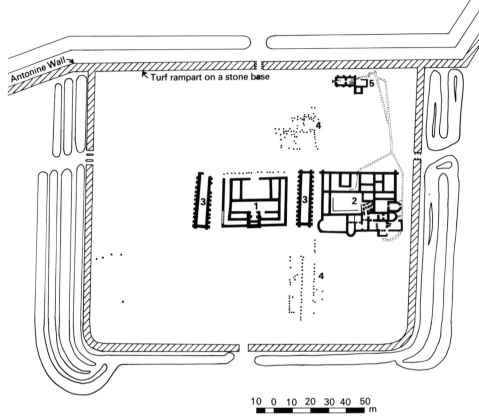

Antonine Wall

Turf rampart on a stone base

10 0 10 20 30 40 50
m

204. Mumrills, Antonine (principal buildings stone). (1) *principia*, (2) *praetorium* with adjoining bathhouse, (3) granaries, (4) postholes of timber buildings in the *praetentura*, (5) internal bathhouse. Scale 1:2000

and on the other stores and workshops, in contrast to the Hadrianic forts, which tended to have either a double or pair of single granaries on one side of the *principia* with the *praetorium* on the opposite side. There were variations in both the size and shape and in the internal arrangements of the Antonine Wall forts.[80] In most cases the *via principalis* ran parallel with the Antonine rampart and the forts faced to the north, which meant that at Mumrills and Castlecary the main street ran along the longitudinal rather than the short axis of the fort. The only exception is at Cadder, where the principal buildings faced east. Several of the forts had an internal bathhouse built against the rear of the rampart in addition to a larger bath building in the annexe.

276

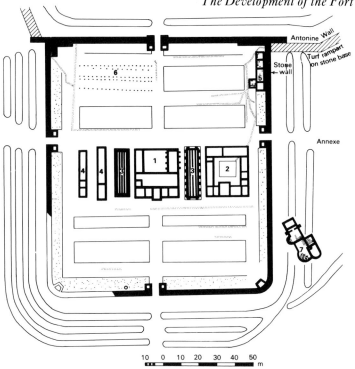

205. Balmuildy, Antonine (principal buildings stone). (1) *principia*,
(2) *praetorium*, (3) granaries, (4) ? stores, (5) internal bathhouse, (6) traces of timber barracks, (7) bathhouse in annexe.
Scale 1:2000

Recent excavations have revealed a very unusual ground plan at
Bearsden. The majority of the internal buildings were timber, except for
two single buttressed granaries sited on opposite sides of the principal street
close to the west gate. No trace of a *principia* was found, and on the site
where it would normally be expected were found only a few postholes; an
adjacent winged building was probably a workshop. The barrack blocks
were particularly short, and lacked verandahs. The apparent absence of a
principia and the considerable amount of granary space for such a small (1
hectare) fort suggests that this may have been an outstation garrisoned by a
small auxiliary detachment, with the commanding officer and the bulk of the
cohort stationed in a larger neighbouring fort.[81] A well-preserved stone-
built bathhouse, with a timber changing room (*apodyterium*) stood in the
annexe to the east of the fort.

When the Antonine Wall was completed in the mid-140s AD the
Hadrianic frontier was abandoned, the milecastle gates probably removed,
and stretches of the *vallum* infilled at regular intervals to allow the free
movement of traffic; despite this withdrawal from the frontier some of the
forts actually on the Wall line may have remained occupied.[82] Forts were

277

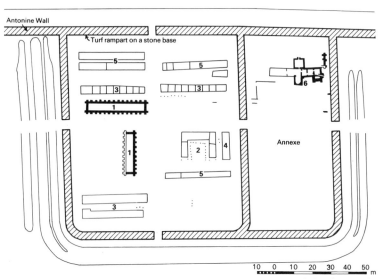

206. Bearsden, Antonine, stone granaries (1), the rest of the internal buildings were timber, (2) *fabrica*, (3) barracks, (4) store, (5) unknown function, (6) stone bathhouse with timber-built changing room in annexe. Scale 1:2000

once again built in the Lowlands of Scotland, often reoccupying Agricolan sites, and spaced along the lines of the two major supply routes between the two walls: Dere Street on the east and via Annandale and Nithsdale into Clydesdale on the west. These new forts were garrisoned by troops drawn from Hadrian's Wall, the Pennines, and probably also from Wales.

Most of the Antonine forts in Scotland show two distinct periods of occupation, the second following upon a brief abandonment. The dating of this activity is far from conclusive, but taking into account what scanty documentary references are available, together with the evidence of the samian pottery, coins and inscriptions, it seems most likely that the Antonine Wall with its outpost forts, and back-up forts in the Lowlands, was held for only twelve or thirteen years before it was given up temporarily, perhaps as a result of a native uprising.[83] A short second occupation lasted only from c. AD 159 until c. 163, when it was finally abandoned and Hadrian's Wall brought back into commission. The forts were destroyed at the end of both Antonine periods, but whether this was because of enemy action or due to deliberate demolition and site clearance by the Roman army prior to an orderly evacuation, is extremely difficult to establish from the archaeological evidence.

A small number of Antonine forts were defended by often elaborate multiple ditch systems, which are particularly striking at the outpost fort of Ardoch, and at Birrens in the Lowlands, and Brough-on-Noe in Derbyshire.

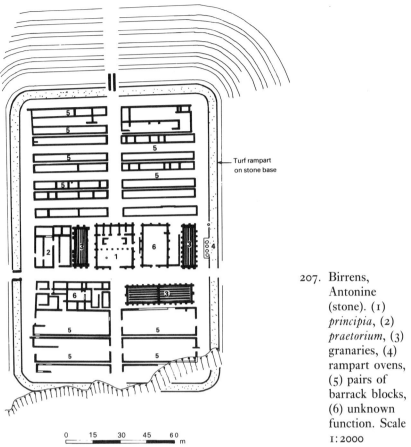

Turf rampart
on stone base

207. Birrens,
Antonine
(stone). (1)
principia, (2)
praetorium, (3)
granaries, (4)
rampart ovens,
(5) pairs of
barrack blocks,
(6) unknown
function. Scale
1:2000

0 15 30 45 60
m

The fort at **Birrens** had a long history. Originally a Flavian foundation the site was reoccupied as a western outlier to Hadrian's Wall. It was then rebuilt during the first Antonine period as one of the forts guarding the Annandale route up to the new frontier. The defences comprised six ditches on the uphill northern side, one on the west, and possibly two on the east: the southern defences had been eroded by the river. The turf rampart on a stone base, so characteristic of Antonine Wall forts, enclosed an area of 1.7 hectares. In 1895 the excavators discovered two periods of stone walling in the internal buildings, but unfortunately the published excavation plan failed to distinguish between the primary and secondary work, and so the plan of the interior remains very much confused. Further excavations in 1962–7 located six 'paired' blocks in the *retentura* and four in the *praetentura*. Each of these pairs of long narrow buildings has been interpreted as one barrack block with a double longitudinal partition.[84] In the second Antonine occupation the fort was rebuilt upon a thick layer of burnt debris from its predecessor, and some of the stone structures still

279

visible amid the debris had their foundations incorporated into the new buildings, which were of inferior workmanship.

An important military strongpoint was held in the Lowlands of Scotland at **Newstead**, which was sited upon the highest part of a ridge overlooking the crossing of the river Tweed by Dere Street, at Melrose. The military importance of the site is reflected in the succession of four exceptionally large permanent fortifications established here, the earliest dating to the campaigns of Agricola, followed by another fort in the late Domitianic period and then by two periods of Antonine occupation. The Antonine defences consisted of two ditches with a stone defensive wall backed by a wide clay rampart, enclosing an area of 4.4 hectares. The stone-built internal buildings had the usual range of buildings in the central range, with the *principia* flanked by granaries and a courtyard *praetorium* beyond, and the *praetentura* was filled with twelve similar-sized barrack blocks, each comprising eleven detached *contubernia*. Unusually a stone wall with a central gateway flanked by guardchambers ran across the *retentura* at a distance of some 32 metres from the rear of the central buildings.

The director of the first excavations here at the turn of the century, James Curle, believed that this wall represented a contraction in the defences owing to a reduction in the size of the garrison.[85] Subsequent excavation by Professor Richmond, however, suggested that this was a dividing rather than a reducing wall, producing a separate walled enclave in the *retentura*. The garrison of the fort is not certain, although centurions of *legio XX* are attested on several undated altars, and so is the quingenary *ala Vocontiorum*.[86] It is therefore thought possible that a composite unit was stationed here, comprising a legionary vexillation with a quingenary *ala*. If this was the case the barracks in the *praetentura* would have housed the legionaries, with the men and horses of the *ala* accommodated behind the dividing wall in the rear of the fort.[87] The relationship between the external fort walls and this cross wall has not yet been examined, however, nor have any structures been found in the *retentura*, and so many questions about the garrison and the internal layout of this fort still remain unanswered.[88]

In the second Antonine period the fort wall was reconstructed and repaired on the same lines, the dividing wall demolished, and triple ditches dug. The garrison at this time is also uncertain although the *ala Petriana*, the only milliary *ala* stationed in Britain, has been suggested.[89] Most of the central buildings and the barracks in the *praetentura* remained in use, with some modifications, and several rectangular stone buildings in the *retentura* may have provided stables or store buildings.

The construction of the new frontier demanded a thorough re-organisation of auxiliary units to man it, and consequently several Welsh forts were abandoned at this time and their garrisons transferred north.[90] At many of the forts retained in service in Wales the earthen defences and timber internal buildings were consolidated in stone at this time.[91]

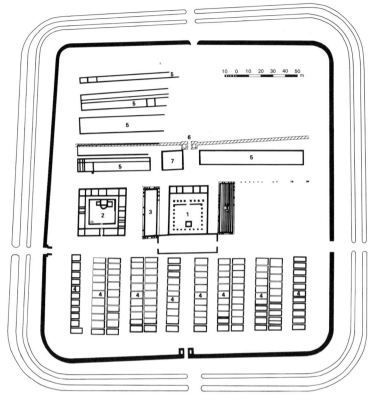

208. Newstead, Antonine 1 and 2 (stone). (1) *principia*, (2) *praetorium*, (3) granaries, (4) barracks, (5) ? stables or stores, (6) dividing wall, (7) unknown function. Scale 1:3000

Particularly striking are the principal gateways at Castell Collen, which were defended by semi-circular projecting gatetowers, the earliest example in a British auxiliary fort, revealing a new trend in Roman military thinking towards highly defensible strongholds. Another example of approximately the same date, also in Wales, but this time with rectangular projecting gatetowers, is seen at Brecon Gaer (see p. 92).

On the Odenwald *limes* in Upper Germany *numeri* of Britons are attested on inscriptions dated AD 145–6[92] rebuilding timber watchtowers in stone. But within less than a decade the Odenwald-Neckar line was completely abandoned to be replaced by a new frontier some 25 kilometres further east. This transfer must have taken place between AD 148, when the commander of the *cohors I Helvetiorum* dedicated two altars at Heilbronn-Böckingen on the old frontier line, and the death of Antoninus Pius (in AD 161), for he is mentioned on an inscription from one of the new frontier forts at Jagsthausen.[93]

The Antonine *limes* consisted of a palisade running dead straight for a distance of 81 kilometres, from Miltenberg on the river Main to Lorch in the Rems valley, defended by stone watchtowers spaced approximately 500 metres apart, with eight new cohort forts and a few associated *numerus* fortlets.[94] The new forts corresponded closely with those left behind, and in most cases the actual auxiliary units involved in the move have been identified from inscriptions, so that their progress from one frontier to the other can be traced.[95]

Although the defensive circuit and the *principia* have been defined by excavation at several of these forts few other details are known of their internal layouts, which makes it impossible to make closer comparisons between them. Like their predecessors, the majority of the new Antonine cohort forts housed *cohortes quingenariae equitatae*, and were internally some 2 hectares in area, with the 4 hectares fort at Welzheim-West garrisoned by a quingenary *ala*; *numerus* forts lay at Miltenberg-East, Walldürn, Welzheim-East and, from the reign of Commodus, at Osterburken.[96] All the forts were defended by a stone wall with angle and interval towers, with gateways flanked by square towers, whose faces usually projected slightly beyond the face of the fort wall; there were usually two ditches. The stone-built *principia* at Welzheim-West and Murrhardt were reasonably well preserved, whilst fragmentary traces were found at Mainhardt and Jagsthausen. The *sacellum* was normally apsidal, and the courtyard was flanked by *armamentaria*; at both Welzheim-West and Murrhardt forehalls were provided.

From Lorch, eastwards along the Rems valley, the frontier of Raetia was also advanced during the reign of Antoninus Pius to join up with the new Upper German *limes*, and a line of new forts and fortlets was added, continuing as far as the crossing of the Danube near Eining.[97] The defences and one or two stone internal buildings have been located in a number of these forts, although it must be emphasised that most of the excavation was carried out at the turn of the century, and often insufficient stratified material was retrieved to enable the structures to be dated accurately.

The strongpoint of the new frontier was at **Aalen**, the base of the *ala II Flavia milliaria*. With an internal area of 5.6 hectares it was the largest auxiliary fort of the Upper German-Raetian *limes*. Traces of only two stone internal buildings have been located. The *principia*, with a trapezoidal groundplan, had a large forehall, *armamentaria*, and an apsidal shrine containing a cellar. To its right were found several stone-built rooms, one of which was hypocausted, of probably an otherwise timber-built *praetorium*.

Like several of their contemporaries in Scotland the Raetian forts of Unterböbingen and Schirenhof were also defended by at least three ditches. Both had stone defensive walls and, like most of the Antonine forts on the German frontier, the headquarters had an apsidal *sacellum*. The rear gate at

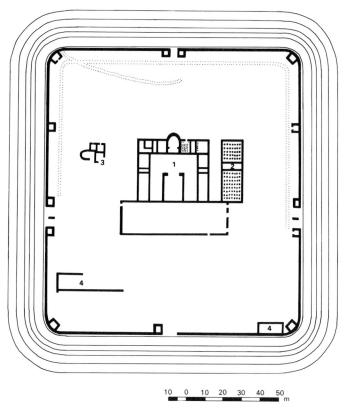

10 0 10 20 30 40 50
m

209. Unterböbingen, Antonine (stone). (1) *principia*, (2) granary, (3) traces of the *praetorium*, (4) unknown function.
Scale 1:2000

Schirenhof was defended by semi-circular projecting gatetowers similar to
those built at Castell Collen, and the rear gate at Theilenhofen also had
projecting gatetowers; here their curved fronts provided a recessed semi-
circular entranceway.

· Elsewhere along this stretch of the frontier rebuilding is attested during
the Antonine period at Gnotzheim, Kösching, Pförring, and probably
Pfünz.[98] To the east of Eining, where the south bank of the Danube again
formed the frontier, the fort of Künzing was rebuilt with a stone defensive
wall towards the end of the Antonine period. The double ditches of the
previous fort were retained, and to them were added three more. Of the
timber internal buildings only the *principia* is known, with a forehall, and
sacellum projecting beyond the rear wall of the building.[99]

The Later Second Century
Marcus Aurelius AD 161–80; Commodus AD 180–92

The later second century was a period of turbulence in which the frontier of Britain was often under threat from the northern tribes beyond, and in Germany also the relative peace which had existed during the reigns of Hadrian and Antoninus Pius was shattered by a succession of wars and native incursions.

Having been repaired and re-garrisoned (probably in the mid-160s AD) Hadrian's Wall and its associated auxiliary forts remained in commission until the fourth century, and during this period there was much rebuilding and modification within the existing defences. Following the withdrawal from the Antonine Wall, Birrens and Netherby were retained as outpost forts on the west of Hadrian's Wall, with Newstead (until c. AD 180) and Risingham on Dere Street. The troops removed from the Antonine frontier were found new accommodation further south, and inscriptions and pottery evidence have shown that there was rebuilding in the AD 160s and 170s at several sites in the Pennines and elsewhere in northern England.[100]

According to his biographer the emperor Marcus Aurelius was faced by troubles in Britain throughout most of his reign,[101] and in the early 180s, at the very beginning of the reign of Commodus, a major uprising is recorded, in which the natives crossed the frontier and killed a Roman commander and the troops accompanying him. The situation was brought under control by the new governor, Ulpius Marcellus in AD 184, and he seems to have been responsible for the reorganisation of the auxiliary garrisons in the frontier zone.[102]

During the reign of Marcus Aurelius the German provinces were threatened by enemy incursions. Information about these attacks is fragmentary and derives mainly from references made by the emperor's biographer; the archaeological evidence for destruction of forts in the frontier zone is slight.[103] The province of Upper Germany was threatened by the Chatti in the 160s, Lower Germany by the Chauci in AD 172, and eastern Raetia and the lower Danubian frontier by the Marcomanni, against whom the emperor waged war in AD 166/7–175. No real traces of enemy action have been found in forts on the eastern edge of the Raetian frontier, although the fort at Straubing was defended by at least four ditches, and three extra ditches may have been added at Künzing (making a total of five) at this time as a precaution.

Under Commodus new fort building is attested at Niederbieber, in the Neuwied basin in the Rhineland, and at Osterburken on the Antonine *limes*.

Niederbieber: This stone fort, situated at the western boundary of the Upper German frontier, some 3.5 kilometres from the right bank of the Rhine, was built c. AD 185–92.[104] Two *numeri* are attested here, although whether they were actually in garrison at the same time is uncertain. With an internal area of 4.9 hectares it was one of the largest forts on the *limes*, comparable in size with the milliary *ala* forts of Heidenheim or Aalen in Raetia, and the garrison here which must have been a particularly strong one, was perhaps comparable in size and status with a milliary *ala*.[105]

210. Niederbieber, c. AD 185 (principal buildings stone). (1) *principia*, (2) *praetorium*, (3) granaries, (4) internal bathhouse, (5) unknown function, (6) hearths marking the position of timber barrack rooms. Scale 1:2000

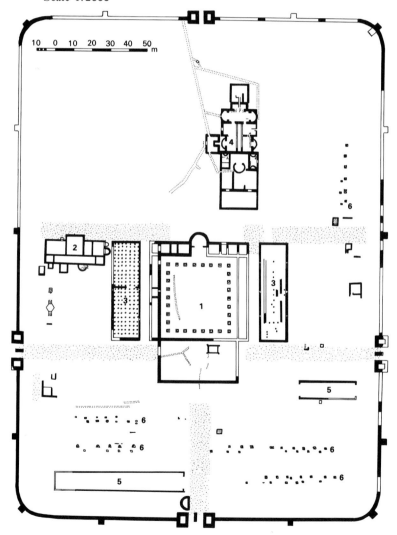

The defences consisted of a stone wall with a single ditch, and beyond it a palisade trench in which may have been set obstacles. The interval and angle towers projected from the external face of the fort wall, as did the gatetowers; a common defensive feature of Roman forts from the mid–late second century onwards. The internal buildings were arranged in a conventional pattern, the *principia* flanked by large unbuttressed granaries, and beyond the stone-built bath suite together with three isolated hypocausted rooms of an otherwise timber-built *praetorium*. An elaborate bathhouse stood in the *retentura*. The barracks were probably either timber or half-timbered upon drystone sleeper walls, for all that remained to define their positions were rows of large and small hearths; small hypocausted chambers at one end of a couple of these blocks probably represent the positions of the officers' quarters.

At **Osterburken** a stone-walled annexe was built to enclose the steep slope which overlooked the existing Antonine cohort fort. When first built the advantages of a good water supply and communications were paramount, but by the reign of Commodus the increasing danger of attack emphasised the tactical weakness of a steep slope above the fort and so the opportunity was taken to include it within the defences, with probably a *numerus* in garrison. Very little of the interior has been investigated, but judging by the steepness it is unlikely that the buildings would have been as closely-packed as they would have been on a level fort platform.

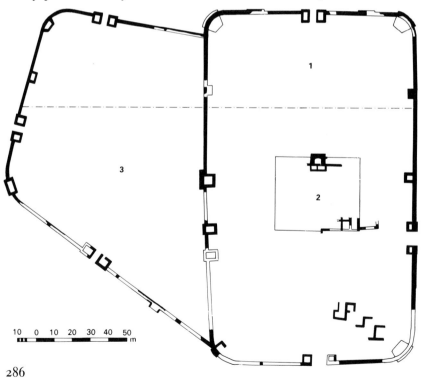

Septimius Severus
(AD 193–211)

The murder of Commodus in AD 192 plunged the empire into civil war, from which Septimius Severus finally emerged the victor in AD 197, having defeated his principal rival D. Clodius Albinus, the governor of Britain, at the battle of Lugudunum.

There is documentary evidence that the northern tribes were once again causing trouble on the British frontier, probably taking advantage of the weaknesses caused by the withdrawal of troops to the continent by Albinus in his struggle against Severus, and the new governor was forced to buy peace from the tribe of Maeatae.[106] The frontier situation probably remained unsettled, for almost a decade later Cassius Dio records the emperor gaining victories in Britain.

At the same time much rebuilding is attested in northern Britain, on Hadrian's Wall, and the outpost forts of Risingham and High Rochester. This programme was not the result of widespread enemy destruction, but rather a necessary programme of modernisation which continued into the middle of the third century. At **Risingham** an inscription was set up over the south gate recording the restoration in AD 205–7 from ground level of the gate and its walls, which had fallen down through old age.[107] The Severan fort wall consisted of very large blocks of fine-grained sandstone with a chamfered plinth, and the gate, built in the same stone, had projecting seven-sided gatetowers flanking a single portal. The only internal building known is a bathhouse at the south-east angle, which was excavated in 1841–2.

A new fort was built at this time at **Bewcastle**, which had originally been the site of an outpost fort for Hadrian's Wall. The whole of the top of a low hill was fortified in an irregular hexagonal shape by a stone wall with a clay backing, enclosing an area of c. 2.4 hectares over the ramparts, with a single ditch in front. The central range of stone buildings was aligned north–south, with the *principia* facing east, and to its right stood two wings of a courtyard *praetorium*. In the *retentura*, built on a completely different alignment parallel to the western defences lay a barrack, and in the south-east *praetentura* the internal bathhouse built in the Hadrianic period remained in use, with modifications, into the Severan period.

Although initially successful in the wars in Britain, by AD 208 Severus' generals were suffering reverses, and the emperor decided to take charge of the campaigns personally, bringing reinforcements with him.[108] Extensive preparations for the new Scottish campaigns were made, which included the

211. Opposite: Osterburken, c. AD 180 (stone). Cohort fort (1) with fragmentary traces of the *principia* (2), and adjoining *numerus* fort (3). Scale 1:2000

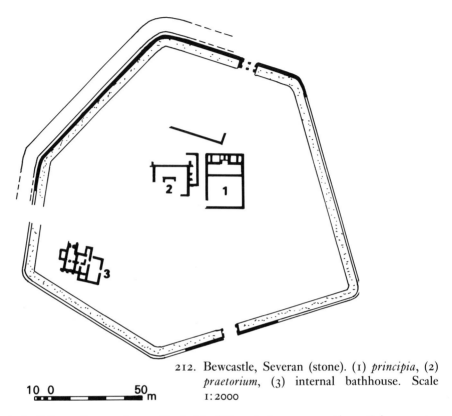

212. Bewcastle, Severan (stone). (1) *principia*, (2) *praetorium*, (3) internal bathhouse. Scale 1:2000

10 0   50 m

rebuilding of granaries at Corbridge[109] and the construction of depots at South Shields on the Tyne, and Cramond on the Firth, to ship supplies by sea.

At **South Shields** the Hadrianic and Antonine auxiliary fort was modified as a supply depot. The *principia* was rebuilt and turned to face in the opposite direction. The adjacent double granary was retained in service and to it were added eighteen single buttressed granaries (two more are inferred) built in three parallel rows occupying the *retentura*, the central range, and half of the *praetentura*. Additionally a wall was built linking the fort wall with the front of the *principia* creating a walled enclosure within this part of the fort. Barrack space was restricted to the front of the *praetentura*, where one double and one single block have been found, which must have housed part of the attested garrison, *cohors V Gallorum*. Thirty lead seals found inside the fort, half of them depicting the heads of the Severan family, and seven more stamped by the garrison probably derived from official stores passing through the base; they were dated AD 198–209. *Cohors V Gallorum* is also named on an undated altar from Cramond,[110] and it is possible that this unit was responsible for the transport of official supplies between the two forts.

288

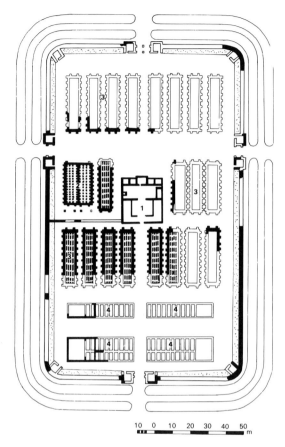

213. Supply base at South Shields, Severan (stone). (1) *principia*, (2) original Hadrianic double granary, (3) granaries, (4) barracks. Scale 1:2000

The fort of Cramond lies at the mouth of the river Almond at its entry into the Firth of Forth. It was defended by a stone wall with a clay bank, enclosing an area of c. 1.9 hectares. Only fragmentary stone foundations of the internal buildings have been found, which included granaries and workshops.

The Severan campaigns from AD 208–11 ended successfully, despite heavy losses inflicted on the Roman army by the natives' guerilla tactics. The establishment of a small fortress at Carpow on the river Tay suggests that Severus intended to reoccupy at least part of Scotland, but after his death in AD 211 his son and heir, Caracalla, concluded a peace treaty with the Maeatae and Caledonians, and returned to Rome;[111] a decision which once more established Hadrian's Wall as the frontier, although Roman troops probably policed an extensive area to the north.

On the German frontier there is little evidence for Severan activity, although by AD 213 Caracalla was engaged in campaigns against the Alemanni. In Upper Germany the frontier was strengthened by the

289

addition of a rampart and ditch behind the palisade, and in Raetia the frontier was rebuilt in stone. These activities are usually attributed to Caracalla, although the dating evidence is slight, and they could well have been the work of one of his predecessors in the latter half of the second century.[112]

9 Fort Types and Garrisons

Despite the obvious similarities in the groundplans of auxiliary forts from the mid-first to third centuries AD, no two excavated forts are exactly identical in their layout, and although the fort builders clearly worked within the guidelines of a standard military manual the forts were far from standardised in their internal details. Vegetius states that 'the dimensions must be exactly computed by the engineers, so that the size of the camp may be proportioned to the number of troops. A camp which is too confined will not permit the troops to perform their movements with freedom, and one which is too extensive divides them too much'.[1] However, although theoretically one might expect to find six specific types of fort size and plan corresponding to each of the six types of auxiliary unit,[2] in practice the builders appear to have had a reasonably free hand to build within certain limits, according to criteria other than just the garrison intended, such as considerations of the natural advantages and constraints of the site, the type and availability of building materials, and even the legionary traditions of building to which they were accustomed.

Although a large number of stone-built forts have yielded inscriptions, often accurately dated, which name the individual auxiliary units in garrison, it is only rarely possible to relate an attested garrison to specific barrack accommodation of the same date, and in timber forts evidence relating to the garrison is hardly ever found.[3] Archaeologists have therefore attempted to identify the type and size of the garrisons of various forts from a comparison of their overall dimensions and area, and from the number and internal arrangements of the barracks.[4]

These comparisons present considerable difficulties, as there are so few examples in which both the garrison and the contemporary fort plan are known exactly to provide a guide and a control. On a rare occasion when it is possible to follow a named unit when transferred from its old base to brand new accommodation (as was the case when the garrisons on the Odenwald-Neckar frontier in Upper Germany were moved to new forts, some 30 kilometres to the east, on the so-called Antonine *limes*) unfortunately too little of their internal details have been revealed by excavation to make any meaningful comparisons.[5] To compound the problems even further, in the few cases where both the primary garrison and internal layout are known, as for example at Künzing in Raetia or Birrens in Scotland, the accommodation provided does not exactly correspond with the theoretical requirements of the known garrison.

To assess the garrison of a fort it is necessary to know its internal area (the space actually available for building), the number of barracks, their dimensions and *contubernium* arrangements, stable provision and the capacity of the granaries, and to be able to compare these with examples where the original garrison is known. This comparison should be made ideally between contemporary sites constructed in similar materials, as otherwise factors apart from the requirements of the garrisons may be reflected.

It is important to ensure that the known garrison is the unit for which the fort was intended, for often more than one type of unit is known to have been stationed at a fort,[6] and it is clear that as the defensive circuit was fixed and generally remained unaltered, adaptations had to be made to the internal accommodation and the sizes of new buildings were restricted by the dimensions of their predecessors even though the size and composition of the garrison may have been substantially changed. This can be seen at Valkenburg (Period 1a) where the existing barrack rooms were enlarged, their divisions altered and the number of barrack rooms reduced from seven to six, apparently reflecting a change from the centuries of a *cohors equitata* to the troopers of a quingenary *ala*.[7] Similarly a barrack in the *retentura* at Corbridge alternated in the number of its barrack rooms at different dates from eight (presumably for cavalry) to ten (for infantry), which implies several changes of garrison, although throughout the defences remained unaltered.[8]

Fort area

The forts at Heidenheim and Aalen, which both at some time housed the 1000-strong cavalry unit, *ala II Flavia milliaria*, had internal areas of 4.8 and 5.6 hectares respectively, and at the other end of the size range it is probable that 1–1.5 hectares was the minimum area needed to house the smallest infantry cohort of 500 men (*cohors quingenaria peditata*).[9] Between these extremes lay a wide variety of fort sizes.

It is usually accepted that two *turmae* of troopers required a barrack block of the same size as an infantry century, and that their horses could be stabled in a similar-sized block. It follows theoretically that a unit of nominally 1000 infantry would require the same fort area as 500 troopers with their mounts, provided that the horses were also stabled within the fort itself. It is possible that legionary detachments may have initially selected and marked out the defensive circuits of, for example the forts on the Hadrianic frontier in Britain, before the actual garrisons had been finally allocated, and that, dependent upon local factors, forts were laid out which could be later designated either to an infantry unit (*cohors milliaria peditata*) such as the one which probably occupied Housesteads, or an *ala quingenaria*, presumed at South Shields; both forts had precisely the same dimensions and internal areas of 1.7 hectares. Other forts at which quingenary *alae* are known ranged widely in internal area from 1.9 to 4 hectares.[10]

Comparison between the sizes of the forts at Künzing and Birrens, whose garrisons are known, is particularly surprising, for a mounted unit nominally 500 strong stationed at Künzing (*cohors III Thracum c.R. equitata*) occupied a fort of 2 hectares internally, whilst at Birrens an area of only 1.7 hectares supposedly housed a unit with twice as many men and horses (*cohors I Nervana Germanorum milliaria*). This discrepancy has been explained by the suggestion that members of some garrisons were seconded for duty in outpost fortlets elsewhere,[11] but such speculation cannot be tested archaeologically, and serves only to confuse further an already unclear picture.

Granary capacity

It is possible in many cases to calculate approximately the grain requirements of a particular size of garrison and to relate this to the storage area available within the excavated fort granaries.[12] Tacitus stated that Agricola secured his forts from protracted siege with sufficient supplies to last one year,[13] and taking this statement as a basis various calculations have been attempted to determine the size of the garrison from a consideration of the capacity of the fort's granaries.[14]

There are, however, too many unknown factors involved to make this kind of calculation really meaningful. Unless the fort has been totally excavated we cannot be certain that the full complement of granaries has been discovered; there may have been granaries additional to those in the central range, situated in other parts of the fort (see p. 152). Despite Tacitus' statement it is uncertain how long the supplies were supposed to last; there may have been circumstances where it was absolutely necessary for a fort to have a year's supply in reserve, whereas in others it is quite feasible that only a few months' or weeks' supply may have been needed, dependent upon the relative security and strategic position which it occupied. It is clear that South Shields, on the river Tyne, was a supply depot for the Severan campaigns in Scotland, but there may well have been other forts which also held reserve supplies to pass onto frontier posts as the need arose. Another unknown quantity is the actual amount of space within the granary devoted exclusively to grain storage, for it is not known what quantities of other foodstuffs were stored there.

A more objective method of assessing granary capacities in relation to garrison and fort size is to equate the amount of granary floor storage space available with the internal area of the fort which it served (where all the granaries are known). Broadly speaking, there is a relatively constant relationship between the two factors,[15] which must reflect the number of men to be fed in the fort (leaving aside the problems caused by the additional requirements of cavalry detachments). Anomalies probably represent supply bases or forts with extra food reserves.

Barrack accommodation

In the absence of epigraphic evidence the most reliable indication of the size and composition of the garrison of a fort is given by the number and layout of the barracks, and their internal arrangements: the provision of stabling, although equally important, poses considerable problems of identification (see p. 176). The probable numbers of barracks and stables required by each of the six auxiliary units of the Roman army are shown in Table 2 below. Unfortunately in only two or three cases can a named garrison actually be matched up with excavated barracks,[16] and only at Künzing in Raetia and Birrens in Scotland can the complete fort layout be compared with the accommodation requirements of the known garrison. However, the barrack layout at neither of these forts conforms exactly with the theoretical requirements in Table 2, and the picture is even further complicated at Birrens, where the design of the barrack buildings themselves is atypical.

At Künzing the groundplan of a 2 hectare fort designed for a part-mounted unit, 500 strong (*cohors III Thracum equitata*), has been uncovered. Much of the investigation here was carried out in very limited trial excavations so it must be emphasised that much of the published plan and the internal arrangements of the barracks are largely conjectural. The eight barracks necessary for this type of unit, all presumed by the excavator to be identical in plan and each with ten *contubernia*, were located in the *praetentura*, and stables are believed to have been provided in two single and two double blocks in the *retentura*, although the evidence is rather inconclusive. There does seem to be accommodation provided here which is surplus to the requirements of the known garrison, which has been tentatively identified as the quarters of a separate unit, such as a small detachment of scouts or a transport corps.[17] The second fort where a named garrison and the barrack layout are both known is at Birrens, believed to have been garrisoned by a milliary part-mounted unit (*cohors I Nervana Germanorum milliaria equitata*), requiring fourteen or fifteen barracks and four or five stable blocks. Both the front and rear portions of the fort were filled with a large number of extremely narrow buildings. This arrangement is almost unique, and it appears that pairs of these buildings were linked together by a central longitudinal passage to form a single barrack block.[18] However, they would still provide insufficient accommodation for the men and horses of the known garrison.

In the absence of inscriptions it is necessary to make certain basic assumptions in order to assess the fort's probable garrison: firstly, that the infantry century was housed in a barrack block containing ten pairs of

Table 2: Barrack and stable accommodation

Unit	Centuries	*Turmae*	Barracks	Stables	Total
ala milliaria	—	24	12	12	24
ala quingenaria	—	16	8	8	16
cohors milliaria peditata	10	—	10	—	10
cohors quingenaria peditata	6	—	6	—	6
cohors milliaria equitata	10	8 (10)	14 (15)	4 (5)	18 (19)
cohors quingenaria equitata	6	4	8	2	10

(alternative figures placed in brackets: see p. 22 above).

contubernia, with each providing accommodation for eight men, and secondly that in a cavalry fort two *turmae*, each with thirty-two men, shared a barrack, again with eight men per *contubernium*, which would mean that a cavalry barrack required at least eight barrack rooms, with the horses of every two *turmae* stabled in blocks similar in size to the men's barracks.[19] On the basis of these assumptions the provision of ten barracks, all with ten *contubernia* at the Flavian timber fort of Fendoch and the Hadrianic stone fort at Housesteads indicates that both were designed to house ten centuries of infantry troops, the nominally 1000-strong *cohors milliaria peditata*. On the other hand barracks with eight or nine *contubernia*, such as those found at Benwell, Wallsend or Carzield, are usually interpreted as cavalry barracks. This equation is not as straightforward as it seems, however, for on the rare occasion when it can be tested against epigraphic evidence, as at Chesters, it does not seem to work. Here the Hadrianic barracks had ten *contubernia*, which would normally point to an infantry unit, but the recent discovery of an inscription has shown the original garrison to have been a quingenary *ala* (*ala Augusta*).[20]

Comparison between barrack lengths from different forts may give a clue to the type of garrison housed in them, although one of the most interesting features to emerge is not the variations in barrack lengths between different forts, but between barracks in the same fort. For example, at Haltonchesters on Hadrian's Wall the barracks in the *praetentura* (which had eight *contubernia*) were six metres shorter than those in the *retentura*, a variation which may mean that the fort housed a mixed unit of infantry and cavalry, a *cohors equitata*.[21]

These problems serve to emphasise just how little we still know, for despite well over a century of excavation in which hundreds of Roman forts have been located and investigated, most of the questions concerning the garrisons of the individual forts and how they were accommodated remain largely unanswered, and will remain so without considerable further archaeological excavation and research. In earlier excavations carried out around the turn of this century a disproportionate amount of attention was paid to the defences and principal buildings, whilst the barracks and stables were often neglected. This may be due in part to the fact that they were often less substantial, frequently remaining timber-built when the rest of the fort buildings were stone, and either the excavators failed to recognise them at all or ignored them because they appeared to be of less interest than the stone buildings in the central range. More recent excavations have redressed the balance to some extent, especially in their recognition of timber buildings and by their more widespread investigation of the interior of earth-and-timber forts. In revealing a greater proportion of the fort's internal layout they have also highlighted an unexpected wealth of differences between individual forts.

Nevertheless, despite the vast amount of work devoted to the subject our knowledge of Roman forts is still very limited. There is no shortage of questions nor, unfortunately, is there any short cut to the answers. For the problem of garrisoning to be pursued comprehensively, it is necessary to uncover the complete plans of forts which are proven by inscriptions to have housed each of the different auxiliary units. These would act as controls against which other sites may be compared.[22] The interior must be totally excavated to ensure that all the barracks are located, as there may be variations in size or in the number of barrack rooms in different parts of the fort. It is also very important to find the stables of cavalry and part-mounted units, an extremely difficult task in the absence of obvious stable drains, but one which may be assisted by careful chemical analysis, as shown by the work carried out at Dormagen in Lower Germany.

There are many other questions to be asked about the design and construction of the fort. Can we detect the hand of different legions at work in fort building along a particular frontier? What exactly did the internal buildings look like? How did the needs of the army change during the two centuries of Roman occupation considered in the preceding pages?

There are also many unanswered questions about the garrisons themselves and their organisation. It is clear, for example, that in the early years of Roman conquest detachments of legionaries and auxiliaries were often brigaded together in temporary frontier positions, such as Hod Hill. From the Flavian period, though, it seems on the whole that the situation was less fluid and that the forts were garrisoned by individual auxiliary units, with the legionaries stationed in bases at the rear of the frontier. This is a difficult period to deal with because the forts were timber-built at this time, and no permanent record of their garrisons were inscribed in stone. However, there may have been more variations in the strength and flexibility in the composition of the garrisons than we suppose. A hint is given at Pen Llystyn in Wales, where a gateway across the *via decumana* apparently separated six of the twelve barrack blocks from the rest of the fort within an internal compound, which may indicate that two of the smallest infantry units were in garrison together. Similarly it is also believed that a quingenary *ala* was housed within a stone-walled compound in the Antonine fort of Newstead in conjunction with a detachment of legionaries. It is at present uncertain how widespread was this practice of combining two units in garrison.

Rarely can comparisons be made between a particular fort plan and a particular type of garrison, even when it is known from inscriptions. In some cases the garrison attested seems to have been too large for the accommodation provided, as seen at Birrens, which may suggest that part of the unit may have been permanently stationed in small neighbouring forts and fortlets to patrol a frontier. This may also have been the case in other frontier regions. On the Antonine Wall in Britain, for example, a number of fortlets of varying sizes were incorporated into the frontier system alongside the more normal-sized auxiliary forts, indicating that perhaps the resources of the army were here somewhat overstretched, and that the auxiliary units were divided into detachments of different sizes to overcome a shortage of manpower.[23] Unfortunately insufficient evidence has yet been gathered to give details of the accommodation provided in most of these fortlets. Other forts may have provided specialist facilities, perhaps serving as workshops like those at Oberstimm, or as food supply depots. As such it is possible that these depots never had a full auxiliary garrison at all but, like the Severan supply depots at South Shields and Cramond, may have shared the same garrison, which was engaged in transporting supplies by sea from the river Tyne to Scotland.

In other cases the attested garrison appears much too small for the known fort size. This is so at Maryport on the Cumbrian coast, where a quingenary cohort is known throughout much of the second century AD, although the fort has sufficient space for a milliary unit. A possible explanation for this discrepancy may be that when the fort was built the attested garrison, *cohors I Hispanorum*, was a milliary cohort, which was subsequently reduced in size when a detachment was sent abroad, leaving the remainder of the unit, now of quingenary status in garrison by itself;[24] how the surplus space within the fort was utilised, and whether it perhaps served as a supply base, providing granaries and storebuildings in conjunction with the adjacent harbour must, like many other questions relating to Roman forts and their garrisons, await further archaeological investigation.

Abbreviations

AA, 1–5	*Archaeologia Aeliana*, 1st to 5th Series. Society of Antiquaries of Newcastle upon Tyne.
Acta Ant.Acad.Scient.Hung.	*Acta antiqua academiae scientiarum Hungaricae*, Budapest.
Ant.J.	*The Antiquaries Journal*, London.
Arch.	*Archaeologia*, London.
Arch.Camb.	*Archaeologia Cambrensis*, Cardiff.
Arch.J.	*Archaeological Journal*, London.
BAR	*British Archaeological Reports*, Oxford.
BBCS	*Bulletin of the Board of Celtic Studies*, Cardiff.
Ber.RGK	*Berichte der Römisch-Germanischen Kommission*, Frankfurt.
Bod.Westf.	*Bodenaltertümer Westfalens*, Münster.
Bonn.J.	*Bonner Jahrbücher.*
BVBL	*Bayerische Vorgeschichtsblatter.*
CIL	*Corpus Inscriptionum Latinarum.*
CLA	*Chartae Latinae Antiquiores.*
Curr.Arch.	*Current Archaeology*, London.
CW, 1–2	*Transactions of the Cumberland and Westmorland Antiquarian and Archaeological Society*, Carlisle. 1st and 2nd Series.
DAES	*Discovery and Excavation in Scotland.*
DAJ	*Derbyshire Archaeological Journal.*
EE	*Ephemeris Epigraphica*, Berlin, 1872–1903.
Fundb.aus B-W	*Fundberichte aus Baden-Württemberg*
Fundb.aus Hess.	*Fundberichte aus Hessen.*
Fundber.aus Schwaben	*Fundberichte aus Schwaben.*
ILS	H. Dessau, *Inscriptiones Latinae selectae*, Berlin 1892–1916.
Jahr.RGZM	*Jahrbuch des Römisch-Germanischen Zentralmuseums Mainz.*
Journal Brit.Arch.Ass.	*Journal of the British Archaeological Association.*
JRS	*Journal of Roman Studies*, London.
JVT	*Jaarverslag van de Vereeniging voor Terpenonderzoek*, Groningen.
LF	*Limesforschungen.* (eds) H. von Petrikovits, W. Schleiermacher and H. Schönberger, Berlin, since 1959.
Mont.Coll.	*Collections ... pertaining to Montgomeryshire*, Welshpool.
Nass.Ann.	*Annalen des Vereins für Nassauische Altertumskunde und Geschichtsforschung*, Wiesbaden.
NCH	*Northumberland County History.*

NL J. E. Bogaers and C. B. Rüger (eds), *Der Niedergermanische Limes. Materialien zu seiner Geschichte*, Köln-Bonn, 1974.
ORL *Der obergermanisch-rätische Limes des Romerreiches.*
P.Amh. *The Amherst Papyri*, B. P. Grenfell and A. S. Hunt (eds), London, 1900.
Proc.Brit.Acad. *Proceedings of the British Academy.*
PBSR *Papers of the British School at Rome.*
P.Hamb. P. M. Meyer *et al.* (eds), *Griechische Papyrusurkunden der Hamburger Staats-und Universitätsbibliothek*, Leipzig-Berlin, 1911–.
PPS *Proceedings of the Prehistoric Society*, London.
Proc.Devon Arch.& Expl.Soc. *Proceedings of the Devonshire Archaeological Exploration Society.*
Proc.Leeds Phil.& Lit.Soc. *Proceedings of the Leeds Philosophical and Literary Society.*
PSAN *Proceedings of the Society of Antiquaries of Newcastle upon Tyne.*
PSAS *Proceedings of the Society of Antiquaries of Scotland*, Edinburgh.
PUBSS *Proceedings of the University of Bristol Speleological Society.*
R.B-W Ph. Filtzinger, D. Planck and B. Cämmerer (eds), *Die Römer in Baden-Württemberg*, Stuttgart, 1976.
RCAHM Royal Commission on Ancient and Historical Monuments.
RFIW V. E. Nash-Williams, *The Roman Frontier in Wales*, (2nd edn by M. G. Jarrett), Cardiff, 1969.
RHW E. Birley, *Research on Hadrian's Wall*, Kendal, 1961.
RIB R. G. Collingwood and R. P. Wright, *The Roman Inscriptions of Britain I*, Oxford, 1965.
RLO *Der römische Limes in Österreich*, RLÖ Wien, from 1900.
Saal.J. *Saalburg Jahrbuch*, Berlin.
Trans.Birm.& Warwicks Arch.Soc. *Transactions of the Birmingham and Warwickshire Archaeological Society.*
TWNFC *Transactions of the Woolhope Naturalists' Field Club.*
VCH *Victoria History of the Counties of England.*
Westdt.Zeit. *Westdeutsche Zeitschrift für Geschichte und Kunst*, Trier.
WMANS *West Midlands Archaeological Newsheet.*
YAJ *Yorkshire Archaeological Journal.*

Notes

Introduction

1. For a more detailed description of the development of the fort plan from the earliest Republican camps and colonies see Chapter 8, pp. 222–90.
2. The changes in recruitment and organisation of the legions during the Republic are discussed by G. Webster in *The Roman Imperial Army* (2nd edn, 1977).
3. Harbour facilities were probably provided at the Welsh forts of Caerhun, Pennal, Neath and Caernarfon. Ravenglass, Maryport and Bowness on the Cumbrian coast and South Shields on the Tyne probably handled supplies destined for the Hadrian's Wall forts; on the Antonine frontier there were ports on the Forth estuary at Cramond and Inveresk, and on the Clyde at Old Kilpatrick. The legionary fortresses generally lay upon navigable waterways to facilitate the transport of supplies.
4. G. D. B. Jones and J. H. Little, 'Excavations on the Roman fort at Pumsaint, Carmarthenshire: interim report 1972', *Carmarthenshire Antiquary* (1973), 3 ff. For a plan of the gold mining area in the vicinity of the fort see *JRS*, 59 (1969), 199 and fig. 25. Military involvement with gold mining has also been detected in north-west Spain; see R. F. J. Jones, 'The Roman military occupation of North-West Spain', *JRS*, 66 (1976), 45 ff. At Charterhouse, in Somerset, an earthwork of c. 1.2 hectares in area, believed to be a Roman fort, has been detected from the air. For its relationship with the Mendip lead mines see K. Branigan and P. J. Fowler, *The Roman West Country* (Newton Abbot, 1976), 183 ff, fig. 46 and *Britannia*, 2 (1971), 278 and fig. 12. For the industry in North Wales see G. Webster, 'The lead mining industry in North Wales in Roman times', *Flintshire Hist. Soc. Publications* 13 (1952–3), 5 ff.
5. *CIL* VII, 1201 from the Mendips and the other from St Valéry-sur-Somme, near Boulogne, stamped 'British lead', by *legio II Augusta* in the Neronian period. For other lead pigs from the Mendips see K. Branigan and P. J. Fowler, *Roman West Country*, 1976, Appendix 4, 230 ff.
6. Lead ore from Brough on Noe, *DAJ*, 59 (1938), 62 ff; lead ingots found near Brough on Humber, P. Corder and I. A. Richmond, 'Petuaria', *Journal Brit. Arch. Ass.*, (3rd Series), 7 (1942), 25.
   A large number of lead seals were found outside the fort of Brough-under-Stainmore in 1936, bearing the stamps of at least six or seven cohorts, an *ala*, and two legions; see I. A. Richmond, 'Roman leaden sealings from Brough-under-Stainmore', *CW* 2, 36 (1936), 104 ff. The fact that such a large number of seals was found, naming several different auxiliary units, shows that the goods to which they had been attached were unpacked here and the seals themselves discarded. This indicates that the fort must have served as some kind of official central collecting point in the area for a wide diversity of goods and materials. One of the commodities involved was probably either lead or silver, for the stamp on the reverse of one of the seals of *cohors II Nerviorum* shows that something was despatched from a *metal(lum)*. This unit was stationed at Whitley Castle and presumably obtained the metal from the lead mines close by on Alston Moor.
7. A. von Domaszewski (ed.), *Hygini gromatici liber de munitionibus castrorum* (Leipzig 1887); E. Birley, *Actes du deuxième Congrès international d'épigraphie grecque et latine* (Paris 1953), 234. For a discussion of the sources used by

Vegetius, see D. Schenk, 'Flavius Vegetius Renatus, die Quellen der Epitoma rei militaris', *Klio*, Beiheft, (1920).

8. Polybius, *Historiae*, VI; Julius Caesar, *de Bello Civili; de Bello Africo; de Bello Gallico; de Bello Hispaniensi.*

9. Josephus, *Bell. Jud.*

10. Flavius Arrianus, *Tactica.* See also F. Kiechle, 'Die "Taktik" des Flavius Arrianus', *Bericht der Römisch-Germanischen Kommission 1964*, 45 (1965), 87 ff.

11. J. F. Gilliam, C. B. Welles and R. O. Fink, *The Excavations at Dura-Europos. Final Report V. Part 1: The Parchments and Papyri* (New Haven 1959).

12. O. Guéraud, 'Ostraca grecs et latins de l'Wâdi Fawâkhir', *Bulletin de l'institut français d'archéologie orientale*, 41, 141 ff; Préaux, 'Ostraca de Pselkis de la Bibliothèque Bodléenne', *Chronique d'Egypte*, 26 (1951), 121 ff; for papyri from Egypt see S. Daris, *Documenti per la storia dell'ésercito romano in Egitto* (Milan, 1964).

13. A. K. Bowman and D. Thomas, *The Vindolanda Writing Tablets*, (Newcastle 1974); A. K. Bowman, 'Roman military records from Vindolanda', *Britannia*, 5 (1974), 360 ff; A. K. Bowman, J. D. Thomas and R. P. Wright, 'The Vindolanda writing tablets', *Britannia*, 5 (1974), 471 ff; R. E. Birley, *Vindolanda: A Roman Frontier Post on Hadrian's Wall*, (London 1977), 132 ff; R. E. Birley, 'A frontier post in Roman Britain', *Scientific American*, 236, no. 2 (Feb. 1977), 46 ff.

14. C. Cichorius, *Die Reliefs der Traianssäule*, (Berlin 1896 and 1900); K. Lehmann-Hartleben, *Die Traianssäule*, (Berlin and Leipzig 1926). For a review of the latter work see I. A. Richmond, *JRS*, 16 (1926), 261 ff, and for a commentary on the more important scenes, I. A. Richmond, 'Trajan's army on Trajan's Column', *PBSR*, 13 (1935), 1 ff. The most recent work is by L. Rossi, *Trajan's Column and the Dacian Wars*, (London 1971), although the photographs do not have the quality of the Cichorius volumes.

15. For inscriptions in stone found in Britain up to 1954, and in other materials up to 1956 see R. G. Collingwood and R. P. Wright, *The Roman Inscriptions of Britain, 1: Inscriptions on Stone*, (Oxford 1965); from 1955–1970 annually in *JRS*, and thereafter annually in *Britannia*. German inscriptions are published in *CIL* and *ILS*.

16. Stamped tiles are particularly common in Germany, and have been used, for example, to identify the garrisons at Valkenburg (Period 4) in Lower Germany, and at Künzing in Raetia.

17. The diplomas have been collected together and published in *CIL* XVI (1936) with a supplement in 1955. For further notes see *JRS*, 54 (1964), 150 ff; M. M. Roxan, *Roman Military Diplomas 1954–1977*, (London 1978).

18. Reported by Robert Smith, and published in Camden's *Britannia*, (ed. E. Gibson), 1722. For a full account of antiquarian interest on the northern British frontier see E. Birley, *Research on Hadrian's Wall*, (Kendal 1961), 1 ff.

19. W. Stukeley, *Iter Boreale*, (1776), 49 ff.

20. A. Hedley, *AA* 1, 1 (1821), 212 ff.

21. For a survey of the Lower German frontier, with a summary of excavation results and full bibliography see J. E. Bogaers and C. B. Rüger, *Der Niedergermanische Limes*, (Cologne, Bonn 1974).

22. J. P. Bushe-Fox, *Excavations at Richborough*, London, I (1926); II (1928); III (1932); IV (1949).

23. I. A. Richmond, *JRS*, 33 (1943), 45 ff; J. K. St. Joseph, *JRS*, 41 (1951), 52 ff; 43 (1953), 91 ff; 45 (1955), 82 ff; 48 (1958), 86 ff; 51 (1961), 119 ff; 55 (1965), 74 ff; 59 (1969), 104 ff; 63 (1973), 214 ff; 67 (1977), 125 ff. Ph. Filtzinger,

'Wehranlagen am Donaulimes in Baden-Württemberg im Luftbild', *Fundber aus Schwaben*, 13 (1967), 106 ff.

24. For developments in fort architecture in the later third and fourth centuries AD see R. G. Collingwood, *The Archaeology of Roman Britain*, (revised by I. A. Richmond) (London 1969), 47 ff; S. Johnson, *The Roman Forts of the Saxon Shore*, (London 1976),34 ff; S. Johnson, *Later Roman Britain*, (London 1980), 70 ff.

25. For the civilian population see P. Salway, *The Frontier People of Roman Britain*, (Cambridge 1965); R. E. Birley, *Civilians of the Roman Frontier*, (Newcastle 1973).

I   The Roman Army

1. Josephus, *Bell. Jud.* III, 6, 2; D. J. Breeze, 'The organisation of the legion: The First Cohort and the equites legionis', *JRS*, 59 (1969), 50 ff.

2. Legionary officers: see E. Birley, 'The equestrian officers of the Roman army', *Roman Britain and the Roman Army*, (Kendal 1953), 133 ff; E. Birley, 'Senators in the emperor's service', *Proc. Brit. Academy*, 39 (1954), 197 ff.

3. Centurions: see E. Birley, 'Promotions and transfers in the Roman army II: the centurionate', *Carnuntum Jahrbuch*, 1963/4 (1965), 21 ff; B. Dobson, 'The significance of the centurion and "primipilaris" in the Roman army and administration', *Aufstieg und Niedergang der römischen Welt II Principat 1*, ed. H. Temporini, (Berlin 1974), 393 ff.

4. A number of legionary *immunes* are listed by Tarruntenus Paternus, *Digest*, 50, 6, 7.

5. Tacitus, *Annals*, iv, 5. For a summary of the number of legions in service see G. Webster, *The Roman Imperial Army*, (London 1969), 113 ff.

6. E. Birley, 'Alae and cohortes milliariae', *Corolla Memoriae Erich Swoboda Dedicata*, (Graz 1966), 55 ff.

7. G. L. Cheesman, *The Auxilia of the Roman Imperial Army*, (Oxford 1914), 25 ff, following von Domaszewski and Mommsen.

8. This figure has been considered too low for a nominally 1000-strong unit and A. von Domaszewski, *Die Rangordnung des römischen Heeres*, 2nd edn by B. Dobson, (Cologne 1967), 35, has suggested an alternative of 42 men per *turma*, giving a total strength of 1008. This interpretation is based upon an inscription from Coptos (*CIL*, III, 6627), which records a vexillation of three *alae* comprising 424 troopers with ten officers. However, only five of the officers mentioned were actually commanders of *turmae* (decurions); the other five were junior officers. Consequently it has been suggested (see G. Webster, *Roman Imperial Army*, 146, note 3) that we may be dealing here only with five commanders with their subordinate officers rather than with ten men in charge of ten *turmae*.

9. R. W. Davies, 'A note on a recently discovered inscription from Carrawburgh', *Epigraphische Studien*, 4 (1967), Appendix, 111.

10. Arrian, *Tactica*, 10 or 18; Hyginus, *de mun. cast.*, 16; Vegetius, *epitoma rei militaris*, II, 14.

11. Hyginus, *de mun.cast.*, 16.

12. E. Birley, *Corolla Memoriae*, 1966, 57.

13. Hyginus, *de mun.cast.*, 28.

14. Hyginus, *de mun.cast.*, 28.

15. *CIL*, XVI, 31; E. Birley, *Corolla Memoriae*, (1966), 60.

16. Hyginus, *de mun.cast.*, 27; R. W. Davies, 'Cohortes Equitatae', *Historia*, 20 (1971), 751 ff.
17. *CIL*, III, 6760.
18. J. D. Thomas and R. W. Davies, 'A new military strength report on papyrus',*JRS*, 67 (1977), 50 ff; H. Schönberger, *Kastell Künzing-Quintana: die Grabungen von 1958 bis 1966, Limesforschungen* 13 (Berlin 1975), 110 ff.
19. E. Birley, *Corolla Memoriae*, (1966), 54, largely following Cheesman, see note 7 above.
20. J. D. Thomas and R. W. Davies, *JRS*, 67 (1977), 60.
21. H. Schönberger, *Kastell Künzing*, 1975, 111.
22. Hyginus, *de mun.cast.*, 26.
23. H. Callies, 'Die fremden Truppen im römischen Heer des Prinzipats und die sogenannten nationalen Numeri. Beitrage zur Geschichte des römischen Heeres', *Bericht der Römisch-Germanischen Kommission 1964*, 45 (1965), 130 ff; J. C. Mann, 'A note on the numeri', *Hermes*, 82 (1954), 501 ff.
24. D. Baatz, *Kastell Hesselbach: und andere Forschungen am Odenwaldlimes, Limesforschungen* 12 (Berlin 1973), 54 ff.
25. Undated inscriptions from Housesteads attest the *cohors I Tungrorum milliaria*; see *RIB* 1578–80, 1584–6, 1591, 1598, 1618–19, and it is mentioned also in the *Notitia Dignitatum*. The *numerus Hnaudifridi* is named on an altar of unknown date (*RIB* 1576) believed to belong to the third century AD, together with a *cuneus Frisiorum Ver*, which is attested under Severus Alexander (AD 222–35) (*RIB* 1594).
26. At least 10 *numeri Brittonum* are known from the Odenwald frontier in Germany, also a *numerus* of bargemen from the Tigris at South Shields, (*numerus barcariorum Tigrisiensium*, named in the *Notitia*), a similar *numerus barcariorum* from Lancaster (*RIB* 601) and a unit of Moors from Burgh by Sands (*numerus Maurorum Aurelianorum*) is also named in the *Notitia*.

2   The Fort Plan

1. For changes in the organisation of the Roman army see G. Webster, *The Roman Imperial Army*, (London 1969), 27 ff.
2. Polybius, *Historiae*, VI; Modern commentaries by E. Fabricius, 'Some notes on Polybius' description of Roman camps', *JRS*, 22 (1932), 78 ff; F. W. Walbank, *A Historical Commentary on Polybius, 1*, (Oxford 1957).
3. Polybius, *Historiae*, VI; G. Webster, *Roman Imperial Army*, (1969), 27 ff.
4. Hyginus, *de mun.cast.*, 21.
5. H. von Petrikovits, *Die Innenbauten römischer Legionslager während der Prinzipatszeit*, Abhandlungen der Rheinisch-Westfälischen Akademie der Wissenschaften, Band 56 (Opladen 1975), 55 ff and fig. 8.1. Nine pairs of barrack blocks were found in the middle *praetentura*, some with 9 and others with 5 double rooms.
6. For the possible function of these rooms see H. von Petrikovits, *Die Innenbauten*, 51 ff.

3   The Construction of the Fort

1. Vegetius, *epitoma rei militaris*, I, 22.
2. Tacitus, *Agricola*, 20.
3. Hyginus, *de mun.cast.*, 56.
4. Such as Fendoch, sited at the mouth of the Sma' Glen. For similar forts founded by Agricola in the 80s AD in Strathmore to control the Highlands see Chapter 8, 256 ff.
5. Vegetius, *epitoma rei militaris*, I, 22; III, 2.
6. Easter Happrew: *PSAS*, 90 (1956–7), 101.
7. Leintwardine and Buckton: *TWNFC*, 39 (1968), 222 ff.
8. Brough on Humber: J. Wacher, *Excavations at Brough on Humber 1958–1961*, (London 1969), 221; Pen Llystyn: *Arch. J.*, 125 (1968), 188 ff; cited by W. S. Hanson, 'The Roman military timber-supply', *Britannia*, 9 (1978), 294.
9. W. S. Hanson, *op. cit.*, 293.
10. W. S. Hanson, *op. cit.*, 297.
11. W. S. Hanson, *op. cit.*, 298.
12. As, for example, Buckton, Castledykes and Wall.
13. Bowness: *CW* 2, 75 (1975), 29 ff; Birdoswald: *CW* 2, 34 (1934), 121 ff. Josephus, *Bell. Jud.*, III, 77, describes the preparation of the site prior to building: 'The camp is not erected at random or unevenly; they do not all work at once or in disorderly parties; if the ground is uneven, it is first levelled; a site for the camp is then measured out in the form of a square.'
14. For tools used in site clearance and defence construction see M. J. Jones, *Roman Fort-Defences to AD 117*, British Archaeological Reports No. 21, (Oxford 1975), 38 ff and fig. 6.
15. Tarruntenus Paternus, *Digest* 50, 6, 7; Vegetius, *epitoma rei militaris*, II, 7.
16. Vegetius, *epitoma rei militaris*, III, 8.
17. Hyginus, *de mun.cast.*, 21.
18. Vegetius, *epitoma rei militaris*, III, 8.
19. Hyginus, *de mun.cast.*, 56; Vegetius, *epitoma rei militaris*, II, 23.
20. Polybius, *Historiae*, VI, 40, 9.
21. Vitruvius, *de architectura*, I, 6; Hyginus, *de mun.cast.*, 56.
22. For Roman surveying instruments see E. N. Shorey, 'Roman surveying instruments', *University of Washington Publications in Language and Literature*, 4 (1926–8), 215 ff; H. G. Lyons, 'Ancient surveying instruments', *Geog. J.*, 69 (1927), 132 ff; O. A. W. Dilke, *The Roman Land Surveyors*, (Newton Abbot 1971), 66 ff.

    A dismantled *groma* is depicted upon the tombstone of a surveyor, L. Aebutius Faustus, from Ivrea in northern Italy (O. Dilke, *Land Surveyors*, (1971), 50). The metal parts of a *groma*, together with measuring rods and compasses were found in the workshop of the surveyor Verus at Pompeii, and reconstructed by M. Della Corte, 'Groma', *Monumenti Antichi*, 28 (1922), 5 ff.
23. Pfünz: *ORL*, 73, Pl. V, fig. 40. In the Raetian fort of Weissenburg was found a foot rule, marked on each of its sides with the different subdivisions of the Roman foot, *pes*, with 12 *unciae*, 16 *digiti*, and 4 *palmi*; see *ORL*, 72, Pl. IV, 6.
24. J. Ward, *The Roman Fort of Gellygaer*, (London 1903), 22 ff and fig. 2. For a detailed study of the various units of measurement and standards employed by the Roman army see C. V. Walthew, 'Possible standard units of measurement in Roman military planning', *Britannia*, 12 (1981), 15 ff.

25. For Roman units of measurements see O. A. W. Dilke, *The Roman Land Surveyors*, (1971), 82 ff; C. V. Walthew, 'Property Boundaries and the sizes of building plots in Roman towns', *Britannia*, 9 (1978), 335 ff.

26. Pen Llystyn: *Arch. J.*, 125 (1968), 129. A similar deposit was found in the *principia* courtyard of the legionary fortress of Inchtuthil on the Tay, where a pit had been dug upon the longitudinal axis of the building, which was displaced approximately 36 Roman feet from the true centre of the fortress, *JRS*, 44 (1954), 84 ff.

27. *ORL*, 11, 31 ff.

28. *CW* 2, 34 (1934), 130.

29. Vegetius, *epitoma rei militaris*, II, 10.

30. Tarruntenus Paternus, *Digest*, 50, 6, 7.

31. Benwell: *RIB* 1340; Carvoran: *RIB* 1820, but see also *RIB* 1778; V. A. Maxfield, *Britannia*, 9 (1978), 496.

32. For example, rebuilding by *cohors II Lingonum eq.* is recorded in AD 139–43 at High Rochester, *RIB* 1276; in AD 141 the *porta decumana* at Pförring in Raetia was rebuilt by the *ala I Singularium p.f.c.R.*, *CIL* III, 5912; and before AD 144 *cohors III Thracum* completed the internal bathhouse at Gnotzheim, also in Raetia; see F. Wagner, *Bericht der Römisch-Germanischen Kommission*, 37–8 (1956–7), 236, no. 81.

33. V. E. Nash-Williams, *The Roman Frontier in Wales*, 2nd end by M. G. Jarrett, (Cardiff 1969), 126 ff and fig. 67; Haltwhistle Common: *JRS*, 41 (1951), 55;Llandrindod Common: C. M. Daniels and G. B. D. Jones, *Arch. Camb.*, 118 (1969), 124 ff; G. D. B. Jones and W. A. C. Knowles, 'Roman Merionethshire: the Dolddinas camps', *BBCS*, 18 (1960), 397 ff.

34. For a summary of these variations in style see D. J. Breeze and B. Dobson, *Hadrian's Wall*, (London 1976), 56 ff and tables 4 & 5; R. Hunneysett, 'The milecastles of Hadrian's Wall—an alternative identification', *AA* 5, 8 (1980), 95 ff.

35. It is believed that *legio II Augusta* was responsible probably for South Shields, Rudchester, Housesteads and Greatchesters, with *legio VI Victrix* responsible for Benwell, Haltonchesters, Chesters, Birdoswald, and possibly also Stanwix and Bowness; see Breeze and Dobson, *Hadrian's Wall*, (1976), 76.

36. D. Baatz, *Kastell Hesselbach Limesforschungen* 12, (Berlin 1973), 36.

37. *CIL* III, 14370.

4   The Defences

1. Vegetius, *epitoma rei militaris*, III, 8.

2. Scenes XI/XII, XIX/XX, XXXIX, LII, LX and LXV show ditch digging. For the tools used see M. J. Jones, *Roman Fort-Defences to AD 117*, British Archaeological Reports No. 21 (Oxford 1975), 38 ff and fig. 6.

3. Cawthorn: *Arch. J.*, 89 (1932), 17 ff.

4. Hyginus, *de mun.cast.*, 49.

5. Duty rosters preserved on papyri show that ditches were cleaned out regularly, *CLA* 7, v, III, 3.

6. This ditch type was less commonly employed, and has been identified at Hod Hill, Stracathro, Ward Law, Waddon Hill and Newstead 3 in Britain, Alphen-Zwammerdam in Lower Germany, and Hesselbach, Vielbrunn and Würzberg in Upper Germany. I. A. Richmond comments that it is uncertain whether this

ditch derived its name from a similar type in Carthaginian agriculture, or because it was a work which deceived, *Punica fides*; see I. A. Richmond, *Hod Hill: Excavations carried out between 1951 and 1958*, II (London 1968), 68, note 5.

7. Examples are known from Balmuildy, Hofheim and Holzhausen. For this type of ditch profile see V. E. Nash-Williams, *The Roman Frontier in Wales*, 2nd edn by M. G. Jarrett, (Cardiff 1969), 153; M. J. Jones, *Roman Fort-Defences*, 108.

8. Such banks are known at the Welsh forts of Caerphilly, Caernarfon, Caer Llguwgy and Bryn-y-Gefeiliau.

9. At Ardoch two ditches of the reduced Antonine fort were added within the triple ditches of the larger Flavian enclosure to give a total of five ditches on the north and east sides, *PSAS*, 32 (1897–8), 32.

10. At Wiesbaden, Hofheim, Heddernheim, Okarben, Kesselstadt and probably also at Langenhain and Butzbach, *ORL*, 31, 10.

11. M. J. Jones, *op. cit.*, 113.

12. Hyginus, *de mun.cast.*, 49 & 50; J. P. Wild, 'A note on "titulum" ', *Arch. Camb.*, 117 (1969), 133 ff; G. Webster, *The Roman Imperial Army*, (London 1969), 171; I. A. Richmond, *Arch. J.*, 89 (1932), 23 ff. *Tituli* are known at Bar Hill, Hod Hill, Wiesbaden, the Saalburg, Brough-by-Bainbridge and Stracathro.

13. Scenes CXXVIII/CXXIX. Internal *claviculae* are known from the Flavian marching camps at Cawthorn, Chew Green, Four Laws and Birrenswark, and external *claviculae* from the Scottish forts of Newstead, Cadder and Ardoch.

14. Theilenhofen: *ORL*, 71 a, Pl. III, 1.

15. For the use of such entanglements see Polybius, *Historiae*, XVIII, 18; Livy, XXXIII, 5, 9.

16. Caesar, *De Bell. Gall.*, VII, 73–80.

17. Caesar, *De Bell. Gall.*, VII, 73; *lilia* are also described by Dio, LXXV, 6.

18. Arzbach: *ORL*, 3, Pl. 2, fig. 1.

19. Vegetius, *epitoma rei militaris*, IV, 3.

20. Hyginus, *de mun.cast.*, 51.

21. M. J. Jones, *op. cit.*, 78.

22. R. E. Birley, *Vindolanda: A Roman Frontier Post on Hadrian's Wall*, (London 1977), 165.

23. Vegetius, *epitoma rei militaris*, III, 8.

24. Vitruvius, *de architectura*, I, v, 3 and 5.

25. M. J. Jones, *op. cit.*, 70 and fig. 14.

26. M. J. Jones, *op. cit.*, 70.

27. J. Ward, *Romano-British Buildings and Earthworks*, (London 1911), 50.

28. B. Hobley, 'An experimental reconstruction of a Roman military turf rampart', *Roman Frontier Studies 1967*, ed. S. Applebaum, (Tel Aviv 1971), 23.

29. Vegetius, *epitoma rei militaris*, III, 8.

30. The rampart turves at the Scottish fort of Strageath, for example, were not cut to a standard uniform size; M. J. Jones, *op. cit.*, 80.

31. Good examples have been found at Bochastle, Great Casterton, Hod Hill and Ilkley, although occasionally the turf cheeks were narrower, as at Pen Llystyn, Chesterton or Brough on Humber.

32. At Valkenburg 1, Altenstadt 4–5 and Butzbach 1.

33. B. Hobley, *op. cit.*, 25 ff.

34. B. Hobley, *op. cit.*, 27 ff.

35. This arrangement is suggested also at Wall 3, Munningen, Rödgen, Valkenburg 2/3, Heidenheim and Heilbronn-Böckingen.

36. The box rampart is known at Wall 3, Verulamium, Clyro, possibly Caerhun 1,

and Stanway; single frontal revetments are known from Bowes, Chelmsford, Metchley 2, Pen-y-Gaer and Barochan Hill.

37. W. S. Hanson, 'The Roman military timber supply', *Britannia*, 9 (1978), 295 ff.
38. See M. J. Jones, *Roman Fort-Defences*, 86 ff for a discussion of the various factors which may have influenced these differences in constructional techniques.
39. Vegetius, *epitoma rei militaris*, III, 8. Similar crenellations along Hadrian's Wall are depicted on the Rudge Cup; see J. D. Cowan and I. A. Richmond, 'The Rudge Cup', *AA* 4, 12 (1935), 310 ff, and the Amiens skillet, J. Heurgon, 'The Amiens Patera', *JRS*, 41 (1951), 22 ff.
40. D. Baatz, *Kastell Hesselbach Limesforschungen* 12 (Berlin 1973), 20 and note 35.
41. Caesar, *De Bell.Gall.*, V, 40, 6.
42. B. Cichy, *Das romische Heidenheim*, (Heidenheim 1971), 41.
43. Hyginus, *de mun.cast.*, 58; for *ascensi* see G. Macdonald, *PSAS*, 67 (1932–3), 286 ff.
44. Pfünz: *ORL*, 73, 4; Oberflorstadt: *ORL*, 19, 3.
45. *CIL* III, 14485 a.
46. Arrian, *Perip.*, 9.
47. *ILS* 2487.
48. Rampart replicas at Baginton and Chesterholm, and experimental earthworks at Overton Down and Wareham; see p. 350.
49. W. S. Hanson, *op. cit.*, 296.
50. Urspring: *ORL*, 66a, 5. The original excavator believed that these timbers were part of the framework supporting the rampart-walk, but for an alternative explanation see Ph. Filtzinger, D. Planck, B. Cämmerer (ed.), *Die Römer in Baden-Württemberg*, (Stuttgart 1976), 543 ff.
51. D. Baatz, *Kastell Hesselbach*, 17.
52. Caesar, *De Bell.Gall.*, VII, 2.
53. Buttresses against the inner face of the fort wall have been detected at Cannstatt, Köngen, Benningen and Welzheim West, *ORL*, 70, 5.
54. J. Collingwood Bruce, *Handbook to the Roman Wall*, 9th edn by R. G. Collingwood, (Newcastle 1933), 18.
55. The portions of walling were found in 1882 and 1887, *ORL*, 36, 3 ff, and figs 1 and 2.
56. Gaps with a minimum width of 1.2 metres have been suggested by D. Baatz, *Kastell Hesselbach*, 20; see also *Saal.J.*, 21 (1963–4), 57 ff and notes 61–2.
57. Stones bearing traces of white plaster with red painted lines have been found at Neckarburken-West, Holzhausen, Niederbieber, Vielbrunn, Saalburg 3, Arnsburg and Heidenheim.
58. *NCH*, 15 (1940), 84 and fig. 14.
59. R. E. Birley, *op. cit.*, 162 ff.
60. Josephus, *Bell.Jud.*, III, v.
61. Vegetius, *epitoma rei militaris*, III, 8.
62. *RIB* 1816, 1818 and 1820. For centurial stones see R. P. Wright, *PSAN* 4, 9 250 ff.
63. *RIB* 1813, 1814 and 1822. Similar stones have also been found at Tomen-y-Mur in Wales, where rampart distances of between 20 and 39 feet are recorded, *RIB* 420–8, and Manchester, 23–4 feet, *RIB* 577–80.
64. Chesters: *JRS*, 52 (1962), 193, no. 14. The stone was found close to the *porta quintana dextra*. A similar stone recording the actual distance completed was found near Brunton Turret on Hadrian's Wall, *RIB* 1445. It was set up by the 'turm (a) L(uci) A(. . . .) Fani', and on the other side an inscription records the

construction of 113 feet of rampart: 'T(urma) L(uci) A(. . . .) F(ani) p(er) Val(lum) p(edes) CXIII'.

65. Josephus, *Bell.Jud.*, III, 79–80.

66. G. Webster, *The Roman Imperial Army*, (London 1969), 180. A platform above the rampart-walk, from which missiles could be discharged, is suggested by I. A. Richmond at Hod Hill, who draws attention to an example of such a structure illustrated on Trajan's Column, I. A. Richmond, *Hod Hill*, 1968, Pl. 45 A.

67. M. J. Jones, *Roman Fort-Defences*, 92.

68. A guardchamber of the west gate at Bowness built at an angle askew to the fort wall suggests a similar explanation, *CW* 2, 75 (1975), 29 ff.

69. Vegetius, *epitoma rei militaris*, IV, 26.

70. S. Johnson, *The Roman Forts of the Saxon Shore*, (London 1976). Projecting towers both at the gates and at intervals around the defences were a common feature of town walls, which were generally designed to be more defensive because of the likelihood of a siege, whilst the fort during the first and early part of the second century provided a base for troops fighting in the open. In his recommendations for town defences Vitruvius, *de architectura* I, 5, states that 'Towers, moreover, are to be projected on the outer side, in order that when the enemy wishes to approach the wall in an attack, he may be wounded in his exposed flanks by weapons on the right and left from the towers.'

71. H. Schönberger, 'Über einige neu entdeckte römische Lager- und Kastelltore aus Holz', *Bonn.J.*, 164 (1964), 39.

72. Vegetius, *epitoma rei militaris*, IV, 4. The gateways at Feldburg yielded 9 cm long iron nails, indicating that the framework of the gates had timbers 8–9 cm thick. The iron binding fragments found at Fendoch are similar to those used for binding the gates at Hadrian's Wall Milecastle 52, *CW* 2, 35 (1935), 253. The doors of a gateway are depicted on Trajan's Column, Scene XLVI.

73. For various classifications of timber military gates see: T. Bechert, 'Römische Lagertore und ihre Bauinschriften', *Bonn. J.*, 171 (1971), 201 ff; A. Fox and W. Ravenhill, 'The Roman fort at Nanstallon, Cornwall', *Britannia*, 3 (1972), 56 ff; W. H. Manning and I. R. Scott, 'Roman timber military gateways in Britain and on the German frontier', *Britannia*, 10 (1979), 19 ff; H. Schönberger, 'Über einige neu entdeckte römische Lager- und Kastelltore aus Holz', *Bonn.J.*, 164 (1964), 40 ff; S. C. Stanford, 'The Roman forts at Leintwardine and Buckton', *TWNFC*, 39 (1968), 240 ff.

74. W. H. Manning and I. R. Scott, 'Timber Gateways', 21; for an alternative interpretation see A. Fox and W. Ravenhill, 'Nanstallon', 1972, 68.

75. A single portal with 2 pairs of posts at Old Kilpatrick on the Antonine Wall; with 3 pairs of posts at the other Antonine Wall forts of Bar Hill and Duntocher and the Hadrian's Wall milecastle at High House and milefortlet at Biglands; 4 pairs of posts at Mumrills on the Antonine Wall, and 5 pairs at the other gate at High House milecastle.

76. See W. H. Manning and I. R. Scott, 'Timber Gateways', 28 ff.

77. In the Stabian, Nolan and Vesuvian gates; H. Schönberger, 'Lager-und Kastelltore aus Holz', *Bonn.J.*, 164 (1964), 39; F. Krischen, *Die Stadt Mauer von Pompeii*, (1941), figs 2, 8 and 9. The timbers of a Flavian gateway at Carlisle were particularly well preserved in waterlogged ground, see D. Charlesworth, 'The south gate of a Flavian fort at Carlisle', in W. S. Hanson and L. J. F. Keppie (eds), *Roman Frontier Studies 1979: Papers presented to the 12th International Congress of Roman Frontier Studies*, British Archaeological Reports, International Series, 71 (i) (Oxford 1980), 201 ff.

78. B. Hobley, *Curr.Arch.*, 24 (Jan. 1971), 17 ff.
79. For a reconsideration of the evidence for prefabrication and the dismantling and removal of gate timbers from one site to another see W. S. Hanson, 'The Roman Military Timber Supply', 298 ff.
80. Baginton: *Trans. Birm. and Warwicks.Arch.Soc.*, 85 (1971–3), 19; Oakwood: *PSAS*, 86 (1951–2), 94 ff; probably also at the north gate at Fendoch, *PSAS*, 73 (1938–9), 116, fig. 3 and Castledykes, A. S. Robertson, *The Roman Fort at Castledykes*, (Edinburgh, 1964), 89.
81. For stone-built gateways see I. A. Richmond and F. A. Child, 'Gateways of forts on Hadrian's Wall', *AA* 4, 20 (1942), 134 ff.
82. When he explored the south gate at Chesters in 1879, John Clayton discovered that: 'Each entrance was closed by a door with two leaves, and each leaf was set in a stout post, on which it swung, and the post was shod with a band of iron. In this instance the iron cylinders were found sticking fast in the pivot holes, traces of the wood which they had encircled being found inside them. The upper pivot of the post worked in a hole that was bored completely through a stone fixed in the structure above. The leaves of the doors were studded with iron nails, and were fastened by means of iron bars; when closed they were kept in position by a stone frame which stood some three or four inches above the sill of the gateway.' *An Account of the Roman Antiquities preserved in the Museum at Chesters, Northumberland*, (London 1903), 106.
83. G. F. Lyon, *A narrative of travels in Northern Africa in 1818, 1819 and 1820*, (London 1821), 65 ff; R. Rebuffat, J. Deneauve and G. Hallier, 'Bu Njem 1967', *Libya Antiqua*, VI–VII (1969–70), 49 ff; R. G. Goodchild, 'Oasis forts of Legio III Augusta on the routes to the Fezzan', *PBSR*, 22(1954), 57 ff, fig. 1, Pl. IIa. I am grateful to Prof. Dr D. Baatz for drawing my attention to this site.
84. *Collectanea Antiqua*, v, 35, cited by J. Ward, *Romano-British Buildings and Earthworks*, (London 1911), 70, fig. 23.
85. W. Stukeley, *Iter Boreale*, 1776, pl. 65, cited by F. G. Simpson and I. A. Richmond, 'The fort on Hadrian's Wall at Halton', *AA* 4, 14 (1937), 158.
86. At Holzhausen, Schirenhof, Pförring, Pfünz and Feldberg.
87. For changing styles in fort gateways see T. Bechert, 'Römische Lagertore', *Bonn.J.*, (1971), 201 ff.
88. They appear from the beginning of the third century at Weissenburg, Passau, Schirenhof and Utrecht.
89. Vegetius, *epitoma rei militaris*, II, 25; Josephus, *Bell.Jud.*, III, v, 6, 3; Ammianus, xxiii, 4, 4 ff.
90. Vegetius, *epitoma rei militaris*, II, 25; Vitruvius, *de architectura*, X; the *carroballista* is also shown on Trajan's Column, Scenes XL/XLI and LXVI/LXVII. Part of a *ballista* tension frame was found at Ampurias in Spain at the beginning of this century, E. von Schramm, *Die antiken Geschütze der Saalburg*, (Berlin 1918), 40 ff and 75 ff.
91. D. Baatz, 'Zur Geschützbewaffnung römischer Auxiliartruppen in der frühen und mittleren Kaiserzeit', *Bonn.J.*, 166 (1966), 194 ff, and 'Recent finds of ancient artillery', *Britannia*, 9 (1978), 1 ff.
92. *RIB* 1280 and 1281.

5   The Internal Buildings

1. Timber shingles were preserved in a well at the Saalburg, see L. Jacobi, *Das Römerkastell Saalburg bei Homburg v.d.H.*, (Homburg vor de Höhe 1897), 233 ff and Pl. 14, 10; *Saal.J.*, 8 (1934), 24, Pl. 4.3. For construction techniques of Roman timber buildings see I. A. Richmond, 'Roman Timber Building', in E. M. Jope (ed.), *Studies in Building History* (London 1961), 15 ff.

2. W. S. Hanson, 'The Roman military timber supply', *Britannia*, 9 (1978), 298. In assessing the quantity of structural timber required Hanson based his calculations upon the fort of Pen Llystyn, and made the following assumptions: that all internal buildings, except the granaries, were single storeyed, with uprights spaced at 1 m intervals, and that the granaries followed the reconstruction proposed by W. H. Manning, 'Roman military timber granaries in Britain', *Saal.J.*, 32 (1975), 112.

   The roofs were assumed to be quarter-pitched, apart from porticoes which had lean-to roofs, having a single couple roof for spans of less than 3.6 m, and a double for anything greater, with rafters at 0.45 m intervals; assuming timber sizes of 10 cm section for the rafters, 23 × 5 cm for ridge poles and 23 × 10 cm for the purlins.

3. I. A. Richmond and J. McIntyre, 'The Agricolan fort at Fendoch', *PSAS*, 73 (1938–9), 151 ff. For further discussion of this interpretation see B. Hobley, *Curr.Arch.*, 24 (Jan. 1971), 17 ff.

4. W. S. Hanson, *op. cit.*, 295 ff.

5. W. S. Hanson, *op. cit.*, 298 ff, Tables 3–5.

6. The mid-late second century forts of Feldburg, Kapersburg, Holzhausen, and possibly also Arzbach, had apsidal stone *sacella* with one or more adjoining rooms of stone, whilst the rest of the building was timber-built. Stone-built headquarters buildings at Zugmantel, Urspring and Stockstadt had timber forehalls.

7. The stone *principia* at Alphen-Zwammerdam and stone buildings of other forts in the Rhine delta such as Valkenburg and Arentsberg were founded upon rammed timber stakes, a method of construction described by Vitruvius, *de architectura*, II, 9, 10 ff; J. K. Haalebos, *Zwammerdam-Nigrum Pullum*, (Amsterdam 1977), 36.

8. Polybius, *Historiae*, VI, 33, 314; Hyginus, *de mun.cast.*, 11 ff; W. Fischer, *Das römische Lager*, (Leipzig 1914), 36 ff.

9. A. von Domaszewski, 'Die Principia des römischen Lagers', *Neue Heidelberger J.*, 9 (1899), 157. Th. Mommsen also pointed out that the term *praetorium* was used for the residence of a provincial governor, or any large house or palace with essentially a private residential function in 'Praetorium', *Hermes*, 35 (1900), 437 ff.

10. Rough Castle: *RIB* 2145. The inscription from Birdoswald, *RIB* 1912, records the reconstruction of three quite independent structures, the *principia*, *praetorium* and *balneum*.

11. R. G. Collingwood, *JRS*, 19 (1929), 214 ff, followed by E. Birley, *CW* 2, 30 (1930), 200 ff. For a fuller discussion of the terminology see R. Fellman, *Die Principia des Legionslagers Vindonissa und das Zentralgebäude der römischen Lager und Kastelle*, (Brugg, Vindonissa Museum, 1958), 75 ff. Other inscriptions referring to *principia* come from Lanchester, *RIB* 1092, and Combe Down, Bath, *RIB* 179.

12. H. von Petrikovits, *Die Innenbauten römischer Legionslager während der Prinzipatszeit*, Abhandlungen der Rheinisch-Westfälischen Akademie der Wissenschaften, Band 56, (Opladen 1975), 75.

13. *CIL* XIII, 7800.
14. G. Macdonald and A. Park, *The Roman Forts on the Bar Hill*, (Glasgow 1906), 8 ff and 133 ff. For inventory of the finds; A. Robertson, M. Scott and L. Keppie, *Bar Hill: A Roman Fort and its Finds*, British Archaeological Reports No. 16, (Oxford 1975), 12 ff and 38 ff.
15. A. Robertson, M. Scott and L. Keppie, *op. cit.*, 42. The total height suggested from the fragments is 2.44 m, although they may have been supported upon sleeper walls.
16. J. Hopkinson, *The Roman Fort at Ribchester*, 3rd edn by D. Atkinson, (Manchester 1928), 17.
17. Saalburg: *ORL* 11, 33. A function as a guardhouse has been suggested by J. Curle, *A Roman Frontier Post and its People: the fort of Newstead in the parish of Melrose*, (Glasgow 1911), 47.
18. G. M. von Groller, *RLÖ*, 10 (1909), 94 ff; H. von Petrikovits, 'Die Spezialgebäude römischer Legionslager', *Legio VII Gemina*, (Léon 1970), 235; H. Lorenz, *Untersuchungen zum Praetorium. Katalog der Praetorium und Entwicklung-geschichte ihrer Typen*, diss., Halle-Wittenberg, 1936, 87.
19. *RIB* 1092.
20. *CIL* XIII, 8824.
21. A. von Domaszewski, 'Die Principia et Armamentaria des Lagers von Lambaesis', *Westdt.Zeit.*, 21 (1902), 21 ff. Tarruntenus Paternus mentions armourers (*custodes armorum*) in his list of legionary *immunes*, *Digest*, 50, 6, 7, and it is presumed that they also served in the auxiliary units, with offices next to the weapon stores.
22. F-R. Herrmann, 'Der Eisenhortfund aus dem Kastell Künzing', *Saal.J.*, 26 (1969), 129 ff; H. Schönberger and F-R. Herrmann, 'Das Römerkastell Künzing-Quintana', *Jahresbericht der bayer Bodendenkmalpflege*, 8–9 (1967–8), 53 ff; F-R. Herrmann, *Die Ausgrabungen in dem Kastell Künzing/Quintana*, Limesmuseum Aalen 8 (1972), 9 ff and figs 8–34.
23. Reculver: *JRS*, 51 (1961), 191, no. 1; I. A. Richmond, 'A new building-inscription from the Saxon-Shore fort at Reculver, Kent', *Ant.J.* 41 (1961), 224 ff.
24. In a more modern study of the legionary *principia* at Vindonissa R. Fellmann has suggested that some cross-halls at least were unroofed. He isolated three variants in the *principia* plan: Variant I with a courtyard and portico on four sides with a rear range of rooms but no intermediate cross-hall, Variant II with two courtyards, one behind the other, divided by a wall or portico, and Variant III with a courtyard and portico, cross-hall, and rear range, see *Die Principia*, (1958), 163 ff.
    Fellman's Variant II category included the legionary examples of Vindonissa, Haltern and Lambaesis and the auxiliary *principia* at South Shields. The excavator at Haltern, F. Koepp, believed that the distance between the rear portico columns of the courtyard and the rear range of the building, amounting to 13–14 metres, was too great a span to have been roofed and so he favoured an open courtyard: roof spans in excess of this distance are known from civilian *basilicae* and from forehalls attached to several military *principia*, and so there is no reason to suppose that the cross-hall here could not have been roofed. The space between the outer courtyard and the rear range in the *principia* at Lambaesis was occupied by a raised terrace approached by steps from the outer courtyard. It was long thought to have represented an example of an open cross-hall, but a cropmark in the grass has since been observed, suggesting that there had originally been a cross wall

present, and so it too was probably roofed—see H. Lorenz, *Untersuchungen zum Praetorium*, (1936), 95. Fellman also included South Shields in this category, as there was a paved pathway running across the cross-hall to the shrine at the rear; but excavation has revealed that the front wall of this cross-hall had stood at least 9 metres high, making its function merely as a screen wall between two courtyards highly unlikely.

25. Fortis, *Viaggio in Dalmazia*, 1774, I, 119, cited by R. Fellman, *Die Principia*, 130 and fig. 54.

26. The group includes less than twenty auxiliary forts, together with the legionary fortresses at Vetera, Novaesium, Carnuntum and Lambaesis.

27. R. Cagnat, 'Les deux camps de la légion IIIe Auguste à Lambèse', *Mémoires de l'Académie des Inscriptions et Belles-Lettres*, 38/1 (1908), 33 ff.

28. R. Fellmann, *Die Principia*, 88 cites Classical authors who indicate that at least in the late Empire the centurions and officers had their *scholae* in the *principia*; Iustin. 11, 6, 6; Ammian 25, 8, 16.

29. For example the cross-halls at Caernarfon, Camelon and Bar Hill were all subdivided into smaller rooms, presumably offices, at this time, a change which has been attributed to the need for more office and storage space for the administrative staff.

30. Exceptions range from 9 rooms at Niederbieber, 7 at Echzell, 6 at Künzing to 3 at a number of forts, including Hesselbach and Ambleside, although in stone-built *principia* with only three rear rooms it is possible that only the principal stone partitions have been detected, and that timber partitions may have been used to further subdivide the rear rooms.

31. An inscription from Reculver identifies the shrine as the *aedes*, *JRS*, 51 (1961), 191, no. 1.

32. R. O. Fink, A. S. Hoey and W. F. Snyder, 'Feriale Duranum', *Yale Classical Studies*, 7 (1940), 1 ff.

33. Tacitus, *Hist.* 3, 13, 2; *Ann.* 4, 23.

34. This description was preserved in the Paris papyrus, U. Wilcken, *Philogus*, 53 (1894), 83, translated by A. von Domaszewski, 'Principia', 162.

35. For the veneration of the *signa*, Statius, *Theb.* x, 176; Tertullian, *Apol.*, 16. See A. von Domaszewski, 'Die Religion des römischen Heeres', *Westdt. Zeit.*, 14 (1895), 11 ff, and I. A. Richmond and J. McIntyre, 'Fendoch', 125.

36. R. E. Birley, *Discoveries at Vindolanda*, 2nd edn, (Newcastle 1975), 18, and *Vindolanda, A Roman Frontier Post on Hadrian's Wall*, (London 1977), 40 and Pl. 14.

37. *RIB* 1904.

38. Tacitus, *Hist.*, 36.

39. R. O. Fink, A. S. Hoey and W. F. Snyder, 'Feriale Duranum', 115.

40. *RIB* 327–8.

41. *RIB* 882–3.

42. Vegetius, *epitoma rei militaris*, II, 19.

43. The pay accounts of two soldiers survive on a papyrus dated AD 81, *P.Gen.Lat.* 1, and show deductions for food, clothing, boots and probably bedding, with possibly contributions deducted for a burial club and regimental dinner. Another papyrus, *P.Berlin*, 6866, shows the pay balances of several soldiers, most of whom had 100 *denarii in deposito*. This sum was probably part of a donative paid upon the accession of either Pescennius Niger or Septimius Severus, G. R. Watson, *The Roman Soldier*, (London 1969), 105 and 220 ff; R. Marichal, 'Le Solde des armées romaines d'Auguste à Septime

Sévère d'après les P.Gen.Lat.1 et 4 et le P.Berlin 6866', *Mélanges Isidore Lévy*, (Brussels 1955), 399 ff.

For compulsory stoppages see Vegetius, *epitoma rei militaris*, II, 20, and for pay in general, G. R. Watson, 'The pay of the Roman Army: the auxiliary forces', *Historia*, 8 (1959), 372 ff; J. F. Gilliam, 'The deposita of an auxiliary soldier', *Bonn.J.*, 167 (1967), 233 ff.

44. Suetonius, *Dom.* 7; G. R. Watson, *The Roman Soldier*, 105.

45. Vegetius, *epitoma rei militaris*, II, 12.

46. The key bore the inscriptions, on one side: ≡BASS CLAUDI | FABI SIG and on the other: 〉BAS; H. Lehner, 'Die Einzelfunde von Novaesium', *Bonn.J.*, 111/112 (1904), 405.

47. H. Schönberger, *Kastell Künzing-Quintana: Die Grabungen von 1958 bis 1966*, *Limesforschungen* 13, (Berlin 1975), 42 ff and fig. 9.

48. Dr D. Baatz has drawn attention to several of these antechambers to *sacella*, which may well represent the foundations for staircases. To his list of Neckarburken-West, Oberscheidental, Osterburken and Echzell may be added Heilbronn-Böckingen; see D. Baatz, *Kastell Hesselbach*, *Limesforschungen* 12, (Berlin 1973), 49 and note 107.

49. A similar sliding door was found at the stone fort of Ambleside.

50. J. Collingwood Bruce, *Handbook to the Roman Wall*, 9th edn by R. G. Collingwood, (Newcastle 1933), 82. These strongrooms in Hadrian's Wall forts are usually believed to have been third century insertions, although their precise dating is often far from clear.

51. *CIL* III 3526 = *ILS* 2355; A. von Domaszewski, 'Die Religion', 13.

52. Tertullian, *Cor.* II, 3.

53. Vegetius, *epitoma rei militaris*, II, 19.

54. J. F. Gilliam, C. B. Welles and R. O. Fink, *The Excavations at Dura-Europos. Final Report V. Part 1: The Parchments and Papyri*, (New Haven 1959); R. O. Fink, *Roman Military Records on Papyrus*, (Cleveland 1971).

55. *CIL* XIII, 7752.

56. *Cornicularius* from Greatchesters, *RIB* 1742; *actuarii* from Ebchester, *RIB* 1101, Ambleside, *JRS*, 53 (1963), 160, no. 4, and Caernarfon, *RIB* 429; *librarii* from Corbridge, *RIB* 1134, and Schirenhof, *CIL* III, 11924.

57. *CIL* XIII, 7753.

58. I. A. Richmond, *Hod Hill: Excavations carried out between 1951 and 1958*, II, (London 1968), 75.

59. H. Lehner, *Bonn.J.*, 122 (1912–13), 325 ff; and *Vetera. Die Ergebnisse der Ausgrabungen des Bonner Provinzialmuseums bis 1929*, Römisch-Germanische Forschungen 4, (Berlin and Leipzig 1930), 50.

A 'division' wall projecting from the rear range into the cross-hall at the vexillation fortress of Longthorpe has been interpreted as possibly being the division of the building for use by both the legionary and auxiliary units thought to have been in garrison—see S. S. Frere and J. K. St. Joseph, 'The Roman fortress at Longthorpe', *Britannia*, 5 (1974), 19 and note 19.

60. At Weissenberg the forehall extended as far as the granaries on either side, and was further connected along the street frontage with the commander's house. Similarly the forehalls at Unterböbingen and Butzbach were linked with an adjacent granary, and at Newstead the granaries on either side were linked into one architectual scheme. The monumental façade of the forehall at Halton-chesters, consisting of stone piers linked by panel walls, directly abutted the end walls of stores, barracks and stables in the *praetentura*. The excavator, I. A. Richmond, compared this linking together of the central buildings with the

scheme at Lambaesis, which was designed 'to form a unified architectural conception', *AA* 4, 14 (1937), 169.

61. Forehalls are known only at Brecon Gaer, Ribchester, Haltonchesters and Newstead.

62. W. Schleiermacher, 'Principia', *Trierer Zeit.*, 18 (1949), 247 ff.

63. Except for the Claudian legionary fortress at Vindonissa, see Fellman, *Die Principia*, 12 ff.

64. D. Baatz, *Kastell Hesselbach*, 1973 32.

65. V. E. Nash-Williams, *The Roman Frontier in Wales*, 2nd edn by M. G. Jarrett, (Cardiff 1969), 51.

66. *ORL* 71a, 8.

67. E. Ritterling, *ORL* 1a, 19.

68. R. Fellman, *Die Principia*, 171, who also considered that the forehalls at Theilenhofen, Gnotzheim, Urspring and Weissenburg were unroofed.

69. D. Baatz, *Kastell Hesselbach*, 1973, 33 and fig. 28.

70. W. Schleiermacher, 'Principia', 1949, 247 ff; R. Fellman, *Die Principia*, 171 ff, following A. von Cohausen's original identification; H. Lorenz, *Untersuchungen zum Praetorium*, (1936), 112 ff.

71. *RIB* 978.

72. R. E. M. Wheeler, 'The Roman fort at Brecon', *Y Cymmrodor*, 37 (1926), 42 ff; Professor Richmond has also suggested that the addition of the forehalls at both Newstead and Haltonchesters coincided with the posting of cavalry to these forts, making their identification as *basilicae equestris exercitatoriae* more probable, *PSAS*, 84 (1949–50), 24.

73. At least half the forts which had forehalls can be shown to have been connected with a cavalry unit. The *ala II Flavia milliaria* is named on a tombstone from Heidenheim and later upon numerous stamped tiles from Aalen. Stamped tiles of *cohors III Thracum c.R.equitata* occur at Künzing in the late first–early second century, and the same unit was responsible for building the internal bathhouse at Gnotzheim by AD 144, and presumably the other fort buildings as well including the forehall. At Ribchester the early third-century forehall may have been built by an *ala* of Sarmatians, which is attested in AD 238–44, and at Brecon Gaer a tombstone of a trooper of the *ala Hispanorum c.R.* was erected in the first or early second century; whether this was still the garrison when the Antonine forehall was built is unknown, although the unit is not attested elsewhere until the Severan period at Binchester.

The second Antonine garrison at Newstead, judging by the barrack and stable accommodation is thought to have been an *ala milliaria*; the *ala Petriana* is the most likely candidate. A tombstone to a *duplicarius* of the *ala Sabiniana* was erected in the first half of the third century, at the same time as the forehall, at Haltonchesters. At Valkenburg the *cohors IIII Thracum quingenaria equitata* is known from graffiti in the fourth period of the fort's occupation, and is thought to have remained in garrison in Periods 5 and 6, when the forehall was built. An inscription mentioning *ala I . . .* provides evidence for a cavalry garrison at Welzheim-West in the Antonine period, and the garrison at Weissenburg, when the fort was rebuilt in AD 153 was *ala I Hispanorum Auriana*. Two inscriptions contemporary with the forehall at Zugmantel name *cohors Treverorum equitata* and *cohortes quingenariae equitatae* are also known at Butzbach and the Saalburg. Three units are attested at Stockstadt, and although it is uncertain which unit was contemporary with the Hadrianic forehall, all three were *cohortes equitatae*; as was the garrison at Eining. *Numeri* are believed to have garrisoned the forts of

Feldberg, Hesselbach 1 and 2, Kapersburg and Niederbieber.

74. Vegetius, *epitoma rei militaris*, II, 23.

75. Vegetius, *epitoma rei militaris*, III, 2.

76. The possible link between an exercise ground and the front of the *principia* is made by U. Kahrsredt, *The Congress of Roman Frontier Studies 1949*, ed. E. Birley, (Durham 1952), 51, in his discussion of the term *campus*, which was applied to the open space in front of the *principia* and also to the exercise ground, R. W. Davies, 'The training grounds of the Roman cavalry', *Arch.J.*, 125 (1969), 75.

77. H. Lorenz, *Untersuchungen zum Praetorium*, 82 ff; R. Fellman, *Die Principia*, 93 ff.

78. Building 11. W. Glasbergen, *De Romeinse Castella Te Valkenburg Z.H.*, (Groningen 1972), 46 ff. Doubt has recently been cast upon this interpretation by H. Schönberger, *Kastell Oberstimm, Limesforschungen* 18, (Berlin 1978), 45 and note 37; and 'Valkenburg Z.H.; Praetorium oder Fabrica', *Germania*, 57 (1979), 135 ff.

79. See above, p. 104. The use of the term *praetorium* for the dwelling is confirmed by the discovery of two altars from the site of the commander's house at Chesterholm which were dedicated to the *Genius* of the *praetorium*, *RIB* 1685–6. See F. Lammert, 'Praetorium', *RE*, 22, 2535 ff and supplement by W. Schleiermacher, *RE Supplement*, 9, 1180 ff.

80. Aurelius Julianus, *RIB* 1909; his son, Aurelius Concordius, *RIB* 1919.

81. Finds of women's and children's shoes have been made at several forts, including Bar Hill, Balmuildy, Chesterholm, Newstead, Hardknott, the Saalburg and Valkenburg; it is often difficult to determine whether they derived from residents within the fort or from civilians living close by in the *vicus*.

82. Civilian parallels include Caerwent Building VII.8, *Arch.*, 57 (1900–1), 30, Pl. XL, and *Arch.*, 58 (1902–3), 122, Pl. VIII; similar houses have been found at Silchester, Wroxeter and Colchester. For further examples of the more elaborate courtyard plan houses see R. G. Collingwood, *The Archaeology of Roman Britain*, revised by I. A. Richmond, (London 1969), 128, and parallels with Italian and provincial town and country houses, H. von Petrikovits, *Die Innenbauten*, 144 ff and notes 199–200.

83. For detailed descriptions of British *praetoria* see R. J. Penny, 'Design influences on commandant's houses in Britain', unpublished B.A. dissertation, University College, Cardiff, 1977.

84. For dining rooms and their identification see I. A. Richmond, 'The Agricolan fort at Fendoch', (1938–9), 128, and fig. 8; *JRS*, 51 (1961), 158, and fig. 9.

85. D. Charlesworth, 'The commandant's house, Housesteads', *AA* 5, 3 (1975), 17 ff.

86. A suggestion made by C. M. Daniels, published by J. P. Gillam, 'The Roman forts at Corbridge', *AA* 5, 5 (1976), 56 ff.

87. I. A. Richmond, *Hod Hill*, 78 ff.

88. B. Hobley, *Britannia*, 5 (1974), 431; *WMANS*, (1973), 14.

89. D. Planck, *Arae Flaviae I*, (Stuttgart 1975), 91 ff.

90. For the career structure of equestrian officers see A. von Domaszewski, *Die Rangordnung des römischen Heeres*, 2nd edn by B. Dobson, (Cologne 1967), 55 ff; G. L. Cheeseman, *The Auxilia of the Roman Imperial Army*, (Oxford 1914), 25 ff; E. Birley 'Alae and cohortes milliariae', *Corolla Memoriae Erich Swoboda Dedicata*, (Graz 1966), 58 ff.

91. E. Birley, *op. cit.*, 57 ff.

92. Kapersburg: *ORL* 12, Stone VI A, No. 4. Corbridge: *RIB* 1143. Unstratified building stones of Severan date recording the reconstruction of *horrea* are known from Birdoswald, *RIB* 1909, Hexham Priory (probably originally from Corbridge), *RIB* 1151, and Greatchesters, *RIB* 1738. An inscription found in Neuwied in Upper Germany, dedicated to the *Genius* of the *horreum*, probably derived from the nearby auxiliary fort at Niederbieber, *CIL* XIII, 7749.

93. T. A. Oxley, *The Scientific Principles of Grain Storage*, (Liverpool 1948).

94. G. R. Coope and P. J. Osborne, 'Report on the Coleopterous Fauna of the Roman well at Barnsley Park, Glos', *TBGAS*, 86 (1967), 84 ff; P. J. Osborne, 'An insect fauna from the Roman site at Alcester, Warwickshire', *Britannia*, 2 (1971), 156 ff; R. A. Hall and H. K. Kenwood, 'Biological evidence for the usage of Roman riverside warehouses at York', *Britannia*, 7 (1976), 274 ff.

95. A. P. Gentry, *Roman Military Stone-Built Granaries in Britain*, British Archaeological Reports No. 32, (Oxford 1976), 4.

96. Marcus Cato, de Agric., XCII; Varro, *Res Rusticae*, LVII.

97. Columella, *de Re Rustica*, I, vi, 9 ff.

98. Varro, *Res Rusticae*, LVII.

99. Columella, *de Re Rustica*, II, xx, 6.

100. Varro, *Res Rusticae*, LXIII.

101. Varro, *Res Rusticae*, LVII.

102. Vitruvius, *de Architectura*, VI, 6, 4.

103. Pliny, *Nat. Hist.*, XVIII, 302.

104. The architectural traditions are discussed by G. E. Rickman, *Roman Granaries and Storebuildings*, (Cambridge 1971), 251 ff.

105. For a detailed discussion and comparative plans of military timber granaries in Britain see W. H. Manning, 'Roman military timber granaries in Britain', *Saal.J.*, 32 (1975), 105 ff. G. E. Rickman, *Roman Granaries*, (1971), 215 ff includes German examples.

106. W. H. Manning, *op. cit.*, 109.

107. W. H. Manning, *op. cit.*, 106.

108. For a detailed discussion and comparative plans of military stone-built granaries in Britain see A. P. Gentry, *Stone-Built Granaries*, (1976), and for German examples G. E. Rickman, *Roman Granaries*, (1971), 215 ff.

109. At Gelligaer and Penydarren in the Trajanic period, G. E. Rickman, *op. cit.*, 221.

110. Okarben and Benningen, both c. AD 90, and Murrhardt, AD 234–60.

111. Ranging from the possible late Flavian examples at Benningen and Okarben to the Severan granaries at South Shields.

112. Square stone pillars were used in the legionary granaries at Neuss and Bonn, and also the auxiliary granaries at Housesteads, Ribchester and South Shields, with irregular boulders at Castlecary. Three rows of stone piers supported the floor at Hüfingen, whilst regular rows of timber posts were used in the stone-built granaries of Niederbieber and Weissenburg.

113. J. P. Gillam, 'The Roman forts at Corbridge', 67.

114. *RIB* 1340. J. P. Gillam, 'Excavations at Haltonchesters', *Durham University Gazette*, (1961), 6.

115. J. Clarke, *The Roman Fort at Cadder*, (Glasgow 1933), 42.

116. W. H. Manning, 'Timber granaries', 114.

117. J. Ward, *The Roman Fort of Gellygaer*, (London 1903), 62 ff.

118. W. H. Manning, 'Timber granaries', 109 ff.

119. At Usk, Baginton, and Crawford.

120. B. Hobley, *Curr.Arch.*, 44 (May 1974), 276 ff.

121. G. E. Rickman, *Roman Granaries*, 236.
122. A. P. Gentry, *Stone-Built Granaries*, 15 and Appendix I, 35.
123. W. Bulmer, 'The provisioning of Roman forts: a reappraisal of ration storage', *AA* 4, 47 (1969), 10.
124. B. Philp, *Curr.Arch.*, 38 (May 1973), 86.
125. F. Haverfield and R. G. Collingwood, 'The provisioning of Roman forts', *CW* 2, 20 (1920), 127, envisaged bins 1.83 m deep with a corridor of 0.9 m between them, covering the entire floor space available. Professor Richmond, in his suggested reconstruction of the timber granaries at Fendoch, postulated bins 1.5 m deep, see *PSAS*, 73 (1938–9), 131 ff and fig. 10.

    In his reappraisal of ration storage, however, W. Bulmer believed that a 0.9 m corridor would be insufficient, and that bins 1.5 m deep may have been used with a sloping base 30 cm off the ground at one end to enable the bin to empty completely. The loss in the amount of storage area by the use of the sloping-base bin would amount to 30%, which he eliminated by raising the back of the bin to a height of 1.98 m. If this were done it would restrict the amount of wall which could be pierced with louvred ventilators, as they would have to be placed at a higher level than the top of the grain (W. Bulmer, *op. cit.*, 9).

    The storage capacity of some German granaries has been assessed by O. Wahle, 'Die Proviantmagazine der Saalburg', *Die Saalburg, Mitteilungen der Vereinigung der Saalburg-Freunde II*, 2 (10th April 1920), 29 ff.
126. The use of sacks would also have helped to ventilate the grain, as, providing they are not stacked too close together, they allow water vapour and heat to dissipate more rapidly than when the grain is stored in bulk, T. A. Oxley, *Principles of Grain Storage*, 24.
127. Plaut *Capt.*, iv, 4, 6; Pliny, *Nat.Hist.*, XVIII, 60.
128. They have been found at Kapersburg, Weissenburg and Wiesbaden, and possibly also at the Saalburg, Ruffenhofen and Pfünz in Germany, and at Templeborough in Britain.
129. Vegetius, *epitoma rei militaris*, III, 2.
130. R. W. Davies, 'Joining the Roman army', *Bonn.J.*, 169 (1969), 208; G. R. Watson, *The Roman Soldier*, 39.
131. G. R. Watson, *op. cit.*, 123.
132. Celsus, *de Medicina*; Paul of Aegina, *de re medica*; Galen, whose writings have been edited in 20 volumes by G. C. Kühn, Leipzig, 1821–33.
133. The best account of the medical service is by R. W. Davies, 'The Roman military medical service', *Saal.J.*, 27 (1970), 84 ff.
134. The *praefectus castrorum* was in overall command of the medical service, Vegetius, *epitoma rei militaris*, II, 10. Tarruntenus Paternus mentions the *optio valetudinarii*, who ran the legionary hospital, in his list of legionary *immunes*, *Digest*, 50, 6, 7.
135. For the various ranks of medical staff see R. W. Davies, *op. cit.*, 86 ff.
136. *CIL* VIII, 2553.
137. Cited by R. W. Davies, 'Roman medical service', 87.
138. Hyginus, *de mun.cast.*, 4.
139. *Valetudinaria* are known from the fortresses of Inchtuthil, Haltern, Vindonissa, Caerleon, Vetera, Novaesium, Bonn, Lauriacum and Carnuntum. See R. Schultze, 'Die römischen Legionslazarette in Vetera und anderen Legionslagern', *Bonn.J.*, 139 (1934), 54 ff; H. von Petrikovits, *Die Innenbauten*, 98 ff.
140. I. A. Richmond, 'The Roman army medical service', *University of Durham Medical Gazette*, (June 1952), 4.

141. C. Koenen, 'Beschreibung von Novaesium', *Bonn.J.*, 111/112 (1904), 399 ff.
142. A. Stieren, *Germania*, 12 (1928), 70, fig. 1 and 175; *Bod.Westf.* 6 (1943), Pl. 30a, 118. Dragendorff linked this find with the description of the *herba Britannica* by the elder Pliny, *Nat.Hist.*, XXV, 20 ff, as a cure for scurvy, which the army of Germanicus learned from the Frisians, C. M. Wells, *The German Policy of Augustus*, (Oxford 1972), 189 ff.
143. *JRS*, 53 (1963), 166, no. 51. Dioscurides, *de mat.med.*, v, 48.
144. Cited by R. W. Davies, 'Roman medical service', 92 and note 62.
145. *Medicus* from Binchester, *RIB* 1028; *medicus ordinarius* from Housesteads, *RIB* 1618; *medicus ordinarius* and *capsarii* from Niederbieber, *CIL* XIII, 11979. Ulpius Telesporus served as a medical officer with the *ala Indiana* in Upper Germany and later with *ala II Asturum* in the province of *Mauretania Tingitana* before returning to civilian life. For his career see *CIL* XI, 3007, and R. W. Davies 'Roman medical service', 88; also R. W. Davies, 'The medici of the Roman armed forces', *Epigraphische Studien*, 8 (1969), 83 ff; 9 (1970), 1 ff.
146. Medical instruments have been found in a number of forts including Corbridge, Newstead, the Saalburg, Housesteads and Straubing.
147. *P.Lond.* 2851 = *CLA* 219 col. 2, 44.
148. D. Charlesworth, 'The hospital, Housesteads', *AA* 5, 4 (1976), 17 ff.
149. J. Liversidge, *Britain in the Roman Empire*, (London 1968), 329. Five medicinal plants were discovered in the legionary hospital at Neuss: K. H. Knörzer, 'Römerzeitliche Heilkräuter aus Novaesium', *Sudhoffs Archiv für Geschichte de Medizin u.d.Naturwiss*, 47 (1963), 311 ff; *Romerzeitliche Pflanzenfunde aus Neuss, Limesforschungen* 10, (Berlin 1970).
150. Aerial photography has detected a small courtyard-plan building behind the principal buildings at Beckfoot, *JRS*, 51 (1961), 56 and Pl. IV, 2.
151. R. G. Collingwood, *The Archaeology of Roman Britain* revised by I. A. Richmond, (London 1969), 31.
152. W. S. Hanson, C. M. Daniels, J. N. Dore and J. P. Gillam, 'The Agricolan supply base at Red House, Corbridge', *AA* 5, 7 (1979), 1 ff.
153. W. S. Hanson, C. M. Daniels, J. N. Dore and J. P. Gillam, *op. cit.*, 80.
154. C. M. Daniels, 'A hoard of iron and other materials from Corbridge', *AA* 4, 46 (1968), 115 ff.
155. R. W. Davies in 'A note on the hoard of Roman equipment buried at Corbridge', *Durham University Journal*, 62 (1969–70), 177 ff, has suggested that the purpose of this burial of scrap iron and bronze under the floor of the building identified as a hospital was to produce quantities of iron rust and verdigris (*aerugo*) which, according to Celsus, *de medicina* 5, 2 and 5, 9 and Pliny, *Nat.Hist.*, 34, 110 ff and 152 ff, was used to dry and cleanse wounds. However, had the medical orderlies wished to promote corrosion in the iron and bronze objects the process would probably have been accelerated by exposing them to the air and the rain, rather than by wrapping them in cloth and burying them; a procedure which has prevented their complete decay to the present day. There would also have been little advantage in including leather, a wooden mug and glass gaming counters.
156. G. E. Rickman, *Roman Granaries*, 1 ff.
157. G. Carettoni, A. Colini, L. Cozza and G. Gatti, *La Pianta Marmorea di Roma Antica*, Rome, 1955. For a detailed discussion of the fragments which depict storebuildings see G. E. Rickman, *Roman Granaries* 87 ff.
158. It is probable that when rolled up in transit the leather tent resembled a butterfly larva (*papilio*). For Roman tents see: J. McIntyre and I. A. Richmond, 'Tents of the Roman army and the leather at Birdoswald', *CW* 2, 34 (1934), 62 ff; W. Groenman-van Waateringe, *Romeins Lederwerk uit*

Valkenburg Z.H., (Groningen 1967), 79 ff; A. Robertson, M. Scott and L. Keppie, *Bar Hill: A Roman Fort and its Finds*, British Archaeological Reports No. 16, (Oxford 1975), 83 ff.

159. Hyginus, *de mun.cast.*, 1.
160. The term *centuria* is attested on an inscription from the legionary fortress of Caerleon, which records the rebuilding of barracks from ground level in AD 255–60, *RIB* 334; a dedication slab from Brough-by-Bainbridge, dated AD 205, *JRS*, 51 (1961), 192, no. 4; fragments of a monument dedicated to the *Genius centuriae* from Feldburg, *CIL* XIII 7494a, and fragments of a statue to the *Genii centuriarum* from the Saalburg, *CIL* XIII 7448.
161. Similar latrines are known at Hod Hill—see I. A. Richmond, *Hod Hill II*, fig. 45 A; at Housesteads, *JRS*, 51 (1961), fig. 11, 161, and Hesselbach, D. Baatz, *Kastell Hesselbach*, 44; several legionary examples are also known.
162. D. Baatz, 'Römische Wandmalereien aus dem Limeskastell Echzell', *Germania* 46 (1968), 40 ff. See 50 ff for other finds of wall plaster in Upper German forts and 'Ausgrabungen im Limeskastell Echzell', *Wetterauer Geschichtsblätter*, 18 (1969), 1 ff, Pl. 3–5. Fine painted wall plaster comparable in quality to the Echzell plaster has recently been found in one of the barracks of the Upper German fort of Hofheim.
163. Similar pits were found at Künzing. Some of the larger ones may have been latrines, with removable wooden tubs, whilst the smaller ones were probably storage pits for valuables, H. Schönberger, *Kastell Künzing*, 27.
164. The lack of spare *contubernium* space at Housesteads has led to the suggestion that the junior officers shared the centurions' rooms, *AA* 4, 39 (1961), 282. The two freedmen who erected a tombstone to the legionary centurion Marcus Favonius at Colchester, *RIB* 200, may have had their quarters within his suite of rooms, and auxiliary centurions also probably had their own slaves or servants. E. Birley, quoted by R. E. Birley, *Vindolanda*, 125, considers that these 'flats provided ample space for a small household'.
165. H. von Petrikovits, *Die Innenbauten*, 36.
166. D. Baatz, *Kastell Hesselbach*, 54 ff and note 132.
167. Examples where more spacious accommodation lies on the right of a pair of barracks are seen at Hesselbach 2, Caernarfon 2, Pen Llystyn and Valkenburg 4–6. But there are as many examples in which the left-hand member of the pair is larger, at Caerhun 2, Baginton 2, Corbridge 2–3, Valkenburg 2/3 and Heidenheim. At Fendoch the officers' rooms in the *praetentura* barracks were generally slightly larger than those in the *retentura*. Many forts do not seem to show any marked differences in size in the officers' accommodation, although it must be stressed that in many cases, Künzing for example, the evidence rests upon rather standardised reconstructions of buildings located only in small-scale trial trenching.
168. B. Cichy, *Das römische Heidenheim*, (Heidenheim 1971), 27 ff.
169. Bunk beds have also been postulated at Künzing and Rödgen in order to fit the requisite number of men into the space available—see H. Schönberger, *Kastell Künzing*, 112; H. Schönberger and H. G. Simon, *Römerlager Rödgen*, *Limesforschungen* 15, (Berlin 1976), 32 and note 48.
170. Josephus, *Bell.Jud.*, III, 5, 95 records that the legionary soldier carried on the march, in addition to his weapons, 'a saw, a basket, a pick and an axe, not to mention a strap, a bill-hook, a chain and three days' rations, so that an infantryman is almost as heavily laden as a pack mule'.

Trajan's Column depicts legionaries on the march carrying stakes over their shoulders to which their kit was tied (Scene III–V), which included cooking utensils, a string bag, a sack probably for provisions, and what may have been a rolled-up leather tool kit.

171. D. J. Breeze, 'Excavations at the Roman fort of Carrawburgh, 1967–9', *AA* 4, 50 (1972), 94. Running down the central axis of a timber barrack at the Flavian fort of Cardean in Scotland, separating the front and rear rooms of the *contubernia*, were two foundation trenches ('median double rib'), which were apparently contemporary. The trenches, which were 0.3–0.6 m apart, have been interpreted as perhaps a constructional device designed to give additional support to a penthouse roof on either side of the building—see A. S. Robertson, 'Excavations at Cardean and Stracathro, Angus', in *Studien zu den Militärgrenzen Roms: Vorträge des 10 Internationalen Limeskongresses in der Germania Inferior*, (Cologne 1977), 68 ff. A similar device seems to have been used in the stone barracks of the Antonine fort at Birrens, where pairs of long, unusually narrow buildings were separated by a narrow cobbled passage or 'eavesdrip'—see A. S. Robertson, *Birrens Blatobulgium*, (Edinburgh 1975), 85 ff.

We need to know much more about the internal layout of such buildings before any firm conclusions can be drawn about the function of this unusual feature. It is presumed that the double wall was pierced at regular intervals to allow access from the front to the rear of the *contubernium*, but unfortunately in neither example have the positions of the hearths or doorways survived to confirm this. It is possible that the contubernial rooms in these atypical barrack blocks lay not one behind the other, but were adjacent, with perhaps chimney flues provided in the cavity.

172. The number of *contubernia* occupied by presumed cavalry units varies from 6 at Valkenburg 1a and 2/3, 8 at Carzield, 9 at Benwell, 10 restored at Chesters and Niederbieber to 11 at Newstead (believed to have accommodated a milliary *ala*) and 12 in the milliary *ala* fort at Heidenheim.

173. Hyginus, *de mun.cast.*, 26.

174. For changes in the fort plan between Period 1 (c. AD 40) and adaptation phase 1a (c. AD 42) see W. Glasbergen and W. Groenman-van Waateringe, *The Pre-Flavian Garrisons of Valkenburg Z.H.*, (Amsterdam 1974), 17 ff.

175. I. A. Richmond, *Hod Hill II*, 80.

176. W. Glasbergen and W. Groenman-van Waateringe, *Pre-Flavian Garrisons*, 8 ff, figs 7 and 8. Similar improvements in the standards have been demonstrated in legionary barracks, where sleeping accommodation for 8 men in the first century amounted to 18 square metres, and increased to 24 square metres in the third century, H. von Petrikovits, *Die Innenbauten*, 137.

177. D. Baatz, 'Limeskastell Echzell. Kurzbericht über die Grabungen 1963 und 1964', *Saal.J.*, 22 (1965), 142, note 142, fig. 2,8.

178. W. Glasbergen and W. Groenman-van Waateringe, *Pre-Flavian Garrisons*, 10 ff.

179. B. Cichy, *Das römische Heidenheim*, (1971), 7 ff.

180. The dimensions of the living rooms at Housesteads and Fendoch are closely comparable, with 27 square metres of floor area at Fendoch and 25 square metres at Housesteads.

181. The numbers of cavalry troopers, and therefore horses, comprising each of the auxiliary *alae* and *cohortes equitatae* are recorded by Hyginus, Arrian, and Vegetius; see p. 21. Hyginus states (*de mun.cast.*, 16) that in addition the commander of each *turma* (*decurio*) had two extra mounts allocated, and his subordinate officers (*duplicarius* and *sesquiplicarius*) one each. This brings the minimum number of horses required by an *ala milliaria* (assuming 32 men per *turma*) to 768 plus 96; the *ala quingenaria* 512 plus 64, and the *cohortes milliariae* and *quingenariae equitatae* to 240 plus 40 and 120 plus 16 mounts

respectively; no allowance has been made for remounts—see R. W. Davies, 'The supply of animals to the Roman army and the Remount System', *Latomus*, 28 (1968), 429 ff. Additionally every unit, whether cavalry or infantry had its own pack animals.

182. C. M. Wells, 'Where did they put the horses? Cavalry stables in the Early Empire', *Limes: Akten des XI Internationalen Limeskongresses*, ed. J. Fitz, (Budapest 1977), 659 ff.

183. J. C. Ewart, 'The animal remains' in J. Curle, *A Roman Frontier Post and its People: the fort of Newstead in the Parish of Melrose*, (Glasgow 1911), 362 ff.

184. C. M. Wells, 'Cavalry stables', 662.

185. The recommended size for an individual stall is 1.8 × 3.4 m; the actual space required by an average modern horse to lie down and rise is 1.8 × 2.7 m. S. Rowland Pierce and P. Cutbush, *Planning: The Architect's Handbook*, (London 1959), 475 ff.

186. The normal breadth of a stable block with one row of stalls is 5.5 m, and with two rows 9.5 m—see J. Wortley Axe, *The Horse: Its Treatment in Health and Disease*, VIII, (1905), 323. Military stables in Austria at the beginning of this century allowed a breadth of between 9 and 10.5 m, giving 3.2 m for each row of stalls with a corridor between them, E. Ritterling, *ORL* 1a, 47 ff.

187. Xenophon, *De Re Equestri*, IV, 3.

188. B. R. Hartley, 'The Roman fort at Ilkley: excavations of 1962', *Proc. Leeds Phil. and Lit. Soc., Lit. and Hist. Sec.* 12, Part 2 (1966), 37, fig. 13, 11.

189. G. Müller, *Ausgrabungen in Dormagen, 1963-1977*, Rheinisches Landesmuseums Bonn, (Cologne 1979), 27 ff.

190. O. Schröder, 'Bodenchemische Untersuchung von Reduktionsverfärbungen', in G. Müller, *Dormagen*, (1979), 129 ff; K-H. Knörzer, 'Verkohlte Reste von Viehfutter aus einem Stall des römischen Reiterlagers von Dormagen', in G. Müller, *Dormagen*, (1979), 130 ff.

191. Xenophon, *De Re Equestri*, V, 2.

192. *P.Dura* 101, XXXIII, 9.

193. I. A. Richmond, *Hod Hill II*, 82 ff.

194. C. M. Wells, 'Cavalry stables', 661.

195. For a theoretical reconstruction of the stable layout see H. Schönberger, *Kastell Künzing*, 58 ff and figs 13 and 14.

196. Polybius, *Historiae*, VI, 39, 12.

197. 1 artab = 23.6 kg. The quantity requisitioned in this papyrus would amount to 472,000 kg per year, *P.Amh.*, 107.

198. R. E. Walker, 'Roman veterinary medicine', in J. M. C. Toynbee, *Animals in Roman Life and Art*, (London 1973), Appendix III, 342, and note 40.

199. *P. Hamb.* 39, 12; R. O. Fink, *Roman Military Records on Papyrus*. (Cleveland 1971), 283 ff no. 76.

200. For receipt for hay from a *turma* on *ostracon* from Pselcis, see R. O. Fink, *Military Records*, 333 ff no. 80.

201. R. E. M. Wheeler, *Segontium and the Roman Occupation of Wales*, (1924), 33 ff.

202. For the *territorium* and *prata legionis* see A. Mócsy, 'Das territorium legionis und die Canabae in Pannonien', *Acta Arch.Acad.Scientiarum Hungaricae*, 3 (1953), 179 ff; 'Das Problem der militärischen Territorien im Donauraum', *Acta Antiqua*, 20 (1972), 133 ff. C. M. Wells in 'Cavalry stables', 664, also draws attention to the extent to which horses may have been put out to graze. H. von Petrikovits, *Das römische Rheinland: Archäologische Forschungen seit 1945*, (Cologne 1960), 63 ff.

203. A good straw bed is calculated to need 3.6 kg per horse per day, or 25.4 kg per week, J. Wortley Axe, *The Horse VIII*, 355.

204. J. Wortley Axe. *op. cit.*, 107.
205. Vegetius, *epitoma rei militaris*, II, 14.
206. Hyginus, *de mun.cast.*, 4.
207. R. W. Davies, 'Roman medical service', 87.
208. R. W. Davies, *op. cit.*, 87.
209. Vegetius, *epitoma rei militaris*, II, 11; Tarruntenus Paternus, *Digest*, 50, 6, 7. For personnel in the legionary *fabrica* see E. Sander, 'Der praefectus fabrum und die Legionsfabriken', *Bonn.J.*, 162 (1962), 139 ff; B. Dobson, 'The Praefectus Fabrum in the Early Principate', in M. G. Jarrett and B. Dobson (eds), *Britain and Rome*, (Kendal 1966), 61 ff.
210. Vegetius, *epitoma rei militaris*, II, 11.
211. Hyginus, *de mun.cast.*, 4.
212. For legionary *fabricae* see H. von Petrikovits, 'Römisches Militärhandwerk', *Archäologische Forschungen der letzten Jahre: Anz. Österr.Akad.Wiss.*, 3 (1974), 1 ff; 'Die Spezialgebäude römischer Legionslager', *Legio VII Gemina*, (Léon 1970), 229 ff; 'Militärische Fabricae der Römer', *Actes du IXe Congrès international d'études sur les frontières romaines*, ed. D. M. Pippidi, (Bucharest 1974), 399 ff; *Die Innenbauten*, 1975, 89 ff.
213. I. A. Richmond, *JRS* 51 (1961), 160.
214. H. Schönberger, *Kastell Oberstimm, Limesforschungen* 18, (Berlin 1978), 30 ff.
215. H. Schönberger, *op. cit.*, 38 ff and fig. 19 for reconstruction drawing of the smoking room.
216. H. Schönberger, *op. cit.*, 138.
217. E. Fabricius (ed.), *ORL* 31.
218. For the identification of these courtyard buildings with a central water tank as *fabricae* rather than *praetoria* see H. Schönberger, 'Valkenburg Z.H.: Praetorium oder Fabrica', *Germania*, 57 (1979), 135 ff. The provision of a large water tank in the centre of a *praetorium* courtyard is most unusual.
219. A. Robertson, M. Scott and L. Keppie, *Bar Hill*, 1975, 86.
220. A. Robertson, M. Scott and L. Keppie, *Bar Hill.*, 59 ff. For leatherwork from Upper German forts see A. L. Busch, 'Die römerzeitlichen Schuh-und Lederfunde der Kastelle Saalburg, Zugmantel und Kleiner Feldburg', *Saal.J.*, 22 (1965), 158 ff.
221. Amongst the list of legionary *immunes* of Tarruntenus Paternus, *Digest*, 50, 6, 7.
222. R. E. Birley, 'A Roman frontier post in Roman Britain', *Scientific American*, 236, no. 2 (Feb. 1977), 44 ff; *Vindolanda Frontier Post*, 123 ff.
223. Vegetius, *epitoma rei militaris*, IV, 8.
224. For the storage of provisions and cooking utensils belonging to individual centuries and *contubernia* see p. 199 ff.
225. W. Glasbergen and W. Groenmann-van Waateringe, *Pre-Flavian Garrisons*, 12 ff.
226. I. A. Richmond, *Hod Hill II*, 89 and note 3; A. H. A. Hogg, 'Pen Llystyn: A Roman fort and other remains; *Arch.J.*, 125 (1968), 142 ff.
227. H. von Petrikovits, *Die Innenbauten*, 96 ff.
228. Arrian, *Tactica*, 34.1; Xenophon, *De Re Equestri*, III, 5.
229. For a full discussion of the possible functions of this arena see B. Hobley, 'Excavations at the Lunt Roman Military Site, Baginton, Warwickshire 1968–71: 2nd interim report', *Trans.Birmingham and Warwickshire Arch.Soc.*, 85 (1971–3), 30 ff; *Curr.Arch.* III, 5 (Sept. 1971), 127 ff.
230. J. P. Gillam, 'The Roman forts at Corbridge', 58 ff.

6 Food and the water supply

1. Polybius, *Historiae*, VI, 39, 12. Ostraca from Pselcis include receipts for food and wine of a *cohors equitata*, which range in date from November (?) 179 to September 205, and which refer to the grain ration of a soldier per month as one *artaba* (approx. 24 kg), R. Fink, *Roman Military Records on Papyrus*, (Cleveland 1971), 78, 79 and 81. For estimates of grain rations see A. P. Gentry, *Roman Military Stone-Built Granaries in Britain*, British Archaeological Reports No. 32, (Oxford 1976), 23 ff.
2. Charred wheat from Theilenhofen, Pfünz and Ribchester, and both carbonised wheat and barley were found at Brough-by-Bainbridge and Niederbieber.
3. Suet, *Aug.*, 24; Polybius, *Historiae*, VI, 38, 3.
4. A. K. Bowman, 'Roman military records from Vindolanda', *Britannia*, 5 (1974), 367.
5. Cato, *Res Rustica*, LXX.
6. *RIB* 1049.
7. R. W. Davies, 'The Roman military diet', *Britannia*, 2 (1971), 122 ff.
8. Vegetius, *epitoma rei militaris*, III, 3; see also document from Pselcis, R. Fink, *Military Records*, (1971), No. 78, 310 ff.
9. R. W. Davies, 'Military diet', 122 ff.
10. A. K. Bowman, 'Military records from Vindolanda', 368; A. K. Bowman, J. D. Thomas and R. P. Wright, 'The Vindolanda writing tablets', *Britannia*, 5 (1974), 478. For the letters from the Wâdi Faŵakhir see O. Guéraud, 'Ostraca grecs et latins de l'Wâdi Faŵakhir', *Bulletin de l'Institut français d'archéologie orientale*, 41, 141 ff.
11. Vegetius, *epitoma rei militaris*, IV, 7.
12. R. W. Davies, 'Military diet', 126 ff and Tables I–III.
13. P. J. A. van Mensch and G. F. Ijzereef, 'Smoke-dried meat in prehistoric and Roman Netherlands', in B. L. van Beek, R. W. Brandt and W. Groenman-van Waateringe (eds) *Ex Horreo*, Cingula IV, (Amsterdam 1977), 144 ff.
14. A. K. Bowman, 'Military records from Vindolanda', *Britannia*, 5 (1974), 366 ff.
15. Newstead amphora: J. Curle, *A Roman Frontier Post and its People: the fort of Newstead in the parish of Melrose*, (Glasgow 1911), 268; Chester amphora: *Britannia*, 2 (1971), 294, no. 26; Mumrills: *JRS* 54 (1964), 184, no. 40; Wallsend flagon: *Britannia*, 7 (1976), 390, no. 56.
16. Vindonissa: M. H. Callender, *Roman Amphorae*, (Oxford 1965), 37 ff, who also lists evidence for a wide variety of commodities contained in *amphorae*, including wines, oil, olives, fish sauces and salted fish, fruits and dried fruits, nuts, pepper, beans, lentils, honey, grain and flour, unguents, hair removers, milk, water, vinegar, urine, medicines and potters' clay. Brough on Noe: *JRS*, 53 (1963), 166, no. 50; suggested reading by R. W. Davies, 'Roman military diet', 131. Chesterholm: *Britannia*, 5 (1974), 467, no. 44 and note 41.
17. R. W. Davies, 'Military diet', 1971, 132 ff; for fruit found at the Saalburg see J. Baas, 'Die Obstarten aus der Zeit des römerkastells Saalburg v.d.H.', *Saal.J.*, 10 (1951), 14 ff.
18. G. R. Watson points out that the lists are not intended to be definitive, and so there may be important omissions, *The Roman Soldier*, (London 1969), 76. Polybius and Hyginus, in their treatises on Roman camps, do not allocate any space for cooking or eating, but this is hardly surprising in the temporary camps, in which every soldier was issued with iron rations.
19. Herodian, IV, 7, 5.
20. *JRS*, 58 (1968), 213, no. 69.

21. *Britannia*, 9 (1978), 480, no. 61.
22. For the barracks at Valkenburg see above, p. 174 and W. Glasbergen and W. Groenman-van Waateringe, *The Pre-Flavian Garrisons of Valkenburg Z.H.*, (Amsterdam 1974), 11 ff. At Oberstimm, see H. Schönberger, *Kastell Oberstimm, Limesforschungen* 18, (Berlin 1978), 108 and fig. 53.
23. Greatchesters: *AA* 2, 7 (1886), 96 ff; Wiesbaden, E. Ritterling, *Nass.Mitt.* Part 2 (1901–2), 56; Straubing: illustrated in *Historischer Verein für Straubing und Umgebung 79 Jahrgang*, (Straubing 1977), 90, no. 37 and fig. 10, 91; Mainz: K. Körber, *Römische Inschriften im Mainzer Museum*, (Mainz 1897), no. 84. For the interpretation of the rearward C as a symbol for the *centuria* see H. Jacobi, 'Römische Getreidemühlen', *Saal.J.*, 3 (1912), 463, no. 13.
24. H. Jacobi, *op. cit.*, 91 ff.
25. Vitruvius, *de architectura*, x, 5. For the use of water wheels for grain milling in the third century at Chesters and Haltwhistle Burnhead see F. G. Simpson, *Watermills and Military Works on Hadrian's Wall: Excavations in Northumberland 1907–1913*, ed. G. Simpson, (Kendal 1976), 26 ff.
26. H. Jacobi, 'Römische Getreidemühlen', 90.
27. L. A. Moritz, *Grain Mills and Flour in Classical Antiquity*, (Oxford 1958), 126.
28. E. Birley, I. A. Richmond and J. A. Stanfield, 'Excavations at Chesterholm-Vindolanda: third report', *AA* 4, 13 (1936), 240 ff and Pl. XX.
29. L. Jacobi, *ORL* 11, 25.
30. *CIL* XIII, 6935.
31. I. A. Richmond and J. McIntyre, 'The Agricolan fort at Fendoch', *PSAS*, 73 (1938–9), 138.
32. For field ovens see A. Fox and W. L. Ravenhill, 'Early Roman outposts on the north Devon coast, Old Burrow and Martinhoe', *Proc.Devon Arch.Expl.Soc.*, 24 (1966), 20; A. Fox, 'Martinhoe and Old Burrow', *Studien zu den Militärgrenzen Roms. Vorträge des 6 Internationalen Limeskongresses in Süddeutschland*, Beiheft der *Bonn. J.*, (Cologne 1967), 18 ff; F. G. Simpson and J. P. Gibson, 'The milecastle on the Wall of Hadrian at the Poltross Burn', *CW* 2, 11 (1911), 429, pl. ii and 432, figs 13–18.
33. A. S. Robertson, *Birrens (Blatobulgium)*, (Edinburgh 1975), 19 and fig. 6.
34. A. H. A. Hogg, 'Pen Llystyn: A Roman fort and other remains', *Arch.J.*, 125 (1968), 123 ff.
35. P. K. Baillie-Reynolds, *Kanovium*, (Cardiff 1938), 36 ff. Similar structures have also been noted at Hod Hill and Slack.
36. Josephus, *Bell.Jud.*, III, 86 and 89.
37. Usk: *Britannia*, 7 (1976), 391 ff, no. 66; Valkenburg: *JVT*, 1940–44, Appendix III, 201 ff, no. 6; Utrecht *Germania Romana*, V, 2 (1930), Pl. 39, 4.
38. Vegetius, *epitoma rei militaris*, III, 2.
39. H. von Petrikovits, *Die Innenbauten römischer Legionslager während der Prinzipatszeit*, Abhandlungen der Rheinisch-Westfälischen Akademie der Wissenschaften, Band 56, (Opladen 1975), 105.
40. Vegetius, *epitoma rei militaris*, IV, 10; Vitruvius, *de architectura*, VIII, 6, 12.
41. H. Jacobi, 'Die Be-und Entwässerung unsere Limeskastelle', *Saal.J.*, 8 (1934), 32 ff.
42. Martial, ix, 19; H. Jacobi, *op. cit.*, 40 ff.
43. Vegetius, *epitoma rei militaris*, IV, 21.
44. H. Jacobi, *op. cit.*, 43 and fig. 13. Silchester pump: *Arch.*, 55 (1896), 232.
45. Saalburg: H. Jacobi, *op. cit.*, 32 ff; Krefeld-Gellep: W. Piepers and D. Haupt, 'Gelduba', *Beiträge zur Archäologie des Römischen Rheinlands*, 3 (1968), 213 ff.
46. Vitruvius, *de architectura*, X, 4 ff; H. Schönberger, *Kastell Oberstimm*, 130 ff,

for reconstruction of the waterwheel see fig. 63.

47. Caernarfon: *RIB* 430; Chester-le-Street: *RIB* 1049; South Shields: *RIB* 1060; Chesters: *RIB* 1463.
48. *CIL* XIII, 11757–9. For discussion of these altars see A. Wolf, *Röm.-Germ.Korrespondenzbl.* 5 (1912), 2 ff.
49. J. Collingwood Bruce, *Handbook to the Roman Wall*, 9th edn by R. G. Collingwood, (Newcastle 1933), 154 ff.
50. B. J. Philp, *Curr.Arch.*, 38 (May 1973), 86.
51. Vitruvius, *de architectura*, VIII, 7, 6, 1; Pliny, *Nat.Hist.*, V, 31, 34 and XVI, 42, 81.
52. H. Jacobi, 'Die Be-und Entwässerung', 56.
53. Pliny, *Nat.Hist.*, XXXI, 31.
54. Vitruvius, *de architectura*, VIII, 6.
55. F. G. Simpson and I. A. Richmond, 'The Roman fort on Hadrian's Wall at Benwell', *AA* 4, 19 (1941), 14 ff. and fig. 2.
56. Vitruvius, *de architectura*, VIII, 2, recommends the collection of rainwater from roofs, and praises its purity. Varro, I, 11, 2, also describes the practice of collecting rainwater to supplement the water supply, and Vegetius states that in the city 'cisterns are to be made to receive the rainwater from the roofs, in all the public and many of the private buildings', *epitoma rei militaris*, IV, 10.
57. D. J. Smith, 'A note on the water supply' in *Watermills*, (1976), 144.
58. Quoted by R. C. Bosanquet, 'Excavations on the line of the Roman Wall in Northumberland: the Roman camp at Housesteads', *AA* 2, 25 (1904), 249. Storage tanks are also known from Künzing, Hesselbach, the Saalburg, Pen Llystyn, Zugmantel and Gelligaer.
59. I. A. Richmond, *Hod Hill II*, (1968), 88; Trajan's Column Scenes, XIV, CXXIV.
60. *P.Gen.lat.1 verso v*, see G. R. Watson, *The Roman Soldier*, Appendix B, 222.
61. R. C. Bosanquet, 'Housesteads', 249 ff. and Pl. XVIII; F. G. Simpson, *Watermills*, 133 ff; D. J. Smith, *op. cit.*, 143 ff.
62. For the use of sponges see Seneca, *Ep.ad Lucilium*, LXX, 20 and Martial, *Epig.* XII, 48, 7.
63. H. Schönberger, *Kastell Künzing*, 88; W. H. Manning, *Curr.Arch.*, 62 (June 1978), 74.
64. For latrine pits and trenches see I. A. Richmond, 'The four camps at Cawthorn in the north riding of Yorkshire', *Arch.J.*, 89 (1933), 68 ff.
65. *P.Gen.lat.1 verso v*=CLA 7, v, see G. R. Watson, *The Roman Soldier*, Appendix B, 225.

7 External structures

1. For training grounds see R. W. Davies, 'The training grounds of the Roman Cavalry', *Arch.J.* 125 (1968), 73 ff; 'Roman military training grounds' in E. Birley, B. Dobson and M. G. Jarrett (eds), *Roman Frontier Studies 1969*, (Cardiff 1974), 20 ff.
2. Vegetius, *epitoma rei militaris*, III, 2.
3. Vegetius, *op. cit.*, II, 23.
4. Vegetius, *op. cit.*, II, 23. For drill halls see p. 125.
5. Vegetius, *op. cit.*, I, 11.
6. Arrian, *Tactica*, 34, 1.
7. Vegetius, *op. cit.*, I, 27; Onasander, *Strat.*, 10, 4 and 6.

8. For practice camps see R. W. Davies, 'Roman Wales and Roman military practice camps', *Arch.Camb.*, 117 (1968), 103 ff; 'Roman military training grounds', 21 ff. For camps on Llandrindod and Haltwhistle Commons, see p. 44 and note 33. For practice forts at Cawthorn, I. A. Richmond, 'The four camps at Cawthorn in the north riding of Yorkshire', *Arch.J.*, 89 (1933), 17 ff.

9. Tertullian, *ad Mart.*, 3. The *testudo* was a defensive device in which a number of soldiers locked their shields together over their heads to provide an impenetrable defence, likened to the shell of a tortoise.

10. At Tomen-y-Mur, Slack, Ambleside, Chester-le-Street, Gelligaer, Hardknott, Maryport and South Shields.

11. For such a calendar of religious observance, the *Feriale Duranum*, see p. 111.

12. *RIB* 815–17, 819, 822, 824–8, 830–1, 838–43. At Maryport the original site of the parade ground, where these altars were found, was sited on the north side of the fort. This was subsequently replaced by a new one on the south, where the *tribunal* is still visible, whilst the former site was overlain by civilian settlement. See M. G. Jarrett, *Maryport, Cumbria: A Roman Fort and its Garrison*, *CW* Extra Series, 22, (Kendal 1976), 8 ff.

13. L. P. Wenham, 'Notes on the garrisoning of Maryport', *CW* 2, 39 (1939), 19 ff. It may be argued that if this was the standard practice every year in every fort, then many more altars of this type should have been discovered; see M. G. Jarrett, 'Roman officers at Maryport', *CW* 2, 65 (1965), 115 ff; G. Webster, *The Roman Imperial Army*, (1969), 269 ff and note 2.

14. Birdoswald: *RIB* 1874–1883, 1885–1896; Auchendavy: *RIB* 2176, 2177; Newstead: *RIB* 2121; Cramond, *RIB* 2135; Castlehill: *RIB* 2195; Benningen: *CIL* XIII, 6449. A similar altar has also been found at Gloster Hill, Northumberland, *RIB* 1206, which is believed to have been a training ground for auxiliary units in the frontier zone, R. W. Davies, 'Training grounds', 93; 'Roman military training grounds', 22. For the special significance of *Campestres* to equestrian units see A. von Domaszewski, 'Die Religion', (1895), 50 ff.

15. *RIB* 1334.

16. Arrian, *Tactica*, 34.

17. For the Straubing parade armour see J. Keim and H. Klumbach, *Der Römische Schatzfund von Straubing*, (Munich 1951); J. Prammer, *Gäubodenmuseum Straubing: Römische Abteilung*, Straubing, n.d. 25 ff. For the Eining parade armour, H-J. Kellner, *Der Römische Verwahrfund von Eining*, Münchner Beiträge zur Vor-und Frühgeschichte, Band 29, (Munich 1978). For a corpus of helmets and parade armour see J. Garbsch, *Römische Paraderüstungen*, Münchner Beiträge zur Vor-und Frühgeschichte, Band 30, (Munich 1978).

18. For the various stages of bathing see *RE*, ii, 2756 ff.

8 The development of the fort plan

1. R. Meiggs, *Roman Ostia*, revised edn, (Oxford 1973). For the colony at Cosa, F. Castagnoli, 'La centuriazione di Cosa', *Mem.Amer.Acad.*, 24 (1956–), 147 ff, and Alba Fucens, J. Mertens, *Alba Fucens I*, (Brussels, 1969). For a general work on Roman colonies see E. T. Salmon, *Roman Colonisation under the Republic*, (London, 1969), and Roman town planning: F. Castagnoli, *Ippodamo di Mileto e l'urbanistica a pianta ortogonale*, (Rome, 1956), and *Orthogonal Town Planning in Antiquity*, (London, 1971); J. B. Ward-Perkins, 'The early development of Roman town-planning', *Acta Congressus*

Madvigiani, IV (1958), 110 ff; and *Cities of Ancient Greece and Italy*, (London, 1974). For land division see O. A. Dilke, *The Roman Land Surveyors*, (Newton Abbot, 1971), 178 ff.

2. Polybius, *Historiae*, VI, 27 ff; also see p. 27.

3. Appian, in his *Iberica*, documents the campaigns of 195, 153–2, 141, 139–7 and 133 BC.

4. E. A. Schulten, *Numantia: Die Ergebnisse der Ausgrabungen, 1905–12*, Munich, published in four volumes, 1914–1931; the two dealing with the Republican camps are *III, Die Lager des Scipio*, (Munich, 1927) and *IV, Die Lager bei Renieblas*, (Munich, 1929). For reviews of these works see: I. A. Richmond, *Antiquity*, 2 (1928), 489 ff, and *Antiquity*, 3 (1929), 368 ff, and C. F. C. Hawkes, *JRS*, 19 (1929), 99 ff. For a general introduction to the sites, in English, G. L. Cheeseman, 'Numantia', *JRS*, 1 (1911), 180 ff.

5. Two earlier camps on this site have been attributed to Claudius Marcellus in 151 BC and Q. Pompeius in 140 BC. Their actual sizes are uncertain, as the defences have not survived, but a polygonal outline dictated by the contours of the hilltop has been proposed by the excavator. Only fragmentary traces of the internal buildings survived, with each camp laid out upon a different alignment. More is known about the earlier camp, whose administrative buildings lay immediately inside the presumed northern defensive line. Part of the headquarters is known, with a narrow courtyard surrounded on at least three sides by small rooms.

6. For recent discoveries in Picardy, for example, see R. Agache and B. Breart, *Atlas d'Archéologie aerienne de Picardie: (Le bassin de la Somme protohistorique et romaine)*, Société des Antiquaires de Picardie, (Amiens, 1975) and review by J. K. St Joseph, *Britannia*, 8 (1977), 472 ff. A number of early military enclosures, ranging in size from 15 up to 120 hectares have been located in this area, often in the vicinity of native hillforts.

7. Caesar, *de Bello Gallico*, VII, 5 (Alesia), VII, 3 (Gergovia).

8. Napoléon III, *L'Atlas de l'Histoire de Jules César*, (Paris 1865–6); J. Harmand, *Une Campagne Césarienne—Alesia*, (Paris, 1967); R. Potier, *Le Génie Militaire de Vercingetorix et le Mythe Alise-Alesia*, (Clermont-Ferrand, 1974).

9. M. J. Jones, *Roman Fort Defences to AD 117*, British Archaeological Reports No. 21, (Oxford, 1975), fig. 1.

10. For this and other sites revealed from the air see O. Brogan, 'The coming of Rome and the establishment of Roman Gaul' in S. Piggott, G. Daniel and C. McBurney (eds), *France before the Romans*, (London 1974), 192 ff. For other Caesarian camps such as Nointel, G. Mathérat, *Gallia*, 1 (1943), 81 ff.

11. This is the case for example at Vetera, Neuss and Mainz. The earliest remains at Vetera consist of two isolated stretches of ditch and the earth-and-timber rampart of a camp whose size and internal layout are completely unknown, and whose remains were overlain partially by at least five other camps, all of pre-Claudian date. Similarly at Neuss there were fragmentary traces of seven superimposed forts or legionary bases of the Augustan–Tiberian period. The earliest, associated with pottery of the third century BC was irregular in shape and defended by two ditches. Only three of its sides were found, enclosing an area of only 6.5 hectares, which suggests that it was designed probably for either an auxiliary unit or, more probably, a legionary detachment. The traces of later camps here suggest that they were probably all polygonal and varied in size from approximately 22 to more than 50 hectares; with the largest of the camps housing up to four legions. Evidence of repairs to the internal timber buildings, together with the vast quantity of pottery found here indicates that

these bases were intended for permanent occupation. Excavations on the south-east side of the legionary fortress at Mainz have also located a succession of defences on the same line, dating from the Augustan period up to the third or fourth centuries AD.

12. The small bronze plate was punched with the inscription L XIX CIII, G. Fingerlin, 'Dangstetten, ein augusteisches Legionslager am Hochrhein', *Bericht der Römisch-Germanischen Kommission*, 51–2 (1970–1), 210 ff and Pl. 13, 1. For cavalry fittings and archery equipment, *op. cit.*, 211 ff and fig. 15.

13. The historian L. Annaeus Florus tells us (ii, 30. 26) that Drusus built fifty *castella* along the Rhine. However, only a relatively small number of sites of this date have been found here, and none is known in detail despite a considerable amount of research, and so it seems most probable that he was, in fact, referring to a more extensive area than just the river bank, probably including the new territory won between the Rhine and the Elbe. For a discussion of the archaeological evidence see C. M. Wells, *German Policy of Augustus*, (1972), 97 ff and note 1; and 157, and note 3.

14. The *fossa Drusiana* is mentioned by both Tacitus, *Ann.*, ii, 8, 1 and Suetonius, *Claud.*, 1. For a further consideration of the role of the fort at Vechten in conjunction with the *fossa Drusiana* see C. M. Wells, *op. cit.*, 101 ff.

15. The results of the excavations here, which took place before the First World War, were published in several volumes of *Mitt.Altert.Komm.f.Westfalen*, between 1899 and 1922. The most modern survey is by S. von Schnurbein, *Die römischen Militäranlagen bei Haltern*, Bodenaltertümer Westfalens 14, (Münster, 1974).

16. H. Schönberger, 'The Roman frontier in Germany: an archaeological survey', *JRS*, 59 (1969), 149. For the dating evidence from coins and *terra sigillata* see C. M. Wells, *German Policy of Augustus*, 229 ff.

17. Tacitus records Augustus' advice to his successor in his will not to extend the empire beyond its present frontiers, *Ann.*, i, 11, 7.

18. The campaigns of Germanicus are well documented by Tacitus, *Ann.*, i and ii. His two major campaigns in AD 15 and 16 were concentrated on the river Ems and resulted in his crossing the Weser, but he succeeded neither in reaching the Elbe or in winning a decisive victory before his recall to Rome.

19. Traces of fortifications or small finds, mostly of Tiberian date, have been found at Bregenz, Kempten, Lorenzberg bei Epfach, the Auerberg and Gauting, H. Schönberger, 'Roman frontier in Germany', 151.

20. One fragment inscribed 'Tigernilo mil(iti) c(o)hor(tis) III Gallor(um) e(quitata)', W. Glasbergen, *De Romeinse castella te Valkenburg Z.H.*, *De opgravingen in de dorpsheuvel in 1962*, Cingula 1, (Groningen 1967), 1972, 70 ff and fig. 31 a–b, and the other inscribed 'c(ohors) III Gallorum', W. Glasbergen, *op. cit.*, 74. Other graffiti, together with infantry belt fittings and bronze horse harness indicate a *cohors equitata* as the garrison of the first fort, W. Glasbergen and W. Groenman-van Waateringe, *The Pre-Flavian Garrisons of Valkenburg Z.H.*, (Amsterdam 1974), Appendix 5, 37 ff.

21. H. Schönberger, 'Roman frontier in Germany', 154.

22. At Hüfingen, probably Ennentach, Emerkingen, Risstissen, Unterkirchberg, Aislingen, Burghöfe, Neuburg, and probably Weltenburg-Frauenberg, H. Schönberger, 'Roman frontier in Germany', 154.

23. G. Ulbert, *Die Römischen Donau-Kastelle Aislingen und Burghöfe*, *Limesforschungen*, 1, (Berlin 1959), 15 ff.

24. Suetonius, *Vesp.*, 4; Tacitus, *Hist.*, ii, 44, records that Vespasian was in command of *legio II Augusta*.

25. The collection, made by a local ironmonger and deposited in the British Museum was published by J. Brailsford, *Hod Hill 1: Antiquities from Hod Hill in the Durden Collection*, British Museum, (London, 1962).
26. This is the interpretation made by their excavator, I. A. Richmond, *Hod Hill: Excavations carried out between 1951 and 1958, II*, British Museum, (London, 1968), 79 ff, although their identification is far from conclusive.
27. 'Vexillation fortresses' are known at Rhyn, Leighton and Clyro in the Welsh Marches, and in the Midlands at Malton, Rossington Bridge, Kinvaston and Newton-on-Trent, with Great Chesterford in East Anglia and Lake in Wiltshire.
28. The reduction in the size of the fortress may be connected with the turbulent period of the Boudiccan revolt, and it is possible that Longthorpe may have been used as a base by Petilius Cerialis, who was heavily defeated by the rebels and may consequently have re-fortified the site in haste in response to the emergency; S. S. Frere and J. K. St Joseph, 'The Roman fortress at Longthorpe', *Britannia*, 5 (1974), 38 ff.
29. For a summary of all the sites both confirmed and presumed see G. Webster, *The Roman Invasion of Britain* (London 1980), 159 ff and Map II, 112.
30. The discovery of only one of the four legionary fortresses of the Claudian period is known, at Colchester (*Camulodunum*) where *legio XX* occupied the recently discovered 19 hectare base. *Legio II Augusta* may well have been based at Chichester initially, close to the supply base and harbour at Fishbourne, before moving to Exeter in the 50s. The discovery of military finds from Leicester also suggests that somewhere under the modern town may once have lain the fortress of *legio XIV Gemina* before its transfer to Wroxeter. The ninth legion occupied a fortress at Lincoln in the late 50s and 60s and was transferred to York in c. AD 72. For Claudian legionary bases see G. Webster, *op. cit.*, 123 ff.
31. The majority of these early sites have been revealed by air photography, and only at Great Casterton in Leicestershire have more extensive excavations been carried out. Here an auxiliary fort of the conquest period, reduced in size in c. AD 60–70, was situated to the north-west of the later Roman town, close to the crossing of the river Gwash by Ermine Street. The rectangular playing-card shaped fort 2.4 hectares in area was enclosed by a rampart with turf cheeks at the front and rear, with a limestone rubble core; there were two ditches. The interior was divided into two by the *via principalis* running down the longitudinal axis. The rear gate was examined and found to have a single portal. Fragmentary traces of timber internal buildings were located flanking the *via praetoria*. Subsequently c. AD 60–70 the fort was reduced in size to 2.1 hectares by the retraction of the south-east defences, and the new timber *porta praetoria* was provided with a double portal and recessed gateway between two towers. An annexe lay between the fort and the river.

Aerial photographs have revealed two superimposed rectangular forts at Baylham House, Suffolk, one of approximately 4.5 hectares enclosed by three ditches, and the other only half this size. At Ixworth, also in Suffolk, triple ditches enclosed a rectangular fort of 2.8 hectares. In close proximity to the Iron Age hillforts of Badbury and Spettisbury in Dorset was built a fort, at Shapwick, which had a slightly irregular plan of some 4 hectares defended by 2 or 3 ditches. At Lake Farm, Dorset, two marching camps or legionary vexillation fortresses, one of 11 hectares, were founded probably early in the conquest, and preceded a small auxiliary fort of 1.4 hectares. Another fort located from the air, at Charterhouse in Somerset, was of regular playing-card shape, 1.2 hectares in area. At Water Newton in Cambridgeshire, in addition to the 2.2 hectare defensive circuit, a long narrow building, possibly a barrack, was visible in the *retentura*.

32. Tacitus, *Ann.*, xii, 31 ff and xiv, 29 ff; *Agricola*, 14 ff. For a summary of the evidence for early campaigns in Wales see M. G. Jarrett, 'Early Roman campaigns in Wales', *Arch.J.*, 121 (1964), 23 ff; V. E. Nash-Williams, *The Roman Frontier in Wales*, (2nd edn by M. G. Jarrett), (Cardiff 1969), 4 ff. For the campaigns of Ostorius Scapula, G. Webster, 'The Roman military advance under Ostorius Scapula', *Arch. J.*, 115 (1958), 49 ff.

33. The southern tribe of the Silures was subdued in AD 74 by Julius Frontinus, and the Ordovices of mid and north Wales by Julius Agricola in AD 78, Tacitus, *Agricola*, 17 ff.

34. The discovery of a small lump of slag rich in silver, together with crucible fragments and a small weight in one of the barracks suggests that the fort may have had a connection with prospecting, extraction and control of minerals; deposits of silver lead lay less than 3 km from the fort; A. Fox and W. Ravenhill, 'The Roman fort at Nanstallon, Cornwall', *Britannia*, 3 (1972), 90 ff.

35. Tacitus, *Hist.*, iv and v. For modern discussions of the episode see W. Sprey, *Tacitus over de opstand der Bataven*, (Groningen 1953); A. W. Byvanck, 'De opstand der Bataven', *Antiquity and Survival*, 3 (1960), 15 ff; P. A. Brunt, 'Tacitus on the Batavian revolt', *Latomus*, 19 (1960), 494 ff; P. G. van Soesbergen, 'The phases of the Batavian revolt', *Helinium*, 11 (1971), 238 ff.

36. Tacitus, *Ann.*, xii, 40.

37. At Vetera the new fortress was built on a lower terrace of the Rhine. The site was flooded and undermined by the river in the Middle Ages and today lies more than 7 metres beneath a deposit of gravel. The remains of the fortress, which were discovered during gravel extraction in 1954, are known to extend across an area of at least 450 × 230 m; the pottery spans the period from the end of the first century until the second half of the third century AD; H. von Petrikovits, 'Legionsfestung Vetera II', *Bonn.J.*, 159 (1959), 89 ff; J. C. Mann, 'Colonia Ulpia Traiana and the occupation of Vetera II', *Bonn.J.*, 162 (1962), 162 ff; J. E. Bogaers and C. B. Rüger, *Der Niedergermanische Limes*, (Cologne 1974), 107 ff.

The new timber fortress at Nijmegen was established on the Hunerberg in c. AD 70. There were several periods of occupation, continuing until c. AD 175, with the Flavian timber buildings being replaced gradually in stone towards the end of the first century; only fragments of the timber buildings have been located; M. Daniëls, *Noviomagus.Romeins Nijmegen*, (Nijmegen 1955); H. Brunsting, *Numaga*, 7 (1960), 6 ff, and 8 (1961), 49 ff; J. K. Haalebos, 'Niews uit Nijmeegse castra', *Numaga*, 19 (1972), 41 ff; for a full bibliography see J. E. Bogaers and C. B. Rüger, *Niedergermanische Limes*, (1974), 79.

38. Milestone from Offenburg, *CIL* XIII, 9082.

39. Four forts are known here altogether. On the left bank of the river Neckar, in Nikolausfeld, two forts have been known since 1913. Fort I: 2 sides of a probable marching camp of early Flavian date, covering at least 8 hectares. Fort II: a 5.5 hectare fort, originally earth-and-timber, rebuilt at the beginning of the second century in stone.

On the opposite side of the river, at Hochmauern, lay an earth-and-timber fort (Fort III), built probably c. AD 72, and to the south of this site excavations in 1971 located part of an earlier layout (Fort IV). Upon this site a large and important civilian settlement subsequently grew up, known as *Arae Flaviae*.

40. There may have been a mixed legionary and auxiliary garrison, as seen perhaps in the Antonine period at Newstead, p. 280. For the probable garrison see D. Planck, *Arae Flaviae 1*, Stuttgart, (1975), 91 ff.
41. Gunzberg: F. Vollmer, *Inscriptiones Baiuariae Romanae*, (1915), no. 196; Kösching: F. Vollmer, *op. cit.*, no. 257; Eining: F. Vollmer, *op. cit.*, no. 331.
42. A. H. A. Hogg, 'Pen Llystyn: A Roman fort and other remains', *Arch.J.*, 125 (1968), 111.
43. Tacitus, *Agricola*, 29 ff. For the probable site of the battle see M. G. Jarrett in P. Clayton (ed.), *A Companion to Roman Britain*, (Oxford 1980), 33 and fig. 27.
44. S. S. Frere, *Britannia*, (London 1967), 109 ff.
45. Other forts in this sequence include Dalginross, Bochastle, Menteith and Drumquhassle, with a further line of forts behind at Stracathro, Cardean, Bertha, Strageath and Ardoch. New sites, such as Drumquhassle, are still being discovered from the air, so that it is probable that the picture may have been far more complicated than has generally been supposed.
46. Most were rectangular, although there are exceptions at Crawford, Loudon Hill and Fendoch, where a narrow site dictated an elongated plan. A few square forts of this period are also known: at Bochastle, Newstead, Easter Happrew and Oakwood in Scotland, Caer Gai, Caerhun and Caersŵs in Wales, and Caermote, Ebchester and Elslack in northern England.
47. This device may also have been used at Castledykes in Strathclyde and Tassiesholm, further south in Dumfries and Galloway.
48. Seen also at Cardean, Elslack, Caermote and Bochastle.
49. It is uncertain whether the Strathmore forts were intended as the final extent of the province or whether they were designed to act as a springboard for a future conquest of the whole island, which had to be abandoned when increasing pressures on the Danubian frontier demanded a reduction in the British garrison.
50. For the archaeological evidence for destruction along the frontier, and the resultant change in troop dispositions see H. Schönberger, 'Roman frontier in Germany', 159 ff.
51. For the development of the *limes* see D. Baatz, *Der römische Limes. Archäologische Ausflüge zwischen Rhein und Donau*, (Berlin 1975). Small fortlets of this date are known at the Saalburg, Altenstadt, Kapersburg and Zugmantel. For Domitian in Germany see H. Schönberger, 'Roman frontier in Germany', 158 ff.
52. H. Schönberger, *Kastell Künzing-Quintana: Die Grabungen von 1958 bis 1966*, *Limesforschungen* 13, (Berlin 1975), 110 ff.
53. At Wiesbaden, Hofheim, Frankfurt-Heddernheim, Okarben and Friedberg.
54. His victories are commemorated upon a sculptured column set up in Rome, which has provided a wealth of pictorial information about the Roman army at war in the early second century AD.
55. For Trajan's campaigns in Parthia see R. P. Longden, 'Notes on the Parthian campaigns of Trajan', *JRS*, 21 (1931), 1 ff; G. Webster, *The Roman Imperial Army*, (2nd edn), (London, 1979), 81 ff.
56. Fortlets are known at Haltwhistle Burn and possible Throp, and forts at Chesterholm and Nether Denton; possibly also at Old Church Brampton, Newbrough and Carvoran, although they are of uncertain date, D. Breeze and B. Dobson, *Hadrian's Wall*, (London 1976), 20 ff.

57. Caerleon: *RIB* 330; Chester: *RIB* 464; York: *RIB* 665.
58. The legionary bathhouses were, however, generally stone-built from the earliest periods, because of the fire risks, as seen for example in the impressive internal bathhouse at the Neronian fortress of Exeter. The stone bathhouse seen in the Trajanic fortress at Chester was probably built originally in the Flavian period.
59. An inscription from Lanchester, *RIB* 604, attests Trajanic rebuilding, and other sites where a stone wall was probably added to an existing Flavian earth/turf rampart at this date include: Loughor, Penydarren, Pumsaint, Templeborough, Melandra Castle, Northwich, Pen-y-Gaer and Ribchester. There are also examples of a new turf rampart replacing a Flavian predecessor at Beulah and Caersŵs.
60. *RIB* 397–399.
61. It is extremely difficult to be sure whether the surviving remains represent original Trajanic work rather than later rebuilding. For other forts of this period on the German frontier see H. Schönberger, 'Roman frontier in Germany', 164 ff.
62. Their excavator, Dr D. Baatz, has estimated that there was sufficient space for 30–32 men in each, possibly housing altogether four centuries of a *numerus*. The organisation of the *numerus* is largely unknown, although it is clear that they were divided into centuries, see above, p. 25; D. Baatz, *Kastell Hesselbach*, *Limesforschungen* 12, (Berlin 1973), 54 ff.
63. Britain: *Scriptores Historiae Augustae. Vita Hadriani*, II, 2; Germany: *op. cit.*, XII, 6.
64. At Birrens, Netherby and Bewcastle.
65. Wallsend, Benwell, Rudchester, Haltonchesters, Chesters, Housesteads, Birdoswald, Castlesteads, Stanwix, Burgh-by-Sands and Bowness-on-Solway were primary forts begun during the governorship of Platorius Nepos (AD 122–c. 126) and completed c. AD 128–38. Before the programme was finished Greatchesters was added behind the Wall, and subsequently Carrawburgh and Carvoran were built. (Carvoran was rebuilt in stone in AD 136–7.)
   Of the Cumbrian coast forts Maryport was already in existence, with Beckfoot and Moresby added to the sequence, the latter in AD 128–38.
   For the chronology of the building work see D. Breeze and B. Dobson, *Hadrian's Wall*, 28 ff and Tables 6 and 7.
66. It has been supposed in the past that the forts which lay astride the Wall were cavalry forts, designed with three principal gates projecting beyond the frontier to permit a speedy exit in times of trouble. The epigraphic evidence is so scanty that the original garrison of most of these forts is unknown, but it seems more likely that this was the plan designed for all the forts in the original Hadrianic fort scheme, where the topography allowed, which was subsequently modified when found in practice to be unnecessary.
67. Internal area: Wallsend, 1.7 hectares; Benwell, unknown; Rudchester, 1.5 hectares; Haltonchesters, 1.4 hectares; Chesters, 1.9 hectares; Carrawburgh, 1.3 hectares; Housesteads, 1.7 hectares; Greatchesters, 1.4 hectares over ramparts; Carvoran, 1.5 hectares over ramparts; Birdoswald, 1.9 hectares; Castlesteads, 1.5 hectares over ramparts; Stanwix, estimated 3.8 hectares over ramparts; Burgh-by-Sands, 2 hectares over ramparts; Drumburgh, 0.8 hectares; Bowness-on-Solway, 2.8 hectares over ramparts; Beckfoot, 1 hectare over ramparts; Maryport, c. 1.9 hectares; Moresby, 1.5 hectares over ramparts.
68. By R. C. Bosanquet; the final report was published in *AA* 2, 25 (1904), 193 ff.

69. Hadrianic headquarters are known at Greatchesters, Carrawburgh, Rudchester, Chesters, Benwell, Wallsend and South Shields.
70. At Watercrook, Neath, Buckton, Caersŵs and Tomen-y-Mur.
71. It is uncertain as to whether the *numeri* were created by Trajan or Hadrian, but if he did not actually create them Hadrian was certainly responsible for their reorganisation, H. Schönberger, 'Roman frontier in Germany', (1969), 166 and note 167.
72. Fortlets enlarged to take auxiliary cohorts include Butzbach, Kapersburg, Zugmantel, Altenstadt and the Saalburg.
73. *Murus Gallicus*, see p. 69.
74. It is not easy to detect the Hadrianic plan beneath later periods of occupation, especially in forts excavated in the last century or in the early years of the present century, and consequently little is known about the internal layouts of these forts.
75. A war in Britain at an unspecified date during the reign of Antoninus Pius is recorded by the Greek Pausanius, *Description of Greece*, 8, 43.
76. *RIB* 1147 and 1148. Both inscriptions probably derived originally from stone granaries. They were reused as paving slabs in later granaries; *RIB* 1147 was found at the north end of the west granary, and the other at the south end of the east granary, corresponding probably to the position of the entrances of the underlying Antonine buildings, J. P. Gillam, 'The Roman Forts at Corbridge', *AA* 5, (1976), 69.

    Lollius Urbicus is later named on inscriptions at High Rochester in the Lowlands (*RIB* 1276), and at Balmuildy on the Antonine Wall itself (*RIB* 2191–2).
77. Antonine forts with Flavian predecessors include Ardoch, Camelon and Strageath to the north of the Wall, Bar Hill and Cadder on the Antonine Wall, and Birrens, Castledykes, Crawford, Newstead and High Rochester in the Lowlands. The Antonine fort at Lyne lay close to the Flavian fort of Easter Happrew, but on the opposite bank of the river to facilitate road communications.
78. With a fort at Bishopton and fortlets at Lurg Moor and Outerwards on the west, and Carriden, Cramond and Inveresk on the east.
79. Internal areas: Old Kilpatrick, 1.7 hectares; Duntocher, 0.2 hectares; Bearsden, 1 hectare; Balmuildy, 1.5 hectares; Cadder, 1.2 hectares; Bar Hill, 1.3 hectares; Croy Hill, 0.6 hectares; Westerwood, 0.7 hectares; Castlecary, 1.3 hectares; Rough Castle, 0.5 hectares; Mumrills, 2.6 hectares; Castle Hill, estimated c. 1.4 hectares. The dimensions of the forts at Auchendavy, Kirkintilloch, Inveravon and Carriden have not been ascertained. Three further sites are presumed from their spacing in the fort sequence, at Sea Begs, Falkirk and Kinneil.
80. Some of the variations may be explained by the fact that the Antonine Wall forts were constructed in two distinct stages. Initially Balmuildy (which has yielded inscriptions of Lollius Urbicus, *RIB* 2191–2), Mumrills, Castlecary and Old Kilpatrick were erected before the Antonine rampart itself; Bar Hill may also belong to this series, as being detached from the Wall it may well have been built before it, although its exact position in the sequence remains uncertain. All were forts large enough to house a complete auxiliary unit, spaced approximately 14 km apart.

    It has been suggested that in its initial planning stages the Antonine Wall was based much more closely on its Hadrianic predecessor, comprising regularly-spaced forts with fortlets between them, a plan which was modified by the introduction of additional forts, some of which, like Duntocher, Rough Castle and Croy Hill, were too small to have housed a full auxiliary cohort, but which served to spread the number of Roman troops more evenly, if albeit thinly, along the frontier. In fact the Antonine Wall had almost the same sized garrison as the Hadrianic frontier, although it was only half as long, D. Breeze and B. Dobson, *Hadrian's Wall*, (1976), 98 ff.

It appears also that both legionaries and auxiliaries were involved in fort building, which may also account for the range of styles employed. Several forts have yielded inscriptions set up by legionary builders (Croy Hill, Bar Hill, Auchendavy, Cadder and Balmuildy), and auxiliary builders are recorded at Rough Castle, Castlecary and Bar Hill.

81. D. Breeze, *Curr.Arch.* 82 (May 1982), 344.
82. D. Breeze and B. Dobson, *Hadrian's Wall*, 82.
83. For a detailed examination of the literary sources and up-to-date archaeological evidence see D. Breeze and B. Dobson, *Hadrian's Wall*, 105 ff; D. Breeze, *The Northern Frontiers of Roman Britain*, (London, 1982), 118 ff. The samian pottery from the northern frontier has been studied in depth by B. R. Hartley, 'The Roman occupation of Scotland: the evidence of samian ware', *Britannia*, 3 (1972), 15 ff. For coins, A. S. Robertson, 'Roman coins found in Scotland, 1961–70', *PSAS*, 103 (1970–1), 133 ff. For the structural evidence from the forts and dating of the various occupations of the Hadrianic and Antonine frontiers see: J. P. Gillam and J. C. Mann, 'The northern British frontier from Antoninus Pius to Caracalla', *AA* 4, 48 (1970), 1 ff; M. G. Jarrett and J. C. Mann, 'Britain from Agricola to Gallienus', *Bonn.J.*, 170 (1970), 185 ff; J. P. Gillam, 'Calpurnius Agricola and the northern frontier', *TAASDN*, 10 Part 4 (1953), 359 ff; D. J. Breeze, 'The abandonment of the Antonine Wall: its date and implications', *Scottish Arch.Forum*, 7 (1975), 67 ff; D. J. Breeze, 'Roman Scotland during the reign of Antoninus Pius', in W. S. Hanson and L. J. F. Keppie (eds), *Roman Frontier Studies 1979. Papers Presented to the 12th International Congress of Roman Frontier Studies*, British Archaeological Reports, International Series, 71 (i), (Oxford, 1980), 45 ff.
84. With each block divided down the centre by a 'median double rib', and consisting of walls spaced 0.6–0.9 m apart, on analogy with the arrangement suggested for the barracks at Cardean, see Ch. 5, note 171.
85. James Curle detected 'black peaty matter' in the area excluded by the new wall and concluded that this part of the fort had been flooded. The Antonine *principia* faced in the opposite direction to the headquarters of the preceding fort, and he linked the construction of the stone wall with this change in direction, believing that the fort had been reduced in size and the *principia* turned around to face the barracks on the east rather than a blank wall, J. Curle, *A Roman Frontier Post and its People: the fort of Newstead in the parish of Melrose*, (Glasgow 1911), 82 ff.
86. Centurions of *legio XX* are attested on *RIB* 2120, 2122, 2123, 2124 and 2127; *ala I Vocontiorum* on *RIB* 2121.
87. I. A. Richmond, 'Excavations at the Roman Fort of Newstead, 1947', *PSAS*, 84 (1949–50), 21 ff; R. G. Collingwood, *The Archaeology of Roman Britain*, (revised by I. A. Richmond), (London 1969), 42. Other examples of cross walls within auxiliary forts are seen at Flavian Pen Llystyn and the Severan supply depot at South Shields.
88. It should perhaps be noted that in the later occupation of the fort it was necessary to rebuild one of the granaries and the western fort wall from foundation level, which suggests that they had been out of commission and

had been almost totally demolished, possibly as a result of a reduction in the size of the fort, J. Curle, *Newstead*, 83.

89. I. A. Richmond, 'Newstead', 1949–50, 24.

90. For forts probably abandoned at this date see V. E. Nash-Williams, *Roman Frontier in Wales*, 22.

91. Rebuilding commencing with the defences and buildings in the central range from c. AD 140 onwards is seen at Brecon Gaer, Caerhun, Caernarfon, Caersŵs and Castell Collen, V. E. Nash-Williams, *op. cit.*, 22.

92. D. Baatz, *BVBL*, 31 (1966), 85 ff.

93. Heilbronn-Böckingen: *CIL* XIII, 6469, 6472; Jagsthausen: *CIL* XIII, 6561.

94. New cohort forts at Miltenberg-Altstadt, Osterburken, Jagsthausen, Öhringen, Mainhardt, Murrhardt, Welzheim-West and Lorch, with *numerus* forts at Miltenberg-East, Walldürn and Welzheim-East, and a further one added to the cohort fort at Osterburken in c. AD 185–192.

95. *ala I Scubulorum* stationed at Stuttgart-Bad Cannstatt (Internal area: 3.5 hectares), was transferred probably to Welzheim-West (4 hectares), where *ala I . . .* is attested; *cohors XXIV Voluntariorum c.R.* transferred from Benningen to Murrhardt, both with an internal area of 2 hectares; the garrison at Walheim (2 hectares) is unknown, but may well have been *cohors I Asturum equitata* which is known at the corresponding fort on the Antonine *limes* at Mainhardt (2.3 hectares); *cohors I Helvetiorum* was transferred from Heilbronn-Böckingen (1.7 hectares) to Öhringen, both forts here (Rendelkastell and Burgkastell, each internally approx. 2 hectares) have yielded tiles stamped by this unit, although it is believed that the unit lay at Rendelkastell until the third century; *cohors I Germanorum c.R. eq.* moved from Wimpfen (size unknown) to Jagsthausen (c. 2.5 hectares), and *cohors III Aquitanorum eq. c.R.* from Neckarburken-West (2 hectares) to Osterburken (1.8 hectares); the garrison at Oberscheidental (1.7 hectares) may have been the *cohors I Sequanorum et Rauracorum eq.*, which is attested at Miltenberg-Altstadt (c. 2.4 hectares) on the new frontier.

96. Internal area: Miltenberg-East (0.5 hectares); Walldürn (0.8 hectares over ramparts); Osterburken (1.4 hectares); Welzheim-East (c. 1.5 hectares).

97. With new cohort forts at Schirenhof, Unterböbingen, Buch, Ruffenhofen, Dambach and possibly Theilenhofen, an *ala* fort at Aalen, and smaller forts at Halheim, Gunzenhausen, Ellingen and Böhming. These small forts may already have been founded by Hadrian, but the dating evidence is insufficient and inconclusive, H. Schönberger, 'Roman frontier in Germany', (1969), 170.

98. Gnotzheim: F. Wagner, *Bericht der Römisch-Germanischen Kommission 1956–7*, 37–38 (1958), 236 no. 81; Kösching, AD 141, *CIL* III 5906 and 11907; Pförring, AD 141, *CIL* III, 5912; an inscription from the *porta principalis sinistra* at Pfünz records *cohors I Breucorum c.R.eq.* under Antoninus Pius, probably rebuilding the fort in stone, *CIL* III, 11930.

99. The rebuilding of defences is also probable at Straubing, Regensburg-Kumpfmühl and Weissenburg, with a new fort constructed at Passau-Altstadt, H. Schönberger, 'Roman frontier in Germany', (1969), 170.

100. Ribchester, c. AD 163–166, *RIB* 589; Ilkley, AD 161–169, *RIB* 636; for rebuilding in the Pennines see J. P. Gillam and J. C. Mann, 'Northern British Frontier', (1970), 25.

101. The general Calpurnius Agricola was sent as governor to quell a war which was threatening in Britain at the beginning of Marcus' reign (*Scriptores Historiae Augustae. Marcus Aurelius*, 8) and again in the AD 170s war was imminent, *op. cit.*, 22. The despatch of 5500 Sarmatian cavalry to Britain in AD 175 may also be seen as a response to an urgent call for reinforcements,

although it may equally well be that Britain, as an island, was chosen to house these hostages in order to make their escape more difficult. See J. P. Gillam 'Calpurnius Agricola', (1953), 359 ff.

102. Cassius Dio, 71, 16.
103. *Scriptores Historiae Augustae. Marcus Antoninus*, VIII, 7 ff, and *Didius Iulianus*, I, 8. For the archaeological evidence for these incursions see H. Schönberger, 'Roman frontier in Germany', (1969), 171 ff.
104. The fort is dated by tiles found in the internal bathhouse stamped by *legio VIII*, bearing the title *pia fidelis constans Commoda*, which it gained in AD 185 and held until the death of Commodus in AD 192.
105. One of the prefects of this *numerus*, T. Flavius Salvianus, is named also on an inscription from Mainz, which records that he held this office in the *militia quarta*, the equivalent stage in an auxiliary officer's career to the command of an *ala milliaria*, *CIL* XIII, 6814.
106. Cassius Dio, 75, 5.4.
107. *RIB* 1234.
108. Herodian, III, 14; Cassius Dio, 76, 11.
109. *RIB* 1143 records the 'officer in charge of the granaries at the time of the most successful expedition to Britain', probably referring to Severus' campaigns.
110. *RIB* 2134.
111. Cassius Dio, 77, 1.1; Herodian, III, 15.
112. H. Schönberger, 'Roman frontier in Germany', (1969), 174.

9 Fort types and garrisons

1. Vegetius, *epitoma rei militaris*, III, 8.
2. For the composition and size of each of the auxiliary units see above, p. 19 ff and Table 1 on p. 22.
3. Occasionally the garrison is named upon stamped tiles, as at Künzing, or recorded on items of equipment, or even wax tablets, as at Valkenburg.
4. I. A. Richmond, in his Albert Reckitt Archaeological Lecture 'Roman Britain and Roman military antiquities', published in *Proc.British Academy*, 41 (1955), 297 ff, proposed type sites for each of the auxiliary units. Some of his original type sites have since been challenged and others, especially on Hadrian's Wall, added by D. Breeze and B. Dobson, 'Fort types on Hadrian's Wall', *AA* 4, 47 (1969), 15 ff and 'Fort types as a guide to garrisons: a reconsideration', in *Roman Frontier Studies 1969*, E. Birley, B. Dobson and M. G. Jarrett (eds), (Cardiff 1974), 13 ff.
5. See above, p. 282 and Note 95.
6. For example Chesters is associated with units of three different sizes, originally an *ala Augusta (quingenaria)*, see P. A. Austen and D. J. Breeze, 'A new inscription from Chesters on Hadrian's Wall', *AA* 5, 7 (1979), 115 ff; and later *cohors I Vangionum milliaria equitata* (*RIB* 1482), *cohors Delmatarum quingenaria equitata* (*JRS*, 46 (1956), 229 no. 14), and *ala II Asturum* (attested on *RIB* 1463 and 1465, and named in the *Notitia Dignitatum*).
7. W. Glasbergen and W. Groenman-van Waateringe, *The Pre-Flavian Garrisons of Valkenburg ZH*, (Amsterdam London 1974), 19 and fig. 8.
8. J. P. Gillam, 'The Roman forts at Corbridge', *AA* 5, 5 (1976), 47 ff.
9. M. J. Jones, *Roman Fort Defences to AD 117*, British Archaeological Reports, 21, (Oxford 1975), 64.
10. Chesters, 1.9 hectares; Weissenburg, 2.7 hectares; Dormagen, c. 3 hectares; Stuttgart-Bad Cannstatt, 3.5 hectares; Welzheim-West, 4 hectares.

11. A suggestion proposed in *Britannia*, 5 (1974), 144 ff and 8 (1977), 458.
12. Estimating 1 kg grain as each man's daily consumption, one man would, in theory, require 365 kg annually, and a garrison of 500 men 182 500 kg of grain. 785 kg of wheat occupy one cubic metre of storage space, and so the space needed to house the grain ration of 500 men for a year would be around 233 cubic metres, if the grain was stored in bulk. If stored in sacks the volume required would be increased by 15% to give the total storage area required in the region of 267 cubic metres, A. P. Gentry, *Roman Military Stone-built Granaries in Britain*, British Archaeological Reports, 32, (Oxford 1976), 25.
13. Tacitus, *Agricola*, 22, 2.
14. Haverfield and Collingwood, on the basis of this statement, attempted to estimate the capacity of 13 British granaries by assuming that the grain was stored in bins 1.83 m high, 1.8–2.4 m wide, with a 0.9 m wide corridor between them. In each case a probable garrison was postulated. Their calculations assured them that the examples studied were able to store twice the quantity of grain required in a year, F. Haverfield and R. G. Collingwood, 'The provisioning of Roman forts', *CW* 2, 20 (1920). See also W. Bulmer, 'The provisioning of Roman forts: a reappraisal of ration storage', *AA* 4, 47 (1969), and Gentry, *Roman Granaries*, 25.
15. Gentry, *Roman Granaries*, 25 ff and fig. 5.
16. The only examples of barracks designed for a milliary *ala* have been found at Heidenheim in Raetia, but here only three of the presumed twelve barracks have been investigated, and no trace of stables was found. At Künzing trial excavations have uncovered most of the fort plan which was garrisoned by *cohors III Thracum eq.*, a quingenary cohort, and at Birrens the barrack plan of *cohors I Nervana Germanorum milliaria equitata* is known. At Chesters one barrack of the quingenary *ala Augusta* has been excavated.
17. H. Schönberger, *Kastell Künzing-Quintana*, *Limesforschungen* 13, (Berlin 1975), 112.
18. See Chapter 5, Note 171 above.
19. Based on the assumptions made by I. A. Richmond, 'Roman Britain and Roman military antiquities', (1955), 30 ff. No allowance here has been made for baggage animals. Every unit whether infantry or cavalry must have had them, but whether they were housed inside the fort or not is completely unknown.
20. P. S. Austen and D. J. Breeze, 'A new inscription from Chesters on Hadrian's Wall', *AA* 5, 7 (1979), 115 ff.
21. There are difficulties in comparing barrack lengths of contemporary forts; for example, there is a discrepancy in length between barracks both supposedly designed for an *ala quingenaria* at Benwell and South Shields, which measure 45.7 and 42.7 m respectively, which probably reflects not a difference in garrison type but construction by different legions, D. J. Breeze and B. Dobson, *Roman Frontier Studies*, 17 ff.

    Differences in barrack lengths between barracks in the *praetentura* and *retentura* of the same fort have been noted at several sites, including Lyne, Valkenburg, Crawford, Fendoch, Haltonchesters, Balmuildy and Templeborough. At Pen Llystyn the barracks were of similar length, but there was quite a variation in the amount of floor space allocated per *contubernium*, between blocks with verandahs (18 square metres) and those without (26 square metres), which may reflect differences between infantry and cavalry troops.
22. Comparison should be made between contemporary forts built in the same materials, and in the same locality.

23. D. J. Breeze and B. Dobson, 'The development of the mural frontier in Britain from Hadrian to Caracalla', *PSAS*, 102 (1969–70), 116.
24. R. W. Davies, 'Cohors I Hispanorum and the garrisons of Maryport', *Britannia*, 9 (1978), 7 ff; M. G. Jarrett, *Maryport, Cumbria: A Roman Fort and its Garrison*, (Kendal 1976), 20 ff.

Select Bibliography of Forts mentioned in the text

Britain

Ambleside	*CW* 2, 14 (1914), 433 ff; 15 (1915), 32 ff; 16 (1916), 57 ff; 21 (1921), 1 ff.
Ardoch	*PSAS*, 32 (1897–8), 399 ff; 102 (1969–70), 122 ff.
Baginton	*Trans.Birm.& Warwicks Arch.Soc.*, 83 (1969), 67 ff; 85 (1971–3), 7 ff; *Britannia*, 4 (1973), 288; 5 (1974), 431; *WMANS*, (1973), 13 ff.
Balmuildy	S. N. Miller, *The Roman Fort at Balmuildy*, Glasgow, 1922.
Bar Hill	G. Macdonald and A. Park, *The Roman Forts on the Bar Hill*, Glasgow, 1906; A. S. Robertson, M. Scott and L. Keppie, *Bar Hill: A Roman Fort and its Finds*, *BAR* 16, Oxford, 1975.
Bearsden	Interim reports in *Britannia*, 5–12 (1974–81); *Curr.Arch.*, 42 (1974), 209 ff; 82 (1982), 343 ff.
Benwell	*AA* 4, 19 (1941), 1 ff; *RHW*, 163 ff.
Bewcastle	*CW* 2, 38 (1938), 195 ff; *Britannia*, 9 (1978), 421.
Birdoswald	Annual reports in *CW* 2, 28–34 (1928–34); 50 (1950), 63 ff.
Birrens	*PSAS*, 30 (1895–6), 81 ff; 72 (1937–8), 275 ff; A. S. Robertson, *Birrens (Blatobulgium)*, Edinburgh, 1975.
Brecon Gaer	R. E. M. Wheeler, *The Roman Fort Near Brecon*, London, 1926; *BBCS*, 22 (1966–8), 426 ff; *Arch.Camb.*, 121 (1971), 91 ff; *RFIW*, 48 ff.
Brough by Bainbridge	*Proc.Leeds Phil. & Lit.Soc.*, 1 (1925–8), 261 ff; 2 (1929), 77, 234 ff; 3 (1932), 16 ff; 7 (1952–5), 1 ff; 9 (1960), 107 ff. Summary reports in *JRS*, 51–59 (1961–9); *Britannia*, 1 (1970), 279.
Brough on Humber	P. Corder, *Excavations at the Roman Fort at Brough-on-Humber*, Hull, 1933–9; J. Wacher, *Excavations at Brough-on-Humber*, *1958–61*, London, 1969.
Brough on Noe	*DAJ*, 59 (1938), 53 ff; Interim reports in *DAJ*, 85–89 (1965–9); *Britannia*, 1 (1970), 283.
Buckton	*TWNFC*, 39 (1968), 222 ff; *RFIW*, 93 ff.
Cadder	J. Clarke, *The Roman Fort at Cadder*, Glasgow, 1933.
Caerhun	P. K. Baillie-Reynolds, *Kanovium*, Cardiff, 1938; *RFIW*, 56 ff.
Caerleon	For full bibliography see G. Boon, *Isca* (3rd edn), Cardiff, 1972; *RFIW*, 29 ff; for current excavations, *Britannia*, from 1 (1970) onwards.

Caernarfon	R. E. M. Wheeler, *Segontium and the Roman Occupation of Wales*, London, 1923; *RFIW*, 59 ff; G. C. Boon, *Segontium Roman Fort*, HMSO London, 1963; interim reports in *Britannia* from 1972.
Caersŵs	*Mont.Coll.*, 46 (1940), 67 ff; 59 (1965–6), 112 ff; 60 (1967–8), 64 ff; 61 (1969–70), 37 ff; *RFIW*, 66 ff.
Camelon	*PSAS*, 35 (1900), 329 ff; interim reports in *Britannia*, 4–9 (1973–8).
Carpow	Interim reports in *JRS*, 53–59 (1963–9) and *Britannia*, 1–8 (1970–7).
Carrawburgh	*AA* 4, 50 (1972), 81 ff; *RHW*, 105 ff.
Castell Collen	*Arch.Camb.*, 69 (1914), 1 ff; 113 (1964), 64 ff; *RFIW*, 74 ff.
Castlecary	*PSAS*, 37 (1903), 271 ff.
Castledykes	A. S. Robertson, *The Roman Fort at Castledykes*, Edinburgh, 1964.
Chesterholm	*AA* 4, 13 (1936), 218 ff; full bibliography in *RHW*, 184 ff; interim notes on more recent work in *JRS*, 59 (1969), 205 and *Britannia*, 1–5 (1970–4); R. E. Birley, *Vindolanda: A Roman frontier post on Hadrian's Wall*, London, 1977.
Chesters	*AA* 2, 7 (1867), 171 ff; 8 (1880), 211 ff; *RHW*, 172 ff; E. Birley, *Chesters Roman Fort*, HMSO London, 1976; *AA* 4, 39 (1961), 321 ff.
Corbridge	Most important for structural sequence and chronology: *AA* 4, 49 (1971), 1 ff; *AA* 5, 5 (1976), 47 ff.
Cramond	*Britannia*, 5 (1974), 163 ff.
Crawford	*PSAS*, 104 (1971–2), 147 ff.
Croy Hill	*PSAS*, 59 (1925), 288 ff; 66 (1932), 243 ff; 71 (1937), 32 ff.
Dover	B. J. Philp, *The Excavation of the Roman Forts of the Classis Britannica at Dover 1970–1977*, Dover, 1981.
Easter Happrew	*PSAS*, 90 (1956–7), 93 ff.
Ebchester	*AA* 4, 38 (1960), 193 ff; 42 (1964), 173 ff; *AA* 5, 3 (1975), 43 ff.
Exeter	P. Bidwell, *The Legionary Bath-House and Basilica and Forum at Exeter*, *Vol. 1.*, Exeter, 1979.
Fendoch	*PSAS*, 73 (1938–9), 110 ff.
Gelligaer	J. Ward, *The Roman Fort at Gellygaer*, London, 1903; *RFIW*, 88 ff.
Great Casterton	M. Todd, *The Roman fort at Great Casterton, Rutland*, Nottingham, 1968.
Haltonchesters	*AA* 4, 14 (1937), 151 ff; 37 (1959), 177 ff; *JRS*, 51 (1961), 164; 52 (1962), 164 ff; *RHW*, 170 ff.
Hardknott	*CW* 2, 28 (1928), 314 ff; 63 (1963), 148 ff; T. Garlick, *Hardknott Castle Roman Fort*, 1973; *JRS*, 55 (1965), 203.
High Rochester	*AA* 2, 1 (1857), 69 ff; *AA* 4, 13 (1937), 171 ff; *NCH*, XV; *RHW*, 242.
Hod Hill	I. A. Richmond, *Hod Hill. Excavations carried out between 1951 and 1958. Vol. II*, British Museum London, 1968.

Housesteads   *AA* 2, 25 (1904), 193 ff; *AA* 4, 38 (1960), 61 ff; 39 (1961), 279 ff; *AA* 5, 3 (1975), 17 ff; 4 (1976), 17 ff; *Britannia*, 9 (1978), 420; *RHW*, 178 ff; E. Birley, *Housesteads Roman Fort*, HMSO London, 1973.

Ilkley   *YAJ*, 28 (1926), 137 ff; *Proc.Leeds Phil.& Lit.Soc.*, 12, 2 (1966), 23 ff.

Inchtuthil   Annual summaries in *JRS*, 43–56 (1953–66).

London   W. F. Grimes, *The Excavation of Roman and Medieval London*, London, 1968, 15 ff.

Longthorpe   *Britannia*, 5 (1974), 1 ff.

Lyne   *PSAS*, 35 (1901), 154 ff; 75 (1940–1), 39 ff; 95 (1961–2), 208 ff.

Maryport   M. G. Jarrett, *Maryport, Cumbria: A Roman Fort and its Garrison*, Kendal, 1976.

Mumrills   *PSAS*, 63 (1928–9), 396 ff; 94 (1960–1), 86 ff.

Nanstallon   *Britannia*, 3 (1972), 56 ff.

Newstead   J. Curle, *A Roman Frontier Post and its People: The Fort of Newstead in the Parish of Melrose*, Glasgow, 1911; *PSAS* 84 (1949–50), 1 ff.

Oakwood   *PSAS*, 86 (1951–2), 81 ff.

Old Church, Brampton   *CW* 2, 36 (1936), 172 ff; *RHW*, 138 ff.

Old Kilpatrick   S. N. Miller, *The Roman Fort at Old Kilpatrick*, Glasgow, 1928.

Pen Llystyn   *Arch.J.*, 125 (1968), 101 ff; *RFIW*, 101 ff.

Penydarren   *Arch.Camb.*, 61 (1906), 193 ff; *JRS* 48 (1958), 131; *RFIW*, 106 ff.

Ribchester   J. Hopkinson, *The Roman Fort at Ribchester*, (2nd edn by D. Atkinson), Manchester, 1928; *JRS*, 35 (1945), 15 ff; *Arch.J.* 127 (1970), 239; annual summaries in *Britannia*, from 1970.

Risingham   *AA* 4, 13 (1937), 184 ff; *NCH*, XV; *RHW*, 235 ff.

Rough Castle   *PSAS*, 39 (1905), 442 ff; *JRS* 48 (1958), 132; 49 (1959), 104; 52 (1962), 163.

Rudchester   *AA* 4, 1 (1925), 93 ff; *RHW*, 165 ff.

Slack   *YAJ*, 26 (1920–3), 2 ff.

South Shields   *AA* 4, 11 (1934), 83 ff; I. A. Richmond, *The Roman Fort at South Shields: Guide*, n.d.; J. N. Dore and J. P. Gillam, *The Roman Fort at South Shields*, Newcastle, 1979; *RHW*, 152 ff.

Stanway   *JRS*, 67 (1977), 126 ff; *Britannia*, 8 (1977), 185.

Stanwix   *JRS*, 31 (1941), 129 ff; *RHW*, 205 ff.

Strageath   *JRS*, 41 (1951), 63; 48 (1958), 90; interim reports in *Britannia*, from 5 (1974) onwards.

Templeborough   T. May, *The Roman Forts of Templeborough*, Rotherham, 1922; C. F. C. Hawkes (ed.), *Greeks, Celts and Romans*, London, 1973, 69 ff.

Tomen-y-Mur   *Arch.Camb.*, 93 (1938), 192 ff; *J. Merioneth Hist.& Record Soc.*, 4 (1961–4), 171 ff; *RFIW*, 111 ff.

Usk	W. H. Manning, *Report on the Excavations at Usk 1965–1976. Volume II: The Fortress Excavations 1968–71*, Cardiff, 1981.
Waddon Hill	Interim notes in *JRS*, 50–59 (1960–69), and *Britannia*, 1 (1970); *Proc.Dorset Nat.Hist.& Arch.Soc.*, 82 (1960), 88 ff; 86 (1965) 135 ff.
Wall	*Trans.Lichfield & South Staffs.Arch.& Hist.Soc.*, 5 (1963–4), 1 ff; 8 (1966–7), 1 ff; 11 (1969–70), 7 ff; interim reports in *Britannia* 2–9 (1971–8).
Wallsend	*RHW*, 159 ff; *Britannia*, 7–9 (1976–8).
Whitley Castle	W. F. Grimes (ed.), *Aspects of Archaeology*, 1951, Pl. xvi; *AA* 4, 37 (1959), 191 ff.

Germania Inferior

Alphen-Zwammerdam	J. K. Haalebos, *Zwammerdam-Nigrum Pullum*, Amsterdam, 1977; *NL*, 49 ff.
Beckinghausen	C. Albrecht, *Das Römerlager in Oberaden*. Veröffentlichungen aus dem Städt Museum für Vor- und Frühgeschichte Dortmund, I (1938), II (1942); *NL*, 119.
Bunnik-Vechten	*JVT*, 29–32 (1944–8), 30 ff; *NL*, 62 ff.
Bonn	H. von Petrikovits, *Das Römische Rheinland. Archäologische Forschungen seit 1945*, Beihefte der Bonner Jahrbücher 8, Köln-Opladen, 1960, 34 ff; *Rheinische Ausgrabungen 3*, Düsseldorf, 1968, 323 ff; *NL*, 196 ff.
Dormagen	*Saal.J.*, 14 (1955), 10; *NL*, 151 ff; G. Müller, *Ausgrabungen in Dormagen, 1963–1977*, Rheinisches Landesmuseums Bonn, Cologne, 1979.
Haltern	*Mitteilungen der Altertumskommission für Westfalen*, 1 (1899), 7 (1922); *Bodenaltertümer Westfalens*, 1 (1929), 13 ff; 6 (1943). S. von Schnurbein, *Die römische Militäranlagen bei Haltern*, (*Bodenaltertümer Westfalens* 14), Münster, 1974; *NL*, 116 ff.
Köln	For full bibliography of the various sites see *NL*, 160 ff.
Krefeld-Gellep	*Rheinische Ausgrabungen 3*, Düsseldorf, 1968, 213 ff; *Rheinische Ausgrabungen 10*, Düsseldorf, 1971, 242 ff; *NL*, 135 ff.
Moers Asberg	*Duisburger Forschungen*, 2 (1959), 162 ff; 20 (1974), 1 ff; *Rheinische Ausgrabungen 12*, Bonn, 1972, 147 ff; *NL*, 128 ff.
Neuss	*Bonn.J.*, 111/2 (1904), 1 ff; 161 (1961), 449 ff; H. von Petrikovits, *Novaesium. Das römische Neuss*, Cologne, 1957; *NL*, 139 ff; *Limesforschungen*, Berlin, 6, 7, 8, 10, 11, 14, 17.
Oberaden	C. Albrecht, *Das Römerlager in Oberaden*, Veröffentlichungen aus dem Städt Museum für Vor- und Frühgeschichte Dortmund, I (1938), II (1942); *NL*, 119 ff.
Remagen	Reports annually in *Bonn.J.*, 105–25 (1900–19); full bibliography in *NL*, 208 ff.
Utrecht	*JVT*, 29–32 (1944–8), 51 ff; full bibliography in *NL*, 58 ff.
Valkenburg	*JVT*, 25–28 (1940–4), 29–32 (1944–8), 33–37 (1948–53),

52–54 (1967–70); *JRS*, 42 (1952), 129 ff; W. Glasbergen, *De Romeinse Castella te Valkenburg ZH*, (*Cingula* 1), Groningen, 1972; W. Glasbergen and W. Groenman-van Waateringe, *The Pre-Flavian Garrisons of Valkenburg ZH*, Amsterdam-London, 1974; *NL*, 40 ff; B. L. van Beek, R. W. Brandt and W. Groenman-van Waateringe (eds), *Ex Horreo*, (*Cingula* IV), Amsterdam, 1977.

Vetera   H. Lehner, *Vetera*, Berlin, 1930; *Bonn.J.*, 159 (1959), 89 ff; *Saal.J.*, 26 (1969), 126 ff; *NL*, 106 ff.

Germania Superior

Altenstadt
: *ORL* B 20 (1912); *Limesforschungen* 2, Berlin, 1962, 75 ff & 92 ff.

Arnsburg
: *ORL* B 16 (1902).

Bad Cannstatt-Stuttgart
: *ORL* B 59 (1907); P. Goessler and R. Knorr, *Cannstatt zur Römerzeit*, Stuttgart, 1921; *R.B-W*, 529 ff.

Benningen
: *ORL* B 58 (1902); *R.B-W*, 234 ff.

Butzbach
: *ORL* B 14 (1894); G. Müller, *Kastell Butzbach*, (*Limesforschungen*, 2), Berlin, 1962, 7 ff; *Saal.J.*, 22 (1965), 17 ff; 24 (1967), 12 ff; 25 (1968), 5 ff.

Dangstetten
: *Archäologische Nachrichten aus Baden*, 6 (1971), 11 ff; *Ber.RGK*, 51–2 (1970–1), 197 ff; *Fundber.aus B-W*, 3 (1977), 278 ff; *R.B-W*, 253 ff.

Echzell
: *ORL* B 18 (1903); *Saal.J.*, 21 (1963–4), 32 ff; 22 (1965), 139 ff; *Germania*, 41 (1963), 338 ff; 46 (1968), 40 ff; *Wetterauer Geschichtsblätter*, 18 (1969), 1 ff.

Feldberg
: *ORL* B 10 (1905).

Frankfurt-Heddernheim
: *ORL* B 27 (1915); *Germania*, 38 (1960), 189 ff; 39 (1961), 164 ff.

Heilbronn-Böckingen
: *ORL* B 56 (1898); *Germania*, 38 (1960), 65 ff; *Limesforschungen* 2, Berlin, 1962, 102 ff; D. Planck, *Archäologische Ausgrabungen* 1975, Bodendenkmalpflege in den Reg-Bez Stuttgart und Tübingen, Stuttgart, 1976, 32 ff; *R.B-W*, 298 ff.

Hesselbach
: *ORL* B 50 (1896); D. Baatz, *Kastell Hesselbach*, (*Limesforschungen* 12), Berlin, 1973.

Hofheim
: *ORL* B 29 (1897); *Nassauische Annalen*, 40 (1912); *Germania*, 38 (1960), 184 ff; *Fundb. aus Hess.*, 5–6 (1965–6), 146 ff; 8 (1968), 76 ff; 14 (1974), 227 ff.

Holzhausen
: *ORL* B 6 (1904); *Nassauische Annalen*, 54 (1934), 233 ff.

Hüfingen
: *ORL* B 62a (1937); *R.B-W*, 303 ff.

Jagsthausen
: *ORL* B 41 (1909); *R.B-W*, 315 ff.

Kapersburg
: *ORL* B 12 (1906); *Germania*, 9 (1925), 39 ff.

Köngen
: *ORL* B 60 (1907); *Blätter des Schwäbischen Albvereins*, 72 (1966), 166 ff; *R.B-W*, 333 ff.

Mainz D. Baatz, *Mogontiacum.Neue Untersuchungen am römischen Legionslager in Mainz*, (*Limesforschungen* 4), Berlin, 1962.

Mainhardt *ORL* B 43 (1909); *Fundb.aus B-W*, 2 (1975), 178 ff; *R.B-W*, 412 ff.

Miltenberg East *ORL* B 38a (1929).

Miltenberg-Altstadt *ORL* B 38 (1910); H. Schönberger, *Die Kastelle in Miltenberg. Führer zu vor- und frühgeschichtlichen Denkmälern*, 8 (1967), 75 ff.

Murrhardt *ORL* B 44 (1894); D. Planck, *Archäologische Ausgrabungen 1975*, Bodendenkmalpflege in den Reg-Bez Stuttgart und Tübingen, Stuttgart, 1976, 39 ff; *R.B-W*, 420 ff.

Neckarburken East & West *ORL* B 53 (1898); *Ber.RGK*, 3 (1906–7), 167 ff; *R.B-W*, 425 ff.

Niederbieber *ORL* B 1a (1936).

Öhringen-Rendell kastell *ORL* B 42 (1897).

Öhringen-Burg kastell *ORL* B 42a (1897); *Ber.RGK*, 53 (1972), 233 ff both: *Fundber.aus Schwaben*, 15 (1959), 46 ff; D. Planck, *Neue Ausgrabungen am Limes*, Aalen Limesmuseum, Stuttgart, 1975, 10 ff.

Okarben *ORL* B 25a (1902); *Wetterauer Geschichtsblätter*, 27 (1978), 1 ff.

Osterburken *ORL* B 40 (1895); *Fundb.aus B-W*, 1 (1974), 497 ff; *R.B-W*, 444 ff.

Rödgen H. Schönberger, *Römerlager Rödgen*, (*Limesforschungen*, 15), Berlin, 1976.

Rottweil *ORL* B 62 (1936); D. Planck, *Arae Flaviae 1*, Stuttgart, 1975; *Fundb.aus B-W*, 3 (1977), 457 ff; *R.B-W*, 483 ff.

Saalburg *ORL* B 11 (1937); L. Jacobi, *Das Römerkastell Saalburg bei Homburg v.d.H*, Bad Homburg, 1897; H. Schönberger, *Führer durch das Römerkastell Saalburg*, 23, Bad Homburg, 1966; D. Baatz, *Limeskastell Saalburg. Ein Führer*, Bad Homburg, 1968.

Stockstadt *ORL* B 33 (1910); F. Rattinger, *Das Römerkastell Stockstadt*, 1968.

Walldürn *ORL* B 39 (1903); *R.B-W*, 555 ff.

Welzheim West and East *ORL* B 45 and 45a (1904); *R.B-W*, 559 ff.

Wiesbaden *ORL* B 31 (1909); H. Schoppa, *Aqua Mattiacae*, Wiesbaden, 1974; *Germania*, 41 (1963), 328 ff.

Wimpfen *ORL* B 54 and 55 (1900); *R.B-W*, 229 ff.

Wörth *ORL* B 36 (1900).

Zugmantel *ORL* B 8 (1909); *Ber RGK 1943–50*, 33 (1951), 145 ff; *Saal.J.*, 10 (1951), 55 ff; 17 (1958), 92 ff; 24 (1967), 40 ff.

Raetia

Aalen	*ORL* B 66 (1904); *R.B-W*, 201 ff.
Buch	*ORL* B 67 (1898); *R.B-W*, 508 ff; *Aufstieg und Niedergang der römische Welt*, *II*, *5.1*, ed. H. Temporini, Berlin, 1976, 442 ff.
Burghöfe	G. Ulbert, *Die Römischen Donau-Kastelle Aislingen und Burghöfe*, (*Limesforschungen* 1), Berlin, 1959.
Dambach	*ORL* B 69 (1901); *Germania*, 39 (1961), 116 ff.
Eining	P. Reinecke, *Das römische Grenzkastell Abusina bei Eining: kurzer führer*, n.d.
Gnotzheim	*ORL* B 70 (1907).
Günzburg	*Bonn.J.*, 157 (1957), 193 ff; *BVBL*, 24 (1959), 86 ff.
Heidenheim	*ORL* B 66b (1900); *Fundber.aus Schwaben*, NF 18, II (1967), 90 ff; B. Cichy, *Das römische Heidenheim*, Heidenheim, 1971; *R.B-W*, 292 ff.
Kösching	*ORL* B 74 (1913); *Germania*, 11 (1928), 26 ff.
Künzing	H. Schönberger, *Kastell Künzing-Quintana: Die Grabungen von 1958–1966*, (*Limesforschungen* 13), Berlin, 1975.
Munningen	*ORL* B 68a (1929); *Saal.J.*, 33 (1976), 11 ff.
Oberstimm	H. Schönberger, *Kastell Oberstimm*, (*Limesforschungen* 18), Berlin, 1978.
Pförring	*ORL* B 75 (1902).
Pfünz	*ORL* B 73 (1901).
Risstissen	*Fundber.aus Schwaben*, NF 16 (1962), 106 ff; G. Ulbert, *Das römische Donau-Kastell Risstissen. Teil 1: Die Funde aus Metall, Horn und Knochen*, Urkunden zur Vor- und Frühgeschichte aus Süd Württemberg-Hohenzollern, Heft 4, Stuttgart, 1970; *Germania*, 39 (1961), 69 ff; *R.B-W*, 466 ff.
Schirenhof	*ORL* B 64 (1897); *Fundber.aus Schwaben*, NF 18/II (1967), 115 ff; *R.B-W*, 498 ff.
Straubing	J. Keim and H. Klumbach, *Der römische Schatzfund von Straubing. Münchner Beiträge zur Vor- und Frühgeschichte*, 3 (1951), 9 ff; *Beilage zum Amtlichen Schul-Anzeiger für den Regierungsbezirk Niederbayern*, 5/6 (1976), 22 ff; *Historischer Verein für Straubing und Umgebung 79 Jahrgang 1976*, Straubing, 1977, 77 ff.
Theilenhofen	*ORL* B 71a (1905).
Unterböbingen	*ORL* B 65 (1895); *Fundber.aus Schwaben*, NF 18/1 (1967), 283 ff; D. Planck, *Neue Ausgrabungen am Limes*, Aalen Limesmuseum No. 12, Stuttgart, 1975, 21 ff; *R.B-W*, 242 ff.
Urspring	*ORL* B 66a (1904); *R.B-W*, 543 ff.
Weissenburg	*ORL* B 72 (1906).

Bibliography

General

Alföldy, G., *Noricum*, London, 1974.

Baatz, D., *Der römische Limes*, Berlin, 1975.

Birley, E., 'The epigraphy of the Roman army', *Actes du deuxième Congrès international d'épigraphie grecque et latine*, Paris 1953, 226 ff.

Research on Hadrian's Wall, Kendal, 1961.

Bowman, A. K., 'Roman military records from Vindolanda', *Britannia*, 5 (1974), 360 ff.

Bowman, A. K. and J. D. Thomas, *The Vindolanda Writing Tablets*, Newcastle, 1974.

Breeze, D. J., review of A. S. Robertson, *Birrens (Blatobulgium)*, Edinburgh, 1975 and H. Schönberger, *Kastell Künzing-Quintana*, Berlin, 1975, *Britannia*, 8 (1977), 451 ff.

Breeze, D. J. and B. Dobson, *Hadrian's Wall*, London 1976.

Cagnat, R., 'Les deux camps de la légion IIIe Auguste à Lambèse', *Mémoires de l'Académie des Inscriptions et Belles-Lettres*, 38/1, 1908.

L'armée romaine d'Afrique et l'occupation militaire de l'Afrique sous les empereurs, Paris, 1912.

Caprino, C., A. M. Colini, M. Pallotino and P. Romanelli, *La Colonna di Marco Aurelio*, Rome, 1955.

Cichorius, C. *Die Reliefs der Traianssäule*, Berlin, 1896 and 1900.

Clayton, P. (ed.), *A Companion to Roman Britain*, Oxford, 1980.

Collingwood, R. G., *The Archaeology of Roman Britain*, (revised by I. A. Richmond), London, 1969.

Collingwood, R. G. and R. P. Wright, *The Roman Inscriptions of Britain 1: Inscriptions on Stone*, Oxford, 1965.

Collingwood Bruce, J. *Handbook to the Roman Wall*, (13th edn by C. M. Daniels), Newcastle, 1978.

Crawford, O. G. S., *The Topography of Roman Scotland North of the Antonine Wall*, Cambridge, 1949.

Davies, R. W., 'The daily life of the Roman soldier under the Principate', *Aufstieg und Niedergang der römischen Welt II Principat 1*, (ed. H. Temporini), Berlin, 1974, 299 ff.

Domaszewski, A. von, *Hygini gromatici liber de munitionibus castrorum*, Leipzig, 1887.

Doppelfeld, O. *Römer am Rhein*, Ausstellung des Römisch-Germanischen Museums Köln, Köln, 1967.

Egger, R., 'Bemerkungen zum Territorium pannonischer Festungen', *Anzeiger der Österreichischen Akademie der Wissenschaften. Philosophisch-historische klasse*, 18 (1951), 215 ff.

Elbe, J. von, *Roman Germany*, Mainz, 1975.

Filtzinger, Ph., 'Ein Beitrag zur archäologischen Luftbildforschung der oberen Donau', *Kölner Jahrbuch für Vor und Frühgeschichte*, 9 (1967–8), 62 ff.

Filtzinger, Ph., D. Planck and B. Cämmerer (eds), *Die Römer in Baden-Württemberg*, Stuttgart, 1976.

Fink, R. O., *Roman Military Records on Papyrus*, Cleveland, 1971.

Fink, R. O., A. S. Hoey and W. F. Snyder, 'Feriale Duranum', *Yale Classical Studies*, 7 (1940).

Frere, S. S., *Britannia*, (3rd edn), London, 1978.

Gilliam, J. F., C. B. Welles and R. O. Fink, *The Excavations at Dura-Europos. Final Report V. Part 1: The Parchments and Papyri*, New Haven, 1959.

Glasbergen, W. and W. Groenman-van Waateringe, *The Pre-Flavian Garrisons of Valkenburg ZH*, Amsterdam and London, 1974.

Goessler, P., F. Hertlein and O. Paret, *Die Römer in Württemberg*, Band 1–3, Stuttgart, 1928–32.

Hanson, W. S., 'The Roman military timber-supply', *Britannia*, 9 (1978), 293 ff.

Haug, F. and G. Sixt, *Die römischen Inschriften und Bildwerke Württembergs*, 1912–14.

Hunt, A. S. and C. C. Edgar, *Select Papyri*, Cambridge and London, 1959–63.

Jarrett, M. G. and B. Dobson, (eds), *Britain and Rome*, Kendal, 1966.

Kellner, H-J., *Die Römer in Bayern*, Munich, 1976.

Lehmann-Hartleben, K., *Die Traianssäule*, Berlin and Leipzig, 1926.

Macdonald, G., *The Roman Wall in Scotland*, (2nd edn), Oxford, 1934.

Mann, J. C., 'The frontiers of the Roman Principate', *Aufstieg und Niedergang der römischen Welt II Principat 1*, (ed. H. Temporini), Berlin, 1974, 508 ff.

Miller, S. N., (ed.), *The Roman Occupation of South-West Scotland*, Glasgow, 1952.

Mocsy, A., *Pannonia and Upper Moesia*, London, 1974.

Nash-Williams, V. E., *The Roman Frontier in Wales*, (2nd edn by M. G. Jarrett), Cardiff, 1969.

Nicole, J., *Les Papyrus de Genève*, Geneva, 1896–1906.

Ogilvie, R. M. and I. A. Richmond, *Tacitus, De Vita Agricolae*, Oxford, 1967.

Petrikovits, H. von, *Das römische Rheinland: Archäologische Forschungen seit 1945*, Arbeitsgemeinschaft für Forschung des Landes Nordrhein-Westfalen Geisteswissenschaften 68, Cologne, 1960.

Die Innenbauten römischer Legionslager während der Prinzipatszeit, Abhandlungen der rheinisch-westfälischen Akademie der Wissenschaften 56, Opladen, 1975.

Richmond, I. A., 'Trajan's army on Trajan's Column', *PBSR*, 13 (1935), 1 ff.

'The Roman siege works of Masada, Israel', *JRS*, 52 (1962), 142 ff.

'Roman military engineering', *Roman Archaeology and Art*, (ed. P. Salway), London, 1970.

Robertson, A. S., *The Antonine Wall*, (4th edn), Glasgow, 1973.

Rossi, L., *Trajan's Column and the Dacian Wars*, London, 1971.

Salway, P., *The Frontier People of Roman Britain*, Cambridge, 1965.
    Roman Britain, Oxford, 1981.

Schulten, A., *Masada, die Burg des Herodes und die römischen Lager*, Leipzig, 1933.

Staehelin, F., *Die Schweiz in römischer Zeit*, Basle, 1948.

Starr, C. G., *Roman Imperial Navy 31 BC–AD 324*, (2nd edn), Cambridge, 1960.

Temporini, H. and W. Haase, (eds), *Aufstieg und Niedergang der römischen Welt*,
    Berlin and New York, from 1972.

Wacher, J., *Roman Britain*, London, 1978.

Walbank, F. W., *A Commentary on Polybius*, *1*, Oxford, 1957.

Ward, J., *Romano-British Buildings and Earthworks*, London, 1911.

Watson, G. R., *The Roman Soldier*, London, 1969.

Webster, G., 'Fort and town in early Roman Britain', *The Civitas Capitals of Roman
    Britain*, (ed. J. Wacher), Leicester, 1966, 31 ff.
    The Roman Imperial Army, (2nd edn), London, 1979.

Wilson, R., *A Guide to the Roman Remains in Britain*, London, 1974.
    Roman Forts, London, 1980.

1 The Roman Army

Alföldy, G., 'Die Hilfstruppen der römischen Provinz Germania Inferior',
    Epigraphische Studien, 6, 1968.

Birley, E., 'Alae and cohortes milliariae', *Corolla Memoriae Erich Swoboda
    Dedicata*, Graz, 1966, 54 ff.

Bogaers, J. E., 'Exercitus Germanicus Inferior', *Numaga* 12 (1965), 98 ff.

Breeze, D. J. and B. Dobson, *The Army of Hadrian's Wall*, Newcastle, 1973.
    Hadrian's Wall, London, 1976, 153 ff.

Callies, H., 'Die fremden Truppen im römischen Heer des Prinzipats und die
    sogenannten nationalen Numeri. Beitrage zur Geschichte des römischen
    Heeres', *Bericht der Römisch-Germanischen Kommission 1964*, 45 (1965),
    130 ff.

Cheeseman, G. L., *The Auxilia of the Roman Imperial Army*, Oxford, 1914.

Davies, R. W., 'A note on a recently discovered inscription from Carrawburgh',
    Epigraphische Studien, 4 (1967), 108 ff.
    'Joining the Roman army', *Bonn.J.*, 169 (1969), 208 ff.
    'Cohortes equitatae', *Historia*, 20 (1971), 751 ff.

Dessau, H. 'Offiziere und Beamten des römischen Kaiserreichs', *Hermes*, 45 (1910),
    1 ff.

Domaszewski, A. von, *Die Rangordnung des römischen Heeres*, (2nd edn by B.
    Dobson), Cologne, 1967.

Frere, S. S., 'Hyginus and the First Cohort', *Britannia*, 11 (1980), 51 ff.

Jarrett, M. G., 'Roman officers at Maryport', *CW* 2, 65 (1965), 115 ff.

Kennedy, D., 'The ala I and cohors I Britannica', *Britannia*, 8 (1977), 249 ff.

Kiechle, F., 'Die "Taktik" des Flavius Arrianus', *Bericht der Römisch-
    Germanischen Kommission 1964*, 45 (1965), 87 ff.

Kraft, K., *Zur Rekrutierung der Alen und Kohorten an Rhein und Donau*, Berne, 1951.

Mann, J. C., 'A note on the numeri', *Hermes*, 82 (1954), 501 ff.

Nash-Williams, V. E., *The Roman Frontier in Wales*, (2nd edn by M. G. Jarrett), Cardiff, 1969.

Nesselhauf, H., 'Umriss einer Geschichte des obergermanischen Heeres', *Jahrb. RGZM*, 7 (1960), 151 ff.

Parker, H. M. D., *The Roman Legions*, Oxford, 1928.

Saddington, D. B., 'The development of the Roman auxiliary forces from Augustus to Trajan', *Aufstieg und Niedergang der römischen Welt II Principat 3*, (eds H. Temporini and W. Haase), Berlin, 1975, 176 ff.

'British auxiliary units—origins and early nomenclature', in W. S. Hanson and L. J. F. Keppie (eds), *Roman Frontier Studies 1979. Papers presented to the 12th International Congress of Roman Frontier Studies*, British Archaeological Reports, International Series, 71 (iii), Oxford, 1980, 1071 ff.

Sander, E., 'Zur Rangordnung des römischen Heeres: Die gradus ex Caliga', *Historia*, 3 (1954), 87 ff.

'Zur Rangordnung des römischen Heeres: Die Flotten', *Historia*, 6 (1957), 347 ff.

'Zur Rangordnung des römischen Heeres: Der Duplicarius', *Historia*, 8 (1959), 239 ff.

Saxer, R., 'Untersuchungen zu den Vexillationen des römischen Kaiserheeres von Augustus bis Diokletian', *Epigraphische Studien*, 1, 1967.

Schleiermacher, W., 'Zu Hadrians Heeresreform in Obergermanien', *Germania*, 35 (1957), 117 ff.

Stein, E., *Die kaiserlichen Beamten und Truppenkörper im römischen Deutschland unter dem Prinzipat*, Wien, 1932.

Thomas, J. D. and R. W. Davies, 'A new military strength report on papyrus', *JRS*, 67 (1977), 50 ff.

Webster, G., *The Roman Imperial Army*, London, 1969, 142 ff.

Wegeleben, Th., *Die Rangordnung der römischen Centurionen*, Berlin, 1913.

2   The Fort Plan

General

Collingwood, R. G., *The Archaeology of Roman Britain*, (revised by I. A. Richmond), London, 1969, 15 ff.

Fischer, W., *Das römische Lager*, Leipzig, 1914.

Nash-Williams, V. E., *The Roman Frontier in Wales*, (2nd edn by M. G. Jarrett), Cardiff, 1969, 145 ff.

Smith, W., (ed.), *Dictionary of Greek and Roman Antiquities*, London, 1849, 244 ff.

Stolle, F., *Das Lager und Heer der Römer*, Strasbourg, 1912.

Ward, J., *Romano-British Buildings and Earthworks*, London, 1911, 18 ff.

Webster, G., *The Roman Imperial Army*, London, 1969, 166 ff.

The Polybian and Hyginian Camps

Fabricius, E., 'Some notes on Polybius' description of Roman camps', *JRS*, 22 (1932), 78 ff.

Hyginus Gromaticus, *Liber de munitionibus castrorum*, (ed. by A. von Domaszewski), Leipzig, 1887.

Oxé, A., 'Polybianische und Vorpolybianische Lagermasse und Lagertypen', *Bonn.J.* 143–4 (1939), 47 ff.

3 The Construction of the Fort

Siting

Moore, D., 'Roman and Norman military sites in Wales: a comparison of two frontiers', *Limes: Akten des XI Internationalen Limeskongresses*, (ed. J. Fitz), Budapest, 1977, 19 ff.

Survey and layout

Dilke, O. A., 'The Roman surveyors', *Greece and Rome*, N.S. 9 (1962), 172 ff. *The Roman Land Surveyors*, Newton Abbot, 1971.

4 The Defences

General

Jones, M. J., *Roman Fort Defences to AD 117*, British Archaeological Reports No. 21, 1975.

Nash-Williams, V. E., *The Roman Frontier in Wales*, (2nd edn by M. G. Jarrett), Cardiff, 1969, 153 ff.

Webster, G., *The Roman Imperial Army*, London, 1969, 166 ff.

Roman defences before AD 43

Kromayer, J. and G. Veith, *Heerwesen und Kriegsführung der Greichen und Romern*, Munich, 1928.

Schönberger, H., 'The Roman frontier in Germany: an archaeological survey', *JRS*, 59 (1969), 144 ff.

Wells, C., *The German Policy of Augustus*, Oxford, 1972.

Rampart replicas and experimental earthworks

Birley, R., *Vindolanda, A Roman Frontier Post on Hadrian's Wall*, London, 1977, 158 ff.

Crabtree, K., 'Overton Down experimental earthwork, Wiltshire 1968', *PUBSS*, 12, 3 (1971), 237 ff.

Hobley, B., 'An experimental reconstruction of a Roman military turf rampart', *Roman Frontier Studies 1967*, (ed. S. Applebaum), Tel Aviv, 1971, 21 ff.

'The Lunt fort, 1966 experimental rampart and ditch: years 1–3' (Appendix 1), *Roman Frontier Studies 1969*, (eds E. Birley, B. Dobson and M. G. Jarrett), Cardiff, 1974, 79 ff.

Jewell, P. A. (ed.), *The Experimental Earthwork at Overton Down, Wiltshire*, The British Association, 1963.

Jewell, P. A. and G. W. Dimbleby, 'The experimental earthwork on Overton Down, Wiltshire, England: the first four years', *PPS*, 32 (1966), 313 ff.

Ascensi

Macdonald, G., 'Notes on the Roman forts at Rough Castle and Westerwood with a postscript', *PSAS*, 67 (1932–3), 286 ff.

Gates

Baatz, D., 'Zur Datierung des römischen militarlagers Hanau-Kesselstadt', *Germania*, 51 (1973), 536 ff.

Bechert, T., 'Römische Lagertore und ihre Bauinschriften', *Bonn.J.*, 171 (1971), 201 ff.

Charlesworth, D., 'The south gate of a Flavian fort at Carlisle', in W. S. Hanson and L. T. F. Keppie (eds), *Roman Frontier Studies 1979 BAR* International Series 71, (i), Oxford, 1980, 201 ff.

Fox, A. and W. Ravenhill, 'The Roman fort at Nanstallon, Cornwall', *Britannia*, 3 (1972), 56 ff.

Manning, W. H. and I. R. Scott, 'Roman timber military gateways in Britain and on the German frontier', *Britannia*, 10 (1979), 19 ff.

Schönberger, H., 'Das Nordtor des Römerkastells Heilbronn-Böckingen', *Germania*, 38 (1960), 65 ff.

'Über einige neu endeckte römische Lager- und Kastelltore aus Holz', *Bonn.J.*, 164 (1964), 40 ff.

Stanford, S. C., 'The Roman forts at Leintwardine and Buckton', *TWNFC*, 39 (1968), 240 ff.

Wheeler, R. E. M., 'The Roman fort near Brecon', *Y Cymmrodor*, 37 (1926), 20 ff.

Artillery

Baatz, D., 'Zur Geschützbewaffnung römischer Auxiliartruppen in der frühen und mittleren Kaiserzeit', *Bonn.J.*, 166 (1966), 194 ff.

Review of E. W. Marsden, *Greek and Roman Artillery*, 1969 in *Gnomon*, 43 (1971), 257 ff.

'Recent finds of ancient artillery', *Britannia*, 9 (1978), 1 ff.

Marsden, E. W., *Greek and Roman Artillery: Vol. 1 Historical Development*, Oxford, 1969.

Schramm, E. von, *Die antiken Geschütze der Saalburg*, Berlin, 1918.

5 The Internal Buildings

General

Nash-Williams, V. E., *The Roman Frontier in Wales*, (2nd edn by M. G. Jarrett), Cardiff, 1969, 157 ff.

Petrikovits, H. von, *Die Innenbauten römischer Legionslager während der Prinzipatszeit*, Abhandlungen der Rheinisch-Westfälischen Akademie der Wissenschaften, Band 56, Opladen, 1975.

Ward, J., *Romano-British Buildings and Earthworks*, London, 1911, 80 ff.

Webster, G., *The Roman Imperial Army*, London, 1969, 205 ff.

Methods of construction

Baatz, D., *Kastell Hesselbach* (*Limesforschungen* 12), Berlin, 1973, 39 ff and fig. 21.

Giffen, A. E. van, 'Opgravingen in de Dorpswierde te Ezinge en de romeinse terpen van Utrecht, Valkenburg Z.H. en Vechten', *JVT*, 19–22 (1948).

Hanson, W. S., 'The Roman military timber supply', *Britannia*, 9 (1978), 293 ff.

Richmond, I. A., 'Roman timber building', *Studies in Building History*, (ed. E. M. Jope), 1961, 15 ff and figs 1–3.

The headquarters building (*Principia*)

Domaszewski, A. von, 'Die Principia des römischen Lagers', *Neue Heidelberger J.* 9 (1899), 141 ff.

Fellman, R., *Die Principia des Legionslagers Vindonissa und das Zentralgebäude der römischen Lager und Kastelle*, Brugg, Vindonissa Museum, 1958.

Lorenz, H., *Untersuchungen zum Praetorium. Katalog der Praetorien und Entwicklungs-geschichte ihrer Typen*, diss., Halle-Wittenberg, 1936.

Mommsen, Th., 'Praetorium', *Hermes*, 35 (1900), 437 ff.

Schleiermacher, W., 'Principia', *Trierer Zeitschrift*, 18 (1949), 243 ff.

Williams, E., unpublished B.A. dissertation, University College, Cardiff, 1970.

The Commander's house (*Praetorium*)

Penny, R. J., *Design influences on commandants' houses in Britain*, unpublished B.A. dissertation, University College, Cardiff, 1977.

Granaries (*Horrea*)

Gentry, A. P., *Roman Military Stone-Built Granaries in Britain*, British Archaeological Reports No. 32, Oxford, 1976.

Manning, W. H., 'Roman military timber granaries in Britain', *Saal.J.*, 32 (1975), 105 ff.

Rickman, G., *Roman Granaries and Storebuildings*, Cambridge, 1971.

The provisioning of forts

Bulmer, W., 'The provisioning of Roman forts: a reappraisal of ration storage', *AA* 4, 47 (1969), 7 ff.

Review of G. Rickman, *Roman Granaries and Storebuildings*, 1971 in *JRS*, 62 (1972), 205 ff.

Groenman-van Waateringe, W., 'Grain storage and supply in the Valkenburg castella and Praetorium Agrippinae', *Ex Horreo. Cingula IV*, (eds B. L. van Beek, R. W. Brandt and W. Groenman-van Waateringe), University of Amsterdam, 1977, 227 ff.

Haverfield, F. and R. G. Collingwood, 'The provisioning of Roman forts', *CW* 2, 20 (1920), 127 ff.

Richmond, I. A. and J. McIntyre, 'The Agricolan fort at Fendoch', *PSAS*, 73 (1938–9), 110 ff.

Wahle, O., 'Die Proviantmagazine der Saalburg', *Die Saalburg, Mitteilungen der Vereinigung der Saalburg-Freunde II*, 2 (10 April 1920), 29 ff.

The hospital (*Valetudinarium*) and the Roman medical service

Davies, R. W., 'The medici of the Roman armed forces', *Epigraphische Studien*, 8 (1969), 83 ff; 9 (1970), 1 ff.

'A note on the hoard of Roman equipment buried at Corbridge', *Durham University Journal*, 62 (1969–70), 177 ff.

'Some Roman medicine', *Medical History*, 14 (1970), 101 ff.

Review of J. Scarborough, *Roman Medicine*, 1969 in *JRS*, 60 (1970), 224 ff.

'The Roman military medical service', *Saal.J.*, 27 (1970), 84 ff.

Jettner, P., 'Valetudinarien römischer Legionen. Geschichte des Hospitals', *Sudhoffs Archiv für Geschichte de Medizin u.d. Naturwiss Suppl.*, 5 (1966), 1 ff.

Knorzer, K-H., 'Römerzeitliche Heilkräuter aus Novaesium', *Sudhoffs Archiv für Geschichte de Medizin u.d. Naturwiss*, 47 (1963), 311 ff.

Milne, J. S., *Surgical Instruments in Greek and Roman Times*, Oxford, 1907.

Nutton, V., 'Medicine and the Roman army: a further reconsideration', *Medical History*, 13 (1969), 260 ff.

Penn, R. G., 'Medical services of the Roman army', *Journal of the Royal Army Medical Corps*, 110 (1964), 253 ff.

Richmond, I. A., 'The Roman army medical service', *University of Durham Medical Gazette*, (June 1952), 2 ff.

Scarborough, J., *Roman Medicine*, London, 1969.

Schultze, R., 'Die römischen Legionslazarette in Vetera und anderen Legionslagern', *Bonn.J.*, 139 (1934), 54 ff.

Webster, G., *The Roman Imperial Army*, London, 1969, 248 ff.

Barracks

Baatz, D., 'Limeskastell Echzell. Kurzbericht uber die Grabungen 1963 und 1964', *Saal.J.*, 22 (1965), 139 ff.

Stables

Axe, J. Wortley, *The Horse: Its Treatment in Health and Disease*, IX, London, 1905.

Davies, R. W., 'The supply of animals to the Roman army and the remount system', *Latomus*, 28 (1968), 429 ff.

Delebecque, E. (ed.), *Xenophon. L'art équestre*, Paris, 1950.

Ewart, J. C., 'The animal remains' in J. Curle, *A Roman Frontier Post and its People: the fort of Newstead in the Parish of Melrose*, Glasgow, 1911, 362 ff.

Müller, G., *Ausgrabungen in Dormagen 1963–1977*, Rheinische Ausgrabungen Band 20, Rheinisches Landesmuseum Bonn, Cologne, 1979, 27 ff.

Pierce, S. Rowland and P. Cutbush, 'Stables' in *Planning: The Architect's Handbook*, London, 1959, 475 ff.

Schönberger, H., *Kastell Künzing-Quintana: die Grabungen von 1958 bis 1966*, (*Limesforschungen* 13), Berlin, 1975, 58 ff.

Wells, C. M., 'Where did they put the horses? Cavalry stables in the Early Empire', *Limes: Akten des XI Internationalen Limeskongresses*, (ed. J. Fitz), Budapest, 1977, 659 ff.

The workshop (*Fabrica*)

Petrikovits, H. von, 'Militärische Fabricae der Römer', *Actes du IXe Congrès international d'études sur les frontières romaines*, (ed. D. M. Pippidi), Bucharest, Cologne and Vienna, 1974, 399 ff.

'Die Spezialgebäude römischer Legionslager', *Legio VII Gemina*, Léon, 1970, 229 ff.

'Römisches Militärhandwerk', *Archäologische Forschungen der letzten Jahre: Anz.Osterr. Akad.Wiss.*, III (1974), 1 ff.

Schönberger, H., *Kastell Oberstimm*, (*Limesforschungen* 18), Berlin, 1978, 30 ff.

Gyrus—vivarium

Hobley, B., 'Excavations at the Lunt Roman military site, Baginton, 1968–71', *Trans.Birm.and Warwicks.Arch.Soc.*, 85 (1971–3), 30 ff.

'A gyrus at the Lunt?' *Curr.Arch.*, III, 5 (Sept. 1971), 127 ff.

6 Food and the Water Supply

The military diet

Davies, R. W., 'The Roman military diet', *Britannia*, 2 (1971), 122 ff.

'The daily life of the Roman soldier under the Principate', *Aufstieg und Niedergang der römischen Welt II Principat 1*, (ed. H. Temporini), Berlin, 1974, 318 ff.

Mensch, P. J. A. van and G. F. Ijzereef, 'Smoke-dried meat in Prehistoric and Roman Netherlands', *Cingula*, 4 (1977), 144 ff.

Grain milling

Jacobi, H. 'Römische Getreidemühlen', *Saal.J.*, 3 (1912), 75 ff.
Moritz, L. A., *Grain Mills and Flour in Classical Antiquity*, Oxford, 1958.
Simpson, F. G., *Watermills and Military Works on Hadrian's Wall: Excavations in Northumberland 1907–1913*, (ed. G. Simpson), Kendal, 1976.

The water supply

Jacobi, H., 'Die Be-und Entwässerung unsere Limeskastelle', *Saal.J.* 8, (1934), 32 ff.
Smith, D. J., 'A note on the water supply', *Watermills and Military Works on Hadrian's Wall* (ed. G. Simpson), Kendal, 1976, 143 ff.

Latrines

Collingwood, R. G., *The Archaeology of Roman Britain*, (revised by I. A. Richmond), London, 1969, 124 ff.
Simpson, F. G., 'The latrine building in the south-eastern angle of Housesteads fort, 1911–12', *Watermills and Military Works on Hadrian's Wall*, (ed. G. Simpson), Kendal, 1976, 133 ff.

7 External Structures

Training grounds

Davies, R. W., 'Roman Wales and Roman military practice-camps', *Arch.Camb.*, 117 (1968), 103 ff.
'The training grounds of the Roman cavalry', *Arch.J.*, 125 (1968), 73 ff.
'Roman training grounds' in *Roman Frontier Studies 1969*, (eds E. Birley, B. Dobson and M. G. Jarrett), Cardiff, 1974, 20 ff.
Wenham, L. P., 'Notes on the garrisoning of Maryport', *CW* 2, 39 (1939), 19 ff.

8 The Development of the Fort Plan

Frontiers

Britain

Birley, E., *Research on Hadrian's Wall*, Kendal, 1961.
Breeze, D. J., *The Northern Frontiers of Roman Britain*, London, 1982.
Breeze, D. J. and B. Dobson, 'The development of the mural frontier in Britain from Hadrian to Caracalla', *PSAS*, 102 (1969–70), 109 ff.
Hadrian's Wall, London, 1976.
Collingwood Bruce, J., *Handbook to the Roman Wall*, (13th edn by C. M. Daniels), Newcastle, 1978.

Daniels, C. M., 'Problems of the Roman northern frontier', *Scottish Arch.Forum*, 2 (1970), 91 ff.

Dudley, D. and G. Webster, *The Roman Conquest of Britain*, (2nd edn), London, 1973.

Frere, S. S., *Britannia*, (3rd edn), London, 1978.

Gillam, J. P. and J. C. Mann, 'The northern British frontier from Antoninus Pius to Caracalla', *AA* 4, 38 (1970), 1 ff.

Jarrett, M. G., 'Early Roman campaigns in Wales', *Jarrett, M. G. and J. C. Mann, 'Britain from Agricola to Gallienus', Bonn.J.*, 170 (1970), 178 ff.

Mann, J. C., (ed.), *The northern frontier in Britain from Hadrian to Honorius:*

Jarrett, M. G., 'Early Roman campaigns in Wales', *Arch.J.*, 121 (1964), 23 ff.

Jarrett, M. G. and J. C. Mann, 'Britain from Agricola to Gallienus', *Bonn.J.*, 170 (1970), 178 ff.

Mann, J. C., (ed.), *The northern frontier in Britain from Hadrian to Honorius: Literary and Epigraphical Sources*, Newcastle, n.d.

Nash-Williams, V. E., *The Roman Frontier in Wales*, (2nd edn M. G. Jarrett), Cardiff, 1969.

Robertson, A. S., *The Antonine Wall*, (4th edn), Glasgow, 1973.

Wacher, J., *The Coming of Rome*, London, 1979.

Webster, G., 'The Roman military advance under Ostorius Scapula', *Arch.J.*, 115 (1958), 49 ff.

    'The Claudian frontiers of Britain' in *Studien zu den Militärgrenzen Roms*, (Proceedings of the VIth International Congress of Roman Frontier Studies), Cologne, 1967, 42 ff.

    'The military situations in Britain between AD 43 and 71', *Britannia*, 1 (1970), 179 ff.

    'A Roman system of fortified posts along Watling Street', *Roman Frontier Studies 1967*, (ed. S. Applebaum), Tel Aviv, 1971, 38 ff.

    The Rebellion of Boudica, London, 1978.

    The Roman Invasion of Britain, London, 1980.

Wilson, D. R., *Roman Frontiers of Britain*, London, 1967.

Lower Germany (*Germania Inferior*) and *Gallia Belgica*

Bogaers, J. E., 'Einige opmerkingen over het Nederlandse gedeelte van de Limes van Germania Inferior (Germania Secunda)', *Ber. ROB*, 17 (1967), 99 ff.

Bogaers, J. E. and C. B. Rüger, *Der Niedergermanische Limes*, Cologne, Bonn, 1974.

Petrikovits, H. von, 'Forschungen und Beobachtungen am Limes: Beobachtungen am niedergermanischen Limes seit dem zweiten Weltkrieg', *Saal.J.*, 14 (1955), 7 ff.

Raepsaet-Charlier, M. T. and G. Raepsaet-Charlier, 'Gallia Belgica et Germania Inferior. Vingt-cinq années de recherches historiques et archéologiques', *Aufstieg und Niedergang der römischen Welt II Principat 4*, (eds H. Temporini and W. Haase), Berlin, 1975, 73 ff.

Rüger, C. B., *Germania Inferior: Untersuchungen zur Territorial- und Verwaltungsgeschichte Niedergermaniens in der Prinzipatszeit*, (Beihefte der *Bonn.J.*, 30, Cologne-Graz, 1968.

Wankenne, A., *La Belgique à l'époque romaine, sites urbaines, villageois, religieuses et militaires*, Brussels, 1972.

Upper Germany (*Germania Superior*) and Raetia

Baatz, D., *Der römische Limes. Archäologische Ausflüge zwischen Rhein und Donau*, Berlin, 1975.

Fabricius, E., F. Hettner and O. von Sarwey, (eds), *Der obergermanisch-rätische Limes des Römerreiches*, Heidelberg, 1894–1937. Part A: description of the *limes* sections, and Part B: description of the forts.

Filtzinger, Ph., 'Bemerkungen zur römischen Okkupationsgeschichte Südwestdeutschlands', *Bonn.J.*, 157 (1957), 181 ff.

Filtzinger, Ph., D. Planck and B. Cämmerer, (eds), *Die Römer in Baden-Württemberg*, Stuttgart, 1976.

Planck, D., 'Neue Forschungen zum obergermanischen und raetischen limes', *Aufstieg und Niedergang der römischen Welt II Principat 5.1*, (ed. H. Temporini), Berlin, 1976, 404 ff.

Schleiermacher, W., *Der römische Limes in Deutschland*, (3rd edn), Berlin, 1967.

Schönberger, H., 'Neuere Grabungen am obergermanischen und raetischen Limes', *Limesforschungen 2*, Berlin, 1962, 69 ff.

'The Roman frontier in Germany: an archaeological survey', *JRS*, 59 (1969), 144 ff.

'Recent research on the *limes* in Germania Superior and Raetia', (eds W. S. Hanson and L. J. F. Keppie), *Roman Frontier Studies 1979. Papers Presented to the 12th International Congress of Roman Frontier Studies*, British Archaeological Reports, International Series, 71 (ii), Oxford, 1980, 541 ff.

Publications of the Congress of Roman Frontier Studies

Congress 1: E. Birley (ed.), *The Congress of Roman Frontier Studies 1949*, Durham, 1952.

Congress 2: E. Swoboda (ed.), *Carnuntia, Vorträge beim internationalen Kongress der Altertumforscher, Carnuntum 1955*, in *Römische Forschungen in Niederösterreich*, Band 3, Köln-Graz, 1956.

Congress 3: R. Laur-Belart (ed.), *Limes-Studien, Vorträge des 3 Internationalen Limes-Kongresses in Rheinfelden-Basel 1957*, in *Schriften des Institutes für Ur- und Frühgeschichte der Schweiz*, Basel, 1959.

Congress 4: unpublished.

Congress 5: G. Novak (ed.), *Quintus Congressus internationalis limitis Romani studiosorum*, Zagreb, 1963.

Congress 6: *Studien zu den Militärgrenzen Roms, Vorträge des 6 Internationalen Limeskongresses in Süddeutschland*, Beiheft der *Bonn.J.*, Cologne, 1967.

Congress 7: S. Applebaum (ed.), *Roman Frontier Studies 1967*, Tel Aviv, 1971.

Congress 8 E. Birley, B. Dobson and M. G. Jarrett (eds), *Roman Frontier Studies 1969*, Cardiff, 1974.

Congress 9: D. M. Pippidi (ed.), *Actes du IXe Congrès international d'études sur les frontières romaines*, Bucharest, 1974.

Congress 10: J. E. Bogaers (ed.), *Studien zu den Militärgrenzen Roms II: Vorträge des 10 Internationalen Limeskongresses in der Germania Inferior*, Cologne, 1977.

Congress 11: J. Fitz (ed.), *Limes: Akten des XI Internationalen Limeskongresses*, Budapest, 1977.

Congress 12: W. S. Hanson and L. J. F. Keppie (eds), *Roman Frontier Studies 1979: Papers presented to the 12th International Congress of Roman Frontier Studies*, British Archaeological Reports, International Series, 71 (i–iii), Oxford, 1980.

9   Fort Types and Garrisons

Breeze, D. J. and B. Dobson, 'Fort types on Hadrian's Wall', *AA* 4, 47 (1969) 15 ff.
   'Fort types as a guide to garrisons: a reconsideration', *Roman Frontier Studies 1969*, (eds E. Birley, B. Dobson and M. G. Jarrett), Cardiff, 1974, 13 ff.
Davies, R. W., 'A note on a recently discovered inscription from Carrawburgh', *Epigraphische Studien*, 4 (1967), 108 ff.
   'Cohors I Hispanorum and the garrisons of Maryport', *CW* 2, 77 (1977), 7 ff.
Richmond, I. A., 'Roman Britain and Roman military antiquities', *Proc.Brit.Academy*, 41 (1955), 297 ff.

Index

Italic numbers indicate illustrations and tables
A number followed by n indicates a reference from the notes

Aalen, 23, 31, 104, 282, 285, 292
Aberdeen, 253
Abergavenny, 144
actuarius, 117, 118–19
Agricola, Iulius, 36, 252–3, 259, 266, 274, 280, 293
ala milliaria, 20, 21, 22, 23, 31, 263, *295*, 314n
　ala II Flavia milliaria, 23, *169*, 175, 263, 292, 314n
ala quingenaria, 20, 21, 22, 280, 282, 292, 293, *295*, 295, 296
Alamanni, 206, 289
Albinus, D. Clodius, 287
Alchurch, Brampton, 146
Alesia, 53, 55, 228
Alphen-Zwammerdam, 42, 53, 102, 105
Alston Moor, 3
altars, 7–8, 111, 113, 206, *207*, 217, *217*, 219, 220
Altenstadt, 57
Ambleside, 37, 91–2, 109, 119, *131*, 131, 144, *147*, 272, *273*
Ammianus, 94
amphitheatre, 219
Andernach, *24*
angle towers, 31, 35, 45, 72–7, 268, 270, 282, 286
Anglesey, 247
Annaberg, 231
Annandale, 278, 279
Antonine Wall, 13, 57, 68–9, 274–7, *275*, 278, 279, 284, 297, 333–4n
　see also names of forts
Antoninus Pius, reign of, 274–83, 284
　in Britain, 274–81 *see also* Antonine Wall
　in Germany, 281–3
　principia plan, 131, *131*
　mentioned, 63, 112, 121, 147
　see also names of forts of this period
Antonius, L. Saturninus, 114, 260
Appian, 223
aqueducts, 204–6
Aquincum, 117, 161
archaeological background, 10–16
Ardoch, 48, 278, 306n
armamentaria, 108–9, 190
Armilustrium, 113

Arminius, 234
armour, 182, 183, *218*, 219, *219*
　see also armamentaria
Arnsburg, 91, 108
Arrian, Flavius, 4, 21, 66, 191, 215, 219
artillery platforms, 94, *95*
Arzbach, 56
ascensi, 57, 65–6, *67*, 94
Assouan, 125
Auchendavy, *217*, 219
Augsburg, 250
auguratorium, 30
Augustus, reign of, 2, 16, 228–34
　campaigns in Germany, 228–9, 230–4
　forts, 230–3
　gateways, 81, *82*, 85, 230
　principia plan, 127, *128*, 130
　mentioned, 19, 62
　see also names of forts of this period
auxiliary units, 19–25, 43–4, 296
Avignon, 90, *90*
axes of fort, layout of, 41, 42

Baatz, Professor Dr D., 69
Bad Cannstatt, 268
Baginton, *248*, 249
　defences, 249
　　ascensi, 66, 67
　　rampart, 58, 59, 61–2, 63, *64*, 65
　　timber gateways, *79*, 79, 85, 85, *86*, 87
　fort plan, *248*, 249
　internal buildings, 114–15, *129*, 130, 140, 173, 186, 249
　　granaries, *146*, 151, 152, 153, *154*, 157, 249
　　gyrus-vivarium, 3, 14, *191*, 191–2, *192*, 215, 249
ballistaria, 94, *95*
Balmuildy, *135*, *193*, 194, 275, *277*
Bar Hill, 275
　defences, 52
　internal buildings, 106, *107*, 187, 188, 189, *189*, 194
　water supply, 204, 213
barracks (*centuriae*), 166–76
　contubernium, 166, *167*, 171–3, *174*, 175, 176,

barracks (*centuriae*)—*continued*
199, 200, 202, 230, 251, 252, 263, 272, 280, 292, 294, 295
examples in relation to fort plan development, 223, 225, 230, 238, 239, 241, 244, 248, 249, 250, 251, 252, 257, 263, 271–2, 277, 279, 280, 286, 288
and garrison, 140, 175–6, 291, 292, 294–7
officers' accommodation, 168, *170*, 170–1, 173, 174
origins in marching camp, 166, *167*, 170
plans, 167–8, *169*, 174, *174*
mentioned, 32, 33, 35, 42
Batavians, revolt of, 250, 252
bathhouse
external, 220, *221*
internal, 193–4
mentioned, 32, 33, 134, 213, 257, 266, 275, 276, 277, 286, 287
Bearsden, 59, 102, 152, 187, 220, 277, *278*
Beaufront Red House, 163, *164*, *190*, 190, *221*
Beckfoot, *15*, 152, 270
Beckinghausen, 81, *82*, 231, *231*
Benningen, 10, *11*, 219, 268
Benwell
fort plan, 271, *272*
internal buildings, 106, 115, 117, 130, 186, 271
barracks, *169*, 271, 295
granaries, 43, 144, 150, 151, 152, 271
hospital, 162, *163*, 164, 271
temple, 219
water supply, 106, 208–9, *209*
berm, 55–6, 69–70
Bewcastle, 134, 287, *288*
Binchester, 40, 161, 213
Bingen, *162*
Birdoswald
altars, 219
construction, 40, 43
defences, 90, *92*
internal buildings, 104, 112, 132, *133*, 188, 190
Birrens
defences, 48, 49, 66, 278, 279
excavation work, 13, 279
food supply, 200, *201*
fort plan, *279*, 279–80
granaries, 144, *147*, 152
history of occupation, 279–80, 284
size of garrison, 292, 293, 294, 297
water supply, 204, 208
Böbingen *see* Unterböbingen
Bochastle, 37
Böhming, 44
Bonn, 14, *18*, 149, 250
Boudiccan rebellion, 243, 247, 249
Bowness, 40, 269, 270
box rampart, *61*, 62–3

Brecon Gaer, 92, *93*, 108, 120, 123, *124*, 125, 135, 194, 281
Breuteuil-sur-Noye, 228
Bridgeness, 274
bridges, timber, 52, *52*, *53*
Brigantia, 244, 250, 252
Britain
archaeological background, 10–12, 14
history of Roman occupation, 2, 239–45, 247–9, 250, 252–9, 266–8, 269–73, 274–81, 284, 287–9
maps, *240*, *254–5*
see also names of forts
British fleet *see Classis Britannica*
Brough by Bainbridge, 58, 111, 112, 115, 117, *118*, *131*, 131
Brough on Humber, 3, 38, 62, 79
Brough on Noe, 3, 40, 145, 177, *178*, 196, 206, 278
Brough under Stainmore, 3, 300n
Bu Njem, 89, *89*, 90, 91, 93
Buch, 87, 121, 190
Buckton, 38, 40, 43, 79, 89
building methods, 97–103
decoration, 102–3
stone and timber combined, 101–3
timber, 97–101
Bumbesti, 66
Bunnik-Vechten, 230
Burghöfe, 239
Burnum, 109, *110*, 110
Bushe-Fox, J. P., 14
Butzbach, 57, 99, 122, 274

Cáceres, 225
Cadder, 79, *102*, 102, 150, 194, 276
Caerhun, 73, 77, 101, 119, 138, *138*, 144, 149, 201–2
Caerleon, 113, 201, 247, 252, 266–7, *267*
Caermote, 57
Caernarfon, 42, 206
internal buildings, 119, 133, 138, *138*, 140, 141, 182, 186, 190, 194
Caerphilly, 48
Caersŵs, 37, 38, 40, 43, 58
Caerwent, *135*
Caesar, Julius, 2, 4, 53, 55, 65, 69, 195, 225, 228, 232
Caledonians, 253, 289
Camden, William, 10, 12, 13
Campestres, 219
campus see parade ground
Camulodunum see Colchester
Cappuck, 48
Caracalla, 198, 289, 290
Cardean, 49, 257, 320n
cardo decumanus, 41, 42
cardo maximus, 41, 42
Carlisle, 58, 266

carnarium, 157
carpentry, 187–8
Carpow, 161, 289
Carrawburgh, 172, 270
Cartimandua, Queen, 250
Carnuntum, 93
Carvoran, 12, 43, *71*, 71–2, 270
Carzield, 295
Cassius Dio, 287
Castell Collen, 92, *93*, 112, 145, *147*, 150, 281, 283
Castillejo, 126, *126*, 147, 223, 225, *226*
Castlecary, 150, 151, 213, 275, 276
Castledykes, 37
Castlehill, 219
catapult platforms, 94, *95*
Cato the Elder, 223
Cato, Marcus, 143, 195
cavalry, 17, 20, 21, 22, 23, 25, 125, 215, 314n
  armour, *218*, *219*, 219
  barracks, 167, 172, 173, 175, 292, 295
  see also ala milliaria;
    ala quingeneria; stables
Cawthorn, 47
Celsus, 159
centuriae see barracks
centuries, 17, 20, 21, 23, 25
  allocation of supplies to, 198–9
  barrack accommodation, 292, 294–5, *295*
  defence construction by, 45, 71–2
centurions, 17, *18*, 45, 71
  barrack accommodation, 168, 170, 173
Cerialis, Petilius, 252
Charterhouse, 3
Chatti, 259, 260, 284
Chauci, 284
Cheshunt Field, 243
Chester, 145, 196, 252, 266
Chester-le-Street, 195, 206
Chesterholm, 6, *6*, 12–13, 37
  defences, 57–8, 61, 63, 71, *74*, *75*
  food and water supply, 195, 196, *197*, 199, 200,
    213
  internal buildings, 104–5, 112, *113*, 118, 119,
    132, 186–7, 188
Chesters, *15*, 206, 220, *221*, 295
  defences, 72, 88, *88*, 91, 309n
  internal buildings, 115, *117*, 130, *131*, 131, 134,
    169, 172, 175
cippi, 53, 55
civilian settlements, 16
Civilis, Julius, 250
classical sources, 3–9
Classis Britannica (British fleet), 3, 43, 150, 155,
  159
Claudius, reign of, 234–45
  invasion of Britain, 2, 239–45
  in Germany, 234–9
  principia plan, 127, *129*, 130

see also names of forts of this period
clavicula, 50, *50*, 51, 228
Clemens, Gn. Pineius Cornelius, 250
Coelbren, 53, 57
cohorts, 17, 20, 21, *22*, 23, 25, 26
  cohors milliaria equitata, 22, 25, *295*
    cohors I Nervana Germanorum milliaria equi-
      tata, 193, 294
  cohors milliaria peditata, 22, 23, 176, 257, 292,
    295, 295
  cohors quingenaria equitata, 22, 23, 176, 282, 295,
    314n
    cohors III Thracum quingenaria equitata, 180,
      263, 293, 294, 314n
  cohors quingenaria peditata, 22, 23, 31, 125, 292,
    295
Colchester (*Camulodunum*), *18*, 239, 243, 249
Colchester Dyke System, 243
Cologne, 260
Columella, 143, 149
commander
  auxiliary, 140–2
  legionary, 17
commander's house *see praetorium*
Commodus, 26, 37, 282, 284, 286, 287
construction, fort *see* fort construction
contubernium, 166, 167, 171–3, *174*, 175, 176, 230,
  292, 294, 295
  and food supply, 199, 200, 202
  mentioned, 251, 252, 263, 272, 280
Corbridge
  defences, 57, 68, 80
  internal buildings, 119, 130, 139, 163, *163*, 173,
    192, *193*, 292
  granaries, 142, 145, *147*, *148*, 149, *150*, *151*,
    151, 152, 156, 288
  transition from timber to stone, 97, *98*, 101
  mentioned, 266, 274
corduroy, log, 35, 57, 60
cornicularius, 117–18
courtyard, 106–8, 202
craftsmen, 183, 185
Cramond, 3, 219, 288, 289, 297
Crawford, 79, 80, *80*, 186, 257
cross-hall, 109–11
Croy Hill, 109, 144
Curle, James, 280

Dacians, Trajan's victory against, 6, 266
  see also Trajan's column
Dambach, 219
Dangstetten, 230, 232
de munitionibus castrorum (Hyginus), 3
defences, 35, 36, 45–95
  angle and interval towers, 72–7
  berm, 55–6
  catapult platform, 94–5
  ditches, 45–52

defences—*continued*
  gates, 77–93
  obstacles, 53–5
  rampart, 56–66
  stone-built, 66–72
  mentioned, 222–89 *passim*
Derbyshire lead mines, 3
Dere Street, 258, 278, 280, 284
diet, military, 195–7
Dioscurides, 161
diplomata (dedication slabs), 6, 7, *8*
discharge diplomas, 8–9, *9*
ditches, 27, 29, 31, 35, 43, 45–52
  clavicula, 50, *50*, 51
  depth of defences, 49–50
  double and multiple, 48, *49*
  marking lines of, 43
  obstacles in, 53, *54*
  titulum, 29, 50, *51*
  tools used for construction, 45, *46*, 47
  types of, 47
  width and depth, 47–8
  mentioned, 225, 228, 230, 231, 234, 244, 258,
    275, 278–83 *passim*, 286
documentary sources, 3–9
Dolaucothi, gold workings at, 3
Domitian, 114, 130, 249, 259, 260–5
Dormagen, *178*, 178–9, 296
Dover, 3, 155, 206, 207
drainage, 177–8, *210*, 210–11
Drumburgh, 270
Drusus, 230, 231, 232
Duntocher, 275
Dura Europos, 4, 111, 117, 120, 179–80

Easter Happrew, 37, 42
Ebchester, 40, 119
Echzell, 80, 81, 219, 274
  internal buildings, 99, 115, 130, 168, *169*, *170*,
    173
Egypt, 23, 181, 195, 196, 214
Eining, 121, 130, 252, 282, 283
epitoma rei militaris (Vegetius), 3–4
Exeter, 247
external structures, 215–21
  bathhouse, 220, *221*
  parade ground, 215–19

fabrica see workshop
Feldberg, 120, 207
Fendoch, 41, 200
  defences, 62, 78, 79, *79*, *80*, 80, 81, 85
  fort plan, *256*, 256–7, 268
  internal buildings, 134, *135*, *146*, 151, 162–3,
    163, *169*, 176, 190, *190*, 295
  principia, 109, 110, 119, *129*, 130
  timber supply for, 100–1
Feriale Duranum, 111, 112–13
festivals, military, 111–12, 113, 217, 219

Fishbourne, 145, *146*
Flavian emperors, reign of, 249–65
  Britain under, 2, 250, 252–9
  gates, 81, *84*, 85, 250, 257
  Germany under, 249–52, 260–5
  organization of legions, 17, 20
  principia, *129*, 130, 250, 257, 263
  ramparts, 57, 59, 62, 63, 250, 251, 257, 258–9
  mentioned, 31, 41, 146, 266, 268, 296
  see also names of forts of this period
food supply, 195–202
  military diet, 195–7
  preparation and cooking, 197–202
    allocation of supplies, 198–9
    bakehouse, 197–8, *198*
    millhouses, 199, *200*
    millstones, *198*, 199, *200*
    ovens, 200–2
forehall, 105, 120–6
  function of, 125–6
  roof of, 121–3
fort area
  in relation to garrison, 291, 292–3
fort construction, 36–44
  responsibility for, 43–4
  site
    choice of, 36–8
    preparation, 38–40
  survey and layout, 40–3
fort plan, 27–35, 222–90
  auxiliary fort, 31, 33, *34*, 35
  classical sources, 27–30
  development, chronological survey of, 222–90
  legionary fortress, 31, *32*, 32, *33*, 33
  numerus fort, 33, *34*
fort types in relation to garrison, 291–7
fossa fastigata, 47, 47
fossa Punica, 47, 47
fossae see ditches
Fosse Way, 244
Frontinus, Sextus Iulius, 252

Galen, 159
garrison, 291–7
  barracks in relation to, 291, 292, 294–7
  fort area in relation to, 291, 292–3
  granary capacity in relation to, 292, 293–4
  praetorium in relation to, 141
  problems of identification, 291–2
  stables in relation to, 292, 294, *295*, 295, 296
  mentioned, 230, 238, 241, 244, 249, 257, 280,
    285, 288
gates, 31, 35, 77–93
  defences in front of, 50, *50*, 51, 52
  groundplan of, 78, 82
  in Hyginian camp, 30
  porta decumana, 30, 35, 41, 77, 244
  porta praetoria, 30, 35, 41, 77, 91, 92

portae principales, 30, 35, 77
portae quintanae, 92, 270
stone, 87–93
  changing styles in, 92–3, *93*
  external appearance of, 89–92
timber, 78–87
  bridge, 78–9, *79*, 85
    reconstruction of, *79*, 79, *80*, 81
  dating, 85
  towers flush with rampart, 79–81
  with internal towers, 81, *83*, *84*, 85
  mentioned, 42, 45, 230, 234, 250, 257, 268, 270, 281, 282, 283, 287
Gaul, 2, 4, *18*, 53, 69, 109, 130, 228
Gelligaer, 13, 37, 42, 213, 267–8, *268*, 274
  defences, 52, *53*, 59, 69, 73
  internal buildings, *135*, 137, 145, 146, *147*, 152, 187
Gergovia, 228
Germanicus, 234
Germany
  archaeological background, 10, *11*, 13–14
  history of Roman occupation, 228–34, 234–9, 249–52, 259, 260–5, 266, 268–9, 273–4, 281–3, 284–6, 289–90
  maps, *229*, *237*, *260*, *262*
  see also names of forts
Glenlochar, 55
Gloucester, *135*
Gnotzheim, 69, 121, *122*, 145, 283
Gosbecks, *243*, 243
granaries (*horrea*), 142–57, 293–4
  capacity in relation to garrison size, 292, 293–4
  design, 144–52
    floor supports and flooring, 145–9
    loading platforms and access, 151–2
    sizes and proportion, 144–5
    stone walls and buttresses, 149–50
    ventilators, 150
  grain storage, 142–4
    classical references to, 143–4
    principles and problems, 142–3
  possible reconstruction, 153–7
    interior, 156–7
    stone, 153, 155, *155*, *156*
    timber, 153, *154*
  siting, 139, 152–3
  mentioned, 32, 33, 35, 99, 225, 230, 250, 276, 277, 288
Great Casterton, 78, *79*, *83*, 85, 170, 329n
Great Chesters, *12*, 48, 115, 118, 199, 206, 270
groma, *41*, 41–2, *43*
Gross-Krotzenburg, 8
guardroom, 117
Günzburg, 252
gyrus-vivarium, 14, *191*, 191–2, *192*, 215, 249

Hadrian, reign of, 269–74, 284

in Britain, 269–73, *see also* Hadrian's Wall
in Germany, 273–4
mentioned, 43, 67
see also names of forts of this period
Hadrian's Wall, 269–72
  archaeological background, 10, 12, 13
  compared with Antonine Wall, 275
  gates, 77, 79, 88, 92
  legions involved in building of, 19, 44
  subsequent history of, 274, 277, 278, 284, 287, 289
  mentioned, 2–3, 26, 69–70, 279, 292–3
  see also names of forts
Haltern, 81, *82*, 230, 231, 233, *233*, 234
  internal buildings, 127, *128*, 130, 145, 161, *162*, 186, 311n
Haltonchesters, 121, 125, 132, 144, 149, 150, *178*, 178, 295, 313–14n
Haltwhistle Common, 44
Hanson, W. S., 101
Hardknott, 13, *216*, 217, 220, 272, 273, 274
  internal buildings, *131*, 131, 147, 151, 273
headquarters building *see principia*
Hedley, Anthony, 12–13
Heidenheim, 23, 31, 65, 104, 130, 263, *265*, 285, 292
  barracks, *169*, 171, *172*, 175, *175*, 263
Heilbronn-Böckingen, *80*, 80, 81, 281
Herodian, 198
Hesselbach
  defences, 62, 69, 80, *80*, 88, *88*, 90, *90*, 91, 273–4
  fort plan, 33, *34*, 44, 269, 273
  internal buildings, 25, 104, 110, 120, 123, *124*, 135, 139, *169*, 176
High Rochester, 13, 69, 94, *95*, 115, 208, 287
Hod Hill, *241*, 241, *242*, 243, 244, 257, 296
  defences, 48, 50, 58, *61*, 66, 72, 94, 241
  gates, 78, 79, *79*, 81, *83*, 85
  internal buildings, 120, 127, *129*, 145, *146*, 152, 162, *163*, 186, 189
    barracks, 167, *169*, 173, 174, 241, 244
    praetorium, 134, *135*, 139–40, 141, 241
    stables, 180, *181*
  water supply, 210, 213
Hofheim, 53, 234, *235*
  internal buildings, 105, 127, *129*, 133, 134, 137, 138, 145, 186
Holzhausen, 73
horrea see granaries
horses *see* stables
hospital, 157–64
  auxiliaries, 161–4
  legions, 159–61
  mentioned, 30, 33, 35, 233, 234
Housesteads
  archaeological background, 12, 13, 271
  fort plan, 270, 271, *271*
  garrison at, 26, 292–3, 295

Housesteads—*continued*
  internal buildings, 186, 192
    barracks, *169*, 176, 295
    granary, *147*, *148*, 149, 151
    hospital, 161, 162, *163*, 164
    praetorium, 134, *135*, *136*, 136, *137*
    principia, 108, 119, 130–1, 132
    water supply, 77, 209–10, *210*, 210–11, *211*, *212*, 213
Hüfingen, *147*, 152
Hyginus Gromaticus, 3, 4
  and construction work, 36, 40, 41
  and defences, 47, 50, 57, 65–6
  and fort plan, 4, 27, *29*, 29–30, 31
  and internal buildings, 126, 159, 166, *167*, 170, 173, 182, 183
  and Roman army, 20, 21, 23, 25

Iceni, 249 *see also* Boudiccan Rebellion
Ilkley, 68, 177, *178*, 178
immunes, 19, 40, 183
imperial cult, 111, 112
Inchtuthil, 31, 32, *32*, 256, 257, 266
  internal buildings, *138*, 141, 142, *160*, 183, *184*
infantry soldiers, 17, 20, *22*, 23, 25
  barracks, 167, 172, 173, 176, 292, 294–5, 296
internal buildings, 97–194, 230–89 *passim*
  barracks, 166–76
  bathhouse, 193–4
  building methods, 97–103
  granaries, 142–57
  gyrus-vivarium, 191–2
  hospital, 157–65
  praetorium, 132–42
  principia, 104–32
  special accommodation, 192–3
  stables, 176–82
  storebuildings, 188–90
  workshop, 183–8
interval towers, 31, 35, 45, 72–7, 268, 270, 282, 286
intervallum, 29, 30, 35, 166, 200, 210, 211
irregular troops, 25–6
Isle of Wight, 239

Jacobi, L., 109
Jagsthausen, 207, 281, 282
Jay Lane, 38, 72, 79, *80*
Jerusalem, siege of, 94
Josephus, 1, 4, 71, 72, 94, 182, 202

Kapersburg, 7, 113, 120, 121, 139, 142, 145, 207, 274
Kent, invasion of, 239
Kirkby Thore, 3
Köngen, 113, *193*, 194
Kösching, 252, 283
Krefeld-Gellep, 203, 204, *205*

Künzing
  defences, 62, 72, *76*, *80*, 80, 81, 83, 283, 284
  fort plan, 263, *264*, 268
  garrison at, 292, 293, 294
  internal buildings, *163*, 163, 187, 188
    barracks, *169*, 176, 263, 294
    principia, 108, 115, *116*, 120, 123, *124*, 125, 130, 263, 283
    stables, 180, *181*, 263, 294
  water supply, 204, 213

Lambaesis, 66, 92, 93, 159, 183, *184*
  principia, 104, 108, 111, 120, *121*, 311–12n
Lancaster, 125
Lanchester, 108
latera praetorii, 30, 35
latrines, 209, *211*, 211–14, *214*
Lauriacum, 120
lead mining, 3
leatherwork, 188
legionary fortresses, 31–3, 159–61, 183, *184*
  see also name of fortress
legions, 17–19, 43–4, 159–61, 296–7
  legio II Augusta, 44, 113, 239, 268
Leiden-Roomburg, 108
Leintwardine, *38*, 38, 62
librarii, 117, 118, 119
lilia, 35, *54*, 55
Lincoln, 62
Llandovery, 57
Llandrindod Common, 44
Llwyn-y-Brain, 37
loading platforms, *151*, 151–2
London, 3, 249, 267
longitudinal sleeper walls, 145, 146–7, *148*, 149
Longthorpe, 146, 151, 244, 245, 313n
Lorch, 282
Loudon Hill, 144
Lugudunum, Battle of, 287
Lunt, The, Baginton *see* Baginton
Lyne, 37, 66, 106, 145, 149
Lyon, G. F., 89, *89*

Maeatae, 287, 289
Maiden Castle, 239
Mainhardt, 282
Mainz, 114, 199–200, 232, 250, 260
maniples, 28
Marcellus, Ulpius, 284
marching camps *see* Hyginus Gromaticus; Polybius; Republican camps
Marcomanni, 284
Marcus Aurelius, 3, 284
Marköbel, 112, 207
Martial, 203
Maryport, 12, 217, 297
Masada, 126, 127
Mauchamp, 228

measurement, Roman units of, 42
medicine *see* hospital
Melandra Castle, 13, 131
Mendips lead mines, 3
metalwork, 163, *164*, 183, 185, 186, 187
Metellus, 225
military documents, 4, *5*, 6
millhouses, 199, *200*
millstones, *198*, 199, *200*
Miltenberg, 69, 282
mineral extraction, 3
Moesia, *5*, 23, 66
Mommsen, Theodor, 13
Mons Graupius, 253
Mumrills, 134, *135*, 139, *193*, 194, 196, 275, *276*, 276
Murrhardt, 113, 125, 282
murus Gallicus, 68, 69

Nanstallon, 79, *79*, 85, 199, 213, 247–8, *248*, 249
  internal buildings, 105, *129*, 130, 137, *138*, *169*
Napoleon 111, 228
Neath, 213
Neckarburken, 25, 115, 268, 269
Nero, reign of, *129*, 130, 247–9
  see also names of forts of this period
Netherby, 125, 284
Neuss, 14, 31, 32, *33*, 33, *160*, 250, 327–8n
  internal buildings, 114, *114*, 127, *128*, 149, 161, 173
Newcastle upon Tyne, 269
Newstead
  Antonine period, 280, 281
  defences, 57, 58, 62, 280
  early excavations, 13, 280
  food supply, 196, 199
  fort plan, *258*, 258–9, 280, *281*
  garrison, 175, 280, 296–9
  internal buildings, 123, 132, 152, 175, 176, 187, 280
  mentioned, 37, 219, 284
Niederberg, 108, 109
Niederbieber, 77, 92, *93*, 284, 285, *285*, 286
  internal buildings, 101–2, *102*, 144–5, 161, 193, 194, 286
  principia, 105, 108, 118, 119, *119*, 122–3, *124*, 130
Nijmegen, 250
Nobilior, A. Fulvius, 223
Novaesium *see* Neuss
Numantia *see* Castillejo; Peña Redonda; Renieblas
numeri, 25, 26, 284–5
numerus forts, 31, 33, 37, 44, 282
  see also Hesselbach

Oakwood, 79–80, *80*, 87, 259, *259*
Oberaden, 81, *82*, 231
Oberflorstadt, 66

Oberscheidental, 44
Oberstimm
  defences, 52, 62, 80, 81
  fort plan, *238*, 238–9
  internal buildings
    barracks, *169*, 174, 199, 239
    granaries, 145, *146*, 151, 152
    hospital, 162, 163
    praetorium, 134, *135*, 139, 239
    principia, 115, 127, *129*
    specialist buildings, 14, 167, 193, *193*
    workshops, 3, 14, 140, 167, 185, *186*, 187, 190, *190*, 196, 239, 297
  water supply, 204–6, 208
obstacles, 35, 53, *54*, 55
Odenwald frontier, 25, 70, 263, 269, 274, 281, 291
Öhringen
  Rendelkastell, *79*, 79, 206, *207*
  Burgkastell, 206
Okarben, 155
Old Burrow, 85
Old Kilpatrick, 79, 108–9, 145, 190, 274
Orange, *90*, 90
Ordovices, 252
Osterburken, 26, 37, 115, 282, 284, 286, *286*
Ostia, 156, *157*, 164, 189, 222
ovens, 200–2

Pannonia, 23
Papcastle, 113
parade ground *campus*, 215–19
part mounted cohorts, 23–5
Paternus, Tarruntenus, 40, 183, 197
Paul of Aegina, 159
Paulinus, C. Suetonius, 247
Pen Llystyn, 38, 42–3, 65, 72, 73, 81, *83*, 296
  food and water supply, 200–1, 207–8
  fort plan, 252, *253*
  internal buildings, *129*, 130, 137, *138*, 141, *146*, 152, 187, 189, 192, *193*
Peña Redonda, 126, *126*, 223, 225, *227*
Penydarren, 146
Pförring, 283
Pfünz, *42*, 42, 44, 66, 283
Phasis, 66
Piercebridge, 213
Plautius, Aulus, 239
Pliny, 144, 161, 206, 207
Polybius, 1, 4, 41, 104, 126, 180–1, 195
  and fort plan, 27, 28, *28*, 29, 30, 222, 223, 225
Pompeii, 81
Pompey, 225
portae see gates
porticoes, 105, 106, *107*, 120, 152
praefectus, 17, 21, 23, 36, 43, 159
praetentura, 30, 32, 33, 35, 235, 239, 249, 257, 269

praetentura—continued
  barracks in, 33, 35, 167, 209, 263, 279, 288
  bathhouse in, 194, 266, 287
  granaries in, 152, 153, 288
  hospitals in, 30, 159, 162
  latrines in, 213
  praetorium in, 139, 140, 238
  stables in, 35, 177, 178
  storebuildings in, 35, 189, 190
  veterinarium in, 30, 182
  workshops in, 30, 183, 186, 238
praetorium (commander's house), 32, 33, 35, 132–42
  additional, 139–40
  ground plan and architecture, 132–6
  in Hyginian camp, 30
  in Polybian camp, 27, 28
  rank of commander, 140–2
  siting, 139
  terminology, 104–5
  yards, compounds and gardens, 137–9
  mentioned, 101–2, *102*, 127, 206, 210, 225, 230, 233, 239, 241, 247, 250, 269, 271, 273, 275, 276, 280, 282, 286, 287
principia (headquarters building), 27, 32, 33, 35, 97, 104–32
  courtyard, 106–8
  cross-hall, 109–11
  entrance, 105
  evolution and development, 126–32
  forehall, 120–6
  rear-range, 111–20
  terminology, 104–5
  weapon stores, 108–9
  mentioned, 42, 91, 101, 102, 139, 140, 142, 144, 152, 159, 162, 167, 170, 174, 179, 180, 185, 190, 191, 202, 208, 210, 230–88 *passim*
Pselcis, 4, 196
Pumsaint, 3, 186

quaestorium, 28, 30

rampart (*vallum*), 27, 29, 31, 35, 43, 45, 56–66, 66–7
  ascensi, 57, 65–6, 67
  external appearance, 63, 64, 65, 65
  foundations, 57–8
  height, 59
  ovens in, 200, 201
  repairs to, 66–7
  revetments, 35, 40, 58, 59–63
    box rampart, 61, 62–3
    British and German compared, 62–3
    clay, 61, 62
    timber, 61, 62–3
    turf, 59, 60, 60, 61, 61, 62
  timber lacing, 58
  width, 58

  mentioned, 223, 228, 230, 231, 234, 250, 251, 257, 258–9, 268, 269, 279, 280
rear range, 111–20
  offices of *signiferi*, 119
  sacellum, 111–15, 117, 119
  tabularium, 117, 118
  treasury and strongroom, 113–15, 117, *117*, *118*, 119
Reculver, 109
Regensburg, 44
Reichs-Limes Kommission, 13–14
Remagen, 105, *105*
Reñieblas, 81, *82*, 223, 224, 225
Republican camps, 1–2, 16, 126, *126*, 222–8
  in Spain, 223–7
  see also Caesar, Julius; Polybius
retentura, 30, 33, 35, 77, 193, 243, 263, 280, 286
  bakehouse in, 197–8
  barracks in, 33, 35, 140, 167, 174, 251, 279, 287
  granaries in, 152, 153, 244, 288
  gyrus vivarium in, 191
  stables in, 35, 178, 180
  workshops in, 167, 183, 239
Ribchester, 106, 121, 146, 149, 151, 213, 219
Richborough, 14, 145, *146*
Richmond, Ian, Professor, 47, 100, 180, 280
Risingham, *8*, 37, 71, 111, 112, 284, 287
Risstissen, 252
roads *see viae*
Rödgen, 62, 81, *82*, *83*, 230, *232*, 232
  internal buildings, 120, 127, *128*, 145, *146*, *169*, 173
Roman army, 17–26
  auxiliary units, 19–25
  irregular troops, 25–6
  legions, 17–19
Rome, plan of, 164, *165*, 189
Rottweil, *251*, 251
  defences, 58, 59, 60, *61*, 61, 66, 72, 81, *84*, 85, 251
  internal buildings, 119, *129*, 130, 138, *138*, 140, 141, 173, 186, 251
Rough Castle, *54*, 55, 104, 151
Rudchester, 130, 131, *147*, 150, 151

Saalburg, The, 13, 14, 43, 219, 273
  defences, *46*, 47, 66, *68*, 69, 273
  food supply, 197, *198*, 199, *200*, 200, 201
  internal buildings, 101–2, 139, *168*, 187
    granaries, 144, *147*, 151, *155*
    principia, 106, *107*, 108, 109, 112, 122, *123*, *124*
  water supply, 202–3, *203*, 203–4, *204*, 207
Sablon, 203
sacellum, *107*, 110, 111–15, 117, 119, 268, 282, 283
Sahum, 199
Saxon Shore, 77, 92

Schirenhof, *93*, 119, 282–3
scholae, 30, 32, 111
Schulten, Dr Adolf, 223
Scipio, 126, 225
Scotland
    Agricola's campaigns, 253, 256–9
    Antonine period, 274–80
    Severan campaigns, 3, 142, 153, 287, 289, 293
Sertorius, 225
Severus Alexander, 111, 112
Severus, L. Septimius, reign of, 16, 287–90
    Scottish campaigns, 3, 142, 153, 287, 289, 293
    mentioned, 115, 130, *131*, 134, 146, 147, 164
    see also names of forts of this period
shrines, 106, 108
    see also altars; *sacellum*
signa, 112–13
signiferi, *114*, 114, 119
Silchester, 203
Silures, 247, 252
site
    choice of, 36–8
    preparation of, 38–40
    restrictions on layout, 41
Slack, 68, 150
Sma' Glen, 256
soakaway pits, 178–9
Soissons, 109, 130
Sorrell, Alan, *15*, 153, *154*
South Shields, 92, *93*, 206, 217, *293*, *297*
    fort plan, 288, *289*
    internal buildings, *107*, 109, 117, 187, 288, 312n
    granaries, 3, *147*, 151, 152, 153, 157, 288, 293
Spain, 1, 4, 81, 126, 223–7
special accommodation, 192–3, *193*
stables, 35, 176–82
    drains in, 177–8
    fodder and bedding supplies, 180–1
    garrison in relation to, 292, 294, *295*, 295, 296
    at Hod Hill, 180, *181*
    at Künzing, 180, *181*
    layout, 177
    problems of identification, 176
    soakaway pits, 178–9
staircases *see ascensi*
standards *see signa*
Stanegate, 266, 269
Stanway, *243*
Stanwix, 23, 270
Stobi, 161, *198*, 198
Stockstadt, 108, 111, 120
stone defensive walls, 66–72
    construction work on, 71–2
    external appearance of, 70–1
    mentioned, 35, 45, 266–7, 268, 270, 271, 273,
        274, 275, 280, 282, 286, 287, 289
storebuildings, 35, 164, *165*, 188–90
Stracathro, 50

Strageath, 66, *129*, 130, 257
Strasbourg, 250
Strathmore, 253, 274
Straubing, 199, *218*, *219*, 219, 284
strongroom, 115, *117*, 117, *118*, 119
Studion, Simon, 10, *11*
Stukeley, William, 10, *12*, 12
Suetonius, G. Tranquillus, 239
sundial, *105*, 105
supply bases, 3, 232
survey, 40–3
Syrene, 112
Syria, 4, 195, *see also* Dura Europos

tabularium, 117, 118
Tacitus, 19, 36, 112, 247, 252, 293
tanning, 187, 188
Templeborough, 133, *135*, *147*, 152
Tertullian, 117, 217
Teutoburg forest, 2, 234
Theilenhofen, 52, *52*, *93*, 93, 112, 113, 121, *122*,
    152, 283
Tiberius, 2, 230, 232, 233, 234
timber lacing, 58
titulum, 29, 50, *51*
Titus, 249, 259
tolleno, 203
Tomen-y-Mur, 55, 217, 219
tools, 45, *46*
towers, angle and interval, 31, 35, 45, 72–7, 268,
    270, 282, 286
training, military, 215, 216
Trajan, 67, 130, 145, 266–9
    see also names of forts of this period; Trajan's
    column
Trajan's column, 6, 7, *39*, 43, 99, *158*, 159, *166*,
    192, 210
    illustration of defences
        clavicula, *50*, 50
        ditches, 45, *46*, 47
        gates, *73*, 78, 81, 85, *86*, 87, 89, 90
        ramparts, 56, 59, *60*, 63, *64*
        towers, 72, *73*, 78, 81, *86*, 90
        weapons, 94
transverse sleeper walls, 145–6, 149
Trawscoed, 53
treasury, 113–15, *118*, 119
tree clearance, 38, 39, 40
tribunal, 30, 111, 126, 217
tribunes, 17, 23, 25
    houses, 32, 141
turmae, 20, 21, 23, 25, 292, *295*, 295

Unterböbingen, *74*, 75, *131*, 145, 282, *283*
Urbicus, Q. Lollius, 274
Urspring, 67, *68*, 101, 120, 123
Usk, *146*, 202, 213, 247
Utrecht, 202

valetudinarium see hospital
Valkenburg
  defences, 57, 65, 72, 81, *83*, 92, *93*
  food and water supply, 196, 199, 202, 214
  fort plan, 235, *236*, 238, 241, 257
  internal buildings, 140, 145, 178, *178*, *179*, 189
    barracks, 167, 168, *169*, 173, 174, *174*, 176, 238, 292
    building methods, *98*, 99, *100*, 100, 103
    principia, 108, 109, 121, 127, *129*, 130, 238
    workshops, 3, 185, *186*, 187, 188
vallum see rampart
Varro, 143, 182
Varus, P. Quinctilius, 2, 234
Vegetius, 3–4, 21, 215, 291
  and construction work, 36, 37, 40–1
  and defences, 45, 56, 58, 59, 63, 71, 77, 78, 94
  and food and water supply, 195, 196, 197, 202, 203
  and internal buildings, 113, 114, 117, 125, 157, 158, 182, 183, 189
ventilators, 150, *150*
Venutius, 250, 252
Veranius, Q., 247
Vercingetorix, 228
Vespasian, 239, 249–52
Vetera, 14, 31, 120, 141, *184*, 231, 234, 247, 250, 327n, 330n
  hospital, *160*, 160–1, *161*, 234
veterinarium, 30, 182
vexillation fortresses, 244
  see also Longthorpe
viae
  via decumana, 35, 42, 180, 185, 205, 252, 296
  via praetoria, 35, 42, 208
  via principalis, 30, 35, 42, 43, 105, 106, 111, 120, 136, 137, 139, 152, 190, 210, 234, 241, 244, 247, 257, 276
  via quintana, 28, 30, 35, 42, 77, 139, 205, 270
  via sagularis, 30, 35
  viae vicinariae, 30, 35
Vindolanda *see* Chesterholm
Vindonissa, 109, 141, *160*, 183, *184*, 196, 197, 234, 235, *236*, 311n
Vitellius, 249, 250
Vitruvius, 41, 94, 133, 143–4, 199, 202, 205, 206, 208
vivarium see gyrus-vivarium
von Domaszewski, A., 104

Wade, General, 12
Wâdi Fawâkhir, 6, 196

Wales, 247, 259, 280–1
  see also names of forts
Wall, 53, 145
Walldürn, 102, 220, 282
Wallsend, 162, *163*, 164, 196, 269, 271, *272*, 295
water supply, 106, 202–14
  affecting choice of site, 36, 37, 202
  aqueducts, 204–6
  drainage, *210*, 210–11
  latrines, 209, *211*, 211–14, *214*
  pipes, 206–8
  rainwater, 209
  tanks, 106, 185, 208–10
  waterwheel, 205–6
  wells, 106, 202–4, *204*, *205*
  in workshops, 185, *186*, 205
  mentioned, 182
Watling Street West, 38
weapon stores, 108–9, 190
weapons, 49–50, 94, 108–9
Weissenburg, 9, *42*, 121, *122*, 123, *147*, 313n
wells, 106, 202–4, *204*, *205*
Welzheim East, 282
Welzheim West, 194, 282
Wheeler, Sir Mortimer, 125
Whitley Castle, 3, 48, *49*, 49
Wiesbaden, 73, 130, 140, 185, *186*, 199, 207, 263, *264*
Wigston Parva, 58
Wilhelm II, Kaiser, *13*, 14
winding gear, 202–3, *203*
workshop (*fabrica*), 163–4, 183–8, 205
  in auxiliary forts, 185–8
  blacksmith, 183, 186, 187
  carpentry, 187–8
  identification problems, 163–4, *164*
  leatherwork, 188
  in legionary fortresses, 183, *184*
  meatsmoking room, 185, 187
  metalwork, 163, *164*, 183, 185, 186, 187
  skilled craftsmen, 183, 185
  tanning, 187, 188
  mentioned, 30, 33, 35, 140, 190, *190*, 233, 239
Wörth, 70, *70*

Xanten, *see* Vetera
Xenophon, 177, 179, 191

York, 252, 266

Zugmantel, 120, 121, *124*, *198*, 207, 208, 274